Passionate Lives

Passionate

❧ Lives ❧

D. H. Lawrence
F. Scott Fitzgerald
Henry Miller
Dylan Thomas
Sylvia Plath
—In Love

by John Tytell

A Birch Lane Press Book
Published by Carol Publishing Group

To Mellon—
enduring love

A Birch Lane Press Book
Published by Carol Publishing Group
Birch Lane Press is a registered trademark of Carol Communications, Inc.

Editorial Offices: 600 Madison Avenue, New York, N.Y. 10022
Sales & Distribution Offices: 120 Enterprise Avenue, Secaucus, N.J. 07094
In Canada: Musson Book Company, a division of General Publishing Company, Ltd.,
Don Mills, Ontario M3B 2T6

Queries regarding rights and permissions should be addressed to Carol
Publishing Group, 600 Madison Avenue, New York, N.Y. 10022.

Carol Publishing Group books are available at special discounts for bulk
purchases, for sales promotions, fund raising, or educational purposes.
Special editions can be created to specifications. For details contact:
Special Sales Department, Carol Publishing Group, 120 Enterprise Avenue,
Secaucus, N.J. 07094.

Acknowledgments of permissions to reprint portions
of previously copyright appear on page 319.

Manufactured in the United States of America

10 9 8 7 6 5 4 3 2 1

Library of Congress Cataloging-in-Publication Data

Tytell, John.
    Passionate lives : D.H. Lawrence, F. Scott Fitzgerald, Henry
Miller, Dylan Thomas, Sylvia Plath—in love / by John Tytell.
    p. cm.
    "A Birch Lane Press book."
    ISBN 1-55972-077-8
    1.Authors, American—20th century—Biography—Marriage.
2. Authors, English—20th century—Biography—Marriage.
3. Romanticism—United States—History—20th century.
4. Romanticism—Great Britain—History—20th century.   5. Authors'
wives—United States—Biography.   6. Authors' wives—Great Britain—
Biography.   7. Marriage—History—20th century.   I. Title.
PS129.T97   1991
810.9'0052—dc20
    [B]   91-29987
                                                              CIP

Contents

Acknowledgments

I am particularly grateful to Berenice Hoffman for her guidance and for her faith in this book, which has matched my own. I am also indebted to Hillel Black, Gail Kinn and Donald J. Davidson for their invaluable editorial assistance. James Laughlin, Joseph McElroy and Ron Sukenick offered advice and encouragement. Barry Wallenstein and Paul Oppenheimer read parts of my manuscript and helped me with suggestions for revision. Other readers who helped as well were Tom Frosch, David Kleinbard, Harvey Fried and Rochelle Ratner. The manuscript was typed by the Word Processing Center at Queens College, under the direction of Muriel DeVack.

Passionate Lives

I do think many writers have what you might call a demonic nature. They are always in trouble, you know, and not only while they're writing or because they're writing, but in every aspect of their lives, with marriage, love, business, money, everything. It's all tied together, all part and parcel of the same thing. It's an aspect of the creative personality. Not all creative personalities are this way, but some are.

Henry Miller, *Paris Review* interview

You said once that marriage is the greatest test in the world. I know now that you were right, but now I welcome the test instead of dreading it. It is much more than a test of sweetness of temper, as people sometimes think; it is a test of the whole character and affects every action.

T. S. Eliot to Isabella Stewart Gardner, July 1915

❧ 1 ❧

The Sublime and
the Suffering

The lunatic, the lover, and the poet,
Are of imagination all compact.
                              Shakespeare

All love is tragic. Requited love dies of satiation, unrequited of
starvation. But death by starvation is slower and more
painful.
                    Lou Andreas-Salomé, *A Struggle for God*

A Submerged Species

THIS IS A BOOK about modern love as it has been lived by a group
of British and American writers—D. H. Lawrence, F. Scott
Fitzgerald, Henry Miller, Dylan Thomas and Sylvia Plath. These
writers express the romantic tradition in our time.

A writer in love implies a mate—Frieda Weekley, Zelda Sayre,
June Smith, Caitlin Macnamara and the English poet Ted Hughes—
so this is also a book about modern marriage among romantics. In
each case, a highly conflicted marriage affected the development
and trajectory of a powerful artistic statement, which is why these
lives merit interest in the first place. The couples whose lives form
this book would have spurned Flaubert's advice that artists should
live quietly so as to save themselves for violent originality in their
work. Instead, they were capable of moments of spectacular and
sometimes frightening excess, full of urgency and extreme psychological gesticulation. The personal desperation, the confused idealism, the flamboyant bohemianism these couples shared and their
willingness to voice these feelings in their work are signs of a
romantic mood that resisted the belief of the modernist literary

3

school, which advocated submerging the direct expression of the writer's personality in order to create "objective" works. T. S. Eliot, a leading theorist of modernism, particularly found the romantic attitudes that had survived the nineteenth century to be distasteful and unaesthetic, a tone no longer commensurate with the bleak twentieth-century spiritual wasteland.

The modern romantics discussed here were on the whole no less attuned to the various malaises of the world around them—in fact, they internalized and personalized them, fusing them into their emotional lives and their artistic vision and expression, becoming in a sense shock absorbers for the upheavals in ideas, psychology, sexual relations and social dislocations that demarcated the history of their century. They risked exposing the emotional center of their private lives in their work, often taking that as the subject through which they signified their individual convictions, their conflicts and anxieties, and the truth of experience as they envisioned it.

Some went further: they wanted not only to describe the world, but to change it.

Living on the farthest edge of risk, past the perimeters of ordinary lives, the writers discussed here nevertheless have helped shape our vision of the human dilemma. They were as capable of stumbling and faltering as all of us, but their lives and writing galvanize us to reimagine ourselves and the ground we stand on. Romanticism is demanding because it upsets existing values and redefines identity. These writers' beliefs broke through inherited assumptions about sexual hierarchy, and they intuitively sought out mates who they felt were spiritual equivalents. In their work, they tried to chart the changing relations between the sexes. In their actual lives, they were victims of a liberation more easily imagined than realized.

Dionysian Models

A series of courtships and their consequences form the narrative center of this book, which is as much about the turbulence of modern marriage as it is about the romantic literary tradition which reflects that turbulence.

The modern romantic tradition begins with D. H. Lawrence, who ran off with his teacher's wife, both of them renouncing all for love and art, only to find themselves in a protracted struggle for personal sovereignty. D.H. and Frieda Lawrence spent eighteen years together in a thrashing relationship that magnifies the clashing expectations of husbands and wives. Lawrence's vision was infused with a romantic idealism that ranged from liberated notions of how women and men should consort with freedom and tolerance to how states should govern. As a visionary, his ambition was monumental: he wanted to change the world by calling with evangelical zeal for the release of the cosmic force of human sexuality and passion that he felt modern industrial society had subverted. His marriage to Frieda became a test case for his romantic vision, a way of measuring its viability. It exposed the tension between the idealized imagination of passion and the jagged actualities of married life—a tension that held true in the marital adaptations of the other writers in this volume, all of whom were in their diverse ways influenced by or aware of Lawrence as a predecessor. Miller would struggle to write a book about Lawrence; Fitzgerald and Thomas read him with intensity; and Sylvia Plath was so moved by him that she named her daughter after Frieda. Miller even tried, in his haphazard manner, to make his way to New Mexico to visit Lawrence, whom he saw as the fountainhead.

The fractured relationships presented here all began with exceedingly romantic overtures. Lawrence demanded that Frieda Weekley give up the security of respectability and that she abandon her three children to elope with him. F. Scott Fitzgerald fell in love with a striking, spirited girl he saw dancing in a country club ballroom and pursued her heedlessly. Henry Miller was immediately mesmerized by a taxi dancer in a cheap Times Square dance hall and remained obsessed with her during the seven years of their marriage and beyond. The first words Dylan Thomas impetuously uttered to Caitlin Macnamara as they sat drinking along with a group of people in an English pub were "I love you," though he had never met her before and didn't know her at all. Sylvia Plath instantaneously identified Ted Hughes as the "smashing love" she felt could rescue her from her inner demons. What happened in these lives when the romantic impulse gave way to the realities of a sustained relationship is the story of all marriages. But the romantic in love is particularly burdened by the undercurrent of a romantic vision of life taken at full tide, a vision of petty realities being swept away in a flood of romantic expectations.

Marriage is one token of an individual's compatibility with the expectations of the world, and all of the marriages treated in *Passionate Lives* were bound by pressures and imbalances that derived from a quest for self-assertion and recognition. These are drives artists associate with themselves, not with the people they marry. Frieda Lawrence insisted on the importance of her role as her husband's collaborator and inspiration. Zelda Fitzgerald insisted on acknowledgment of her own spirit and talent. June Miller tried to control her husband's work and to assert her supremacy over him. Caitlin Thomas demanded that she not be cast into the periphery of Dylan Thomas's life. Sylvia Plath might have foreseen the competition that would be present in marriage to a poet of equal power and greater renown. Rivalry and competitiveness marked these marriages, and the way that these dissonances expressed themselves became the subject matter of the writers. Invariably, the appropriation by these writers of life for art, of their lovers' moods, mannerisms and words for their stories and poems, caused a festering resentment and a countervailing demand for recognition. In a sense, these writers are the logical historians of the contending demands and expectations between men and women that speak so directly to issues in marriage in our time.

Ultimately, their conflicts transcended marital difficulties and became a tremendous argument with the body politic, the authorities from publishers to politicians that determine social reality. The artist is usually a most singular minority of one with the resolution to resist the dictates of superior forces. Censored, publicly condemned, Lawrence, Miller and Thomas were buffeted by such forces, but strengthened by the bohemian belief that everyone was spiritually dead except the artist, who became a law unto himself.

Imbued with a romantic vision of the artist as bohemian, refusing to entertain notions of bourgeois respectability, these writers were for the most part self-exiled wanderers, literary nomads avoiding confrontation with conventional patterns of existence. Lawrence, Miller and Thomas were afflicted by great difficulties in acquiring enough money to live and write, and their marriages were plagued by want and poverty. Fitzgerald, who showed quickly that he could earn large sums, always spent much more than his income and lived in debt. Lawrence found the patronage he sought from wealthy women, which drove Frieda to enraged jealousy. Miller did his best to evade the question of a regular income, living hand-to-mouth for decades, often depending on stipends from June, who resorted to dubious means to obtain those sums. Thomas was hounded by bill collectors and terrified by the prospect of poverty, though he left it to Caitlin to manage their household on virtually nothing. In different ways, these writers tended to drain their financial resources, ironically making themselves more dependent on systems they castigated.

The financial difficulties that strained their domestic lives were serious, but were not the major cause of dislocations in these marriages. These writers all experienced a self-lacerating torment that became a fuel for art. They romanticized physical and psychic illness as a contradictory, destructive capacity that led to creativity. Traditionally, we see such figures as disabled, but a writer caught in the vortex of mental anguish or the transport caused by alcohol or the impending sense of his own mortality may be endowed with a power that has its own relentless energies. The Greeks would have called it possession, and the possessed artist acts in unconscious obedience to some primal part of the self, some ancient, buried impulse that often dictates images and stories that the artist transcribes, signaling a message desperately through the flames of inner tribulation. The work results from a sort of manic frenzy in which the artist acts as a transfer point for energies whose painful origins function as a catalyst for release and expression. The critic Edmund Wilson, in his famous essay "The Wound and the Bow," speculated that the diseased, broken modern artist has been somehow strengthened by his pain and has formed the power of his insight as part of his healing.

Wilson connected Fitzgerald to Shelley, and to D. H. Lawrence and Dylan Thomas, as three cardinal instances of the literary surrogate of the Dying God, particularly Dionysus, the reveling agricultural god of the grape, who lived through his senses until he was torn apart by his revelers only to reemerge and repeat the cycle the next year. The literary surrogate is used as a totem to gratify some deep instinctive need, some buried primitive imagery of sacrifice and recycling, of the suffering god who transcends death.

Comparing modern writers to gods and their works to magical rites ignores the reality that lives are not lived as ritual reenactments of myths. The paradox lies in the intoxication of creative productivity and the destabilizing psychic costs to the writers themselves and to the people who lived with them.

Supremacists of the Heart

The god question, however, is central. An international movement in philosophy and the arts, Romanticism was very much about waning beliefs and resurrected gods. One of the chief resurrected divine principles was pagan and Dionysian, an incorporation of the desire to express emotion and let it govern action.

We can become so taken by the spectacle of romantic anguish that we fail to measure the seriousness implicit in the romantic position, the extent to which by questioning our safest suppositions it shapes our future assumptions. Lawrence, Fitzgerald, Miller, Thomas and Plath participated in a process of pushing the acceptable beyond the limits of community approval. They were the most recent offshoots of a tradition whose subversive dissidence had taken root in the nineteenth century.

"Romanticism" is an all-embracing term that attempts to encompass a broad variety of attitudes. It was set in motion by the awareness that the industrial age which emerged at the end of the eighteenth century fundamentally alienated human beings from the natural world, the source of all divinity, which had previously sustained them. It found wellsprings of energy in the egalitarian principles released by the American and French revolutions. It pitted the individual against entrenched systems and community standards. In subscribing to the power of the individual, it also subscribed to the power of individual emotions, of heightened sensibility and of personal expression. It valued disorder as a force for upsetting the existing order and creating new possibilities and prospects. Friedrich Nietzsche, who died in 1900, at the very beginning of a new era, uttered the ultimate romantic heresy, the belief that Christ was now dead as a god, supplanted by Darwin and the illusion of progress. Deprived of the security of former beliefs, the Nietzschean man would seize the opportunity to reevaluate all past values, but Nietzsche knew that such an examination would only alienate him and that, without the comfort of his gods, man would endure alone and in agony. Debilitated by illness and succumbing to insanity a decade before his death, Nietzsche epitomized the dark psychic costs of Romanticism, a creativity that seemed inextricably linked with sickness and suffering, and he is a prototype for the writers explored in this book.

Nietzsche once asserted that philosophical systems should always be approached in terms of the lives of those who had devised them, a productive view when it is applied to literature, and the lives of the Romantic writers usually tell us much more about the movement they inspired than does theoretical inquiry. The Romantic movement that broke new ground in England early in the 1800s with the work of Blake, Wordsworth and Coleridge gained momentum with the emergence of the next generation of Romantic poets: Byron, Shelley and Keats.

For the romantic sensibility of these poets and their followers, barriers and obstacles, including society's prohibitions and injunctions, became incentives for love. The Romantics were the first to advocate couples marrying only for love instead of bartering their futures in marital arrangements designed to perpetuate property rights. They reinvented the medieval notion of romantic love, but did not give the concept exact definition. Instead, they believed in love as a fundamental principle of life. Some confused it with honor and were willing to die for it, as the Russian poet Pushkin demonstrated when, provoked by his wife's insatiable flirtatiousness, he fought a fatal duel. To die for love became an extreme romantic posture, epitomized by the hero of Goethe's *Sorrows of Young Werther,* whose suicide as a result of an infatuation set a romantic fashion for a time among real-life Werthers.

More than any other nineteenth-century figures, the lives of Byron and Shelley inform us of the creative license, the agony of idealism and the personal confusions that characterize Romanticism. They are seminal Romantics who died as a result of an excessive sense of romantic daring. Both poets were prodigal representatives of the romantic premium on youth and on the hero in exile. When they met abroad in the spring of 1816, Byron was twenty-eight. Shelley, then twenty-three and still a relative unknown, believed he would succumb to disease at an early age. In Geneva and later in Italy, they catalyzed each other with their conversation and poems, Byron working on *Don Juan,* his satiric masterpiece, and Shelley on *Prometheus Unbound,* his paean to moral perfection and the liberation of the benign spirit from the bonds of tyranny. With a speculative mind capable of expressions of lofty idealism, Shelley worked feverishly and produced a dazzling variety of poetic works and verse dramas, none of which brought him the large audience he simultaneously criticized and desired.

Inconsistency would not have perturbed Shelley. To the Romantics, it was a characteristic to be valued, even courted, as a wellspring for change and renewal—which is a basic romantic drive. At its worst, however, inconsistency could be used to rationalize a romantic elitism, the belief that those capable of romantic love are quite beyond conventional standards.

Shelley exemplified that attitude. When he eloped with Mary Godwin to Switzerland, he invited as their companion his wife

Harriet, whom he had married when she was sixteen. The gesture was typical of Shelley, who had once tried to persuade Harriet to sleep with his best friend as a sign of their mutual compatibility. In the end she would drown herself, the case of an ordinary woman who had expected to marry a clergyman driven beyond her endurance by a firsthand acquaintance with romantic principles.

In choosing Mary Godwin, Shelley, who courted her during long discussions in the afternoon over her mother's gravestone, was defining the tradition to which he wished to belong. Her mother was Mary Wollstonecraft, whose pioneering work, *A Vindication of the Rights of Woman,* rejected Rousseau's cavalier observation that women were designed to please men and therefore did not require the same education. Her insistence on the rational and intellectual capacities of women had not prevented Wollstonecraft from falling under the spell of an American adventurer who deserted her after she had his child. A despairing example of the romantic stress on emotion at the expense of reason, she tried to throw herself off a bridge. Restored to her senses, Wollstonecraft married one of the key freethinking intellectuals of her era, the anarchist William Godwin, and died after giving birth to their daughter, Mary, who entered literary history not only as the wife of Shelley but as the author of *Frankenstein.*

An awful sailor, inattentive, awkward, preferring to read while steering, Shelley also could not swim. None of this cautioned him against the absurdity of sailing his own boat. His small schooner, *Ariel,* went down in a sudden summer storm as he was sailing back to his home in Leirci after visiting Byron and the poet Leigh Hunt in Livorno. As husband, sailor and poet, Shelley is an incarnation of romantic escapism, a quality that colors a movement whose priorities were extremely individualistic.

If Shelley sought in love the expression of the romantic ideal, Byron approached it more cynically. An English lord who captivated high British society, extremely handsome, self-centered and sardonic, devastatingly attractive to women and often scandalous in his behavior, he played out his life on as theatrical a stage as the heroic characters in his poems, falling victim to a fatal fever as a participant in the Greek war of independence against the Turks. In Byron we see the Romantic hero writ large in all his contradictions and attractiveness. His name entered the language as a descriptive word, and Byronic attributes—defiance of convention, an excess of moodiness and melancholy, an affinity for dangerous liaisons and an identification with dauntless valor and idealistic causes—were admired and imitated.

The circle around Byron and Shelley in Italy had been a chaos of sexual and emotional discovery, as if centuries of repression had suddenly been released from some Pandora's box, producing a stew of illicit affairs, miscarriages and illegitimate births. Romantic love was often irresponsible, as it overstepped the bounds of social convention, and potentially damaging—its passion as connected to pain as to pleasure.

While the Romantic era promised considerably more than it could deliver, it shaped the way we see ourselves. It extolled individuality, imagination, spirit. It reveled in a love of untamed nature and in the "sublime" link between nature and man. It reinvented terror and passion and rediscovered the primitive and mysterious. Inspired by the American and French revolutions, it prized liberty and nonconformity and broke with traditional authoritarian values. It called attention to folklore and folkways. It esteemed the commonplace and everyday and it gave new importance to the experiences of childhood. In elevating the emotions and a belief in the "self," it explored human psychology and the intensity of feelings. It opened a door and permitted a new view of individual possibilities and the hope of a more equal basis for relationships between men and women. And in doing all that, it effected a glacial shift in consciousness.

The Victorians were as fascinated as the Romantics had been by the kind of sweeping passion that could transform all experience, but they were at the same time afraid of such unrestrained emotion. Inhibited, sentimental and secretive, they developed a facade of propriety and took their passions underground. Poets like Tennyson were still pining and swooning, full of tearful effusions and rhetorical flights, trying their best to use their rediscovery of medieval chivalry to obscure tensions that lived below the surface. In one of the great love stories of the nineteenth century, between Elizabeth Barrett and Robert Browning, the lovers are reputed never to have seen each other entirely in the nude. Still, it was the intensity of their romantic passion that saved her from the fate of the Victorian female invalid and liberated her creative powers. The Queen who dominates the period with her punctilious morality and rectitude secluded herself from public view for three years in an extravagant expression of passion and grief when Prince Albert died. When Victoria reemerged, she consolidated her empire with the help and guidance of gifted politicians like Disraeli and is remembered as much for her power as her puritanism.

By the end of the nineteenth century, which roughly coincided with Victoria's death, views of women and women's views of themselves had begun to change in response to agitation for suffrage and divorce reform. But Victorian scientists were still insisting that the brain capacities of women were smaller than men's, and that most of the medical ailments suffered by women could be traced to some dysfunctioning of the reproductive organs. The Victorian pretense that women felt no innate pleasure in sexual intercourse, and whatever sexual desire they experienced was pathological, was being refuted by the studies of Krafft-Ebing, Havelock Ellis and Freud. Theory was rapidly moving beyond what people could imagine for their daily lives, and even Freud confessed that ultimately he could not understand women, that they were probably incapacitated by genital physiology.

Some women near the end of the nineteenth century refused to subscribe to so biologically determined a view. Inspired by the French novelist George Sand, and by the heroines in Ibsen's plays who struggled so to free themselves, they began to enact new lives.

It is at this junction—at the boundary line between old expectations and new imaginings for the sexual and emotional lives of women—that the husbands and wives whose marriages are described in these pages meet and pursue their own directions. All of these writers faced obstacles that were inherent in their own contradictions, insofar as they advocated varying degrees of equality in the relations between men and women that they were reluctant or incapable of subscribing to fully in their lives. Driven by their egos and inner conflicts and by the supremacy of their devotion to their work, they allowed practice to lag behind theory. Nevertheless, they make some claim as innovators.

As romantics these writers believed in dreams, intuition and imagination. Lawrence, Miller and Plath used raw risk and emotional vulnerability for the sake of vision and sensibility. Less challenging but still essentially romantic, Fitzgerald and Thomas were caught in different aspects of the romantic dream. Although each of these figures was extremely self-destructive, they performed a crucially redeeming function for us all, acting as a kind of singular alter ego for lives that are of necessity more restrained and constricted. Perennial outsiders obsessed by the need for self-expression, they replaced the usual choices of career or comfort by the prospects of the gypsy, the pirate or the lover. Truly romantic lives are perhaps best appreciated vicariously. They inevitably contrast with our own inhibitions and aspirations, and help us measure the more circumscribed and cautious conditions under which we live.

In a more positive sense, these modern romantics have changed our conceptions of who we can be and how we can act. They have allowed us to appreciate both the costs of and values of risk. Instead of cowering before their inconsistencies, repressing their neuroses, and denying their deepest desires, they released them and allowed themselves a wider latitude in human affairs than was sanctioned by their historical moment in time. As models of our evolving freedom, they left us a visible record in their writing, a history of their travails with the world. With all their imperfections, their self-aggrandizing needs, their peculiar avocation for painful encounter in the name of consciousness and liberation, they had their art as psychic ballast, an ordering purpose in the heart of emotional chaos. We stand served by that art and human struggles out of which it was formed.

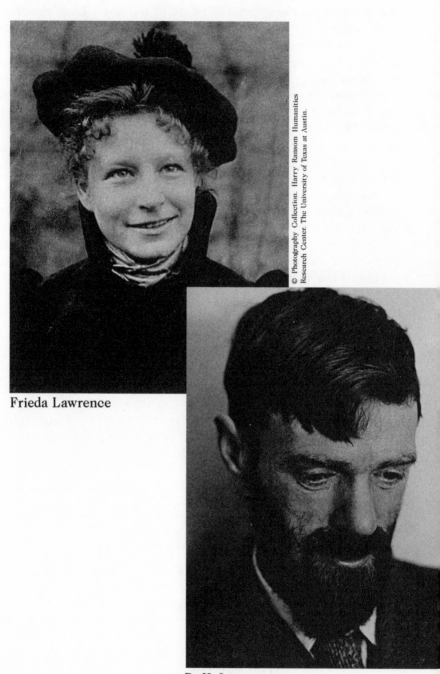

© Photography Collection. Harry Ransom Humanities
Research Center. The University of Texas at Austin.

Frieda Lawrence

D. H. Lawrence

✿ 2 ✿

D. H. Lawrence and Frieda

Man, the doer, the knower, the original in *being* is he the lord
of life? Or is the the woman, the great Mother, who bore us
from the womb of love, is she the supreme Goddess?

Fantasia of the Unconscious

The Infirm Prophet

D. H. LAWRENCE was the outraged prophet who presumed to
have answers to irresolvable questions in a perilous time. He
was not surprised by the catastrophe of the First World War, but
nevertheless soon felt stunned and crushed by its terror and
violence. The war represented that historical moment when, in
Yeats's terms, the center ceased to hold and all human relations
were altered. It left Lawrence with a deep suspicion of political
systems. If reasonable men could lead the world into so devastating
a debacle, then reason itself was suspect. Lawrence believed in the
power of the body, of flesh and blood as opposed to mind. "We can
go wrong in our minds," he once wrote, "but what our blood feels
and believes and says, is always true. The intellect is only a bit and
a bridle." He worshiped nature and its beauties with more passionate conviction than any writer of his moment. He hated industrialism and saw the First World War as its shameful progeny. His
own political prescriptions, however, were often confused, though
he preached them with messianic fervor.

He was quick to sense that the power factors affecting relationships between the sexes were being redefined, and he imagined
situations in his fiction vital enough to constitute basic representations of the changes he felt. Feminists have criticized him for not
going far enough, for not permitting the women he invented to
triumph or persevere on their own terms.

The role of the prophet presents certain handicaps for any

creative artist. The danger is that one's own human vulnerabilities and infirmities may be forgotten or minimized in the omniscient glow of propositions and solutions, that the feedback system, the appreciation by a group of actions one has proposed in a time of great questions is intoxicating and blinding.

Lawrence was a consumptive who successfully denied the disease in his own body despite a succession of severe illnesses, at least two of which nearly killed him. The denial was necessary for Lawrence, his means of positively affirming whatever life would be available to him, a way of mobilizing resistance. Yet the tuberculosis which inhabited his lungs had its dark debilitating implications, contributing to the intensity of his awful adrenal rages.

Part of Lawrence's illness involved a rather complex attitude to his own mother, a view which we try to simplify, and in some sense vulgarize, with the "oedipal" rubric. For Lawrence, this involved a struggle with maternal authority. He loved his mother, perhaps even unnaturally in his deepest fantasies, but at the same time he needed to repudiate the narrow fundamental Christianity that defined her world and to free himself from her. He tried his best to exorcise her in his first great novel, *Sons and Lovers*. Eloping with Frieda Weekley, herself the mother of three children, while a romantic assertion of free will in the face of convention, served only to raise the stakes of Lawrence's own inner conflict. Suddenly he became legally and emotionally bound to a woman who he realized was another version of the "devouring mother."

We tend to idealize our prophet figures, to put them on pedestals. We forget that their insights often result from their infirmities, from perceptions caused by their suffering. Lawrence's vision developed because of his own suffering, the result of a marriage that challenged him. Life with Frieda provoked him to raise unprecedented questions about marriage and its possibilities for enlightened women. By managing to imagine powerful men and women in his fiction, he dramatized many of the issues that have divided the sexes ever since.

Frieda Weekley became the single most important element in Lawrence's emotional world. She advised him on what certain of his fictional characters could say, as well as on his relations with friends and potential patrons. Bossy, meddling and manipulative, she could be a dominating figure. She was five years older than Lawrence when they met, and more experienced in the ways of the world. Settled in a dull marriage, she had enjoyed two secret lovers—a businessman and a wild, often drugged psychiatrist. When they met, Lawrence had barely finished his university studies and his life was still to a large extent confined and provincial. He had published poetry and stories and a first novel, *The White Peacock,* and *The Trespassers* would be issued shortly. Though this second novel delved into love outside marriage, most of his experience with women had been with resistant Victorian maidens. He had little first-hand knowledge of passion.

Frieda opened the floodgates of Lawrence's creativity to the extent that he later felt dependent on her good will, her cooperation and their mutual harmony. This dependence, in part the sort a son might feel for his mother, became the source of Frieda's power. She began to believe she was as responsible for the genius of Lawrence's fictional world as he was. Such presumption became a crucial lever in their relationship and a cause of great conflict.

Luncheon at the Weekleys'

It was a sunny afternoon in the beginning of April, 1912. D. H. Lawrence came to lunch at the home of one of his former teachers, Professor Ernest Weekley. Lawrence wanted a recommendation to a German university, where he hoped to find employment as a teacher of English. The eager young man—Lawrence was twenty-six—had arrived early. His dour professor, still immersed in his study, asked his wife, Frieda, to entertain his guest for an hour.

The visitor was a man whose fiction would cause more notoriety in England than any since Thomas Hardy's in the 1890s, when the conventions of the old-fashioned Victorian novel were first being challenged. In novels like *Sons and Lovers, The Rainbow, Women in Love* and finally *Lady Chatterley's Lover,* the intimacies of human relations as Lawrence chose to depict them seemed too heated to suit standards of public taste and decency. His novels would reflect the new feminist conceptions of what a woman could do with her life in the post-Victorian era, but they presented, as well, the stratagems that powerful men invented to maintain their power. Lawrence was throttled as an immoralist in the editorial and literary pages of the newspapers, but nothing he wrote would seem as scandalous as the single action he took in the following month of eloping with Frieda Weekley.

There was nothing unusual in Professor Weekley's request that his wife occupy his former student, but in its salient way it suggested a central feature of their marriage. Like the good Victorian that he was, Weekley preferred his work to any other possible devotion. And he was an assiduous worker, a philologist and etymologist. Absorbed in his books and in the past which they preserved, he was reserved, reflective, abstracted, a man who could seem smug or pontifical, with the habitual air of authority which can be the occupational hazard of the lecturer. Weekley was a master of words, and the stuffy omniscience that such mastery implied could become overbearing.

While Weekley kept Lawrence waiting, he was adding the finishing touches to *The Romance of Words,* which would become the most successful of his many books. Forty-five years old, graying at the temples, he was professor of French and chair of the Department of Modern Languages at Nottingham University College, a provincial school in the middle of England with a mediocre reputation. He would spend forty years there, a solid reliable fixture who became the dean of faculty, all the while complaining that his lectures were too draining. Weekley was burdened by his considerable administrative duties and, beyond these, the demands of his own research and writing. And then, fatigued after his daytime perambulations in the history of language, he taught in the evenings for extra compensation.

Lawrence had been a student in one of those evening classes, composed mainly of workers from the Nottingham region, shopkeepers and employees of the large lace manufacturers seeking to improve themselves. A sympathetic, democratic audience, it fulfilled the civilizing mission of Victorian England as well as the opportunity that the epoch promised and sometimes delivered. Lawrence was an auditor with something in common with Weekley, for he was also a schoolmaster, though a dissatisfied one who taught unruly adolescents.

Nottingham was coal country. Once a pastoral, agricultural area with Sherwood Forest on its perimeter, it had provided some of the raw material for England's industrialization. The mood of Nottingham was determined by its black slate roofs, the preponderance of factories and warehouses, chimneys belching black smoke, and the omnipresent soot of pollutants that had once so enraged the poet William Blake. Lawrence described the region in one of his last essays as a place mutilated by capitalism, ruined by a privileged investor class that saw workers as tools. The word Lawrence reiterates in his essay "Nottingham and the Mining

Countryside" is "ugly": "meanness and formless and ugly surroundings, ugly ideals, ugly religion, ugly hope, ugly love, ugly clothes, ugly furniture, ugly houses, ugly relationship between workers and employers."

The result was squeezed living quarters and the architecturally hideous towns that would reappear in his fiction. In *The Rainbow,* he would call Nottingham Wiggeston and compare its homogeneous, amorphous and repetitive red brick structures to a rapidly spreading skin disease. The Weekleys, however, lived in the more exclusive Mapperley section where the houses had front lawns and large gardens. They could afford domestic servants and a cook. It was a quintessential bourgeois area in which the primary concerns of women like Mrs. Weekley were presumed to be the well-being of their husband and children. Frieda Weekley played the role of the respectable *Hausfrau* quite well, but during her marriage she had taken some minor risks against the strictures of domestic propriety.

She was thirty-one years old, fourteen years younger than Weekley. She was a member of the von Richthofen family, aristocrats who had lost their land in Silesia and who had worked mostly as diplomats, soldiers or civil servants, part of the German ruling class. Her father was a baron who had lost the use of his right hand while battling for Bismarck during the Franco–Prussian War, the conflict in 1870–71 that marked the emergence of a strong, unified German state, an eventuality feared by other Europeans since the decline of the Roman Empire. Baron von Richthofen had settled in the town of Metz in the Lorraine after the war, part of an occupying army governing an area that was as Gallic as it was Teutonic. Trained as an engineer, he worked on the administration of the canal system around Metz and participated in regimental activities. Metz was an army town during Frieda's childhood, half its fifty thousand inhabitants being in the military, so the strict Prussian warrior code was a dominating force. It was a code that stressed authority and control and elevated the importance of the army—the Kaiser, for example, always wore his uniform when he appeared in public. Baron von Richthofen worked in the Prussian civil service, a stepchild of the military designed as a means of raising money for armies and organizing conscription. The ensuing atmosphere seemed patriarchal, autocratic, harsh and inflexible. The important issues of the day, Bismarck had decreed, would not be settled by speeches and majority votes but by "blood and iron."

It was a creed that would lead directly to the first major international catastrophe of the twentieth century.

Frieda had a sense of the arrogance of German power and the assumption of cultural superiority that emanated from the Kaiser's court. One of her father's uncles served as ambassador to Sweden, and another, Oswald von Richthofen, was Prussian secretary of state in Berlin. Frieda lived in Berlin with Uncle Oswald for a year, attending diplomatic receptions and state balls. The Kaiser himself is said to have remarked on her beauty. But her immediate prospects were not very promising. Her father had dissipated his patrimony by gambling and a costly affair with a mistress, and there would be neither dowry nor expectations of inheritance for either of his three daughters.

She had met her future husband when she was only eighteen. He was on a walking tour of the Black Forest, and she was the green-eyed, golden-haired beauty of Teutonic myth, a naive but high-spirited girl with little real experience of life or love except for the few mild flirtations with the junior officers of Metz that she had enjoyed. Though Ernest Weekley was older, he had even less experience.

On the morning of Lawrence's visit, Frieda had already lived in Nottingham for over a decade. She welcomed the opportunity to greet her husband's former student. He wanted assistance in traveling to her native land, and that implied an interest in her heritage, a common ground, a bonding potential that would cause her to be more than merely courteous. Even more intriguing had been her husband's remark, made earlier that morning, that they were expecting a genius for lunch. Weekley said it with a typically sardonic edge—the cynical superiority that the schoolmaster assumes to humble an ambitious student—but Frieda ignored the potential irony. Perhaps her husband's comment reminded her of her own father's perennial cynicism, which she hated, and she had accepted the remark at face value.

They spoke in the piano room, watching the children play croquet on the lawn as the curtains fluttered over the open French windows. Full-bodied, as statuesque as the women in Rubens's paintings, Frieda was immediately taken by her interlocutor's leanness, his deft, light but certain movements. In her *Memoirs,* she characterized his manner as "sovereign," which implies taking what he had the right to take, though this may simply be her rationalization for giving what she would want to give. She felt an elemental honesty about his presence, and he spoke with a refreshing directness. What he said seemed to come straight from his heart, not from his head, and it was said without affectation or pretension; even when he verged on matters that could shock the Victorian ear, there was a natural ease about his language and its flow.

Frieda was provoked by his assertion, practically the first thing he said, that he was finished with his attempts at understanding women. "Understanding," of course, is the business of a novelist, though it may often take the form of his own subjective view of the world. For a man to state that he is finished with the attempt to understand women suggests impatience, a frustration that may mask the desire for further contact. What surprised Frieda was his emphasis, bordering on vehemence. His voice rose stridently, and the energy and concern carrying it was so utterly different from the circumspect and phlegmatic modulations of her husband. Lawrence's talk was inspired, grandiose: "I shall change the world for the next thousand years," he would tell her on their next meeting. Such remarks stirred her.

The Quivering Greyhound

Lunch with Professor Weekley and his wife consumed the afternoon. Animated and ebullient, Lawrence did most of the talking, describing life in Eastwood, a mining community nine miles north of Nottingham where he had spent his childhood. He noticed that Mrs. Weekley never addressed her husband, that she barely seemed aware of Weekley's presence; this was discomforting, and made conversation awkward. Frieda made such an impression on Lawrence that he chose to walk back to Eastwood instead of taking the train. Leaving just before dusk, he tramped for hours through darkened fields, thinking about Frieda Weekley, wondering whether the distance he sensed between the couple could be taken as a sign of hope.

Women had always been central in Lawrence's life, beginning with his mother, as the most casual reader of Sons and Lovers will discern. Lawrence himself, in a letter to Jessie Chambers, his teenage sweetheart, claimed that his love for his mother was excessive, unnatural, that he loved her as a lover, not as a son. We may accept this more as fantasy than fact, especially given Lydia Lawrence's self-righteousness and her defined puritanical consciousness, and because Lawrence expressed his feelings to Jessie in a perverse and bitter mood, in his grief just after his mother's death; but there are other elements of the oedipal configuration evident in his parents' marriage and the way their son, David Herbert, saw it.

A small, slight woman who wore only black, white or gray, Lydia was from a higher social class than her husband, who wooed and won her at a dance. She had been a schoolteacher who wrote poetry and read novels. The man she would marry was a coal miner who had worked in the pits since he was seven, and who could barely read a newspaper. For Lawrence, his mother represented promise and sensitivity; his father suggested a grimier, more coarse and brutal reality. There were five children, but the marriage was a protracted battle of wills—surely a model for Lawrence's subsequent contest with Frieda. Lydia Lawrence fought her husband, who was often drunk, mulish and abusive. When she berated him, he sought the barroom to drink with his friends. Lydia won the sympathy of her five children, which in her son's case may have taken its classically oedipal turn. He admitted a phobia about his father: he could not as a young man stand his father's physical presence and would leave any room he entered.

Lawrence had a deprived, Dickensian childhood. His father was a poor provider, always quarreling with his superiors at the mine and paying for his insubordination by getting the worst sites. There was barely enough money for food, and an improper diet probably contributed to Lawrence's consumptive nature. "A delicate pale brat with a stuffy nose," he characterized himself in an autobiographical sketch. He had been fragile and sickly, a chalk-faced skinny boy in knee britches and high socks troubled by a persistent, hacking cough. He was too frail to play soccer with his male classmates, who rejected him unilaterally because of his puniness. His friends were girls, and his interests were botany and flowers. School seemed a sort of prison, mostly because of the harassment of the other boys, but there was some escape from the insularity of Eastwood when at twelve he won a scholarship to the high school in Nottingham.

Lawrence's early manhood was marked by a series of traumatic experiences. In the summer of 1901, when he was sixteen, he obtained a clerk's position in a surgical supply factory in Nottingham. The young women who made the bandages and elastic hose began to tease him, a case of the coarse hating and feeling the need to defile the refined, really the story of Lawrence's parents, reversed and on a broader scale. Finally, a group of these women accosted him in a downstairs storeroom, attempted to strip his trousers and expose him. Lawrence fought the girls off, but the incident agitated him, and caused him to begin retching to purge something profoundly soiling and humiliating. Later on, when he would write *Sons and Lovers,* he would repress this incident, instead making his hero Paul eminently successful with the factory women. It was an early sign of the way Lawrence would use his fiction to recast reality.

Two months later, his older brother Ernest, the great hope of the family, who worked in London and had prospects of a business career, developed pneumonia and died. Lydia Lawrence felt crushed and embittered. The damage was compounded when Lawrence himself came down with pneumonia and struggled to survive during the winter of 1901–02. In the spring, as a recuperative measure, he began spending time at Haggs Farm, located about two miles from Eastwood. The Chambers family who farmed the land was a large, nourishing group who offered a healthy contrast to the pallid miners of Eastwood. Lawrence was first drawn to Alan Chambers, one of the sons who helped with the haying and gardening, but gradually grew closer to his sister Jessie, a year younger than Lawrence. She was a shy, serious girl interested in books and writing, who kept a journal (which Lawrence would later use when he cast her as Miriam in *Sons and Lovers*). The friendship became a protracted courtship, although Jessie was introverted, stiff and unable to relax, with rigid moral views (similar to those of Mrs. Lawrence, who discouraged the relationship because she believed Jessie was not good enough for her son—the characteristic maternal complaint). The major problem, however, was the sexual tension between the two young people, which could not be resolved. Jessie insisted on preserving her chastity despite a decade of Lawrence's efforts to dissuade her, the result of the natural inclination of a young man frustrated by his yearnings for sexual knowledge. In *Sons and Lovers* Lawrence would refer to his need as the baptism of fire in passion which Jessie/Miriam could not provide him. The same barrier arose with the next woman Lawrence pursued, Louie Burrows, whom he met while both were pupil-teachers in Eastwood. Even after their engagement, Louie refused to allow Lawrence to cross the line between suitor and lover, and the engagement was subsequently dissolved.

We must remember that these young women inhabited a world dominated by Victorian values and a public posture for women of rectitude and reserve. Sex might be endured for the sake of family, and a married woman in nineteenth-century England could expect a dozen pregnancies, but sex was not supposed to be enjoyed. In novels and social teas it was referred to as the "inconsiderateness" of men.

Women often saw sex as a debt to be paid, a means of insuring harmony, and some women, then as now, loathed it. The formality of marital relations in that era is difficult for us to understand, and women who addressed their husbands by their surnames are as remote from our concerns as the eighteen-button gloves those same women wore when leaving their houses. Even if a woman felt free enough to engage in sex outside of marriage, she was encumbered by fashion. To face the day, she would be stuffed and padded in a package of corsets and petticoats held together by innumerable hooks and buttons. Such impediments served to frustrate occasions of sexual spontaneity and reflected the idea that sexual intimacy could only be countenanced in formal wedlock.

In the fall of 1906, when Lawrence was twenty-one, he entered Nottingham University College, where he would spend two years in a teacher training program. Weekley was one of the few lecturers who appealed to him, though it was more gratifying to work on his own poems and stories than on the academic curriculum. He had begun *The White Peacock,* and would continue it fitfully over the next four years, the story of a vain, flirtatious woman who marries a local squire.

He was still seeing both Jessie and Louie, with Jessie suffering considerable torment because of her rival. The women in his life, Lawrence confided in a letter, were sickly sentimentalists who draped themselves in the "woolly fluff of romance." In Lawrence's courtships, his own writing was an object of centrality, as if it was his imaginative vision, his creativity, his very genius that he was asking Jessie or Louie to love. It was essential for Lawrence that any woman he loved could respond to his writing and become, as Jessie did with her journal, and later Frieda, a collaborator. For Jessie, though she married subsequently, Lawrence was the love of her life; she tried to tell her version of their tortured, unfulfilled love in a novel of her own, which she destroyed, and then in a memoir.

In the summer of 1909, Jessie sent a group of Lawrence's poems to Ford Madox Hueffer, who was editing *The English Review*. The magazine was only a year old, but it had quickly established itself as the leading literary organ of the moment. Its first issue had included a poem by Hardy and fiction by Henry James, Joseph Conrad and H. G. Wells. Hueffer, a literary impressario at that time, decided to print the poems, and later would take others and some stories. He asked to meet Lawrence and then introduced him to such writers as Wells, W. B. Yeats and Ezra Pound, and helped to find a publisher for *The White Peacock*.

Lawrence was now teaching in the Davidson School in Croydon, a suburb near London, "a quivering greyhound set to mind a herd of pigs," he remembered, and he was beginning to establish a reputation in the world of letters. He was also interested in another of his fellow teachers, another ambitious writer, Helen Corke, but she had suffered through a disastrous affair with a married man and only wanted Lawrence's intellectual companionship.

Lawrence's sexual initiation occurred in the summer of 1910 at the hands of a married woman, in the oedipal sense perhaps a projection of his own mother. A small, blond woman, Alice Dax was married to the local pharmacist and held advanced views on matters of dress and feminism. She claimed to a friend that she "gave" Lawrence sex—the usage is so eminently Victorian, to "give" sex as if it were a poultice or some sort of medicine—to relieve his anxiety over a poem he was unable to complete in her upstairs study. We may smile at such a sacrifice for art; it is an argument for ardor that even John Donne or Andrew Marvell did not imagine. Just why Lawrence had been permitted upstairs, in such proximity to the bedroom, when Mr. Dax was busy mixing his preparations at his pharmacy, we cannot know, but apparently Mrs. Dax had a more potent prescription than her husband, because Lawrence completed his poem. The relationship with Mrs. Dax ended Lawrence's virginal state, but such intimate visits were difficult to arrange in Eastwood. There was also the complication that Mrs. Dax fell in love immediately. They managed a weekend in London, where they saw a performance of Strauss's *Elektra*, which inspired them to make love again, but the affair was cut short by the discovery that Lawrence's mother had cancer.

The oedipal mother instinctively discourages her rivals. In good health, Mrs. Lawrence objected to Jessie and Louie; now, in grinding pain during the fall of 1910, she became her son's exclusive concern and her agony became his. Lawrence presented his mother, gray and drained, with the first copy of *The White Peacock,* but she was too far gone to appreciate its significance.

A year after his mother's death, still teaching at Croydon, working on an early draft of *Sons and Lovers,* Lawrence again succumbed to pneumonia. For a month he could not even sit upright in his bed. The illness, coming so soon after his mother's death, increased his own awareness of his mortality. His doctor warned him to stop teaching or risk consumption. As he recuperated, he worked on the manuscript of *The Trespasser,* his second novel. Lawrence soon realized the extent to which teaching delayed and frustrated his intentions to write. Though he felt confident that now he could support himself as a writer, such a prospect was daunting. He also had the idea of teaching English in a German university where there might be fewer demands on his time than at the Davidson School. It was with this purpose that he had come to lunch with the Weekleys.

The "Free Love" of Otto Gross

For Lawrence, his afternoon at the Weekleys' resulted in love at first sight. Mrs. Weekley was, of course, a married mother of three children, and she seemed quite settled in her propriety. The facts of her existence, however, may not have been sufficient to discourage Lawrence. As he told Jessie Chambers in the formulation of a kind of personal motto, "With *should* and *ought* I shall have nothing to do!"

Upon returning to Eastwood, he sent Frieda a note claiming that she was the most wonderful woman in England, to which she tartly replied that it was clear that he did not know many Englishwomen. She did suggest, though, that he pay her a second visit in a few days, strategically naming the day as Easter Sunday, knowing that her husband would be in London visiting his parents. Lawrence appeared and the couple had a few hours to themselves. The children were in the garden hunting for Easter eggs and the servants had a holiday. In her *Memoirs,* Frieda remembered that Lawrence saw through the false cheer of her domesticity, "through my bright and hard shell." What she pretended not to understand was why Lawrence was at all interested, since she did not see herself as particularly desirable or attractive.

According to Frieda, she was a living somnambulist stultified in marriage and conventional responsibility. Originally, she had been drawn to Weekley because of his stature and dignity. But she would learn very quickly that his authority was a matter of appearances. In her *Memoirs*, which she partly fictionalized, inventing pseudonyms for herself and Weekley, Frieda related the disappointment of her wedding night. It exists as her symbolic fable, the explanation of the failure of her marriage, inhibited by the fear of passion and made mechanical by Weekley's fears. Just before the newlyweds retired to bed in an inn in Lucerne, Weekley descended from their room to get something to drink. Was he insecure, did he need alcohol to bolster his spirits? Perhaps because she realized his lack of imagination, Frieda partly undressed and climbed to the top of an old cupboard, dangling her legs and waiting. The cupboard was decorated with a stiff Eve—the petrified Victorian bride—and an Adam who reminded Frieda of an unevolved "missing link." She wondered what Weekley would do when he returned and could not find her, but the prospect of her perched on the cupboard might be too unsettling, too playful a gesture. Dutifully, she climbed back into the bed, into a recess that made her feel as if she were sinking into the earth. Another version of this story is told by Lawrence in a short play called "Fight for Barbara." There, Weekley "stood in the doorway looking frightened to death," unable to comprehend why his wife was on the cupboard.

According to Frieda, when they finally did make love later that same night, Weekley treated her like a cross between a child and "an old dowager Empress," suggesting some version of Queen Victoria. She remembered her virginal passage as more than horrible; instead of the "unspeakable bliss" she expected, she was left with an "unspeakable torment of soul." Reading the chapter, one senses that Frieda is constantly overreaching, making matters seem worse than they may have been. The prose is ejaculatory and grandiose. She labored for fifteen years over her *Memoirs,* and she complained during her years with Lawrence of the difficulties she felt in expressing herself in English. For all her exaggerations and theatricality, she does present the picture of a woman at odds with the conventional image of the Victorian wife who submits passively to her husband's sexual will because it is expected of her. Frieda Weekley may have been submissive to the respectability that marriage conferred, but she dared to try to stimulate and engage her husband sexually, aspiring to sexual equality and pleasure. In that way, she was a more robust participant in the romantic tradition than most of her female predecessors and was making a demand that would carry over into the future.

The security Weekley once represented became, over the four-teen-year course of marriage, overprotective and smothering, contradicting a vital ingredient in her character. As a child she had been a tomboy, reckless, exhibiting a wild, rebellious side that made her parents fear for her safety. After her marriage, she made several trips back to Germany to visit her family. On one of those trips, she reveals in her *Memoirs,* she encountered a "remarkable disciple of Freud and was full of undigested theories." Frieda was twenty-six when she met Otto Gross through her older sister, Else Jaffe, in Munich during the summer of 1907.

The three von Richthofen sisters were remarkable women for their era. Each had a rebellious nature and intellectual aspirations, and each eventually married an accomplished man. Else was then separated from her first husband, Edgar Jaffe, a mild-mannered and excessively tactful man, a professor at Heidelberg who had been a student of the renowned German sociologist Max Weber. Else, too, was an intellectual. She had also been a student of Max Weber's and had received her doctorate in sociology. She lived in Schwabing, a bohemian sector of Munich, where Gross would hold court in the Café Stephanie or the famed Simplicissimus bar throughout the night, advocating electrifying new theories of erotic release while he was supercharged with cocaine. Frieda was enthralled, excited by the atmosphere in the cafés, in such direct contrast to the complacency of life in Nottingham, and by the man who was the center of attention.

Freud's biographer, Ernest Jones, described Gross as the "nearest approach to the romantic idea of the genius" he had ever met. A tall, slender, blond man with a loping stride, as if in relentless pursuit of some disappearing truth, Gross was a charismatic psychiatrist, a man who inspired characters in half a dozen German novels of the period, and who damaged the reputation of the psychoanalytic circle around Freud because of his excesses. Gross showed his utter disdain for convention with his disordered, unkempt appearance. He was not handsome in the usual sense—he had a receding chin, a large hooked nose, gaps in his front teeth—but because of his mental agility he had enormous appeal for women. Like Nietzsche, Gross was a wunderkind who became so debilitated by his own illnesses that he had to resort to drugs as a palliative. Secretly addicted to morphine, and experimenting as well with opium and cocaine, he was a psychosexual explorer who practiced an irresponsible kind of "free love" in the pursuit of sexual liberation.

From one point of view, usually that of the deserted woman, "free love" is irresponsible, or at least fickle and without lasting commitment, but in the waning moments of the Victorian mood in Europe, the concept had some eager adherents. "Free love" was experimental, a radical subversion of traditional morality and social expectations governing courtship and marriage. It meant that men as well as women could free themselves of the obligations of monogamy and that sexual relations could occur on a more spontaneous basis. According to Gross, the old formalities of the Victorian sexual code resulted in crippling repression and neurosis which could only be relieved by new attitudes toward sexuality. Gross wrote four books and a number of articles that contributed to the fledgling science of psychiatry, but he was as well an archetype of the physician who gains the confidence of his patient (who was almost always female), seduces her and encourages her to fall in love as the central part of the "cure." Like some primitive shaman, the doctor's body and being would grapple with the disease and defeat it. And while in love, the patient often does have the strength to sustain an illusion of health, and the confidence to ascribe value to actions.

In 1907, this therapy had considerable theoretical appeal. Actually, however, Gross was a master manipulator of women, an obsessive progenitor of children born out of wedlock who habitually denied paternity, a kind of Jim Jones of the psychiatric community who saw himself surrounded by a cult of admiring women who revered and would even die for him. Married himself to a friend of Frieda's older sister, he persuaded his wife to have a child with one of his male acolytes with whom she would live. Frieda did not know in the summer of 1907 that her sister Else was pregnant with Gross's child and that they had reached the end of their affair. Not too many years later, ostensibly as acts of euthanasia, Gross would give poison to at least two and possibly three of his patients, women who were in love with him, to facilitate their suicides.

Gross's faith in the Freudian vision that individuals could change themselves and thus effect broad social changes made him a man of special appeal. When he met Frieda, he immediately flattered her by announcing she could be the harbinger of a new sexual code, one that was not monogamous. Gross stirred the dormant sexual animal in Frieda. Their union, he promised, would be a model for a great trust in the future, an act of rejuvenation. He told her that she belonged to an aristocracy of the beautiful and that her beauty was an invaluable, incomparable gift.

The good Professor Weekley, steeped in his arcane researches, serious about his work and supporting his family, was perhaps not as aware of such gifts. There are signs, as well, that he was not ardent, that despite the fact of his three children, he was afraid of the woman in Frieda, distrustful of sexuality in general, and knew little about pleasing women sexually.

Frieda returned to England after having become Gross's lover. He pursued her with epistolary appeals. He called her his source of strength, a fount of elemental warmth, "a wave of blissful liberating sensuality." He pleaded with her to join him in Munich with her children so that she never again would have to return to Weekley. She did meet Gross at a conference on neuropsychiatry in Amsterdam in September of 1907—her sister Else also attended, providing a convenient excuse. And Frieda spent another momentous night with Gross on a ferry crossing back to England, which engendered more fervent letters exhorting her to desert Weekley and leave the "annihilating, strangling, smallness of life in England." Believing, erroneously, that she had become pregnant by Gross, Frieda was on the verge of leaving Weekley until she was dissuaded by her sister, who by this time knew the ruinous fiasco that would result. Actually, Gross's future was one of unmitigated disaster. He would be found after World War I in a warehouse in Berlin, suffering the intense paranoia of advanced drug addiction and dying of malnutrition. Still ambivalent about Gross and not quite inclined in 1907 to risk the penalties that would follow a radical break with the prevailing morality about the marriage vows, she had written to Gross that she did not have the right to destroy a good man, but Gross had insinuated an idea that she would be ready to realize with Lawrence, more precipitously than she could have anticipated.

One of the cruel ironies usually disregarded by lovers is that romantic infatuations are notoriously brief. Initially, Frieda saw Lawrence as a temporary distraction, a way to alleviate the boredom of being the good Mrs. Weekley, a quick escape into temporary pleasures with a man of ideas. For Frieda, a brief fling would not constitute a profound betrayal or a *compromise* of her role as matron and mother.

Yet the heady notion of liberation that Gross had stirred in her simmered in Frieda's heart as part of her discontent for five years. She seemed to be waiting for a man who would arouse her as Gross had before she would act decisively. Meeting Lawrence, she would be swept away by the power of his language. She had been drawn to Gross, who was ungainly, even ugly. Lawrence, with his stooped shoulders and narrow chest, was equally unprepossessing, but, like Gross, he had a powerful and supple mind, which for a woman of substance can often seem an overwhelming inducement for love.

The actual idea of elopement, however, was Lawrence's. Initially, Frieda presumed a more conventional alliance, one with which she could safely deceive her husband while keeping her family intact. She had managed such an affair, before meeting Gross, with a Nottingham businessman named Will Dowson, who had a motorcar, a rare convenience for lovers at that time. She met Lawrence at a railway station in Derbyshire, midway between Nottingham and Eastwood, bringing along her two daughters to avoid raising any suspicion. She was charmed by Lawrence's attentiveness to the two young girls, his ability to play with them as they walked through the early spring woods and fields as if he were their age. Frieda proposed that Lawrence visit the following Sunday afternoon, knowing that once again her husband would be traveling to London. Lawrence came, and Frieda, eager that their touches and furtive kisses lead to some more passionate encounter, invited Lawrence to spend the night.

She was surprised when Lawrence refused, arguing that he wanted a fuller commitment, that he would not disguise his love from Weekley. Drawn by absolutes and extremes, the romantic is a voluptuary of demands and ideals. Lawrence knew an affair could have only led to an inferior pleasure, frustrating and vitiating. He wanted all of Frieda and at once, and the ardor of his demand was intoxicating. He asked Frieda to declare their love, and to allow him to accompany her on an imminent trip to Germany that she had planned. Dramatic, theatrical love seems more romantic when blocked by obstacles. Frieda had known Lawrence for little more than a month, but she felt, as she wrote in her *Memoirs,* that she was submitting to "a force stronger than myself." When Weekley returned from London on the next day, she announced her intention to go to Germany with Lawrence. Leaving her son with her husband, she took her two daughters to the home of Weekley's parents in London, dimly aware that her former life with her children could never be resumed. Then she met Lawrence at the Charing Cross Station where he "lifted me body and soul out of all my past life."

A Modern Romance

Baron von Richthofen had organized a large family party in Metz on May 4, 1912, to commemorate his retirement after fifty years of government service. Nervous about arrangements and still unsure of her actions, Frieda hid Lawrence in his own hotel room, communicating to him coyly through notes. Lawrence wrote his friend Edward Garnett, a publisher's reader who had helped with the acceptance of *The Trespasser,* his second novel, that what he and Frieda needed was a period of naked intimacy, what he called "free-breathing space." He would not find it in Metz. Before the departure, he had felt uneasy, fearing that some unknown force might strike from below. His image, unconsciously phallic, was an eel biting from the mud, a possible projection of Frieda's husband or father. He would dream of fighting with Weekley, and Frieda of Lawrence fighting with her father and beating him. The content of these dreams leads to obvious Freudian interpretations, but there is as well the romantic connotation of the knight in armor engaged in mortal combat for the hand of his lady.

The would-be lovers spent a week in Metz with few opportunities alone. "Making history" was not the most comfortable matter, Lawrence confided in a letter to Garnett, though he compared this week of separation to a necessary vigil, a ritual of preparation for life with Frieda. She introduced Lawrence to her two sisters; both approved of him. Frieda's parents would learn of the elopement through a barrage of telegrams and imploring letters from Weekley, but they would only meet Lawrence after a melodramatic incident in which he was apprehended as a British spy. Lawrence and Frieda had been walking along the fortifications outside Metz, which was still a military outpost. They spoke in English and were overheard by a policeman. Lawrence's release was expedited through the military connections of Baron von Richthofen, but Lawrence had to leave Metz. The incident put Lawrence in the position of the Romantic outsider, hostile to governing systems and the military arm enforcing them. This is a perspective familiar to nineteenth-century Romantics, but modern writers tend to be even more alienated and embittered, perhaps because modern war has been so much more consequential and terrifying.

Frieda's sister Else persuaded her friend Alfred Weber to lend his vacation apartment in the village of Icking, south of Munich, to Frieda and Lawrence. With very little money and like the proverbial lovers who lived on air, they made meals of eggs, black bread, berries and beer. The apartment had a balcony where Lawrence could work on his revisions of *Sons and Lovers*. Below, there were peasant women working in wheat fields, bullocks pulling carts, the pale milk-green Isar River, and, beyond, the snow-covered peaks of the Alps. Finally, they were together and in love: "I never knew what love was before," Lawrence declared in a letter. Frieda appreciated the romance of being with the son of a coal miner who showed her the poems he was writing, poems in which he would romantically declare that "you are the call and I am the answer." Lawrence for his part admired Frieda's aristocratic lineage, though, on deeper levels, the fact that she was a married mother satisfied both his rebelliousness and his oedipal yearnings.

Even idyllic love has its torments. The lovers had fled to another country, but the letters from home kept arriving. Impetuously, perhaps to relieve herself of guilt or to shift the blame from Lawrence, Frieda sent her husband the love letters she had received from Otto Gross five years earlier. Did she imagine that they would so horrify him that all relations between them could end instantly? Weekley's appeals were on behalf of the children. For the sake of their misery over losing their mother, he would be able to forgive both Gross and Lawrence as temporary aberrations. Frieda would suffer enormous pain over her separation. As time went on, her pain over the loss of her children became a serious point of emotional contention. Curiously, it was the one thing with which Lawrence could not sympathize, as if Frieda's children represented an intolerable nerve, a reminder of his close attachment to his own mother, and of the fact that he had helped Frieda violate the ultimate taboo—that against the mother who abandons her offspring. Lawrence's attitude toward Frieda's children illustrates his romantic escapism. The responsibilities of children represent an intrusive reality powerful enough to disturb any self-contained romantic illusions.

"I wanted love and now I have more than I can bear," Frieda wrote to Lawrence's friend, Edward Garnett. Lawrence told another

friend that he would always be a priest of love, but there were
elements of ambivalence during the delirium. Frieda was reading
Anna Karenina, which so closely paralleled the choices she had
made for love and passion over family and past associations. She
sent the book to Weekley as another explanation of her acts. But
inserted between the pages of *Anna Karenina,* Frieda had left a
letter from Will Dowson, the Nottingham lace manufacturer with
whom she had had an affair. Dowson had asked Frieda why she had
not eloped with him, and with clear malice Weekley sent this letter
back—to Lawrence!

Frieda also read the evolving manuscript of *Sons and Lovers* and
commented freely, especially on the dialogue and reactions of Mrs.
Morel and Miriam, the characters based on Lawrence's mother and
Jessie Chambers. Lawrence was still corresponding with Jessie,
and he invited her to visit, an offer she was unprepared to accept.
While the invitation was a typical gesture, an open expression of
Lawrence's desire for community, it also seems peculiar, reminiscent of Shelley's invitation to his wife to accompany him when he
ran off with Mary Godwin. Jessie could not countenance the
possibility of another woman for Lawrence. She had already
chastised him for pursuing Louie Burrows, and she could never
have tolerated Frieda, who would have overpowered her
immediately.

After two months in Icking, Lawrence and Frieda decided near
the beginning of August to walk through the Alps to Italy. At one
time poets walked great distances as a means of sociology, a way of
learning the habits and contours of a place firsthand. For European
Romantics, the colossal beauties of the Alps could lead to a
tremendous vertigo. The overwhelming impact of the mountain
scenery could cause a writer to see beyond ordinary capacities, to
transcend the limitations of conditioning, to release what before
seemed inexpressible. For Lawrence and Frieda, the trek through
the Alps was a way to purge themselves of the past and, in a sense,
prepare themselves for a new life together.

Outfitting themselves with rucksacks and a portable stove,
Frieda and Lawrence sent most of their possessions ahead by rail.
In a very real sense, they were fleeing civilization (and Weekley's
letters) as Melville or Gauguin had fled to the South Seas. They
were practically destitute vagabonds. Frieda's mother had appeared
just prior to their departure, admonishing Lawrence for treating a
baroness like a barmaid. Most of the time Frieda seems to have

enjoyed the poverty: They sang songs as they walked, they bathed in cold streams, and slept in huts, haylofts, over a pigsty one night, or in dirty inns during the month they took to reach the Lago di Garda in Italy. The simplicity that delighted Lawrence was his antidote to the poisons of industrialization, a conflict that he would dramatize again and again in his fiction. Lawrence believed that during the course of their trek they formed an indissoluble bond; for Frieda, Lawrence was the type of man who needed to be born twice—first through his mother and then with the woman he loved—and his rebirth occurred during their passage through the Alps.

The couple settled in Gargano, a town that could only be reached by water—Lawrence having providentially received a fifty-pound advance for *Sons and Lovers*. Frieda would lie in bed till midday; she was messy (some might say slovenly), as unconcerned with the domestic disorder around her as her lover Otto Gross had been, and she had been accustomed to having servants care for her. Lawrence cheerfully assumed all domestic chores, scrubbing floors, marketing and preparing meals. He was completing the final version of *Sons and Lovers* and beginning *The Sisters*, a book that would become *The Rainbow*. His concentration was extraordinary, and he could leave off writing to join a conversation and then resume almost as if there had been no interruption. The only problem was Frieda's desire to return to see her children.

Early in the summer of 1913, the lovers returned to England so that Frieda could begin negotiations with Weekley about the children and a divorce. *Sons and Lovers* had been published, generally favorable reviews were appearing, and Lawrence was being taken seriously as a novelist. Frieda's distress over her separation from the children had caused a breach between Frieda and Lawrence in Italy, a diminishment of the fund of sympathy that connects a couple, even a couple in love. Frieda's torment is comparable to that suffered by Marie d'Agoult in France almost a century earlier. She also had abandoned her children to flee with her lover, the pianist and composer Franz Liszt. "When one has smashed everything around oneself," Marie d'Agoult realized, "one has also smashed oneself."

Lawrence's lack of sympathy for Frieda's sacrifice is surprising given the quality of compassion he was able to exercise as a novelist. Emotionally, he needed Frieda as his buttress. He resented her agonies over the loss of her children, her complaints, self-pitying remarks, depressions. A poem he wrote shortly after their elopement, "She Looks Back," sheds some light on the threatening place of children in his scheme of things. In it, he cursed Frieda's motherhood, recollecting the devastating potential and even murderous capabilities of mother love—the kind of love he had experienced with his own mother and had so powerfully described, with the help of Frieda's commentary, in *Sons and Lovers*. The conflict over children may have been exacerbated by her desire to have a child with Lawrence to fill the void left by her abandonment of her children, but her desire was unshared by Lawrence. Her loss, particularly in view of Weekley's having forbidden Frieda to see the children—the condoned punishment for a wayward mother—was an intolerable barrier to her happiness, though not enough to make her return to the fold. It remained a constant source of discord between Frieda and Lawrence. Lawrence was so blinded by his own consuming vision of the world that he told Frieda at one point to overcome her feelings about the loss of her children because he was going to make the world a better place for them—secure in the belief that his ameliorative vision would console her.

Their quarrels intensified. Frieda was a confident, outgoing woman who pushed self-doubts aside. She would vent her disappointments openly, would rage and scream when angered, and would begin a fight and recover within minutes with remarkable resilience; Lawrence would brood, would repress and control his anger, and then would resent Frieda for bruising his feelings.

There were, at least, some distractions from marital stress. Lawrence was beginning to meet other writers, artists and intellectuals who would form the nexus of his social circle in England, where he would be forced to spend the war years. Most important, because of the perspective they provide on the details of life with Frieda and Lawrence, were a young couple they had met in London, Katherine Mansfield and John Middleton Murry. The two couples felt an immediate bond because both were living together without the sanction of marriage. Son of a clerk, a small, nervous, shy man, good-looking but with thinning hair and hazel eyes that seemed disconnected, staring into unfocused vacancy, Murry had been a scholarship student at Oxford. Recently graduated, he met Mansfield when she was twenty-four. A delicate pale woman who dressed habitually in black, with sleek black bobbed hair brushed stylishly close to her forehead, she projected caution and moved her body with great deliberation and restrictive control as if it were so fragile it could break. Frieda found her exquisite. Daughter of the chairman of the Bank of New Zealand, Mansfield had married a man and deserted him on the next day. Still undivorced, she was living on a small trust allowance provided by her father. She was cynical about love, and perhaps about life as well, partly because of the tuberculosis she harbored in her lungs, and partly because an abortion had left her without the capacity to bear children.

Diffident, sardonic in temperament, with the capacity to make himself entirely dependent upon a woman, Murry was writing a very bad novel called *Still Life*—"wriggling self-abuse," Lawrence called it. Mansfield had already published an excellent collection of acerbic short stories, *In a German Pension*.

Beside writing, Mansfield, Murry and Lawrence shared a common physical disability that on some deep psychic level had to affect their outlooks: they were all incipient consumptives. Through the nineteenth century, tuberculosis had been regarded as the romantic disease. The patient would often spend years aware of an impending wasting-away from within, with bronchial problems and attacks of coughing that often ended with spitting blood as a visible reminder of eventual doom.

Frieda was the exception in this quartet, exuding vigor and health, the gushing enthusiastic blond even in her more indolent moments. She felt especially at ease with Mansfield and Murry because they were still full of the spontaneity of their love. On one occasion when the two couples were on a London bus, Frieda was delighted by the discovery that Mansfield and Murry were sticking their tongues out and making faces at each other. The act was playfully irreverent and without pretension. Frieda felt that Mansfield and Murry needed to be helped out of their troubles and she did try to make a younger sister out of Mansfield. Actually Mansfield would become an intermediary for Frieda with her children. Frieda managed to see them early one morning by intercepting them on their way to school. She was shocked when she tried to see them this way again, realizing that they had been instructed not to even speak to her. Frieda had eight months with Lawrence in Germany and Italy in which to remember the impassive, suspicious, confused faces of her children. When Frieda and Lawrence returned to England, it was because Weekley had agreed to a divorce, and Frieda saw her children for a tense half hour in a lawyer's office. Very quickly afterward, in May of 1914, Frieda married Lawrence, with Mansfield and Murry serving as witnesses. Frieda gave Mansfield the wedding ring she had worn for so many years with Weekley; it was, to say the least, a curious gesture, making her younger friend become the visible reminder of a past from which she had tried to flee.

The Promise of *The Rainbow*

Condemned by the bourgeois world as illicit lovers, so intent on gratifying their pleasures that they would sacrifice family and hearth, Frieda and Lawrence found an identity that satisfied their rebellious natures. Though they could never escape the consequences of the elopement—Frieda's loss of her children—their new legality may have subtly affected the way they saw themselves; their more permanent union may have made their liaison less romantic. But other factors contributed to the tensions which began to emerge in their relationship, latent hostilities that became so disruptingly evident as to end in recrimination and physical assault. One such factor was the war, which began a few months after the marriage ceremony, and the growing dismay that Lawrence began to feel as a result, a loss of faith in future possibilities which became the touchstone of his generation, as expressed by Eliot in "The Waste Land" or Pound in "Mauberley."

Related to Lawrence's despair over the war was his own need to express a vision of the world through his writing that could in some meaningful manner improve it. Such didactic intentions are apparent in the earliest of fictions, beginning with Defoe and Swift, and continuing from Fielding to Thackeray. In Lawrence's case, however, the need to improve matters seemed more urgent and resulted in shrillness. As long as he could believe in his own powers, the messianic impulse could be a creative catalyst. At other times it could as easily sour into dark delusion.

Lawrence became more autocratic in his views during the war, denouncing democratic options and advocating a tyranny of the elect. When Lawrence's messianic illusions were exposed as unconvincing delusions, the disillusioning result could lead to a poisoning of perspective. The desire to overwhelm the world with a vision revealing its banalities, follies and evils has typically been relieved by a comic approach, a dominating mode in fiction from Fielding through Dickens, but the ameliorating possibilities of such a comedy are absent from Lawrence's fiction.

His friend Katherine Mansfield would observe that Lawrence

took himself "dreadfully seriously," that he had lost his sense of humor, that he saw himself as a symbolic prophet crying "woe" in the wilderness. This howling advocacy is reflected in his fiction as the pressure for reform, a reliance on the need for political change that makes some of his characters seem hysterical or bombastic. It is a pattern which is confirmed by a story told by one of Lawrence's friends, Henry Savage, who was basking in the sun with Lawrence one day on some cliffs near Kent. Suddenly, Lawrence struck his chest violently, declaring that he had something in it that was "harder than concrete. If I don't get it out it will kill me." Savage did not believe Lawrence was referring to his tubercular condition, but that Lawrence "meant the dark, strange forces" that began to find expression in *The Rainbow*, the novel he began writing during the war.

Lawrence wrote the first draft of *The Rainbow* just before beginning his *Study of Thomas Hardy*, so it is no surprise that the finished version of his novel had such deep affinities to Hardy. Both writers told stories about ordinary people caught in heroic struggles with destiny; both used nature as an active agent, not merely as the source of metaphor or scenic backdrop, but as a purgative force; and both raged against the consequences of industrialism. As a novelist, Lawrence has often aroused ambivalent critical responses. Initially, his Victorian audience, like Hardy's, was unprepared for his sexual emphasis. Later readers felt uneasy about his overt narrative intrusions, a heavy-handed omniscient preachiness that also seemed sententious when his characters voiced his evangelical beliefs.

The Rainbow is characteristic of Lawrence's strengths and weaknesses, an irritating repetitiveness, voluminous speeches that can become superfluous or even boring, and scenes of surging lyricism like the one at the end of the novel when Ursula Brangwen runs through the woods in the rain, or, earlier, when Anna, her mother, dances pregnant and naked in her bedroom, a sort of fertility ritual which Will, her husband, cannot fathom. Lawrence is always best when moving his characters through some phenomenon of nature or agricultural activity, and scenes like the one in which Anna and Will Brangwen pick corn in the moonlight are still lambent and inspiring. Ostensibly a history of the Brangwen family through three generations, *The Rainbow* dramatizes the struggle of will between men and women, and reflects his own emerging difficulties with Frieda.

In Lawrence's work, sexual desire—whether for initiation, pleasure, preservation, or dynastic continuity—becomes a vital expression of his will. Early in *The Rainbow,* a concentrated sexual drive is expressed by Tom Brangwen, who has inherited the Brangwen lands and works them alone. He courts and marries Lydia Lensky, a Polish widow with a daughter, Anna. Like Frieda Weekley, Lydia Lensky is older than Tom, and she is descended from aristocrats who have sold their land for money, which was then dissipated. Anna has all the wild independence of Frieda, and her dissatisfaction with the possibilities for women in the last stages of the Victorian era is expressed in her disdain for housework, her lax domesticity. At one point Anna spills her tea on her pillow, which she then carelessly rubs with her handkerchief, turning the pillow over. Lawrence had been disturbed when Frieda spilled her tea in this manner on one of their first mornings together in Icking. A few days later, Frieda broke the heel of her shoe when walking and wanted to throw the shoe into a lake. Lawrence appreciated the aristocratic disdain for the material in both these acts, which he admired as manners but which on a deeper level provoked him, and made him remember the deprivations of his own childhood, when his mother had to scrimp and save for a pair of shoes.

Through Ursula Brangwen, Anna's daughter, Lawrence projected the central quality he so admired in Frieda, an animating willfulness that enabled her to resist expected social roles. Anna and Ursula are formed out of the stuff of Lawrence's experiences with Frieda, but they reflect and to some extent become spokeswomen for Lawrence's own views, his anticlericalism, his hatred of the military, and his ability to expose and wither illusions cherished by others. While Anna accepts the Victorian notion of marriage, of the woman serving and comforting the man and mothering his children, Ursula will wrestle with such conventions, and by ultimately rejecting them will repudiate the model of female subservience represented by her parents' marriage.

The qualities with which he imbues Ursula, here and later in *Women in Love,* underscore the extent to which Lawrence is a transitional figure, repudiating the notion of women as mere adjuncts of their husbands, urging them toward rebellion and independence, and yet insisting with evangelical fervor on the "natural order" of male dominance in the sexual equation. In both novels, his theme is the recurrence of love and conflict within marriage. It was a recurrence he lived with daily in his marriage and that he rearranged and put into his own perspective in his work—the artistic prerogative by which writers universally impose a form of dominance on reality.

The wedding of Anna and Will Brangwen is the central action of the early part of *The Rainbow*. Presented from an essentially male perspective, it is colored in elemental, almost brutal tones. Tom Brangwen, Anna's stepfather, gives Anna away to his nephew Will, and the wedding party is dominated by Tom and his two brothers Alfred and Frank:

> Tom Brangwen wanted to make a speech. For the first time in his life, he must spread himself wordily.
>
> "Marriage," he began, his eyes twinkling and yet quite profound, for he was deeply serious and hugely amused at the same time, "marriage," he said, speaking in the slow, full-mouthed way of the Brangwens, "is what we're made for—"?
>
> "Let him talk," said Alfred Brangwen, slowly and inscrutably, "let him talk." Mrs. Alfred darted indignant eyes at her husband.
>
> "A man," continued Tom Brangwen, "enjoys being a man: for what purpose was he made a man, if not to enjoy it?"
>
> "That a true word," said Frank, floridly.
>
> "And likewise," continued Tom Brangwen, "a woman enjoys being a woman: at least we surmise she does—"
>
> . . . .
>
> "Therefore we have marriage," continued Tom Brangwen.
>
> "Hold, hold," said Alfred Brangwen. "Don't run us off our legs." And in dead silence the glasses were filled. The bride and bridegroom, two children, sat with intent, shining faces at the head of the table, abstracted.
>
> "There's no marriage in heaven," went on Tom Brangwen, "but on earth there is marriage."
>
> "That's the difference between 'em," said Alfred Brangwen, mocking.

By this point Tom Brangwen has had much too much to drink to be able to articulate his feelings, and he cannot admit or express his buried desire—is it an inchoate lusting for his own youth?—to possess his stepdaughter. He is not even sure, as Lawrence puts it, "whether he was going to be married now, or what he had come for," but he is indeed attending his stepdaughter Anna's wedding. Lawrence has anticipated so incestuous a possibility for his readers much earlier, in a scene where Anna's mother gives birth to a son by Tom Brangwen. Petulant, disturbed by her mother's screams, Anna begins to cry herself and refuses to go to bed when Tom orders her to do so. Impatient, he forces her to undress:

> Her body was held taut and resistant, he pushed off the little dress and the petticoats, revealing the white arms. She kept stiff, overpowered, violated. He went on with his task. And all the while she sobbed, choking: "I want my mother."

The scene dramatizes arbitrary paternal authority, and it exists as a paradigm of the male dominance that lies at the heart of all of Lawrence's fiction.

The Rainbow presents the struggle of the sexes and it explores the institution of marriage as it was being redefined by feminist anxieties at the turn of the modern era. Marriage becomes the field, in some cases the battlefield, where lines of power and dominance are drawn, and then respected or violated. Almost as soon as Anna and Will Brangwen are married, a tension forms between them. This tension is what most interests Lawrence; it troubled him with Frieda as well.

As Lawrence told his friend John Middleton Murry, his work depended on Frieda's "active goodwill," so the tension between them could inhibit his creativity if it became excessive. There may be an inevitability about that tension as Lawrence saw it similar to the sort of fundamental difference we can ascribe to biology or to myth—take, for instance, Lawrence's own view, in his *Fantasia of the Unconscious,* that men are "polarized upwards," that is, given an outlook that welcomes the sun and wants to work in its light, while women are "polarized downwards," toward the center of earth because of their attachment to hearth and home. Such views outrage contemporary women who see in them an archaic over-simplification more related to the conditioned differences they are trying to overcome than to any innate determinations.

Lawrence situates his sexual polarization in practically each couple he invents in *The Rainbow* and *Women in Love,* the novel which continues Ursula's story. In *The Rainbow,* this opposition manifests itself soon after the wedding of Anna and Will Brangwen, who begin to dispute over religious values. Anna, evidently speaking for Lawrence, argues that Christianity is mostly sham, a hollow practice which she finds unfulfilling. She jeers at Will, who she feels can mechanically accept religion as a social obligation. For Anna, as for Lawrence, this acquiescence leads to spiritual death. Lawrence uses the image of an attacking hawk for Anna and then for Will, who retaliates after feeling wounded. The couple displace their hostilities to domestic matters—his irritation at her sewing machine, her annoyance at his scattered garden tools—until one day "it seemed as if everything was shattered, all life ruined, desolate and laid waste." A day later, things seem marvelous again. It is such rapid emotional or ideational oscillation, from love to hate, from pain to pleasure or beauty to horror, that we recognize as the gothic element in the romantic spirit. Since it was as present in Lawrence's prose as in Frieda's outbursts, it must have been an important part of the music of their communication. Anna's submission is interesting in light of Lawrence's resistance to Frieda's desire to have a child with him. He was well aware that women's place in society was shaped by domestic bonds and that those bonds, reinforced by bearing children, could dictate limitations on their freedom of spirit. He may have felt, in opposing Frieda, more than his need to have her exclusive attention; he may have feared that Frieda would revert to the conventional role of mother and thus dampen some of the fire he found so vital in her. Stormy though their marriage was, Frieda's untamed vigor engaged and energized him.

The contest in *The Rainbow,* the struggle to dominate through will, recurs later in the novel in Ursula's rejection of Anton Skrebensky, whom she loves but will not accept because he is a soldier. For Ursula, or really for Lawrence, who uses his women to express his deepest views, Skrebensky is also spiritually dead, because as a military man he has sacrificed control over his own destiny.

Instead Ursula, seventeen and finishing high school, is attracted to Winifred Inger, one of her teachers, who with her "indomitably proud nature" seemed as "free as a man, yet exquisite as a woman." For Lawrence, emerging himself from a long century of Victorian repression, bathing scenes were always ripe with sexual overtones, as in *The Rainbow* where Will teaches Ursula how to swim. In a scene which surely must have shocked Lawrence's post-Victorian audience (more than any other in the novel except, perhaps, for the one near the end where Ursula and Skrebensky make love on a beach on the Lincolnshire coast), Winifred and Ursula bathe in the nude at night after a thunderstorm. The scene typifies all of

Lawrence's potential as a novelist as he finds a place for his characters to exult in nature. But it demonstrates, as well, his characteristic limitations, his tendency to overemphasize, to become too overtly symbolic, to make his characters seem more the puppets of his viewpoints than autonomous beings, especially when Ursula says she cannot see the path to the water because of the dark, and Winifred proposes to carry her into the water (a scene that was excised from the American edition), a case of Lawrence programming the initiation to suit the terms of his own gospel. By having Ursula accept Winifred as her lover, even though they only sustain the relationship for a short time (Winifred marries Ursula's uncle), Lawrence is challenging Victorian morality in a way that Thomas Hardy would not have dared. Nineteenth-century English novelists knew that any portrayal of female lovers risked censorship and condemnation. By having Ursula reject Anton Skrebensky, who wants to marry her and take her to India for a life in the colonial service, Lawrence frees her for the possibilities of an unconventional existence, which he will explore in *Women in Love*.

For the character of Ursula, Lawrence had been inspired by Frieda's arrogant superiority and sweeping generalizations as much as by her energy and power, but he may have succeeded in creating a figure beyond popular comprehension at the time. Even Lawrence remembered that when he was beginning his novel, it seemed like a book written in a strange foreign language which he hoped to be able to decipher. The critics clearly did not sympathize or understand. The *New Statesman* called it "dull, monotonous, pointless." The *Daily News* condemned its "wilderness of phallicism." The critic Clement Shorter found it a viciously suggestive "orgie of sexiness." James Douglas, in *The Star,* argued that the book had no right to exist, that the characters were less than human, lower than animals in a zoo. The reviews were part of a general cultural backlash, a stiffening of Victorian resistance that had begun with Hardy's novels and Wilde's plays in the 1890s. Many people would no longer wear their starched collars or their stiff straw hats; they removed corsets and padding from hips and buttocks, hemlines rose from the dust, daring ladies slashed their evening skirts up to the knee and wore plumed headdresses and clashing colors. Such women faced condemnation, public insult and an arthritic resistance. Reverend James Marchant organized his Crusade for Social Purity and advised young men to take cold baths, avoid modern fiction and practice abstinence. The writings of Havelock Ellis and Freud on sex were castigated from pulpits. Books by Balzac and Dickens were regarded as unfit for London schoolchildren, and a series of public morals conferences in London, Dublin and Edinburgh was organized to exert pressure against "sex novels" and contraception. There was a feeling that religion and the family were endangered by indecency and that the social stability of the country was being adversely affected. The result for the arts was that whatever artists created was considered suspicious by the middle classes, and artists were generally classed as dangerous dissidents.

Supported by an 1857 law governing the printing of pornography, a Scotland Yard inspector seized one thousand copies of *The Rainbow* from Lawrence's publisher, Methuen, on November 4, 1915. At an official hearing, a lawyer representing an organization called the National Purity League declared that the novel was a "mass of obscenity of thought, idea and action." Algernon Methuen, practically weeping, hoped that the scandal would not ruin his chances at becoming a baronet. He publicly apologized for printing the novel, admitting that he had not known the dirty thing he had handled, blaming Lawrence for not revising the book according to his suggestions. It was a scene directly out of some Victorian melodrama, but what followed seemed more like a medieval ritual exorcism. All the bound and unbound copies that had been printed were transported to a street outside the Royal Exchange, and there were burned by the public hangman. This burning of the books was the perfect opportunity for writers to deplore, denounce and demonstrate, but there was no protest, not even from the Society of Authors. The only positive notice of the book had been written for the *Glasgow Herald* by Catherine Carswell, Lawrence's friend, who was then dropped as a contributor. And with the exception of a single short story, nothing Lawrence would write would appear in England for the next five years.

The proceedings against *The Rainbow* occurred just after the first Zeppelin raid on London, an event that ended the island insularity of the British and announced the brutal beginnings of World War I. Lawrence wanted to leave England to found a utopian community he called Rananim, his "colony of lost souls," and he needed a physical deferment to get his passport. Standing in line for his examination, having his testicles squeezed by the attending physician, brought him face to face with what he felt was the mob spirit behind mobilization, the "bullying, servile conformity, the loss of individual 'manly isolation.'" For Lawrence, the "old world ended" and the reign of "bloated ignominy" began. The war was "utterly wrong, stupid, monstrous and contemptible," he told a friend, and such a recognition effectively left him "torn off from the body of mankind," which was zealously supporting the war effort.

The war, prolonged and without resolution, a stalemate of bloody atrocity, became "just hell" for Lawrence: "I don't see why I should be so disturbed—but I am. I can't get away from it for a minute: I live in a sort of coma like one of those nightmares when you can't move." In his Whitmanesque poem "New Heaven and Earth," it is clear that Lawrence, as sensitive to historical change as to the nuances of a friend's gossip, was terribly affected by the war, that it caused a kind of hysteria alleviated by the act of writing, which, in turn, helped him internalize the pain:

> When I heard the cannon of the war, I listened with my own ears to my own destruction.
> When I saw the torn dead, I knew it was my own torn dead body
> It was all me, I had done it all in my own flesh.
> I shall never forget the maniacal horror of it all in the end when everything was me....

Brittle Friendship

Lawrence grew a beard, he quipped in a letter, a convenient bush under which to hide. Actually, it was an incendiary red, and some of his friends thought it created a diabolical aura. The beard represented a shift in perspective, an identification with his coal-mining father who announced with frequent pride that no razor had touched his face, a mark no doubt of the insubordinate spirit that insured his poor prospects in the pits. Lawrence's red beard was a flaming expression of his anger at what he decided was the colossal stupidity of the war and its carnage.

Some of this anger, Frieda felt, was deflected to her. After all, she was German and had relations on the front lines: a cousin, Manfred von Richthofen, was to become known as the "Red Baron," the German ace who downed seventy-five planes. The English were quite naturally full of anti-German feeling. Beethoven and Brahms were banned from British concert halls. People with German-sounding names like the novelist Ford Madox Hueffer or Prince Louis Battenberg, whose wife was the granddaughter of Queen Victoria, decided to change their names—from Hueffer to Ford and from Battenberg to Mountbatten. Relations with Frieda became more tense, the internecine quarreling more frequent, as Lawrence became morose because of the war news and the trouble over *The Rainbow,* and also because it became evident that Frieda, with her emphatic and sometimes truculent assertiveness, was becoming a point of contention in Lawrence's relations with others.

In the war years, a brittleness about Lawrence made friendship tenuous. Lawrence had the ability to share his deepest feelings with complete intimacy and apparent honesty, and to use his own admissions as a way of drawing people out of their shells, quickly hoping to win their confidence to the point where they would reveal themselves. For Lawrence, this proved a way to make his life a dramatic medium as well as a means of gathering materials for the novels he was writing, which reflected his friendships. Most of these coaxed alliances, with Bertrand Russell or E. M. Forster or Murry, foundered on the shoals of British reserve and phlegmatic notions of privacy, frustrated by those who felt uncomfortable with personal revelation.

The problem of strained friendships was prompted by Lawrence and Frieda, who could conspire with a harsh insistence to view others unsympathetically, which could seem uncivil or at least impolite. With the strict moral fervor that often characterizes the radical temperament, they were forever concerned with what they judged "dodging," that is, evading the truth as they saw it with illusions. They could be extreme and censorious; when they disliked they raged and reviled, but what they liked they worshiped and celebrated. Lawrence's friend Richard Aldington shrewdly remarked that Lawrence's role was that of the heretic, the man who smashed other people's values and left them with nothing to believe in except the force of his personality. Of course, in the violent upheaval of the war itself—with its ten million fatalities and its twenty million wounded—the old absolutes of religion and country were open to question, especially by artists and intellectuals who could no longer subscribe to a system of beliefs that had resulted in such a conflagration in the first place.

Aldington observed that Lawrence was a master of the lost art of talking, who spoke his novels out while composing them. His predecessors, Coleridge and Wilde, the great talkers of the beginning and end of the nineteenth century respectively, were usually more graceful. Even Wilde found humorous ways to make his vitriol accommodating. Lawrence could also be quite compelling, but was more antagonistic. His voice was one register of the agitation he felt as it rose to a thin, reedy scratch or as his laugh suddenly warped into a nervously high-pitched giggle. His friend, Lady Cynthia Asquith (whose father-in-law was prime minister of England), remembered his brilliant blue eyes, his lithe springing step and the "flashing phrases" of his challenging talk with "startling beauty of utterance." It was delivered with a voice that shifted from harshness to softness: "one moment he was lyrically, contagiously joyous; the next sardonic, jibing."

In 1915 and 1916, Lawrence and Frieda lived in a series of damp, simply furnished country cottages in Chesham, Greatham and Hampstead, in the English countryside, spending about six months in each place. They had very little money, supplemented by occasional gifts from some of Lawrence's wealthier friends: fifty pounds from Amy Lowell, a rich American who was grateful for the poems Lawrence contributed to her Imagist anthology; the use of poet Alice Meynell's cottage in Greatham, which was more comfortable than any of Lawrence's other residences during the war years, and where at least Frieda was not obligated to draw water from a spring at the top of a hill or depend on outdoor privies in the rawness of the English winter. Frieda accepted the material deprivation, the nomadic bohemianism of life with Lawrence without complaint, with cheerful stoicism, and readers of her fervent book about life with Lawrence, *Not I but the Wind,* will detect her pleasure in the simplifications afforded by poverty.

Another friend willing to help Lawrence was Lady Ottoline Morrell, whose family had owned the coalfields in Eastwood where Lawrence's father worked in the pits. Married to a member of parliament, she lived in an elegant home in London's Bedford Square and owned Garsington, a regal five-hundred-acre estate near Oxford, where peacocks paraded and which she hoped to turn into a refuge for artists and pacifists. The eccentric renegade in her family, Lady Ottoline sought the company of artists and intellectuals, and she was the mistress of the philosopher Bertrand Russell, who shaped her pacifist outlook. She was not beautiful—she had a long, narrow thickly powdered face, a long neck and an angular body that made her enemies call her horsey—but she made Frieda jealous. Extravagant, quixotic, a tempestuous redhead, a modern

Messalina according to the poet Siegfried Sassoon, she responded to Lawrence's intensity and recognized his imaginative insight into people (a power he would characteristically use to her disadvantage when he lampooned her as Hermine Roddice in *Women in Love*).

Lady Ottoline introduced Lawrence to the novelist E. M. Forster, and to Bertrand Russell. Both Forster and Russell were linked with the Bloomsbury group—Virginia and Leonard Woolf, the philosopher G. E. Moore, the economist John Maynard Keynes, the biographer Lytton Strachey, and the art critic Clive Bell, who were all in some way associated with Cambridge. The artists and intellectuals of Bloomsbury were well born and highly mannered. Precious, self-consciously esthetic, they often seemed to regard wit as more important than feeling. For the most part, they were discreetly homosexual in character, with an effeteness that aroused a shrill repugnance in Lawrence, even as he may have contained or repressed some of his own inclinations to be close to members of his own sex. Always the mystical romantic, Lawrence believed that the power in sexuality depended on an individual's ability to use it as a means of self-discovery; unless this was an active principle, sex could become mechanical, stale and meaningless. He had decided that homosexuality was masturbatory, merely the projection of a mirror image instead of the struggle that could lead to a rebirth.

As an elite pressure group, for Bloomsbury to unite behind the work of a young writer—as it did with T. S. Eliot—could only help insure reputation and success. Forster had a high regard for Lawrence's talent, which he astutely realized depended on the balancing of the capacities of the preacher and the poet. He would declare Lawrence to be the "greatest imaginative novelist of his generation." But his own circumspection, his typically English personality with his guarded inhibitions—the guilt in his own Victorian closet—made him cringe when he heard the outspoken vehemence of Lawrence's opinions. On one occasion, when he was visiting the painter Duncan Grant, a Bloomsbury favorite, Forster was shocked to hear Lawrence criticize and condemn Grant's work. Such honesty was inadvisable in genteel circumstances, and the Bloomsbury contingent would do their part to exclude Lawrence. Forster came to Greatham to visit Lawrence and Frieda, but all Lawrence could discuss (with an intuitive grasp of exactly how to discomfit his guest) was revolution, a classless society and sex. Forster, who had a comfortable independent income and who only wanted to find a young man of a lower social class to love discreetly,

was astonished at the insistence of Lawrence's views and the way
Frieda so completely agreed. He wrote a note to the "Dear Lawrences," dryly referring to them as one communal unit until they
thought it "worthwhile to function separately," complaining about
Lawrence, the "deaf impercipient fanatic who has nosed over his
own little sexual round until he believes there is no other path for
others to take."

Forster's note expressed the spleen of a diffident patrician who
had been taunted by bohemians, but it occurred after substantial
provocation, as a way of retreating from a relationship that had
proved too combative. With Bertrand Russell, matters were even
more tempestuous. Lawrence was thirty and Russell forty-three
when they met. A lecturer at Cambridge and the author, along with
Alfred North Whitehead, of the influential treatise, *Principia
Mathematica,* Russell is the grandson of a prime minister who
served twice during the nineteenth century, and Russell himself
was heir to an earldom. Yet the lord and the coalminer's son had an
ideological outlook that suggested compatibility. Russell had lost
faith in human possibilities because of the cataclysm of the war,
and his own emotional life was turbulently unsettled because he
was in love with Lady Ottoline, who was already married. At first,
Russell responded to Lawrence's habit of challenging the assumptions which most people took for granted, and he saw in Lawrence a
potential acolyte.

The crucial encounter occurred at Cambridge where Russell
invited Lawrence to meet the ruling eminences, G. E. Moore and
Keynes. Full of the revolutionary ideas with which he had assaulted
Forster, Lawrence was at the same time intimidated—he called it a
life crisis—by meeting the Cambridge intellects on their own
ground. His declarations of the need for a fundamental socialism
and a nationalization of land, industry and railroads without
capital compensation for existing owners made little impression on
Moore or Keynes. For his part, after a dinner meeting, and
expostulations which Keynes heard as shallow noises, Lawrence
realized that he could not stand the taciturn reticence of the
reserved dons who listened to him as if they were dead. He was
irritated by Russell's stiff formality, the dry nasality of his voice. At
a breakfast in Russell's rooms, Lawrence was repelled by Keynes,
who arrived quite congenially in pajamas. Lawrence knew that
Keynes and Duncan Grant, the painter whose work Lawrence had
criticized, were lovers. Lawrence crouched on a couch and sulked

in front of the fire, irritable and glum. Keynes thought it was the hostile jealousy of the outsider, but it may have been more an implicit rejection of Keynes's homosexual airs.

Both Lawrence and Frieda had been seriously ill with influenza before the trip to Cambridge. After the visit he was affected with a mood of black melancholy. When Russell came to Greatham to return the visit, and ostensibly to plan a series of joint lectures (with Lawrence intending to speak on immortality) friction grew between them. As usual, Frieda took Lawrence's side and found Russell patronizing. She accused him of using his intellect to maintain his feeling of superiority. Frieda regarded herself as Lawrence's collaborator, a view that Lawrence encouraged. Russell believed Lawrence was essentially timid, mere bluster compared to Frieda's thunder. Russell may have been trying to keep his distance from Frieda, in effect shutting her out, perhaps because of Lady Ottoline's view of Frieda as a "monster of vulgarity."

Matters were complicated by Lady Ottoline's offer to let the Lawrences live in one of the cottages on the Garsington grounds, an idea that Frieda opposed because she suspected Ottoline had designs on Lawrence. While at Greatham, Russell felt signs of Frieda's intense jealousy. Lawrence had written Lady Ottoline a long letter about her offer, which Frieda tore to pieces. Russell remembered Frieda approaching Lawrence, who was working in his flower beds. She was jeering. Lawrence threatened to "hit thee in the mouth" unless she desisted.

Russell and Lawrence traded a series of letters full of argument and accusation. Russell maintained that for Lawrence, "truth" was more important than fact: indeed, the leading rationalist of his generation had met its leading intuitionalist. Russell charged that Lawrence had become misanthropic, an insight which seems justified if we consider some of Birkin's outbursts in *Women in Love,* the novel Lawrence was writing. Russell also claimed that Lawrence's conception of socialism was an anticipation of fascism, that the benevolent Caesar that Lawrence imagined as a perfect leader was really a projection of himself, and that Lawrence had no real desire for reform but only to create a forum where he could be heard and admired. The real source of his ideas, Russell added, perhaps gratuitously, was Frieda, for whom he was only an elegant spokesman. Russell had mentioned that the correspondence with Lawrence was frustrating enough to drive him to suicide, and Lawrence's response, only partly tongue in cheek, was to request that Russell leave him enough to live on in his will. The ultimate rejoinder, however, was Lawrence's portrait of Sir Joshua Malleson in *Women in Love,* a dry, rigid, pedantic puppet of a man based on Russell.

Russell and Lawrence had engaged in a heated dialectic between peers; they represented the opposed polarities of mind and heart that Lawrence characteristically dramatized in his fiction. Perhaps the most significant quality to emerge as a result of the conflict was Lawrence's formulation of what he would call "blood-consciousness":

> There is another seat of consciousness which exists in us independently of the ordinary mental consciousness. One lives, knows, and has one's being in the blood, without any reference to nerves and brain. This is one half of life belonging to the darkness. When I take a woman, then the blood-percept is supreme. My blood-knowing is overwhelming. We should realize that we have a blood-being, a blood-consciousness, a blood-soul complete and apart from a mental and nervous consciousness.

The passage sounds primal in its insistence that irrationality governs our decisions, that choices spring from "beyond" or "behind," from the "wind that blows through me," as he once put it, not from the rational processes perceived by Russell. Lawrence's position derives more directly from the romantic tradition of faith in intuition and emotions than it does from a scientific belief in the theories of the unconscious. What he expresses is, however, far earthier than the ideal of romantic love implicit in Shelley's "universal thirst for a communion...of our whole nature" or Keats's "holiness of the heart's affections." The bold, elemental passion of his blood-steeped vision was at the vital center of the sexual encounters of the characters in his fiction and stamped his consciousness on the consciousness of his readers, critics and disciples.

Modern Marriage

The visits of Forster and Russell indicate that there were fissures in the seams connecting Frieda and Lawrence. Forster found the couple too unified, speaking as it were with one voice, which made him all the more distrustful; Russell felt that Frieda spoke through Lawrence. Russell also saw the quarreling which Lawrence's biographer, Harry T. Moore, unconvincingly later tried to minimize, presenting the fights as the intermittent punctuation of longer periods of "quietness" and "gaiety," an Arnoldian pastoral of sweetness and light, familiar to readers of hagiography.

Close witnesses of the Lawrences' clashes—which were becoming more frequent and violent—were Katherine Mansfield and John Middleton Murry, who in 1916 lived near the Lawrences for five months in Zenmor, on Cornwall's northern coast. Since the two couples had met in London three years earlier, Lawrence had been trying to keep Murry in his orbit as part of the select group with which he could launch his idealistic community, Rananim. A year earlier, at Chesham, he had succeeded in persuading Murry and Mansfield to move into a cottage just two miles away, and he had helped them decorate it. There had been frequent opportunities for meeting, teas and dinners, and time to talk about writing.

Mansfield was unhappy in England. Like Lawrence, she suffered from the long, damp English winters. She fell in love with one of Murry's friends, a French officer named Carco, and she abandoned Murry to be with Carco in the south of France. Disillusioned, she returned to find Lawrence nursing Murry during an illness, caused by his grief during her absence. After she returned, however, things were never quite the same. Lawrence saw the relationship as "false and deadly," according to Murry, a foil to his own with Frieda, which was "real and life-giving."

Murry was insecure and disconsolate. Katherine could be peremptory and superior because she wrote fiction and he was merely a critic and journalist. Once, when he needed quiet to write a book review, she berated him for being a little whining dog (a view which Lawrence later corroborated by calling him a "mud-worm"). Another time, at a Christmas party hosted by Gilbert Cannon, a novelist, and attended by the Lawrences, she was caught making love to a young painter in the music room.

By the time Mansfield and Murry came to Zenmor in 1916, Katherine's only brother had been killed by a grenade in a training accident, deepening her bitterness. In her journal she noted that not one of her friends who went to the war ever returned.

At Zenmor, the two couples lived in close proximity, in separate stone houses only a few feet apart. The area was windswept, gray and dotted with boulders that emphasized the primitive quality of the two isolated houses that faced the sea. Lawrence painted the walls of his house pale pink, his cupboards bright blue. Over the fireplace he hung an embroidery by Lady Ottoline depicting a tree with big, bright flowers and animals underneath—an Edenic scene, perhaps, but for Frieda a reminder of the hand of a meddling woman. Once again, Lawrence helped the Murrys decorate their house, which would turn out to be only another temporary respite for a couple who had moved sixteen times in four years.

Lawrence was working on the revisions for *Women in Love,* in which Gudrun and Gerald Crich were to reflect Mansfield and Murry. In a picturesque tower above her house, Katherine Mansfield was blocked, incapacitated in her writing. Murry was working on his book on Dostoyevsky, a writer Lawrence did not like and so the cause of considerable discussion. Frieda was still enmeshed in the quarrel with Lady Ottoline, and she wrote her again, condemning her for wanting "some sort of unwholesome relation" with her husband. Quite maliciously repeating what Weekley had done when he sent a love letter of Frieda's to Lawrence, Lady Ottoline returned Frieda's letter to the Murrys, sending it in care of Lawrence, and managing by this ruse to poison relations among all of them.

Katherine Mansfield was now convinced of Frieda's "ultimate vulgarity." In her view, Frieda was obsessed by sex, which she imagined in every gesture, in every story, even in running brooks and trees. Lawrence, Katherine concluded, was willing to overlook any of Frieda's deficiencies, even her flirtatiousness. He had "queer blind places" for Frieda, even though she was beginning to age and get heavier—"what a great fat sow she is," Mansfield reflected in a letter to Lady Ottoline; what an "immense German Christmas pudding," she added in a subsequent letter. To complicate everything, Frieda began to express a subtle but continued attentiveness to Murry. In 1916, this sexual interest was only being explored as a possibility. Lawrence was aware of the attraction because he described it, in stories like "The Borderline" and "Jimmy and the Desperate Woman," but Frieda and Murry would only consummate their desires immediately after Lawrence's death in 1930.

In *Son of Woman,* the book that Murry wrote about Lawrence, he claimed that Lawrence had become impotent during the long period at Zenmor, and that this was the reason Frieda turned to him. He does not say whether Frieda discussed Lawrence's impotence, but his own particular discretion would have prevented such disclosure. For her part, Frieda hardly needed a reason. She was jealous of Lady Ottoline and may have been striking back at Lawrence. Frieda regarded affairs as distractions, and Otto Gross had ended her belief in monogamy. She had a number of brief liaisons during the first stages of her courtship period with Lawrence, a flirtation with a former suitor at Metz during the week of her father's anniversary, and another one with Harold Hobson, a handsome young man who walked partway across the Alps with her and Lawrence.

Murry was not ready for any sexual connection with Frieda in 1916 because he was so afraid that Mansfield, though she was openly promiscuous herself, would leave him. He was also not ready to betray Lawrence, whom he regarded as his best friend, a person who had surrounded him with a "warm and irresistible intimacy," an atmosphere which he compared to that established by a loving gardener determined to make a plant grow. He was bewildered, however, by certain overtures, particularly Lawrence's declaration of the need for what he called a blood brotherhood to be confirmed by some sacrament. Whether what Lawrence wanted was an active homosexual exploration, Murry did not know or admit; possibly it was more than he could conceive. It is clear, however, from manuscript versions of *Women in Love,* that Lawrence was aware of such a possibility, especially in the "absolute recognition" scene in the Alps that occurs between Gerald Crich, the industrialist, and Rupert Birkin, the school inspector.

In this suppressed first chapter, Lawrence tells us that though Birkin was always drawn to women, he saw them as sisters, "and it was for men that he felt the hot, flushing, roused attraction which a man is supposed to feel for the opposite sex." While working on *Women in Love,* in which Birkin marries Ursula Brangwen and manages to domesticate the feminist out of her, Lawrence seems to have been stumbling toward some notion of spiritual brotherhood, perhaps a version of what Whitman meant by adhesiveness (originally a phrenological term for nonsexual love). Lawrence had been disgusted by the overt homosexuality that he had seen in the Bloomsbury group, but in his own uncertain, groping state— because of what he wanted to write and the difficulties he was experiencing with Frieda—he seemed to be searching for some form of emotional fulfillment with Murry. He had agreed with Lady Ottoline, after one of his fights with Frieda, that "one should go to different persons to get companionship for different sides of one's nature."

What Lawrence could not realize in his life, he could often

project in his fiction. He would come to terms with the "unfinished meaning" of the conflict with Murry in the famous scene in which Gerald Crich and Birkin wrestle in the nude. As the two men lie exhausted in the mud after a scene in which Lawrence's great strengths as a novelist are evident (his ability to create splendid human motion and emotion in a natural landscape), Gerald clasps Birkin's hand and Birkin admits that the physical closeness helps preserve his sanity. The scene exemplifies the extent to which Lawrence yearned for the sort of male bonding that transcends mere friendship and is consummated in love.

In *Women in Love,* he makes Rupert Birkin denounce the restrictive nature of marriage, "each couple in its own little house, watching its own interests and stewing in its own little privacy." The two men, in a discussion that points to the tendentious preacherly aspect of Lawrence's fiction, argue about the nature of modern marriage and its possible evolutions. The passage is such a sharp departure from the Brangwen wedding scene in *The Rainbow,* quoted earlier, in which Tom Brangwen loutishly assumes the primeval value of marriage is a social means of perpetuating the species. Birkin wants something that is different and more radical than merely the abolition of monogamy:

> "You've got to take down the love-and-marriage ideal from its pedestal. We want something broader. I believe in the *additional* perfect relationship between man and man—additional to marriage."
>
> "I can never see how they can be the same," said Gerald.
>
> "Not the same—but equally important, equally creative, equally sacred, if you like."
>
> Gerald moved uneasily. "You know, I can't feel that," said he. "Surely there can never be anything as strong between man and man as sex love is between man and woman. Nature doesn't provide the basis."
>
> "Well, of course, I think she does. And I don't think we shall ever be happy till we establish ourselves on this basis. You've got to get rid of the *exclusiveness* of married love. And you've got to admit the unadmitted love of man for man. It makes for a greater freedom for everybody, a greater power of individuality both in men and women."
>
> "I know," said Gerald, "you believe something like that. Only I can't *feel* it, you see." He put his hand on Birkin's arm, with a

sort of depreciating affection. And he smiled as if triumphantly.

For contemporary feminists, such an encounter may be regarded, as Kate Millet put it, as an instance of the "godlike and indifferent Laurentian male." In *Sexual Politics,* Millet stated that in Lawrence's mind "love" had become "the knack of dominating another person," that it was simply synonymous with power. Millet emphasizes Lawrence's "phallic consciousness" and what she regards as the totemistic sacrifice of women in later novels like *The Plumed Serpent,* overlooking that, in that novel at least, Lawrence was also responding to the rise of the new fascist order that he observed when he lived in Italy in the early 1920s.

Women in Love also stresses Lawrence's belief in the curative force of love as he conceived it. Gerald, who rejects the holistic nature of love, finds only destructiveness in his marriage and finally wanders off alone to die. Birkin, the proselytizer of "sex love," moves forward in his marriage to Ursula, toward both extraordinary tenderness and fulfillment. Lawrence was projecting an idealized version of married love that, again, expresses the artist's ability to control and bend reality to his imaginative powers. His commitment to the perfect male and female union delineated in so much of his work left no space for the intrusion of the everydayness of life, for the humdrum facts of chores, misunderstandings, selfishness and irritability, and the abrasiveness of clashing temperaments and conflicting needs.

Physical Force

At Zenmor, beside the work of *Women in Love,* Lawrence was occupied with gardening, carpentry, mending and embroidery, wood-gathering and the housework and cooking, which Frieda now shared with him. Evenings, he would read poetry aloud, organize a game of charades or mimic a clerk in a shoe shop, a revivalist minister, a prim schoolmaster, a miner's wife. In January 1916, a month after the Murrys settled in Zenmor, Lawrence became seriously ill with a chest inflammation so severe that his left side became numb. He had been the perennial patient, chronically ill with bronchitis since childhood, but this illness left him in a state of nervous prostration. As always, Frieda had been the cheerful nurse.

He was only thirty, but there had been a subtle change in Lawrence's resilience. The war news was increasingly distressing, the "spear through the side of all sorrows and hopes," a source of "colossal and deliberate horror," he told Lady Asquith. He was living on the "edge of a precipice" and was now subject to ugly rages, frenzies which could last for hours until he would fall exhausted into bed, particularly if and when he was contradicted by anyone, or opposed or goaded by Frieda. Murry noted that whenever anyone disagreed with Lawrence, he ascribed his opponent's error to a sexual dysfunctioning. His anger, Murry recalled, was like a big, black, shrieking railroad engine. Another visitor, Eleanor Andrews, remembered that Lawrence would become vituperative at the slightest note of adverse criticism. A good part of Lawrence's obvious rage with Frieda and the world must be related to his chronic illnesses, his own awareness and denial of his incipient tuberculosis and the brevity of life afforded to someone with such a disability.

At Zenmor, Frieda felt particularly isolated, eventually not even able to speak to the Murrys, who lived only a few feet away. She felt that everyone in Lawrence's circle had turned against her—Forster, Russell, Lady Ottoline, the Murrys—partly because she was German, partly because she had abandoned her children for love, but mostly because she was not an artist. She told. S. S. Koteliansky, a Ukranian Jew whom the Lawrences had met in London, that she took "my ideals and life quite as seriously as he [Lawrence] does his." She claimed that her position was not conceited, but based on the notion that women counted fully as human beings. She knew that Koteliansky in particular did not like her, and in another letter she admitted to him (because he was also a foreigner) that she had great difficulty expressing herself, that when she spoke she felt like a fool, and finally that "everybody is Lawrence's friend and nobody seems to like me." She told Forster that she was regarded as "die zweite flöte," or, as we would say, a second fiddle, and she was particularly angry with Lady Ottoline, whom by now she regarded as her enemy, who "thought that Lawrence ought to leave me, that I am bad for him, that he does not care for me." Actually, Frieda was not being paranoid. Ottoline had written to Russell that Frieda was "a mad Egotist. I wish she would die or go off with another man who would beat her." The remark seems eerily prescient since Lawrence was the man she had gone off with and the man who would beat her. Lady Ottoline's reflection, however, suggests that the pugnaciousness of Frieda's manner invited physical assault.

The Murrys now found themselves living next door to a domestic imbroglio which they—ironic, reserved, evasive and deceptive in their relations with each other—were temperamentally unable to understand. The Lawrences were fighting continually, throwing dishes and pots, and striking one another. The culminating episode occurred early in May of 1916, described by Mansfield in a letter to Lady Ottoline. In the afternoon, Frieda made a disparaging remark about Shelley, which Lawrence angrily refuted, stating that she knew nothing about Shelley, that she had only read one of his poems. Lawrence went to the Murrys for dinner without Frieda, who remained outside, obsessively pacing. Suddenly, "green with fury," Lawrence ran outside and attacked her. Screaming for protection, Frieda burst into the Murrys' kitchen with Lawrence following, both of them sobbing.

The Lawrences recovered, Mansfield remembered, in half an hour. The next day Frieda remained in bed while Lawrence catered to her, bringing her food, putting flowers in her hair, singing songs. There is a note of envy in Mansfield's account, loathing and amazement that the Lawrences could so beat one another one day—"brutalize one another beyond words" is how she put it to Lady Ottoline—and then become playfully reconciled lovers the next day. Mansfield was convinced that Frieda, whom she now despised, took some "awful relish in such altercations. What may have seemed fraudulently melodramatic to Mansfield, as out of place as soap opera masquerading as grand opera, may have been for the Lawrences the only way to release unbearable tensions that had developed in their marriage.

To a certain extent they had been collaborators in planning Lawrence's fiction. Lawrence valued Frieda's views and had used her mannerisms and opinions as raw material. While Frieda had no talent as a novelist, she was quite capable of overestimating her contribution to Lawrence's creativity. What she had actually created during her life was her three children, but they had been denied to her because she had chosen Lawrence. He had withheld sympathy for this loss, a matter which Frieda could never really forgive. There is a pathetic aspect to Lawrence's position, a reflection of his own father's brute, inarticulate domination and brooding threat of force. The instinctual raging of Lawrence's

moods is an expression of blood-consciousness, which makes him
look a bit loutish, exposed and compromised in the excess of his
emotions.

The battle that Katherine Mansfield described was not the only
occasion of physical violence. Later, after the Murrys moved to the
southern coast of Cornwall, using the inclement weather of Zen-
more as an excuse, Frieda smashed an earthenware dish on
Lawrence's head after a fight caused by complaints about missing
her children. Lawrence was bruised, the plate broken after it fell,
but he could have been seriously hurt The broken earthenware
vessel is a reminder of the fragility of the romantic mood, of the
dark anger that is as much a part of passion as ecstasy.

The abuse was as mutual as it was chronic, which lends an
almost archetypal, larger-than-life quality to the relationship.
Murry believed that, for Lawrence, Frieda was an incarnation of
the female principle, "a sort of Magna Mater in whom he deliberately engulfed and obliterated himself." Lawrence regarded Frieda
as a prophetess, an instinctive oracle of blood-consciousness:
"When I take a woman the blood precept is supreme," he had told
Russell. Such a view was intimately connected to the sexual nexus
between Lawrence and Frieda, a tie which became vitiated due to
Lawrence's illness and the unresolved hostilities they felt for each
other. Russell had charged that Lawrence saw sexual relationship as
perpetual struggle and that the energy he needed was derived from
the conflict. Russell's remark is perceptive as far as it goes,
associating Lawrence with the tradition of romantic impetuous-
ness that the poet Shelley epitomized, a willingness to sacrifice
sensibility, friendship, even love for the sake of recognition and art.
For Lawrence, intensity was an opening to creative discovery that
had to be pursued no matter what the cost.

The emotional variables in any sexual relationship are volatile
and mysterious. Lawrence never underestimated those variables or
the importance of sexual union. He mystically believed that in
1915, in Chesham, Lawrence had been taking Frieda from the rear
as a male dog might take a bitch (which Lawrence uses in his
"Excursus" chapter in Women in Love). Was this his final desperate
lunge of passion, the last lusty exertion in which the male could
somehow quell or humiliate his mate? In a letter to Katherine
Mansfield, Lawrence related that by the time they had all settled in
Zenmor a year later, the sexual connection had failed, and that
Frieda had become the "devouring mother." Since she assumed

such a role (nursing his illness or impotence?), "it is awfully hard, once the sex relation has gone this way, to recover." He continues, in his letter, to state the problem with a brutal clarity: "I do think a woman must yield some sort of precedence to a man, and he must take his precedence. I do think men must go ahead absolutely in front of their women, without turning round to ask for permission or approval from their women. Consequently, the women must follow as it were unquestioningly. I can't help it, I do believe this. Frieda doesn't. Hence our fight."

Lawrence's perspective sounds curiously Victorian for a writer with the reputation he had for sexual and marital exploration in his fiction. Frieda found it "antediluvian." Catherine Carswell, who visited the Lawrences after the departure of the Murrys, and who is the source of the broken plate story, claims that Lawrence never intended to damage Frieda's spirit, which he argued would be like breaking the floor joists and crashing to the cellar. Carswell believed that Frieda was the case of "mindless Womanhood, wilful, defiant, disrespectful, argumentative, assertive, vengeful, sly, il-logical, treacherous, unscrupulous and self-seeking." She was capa-ble of hatred and mockery. While she sought the approval of men, she was independent enough to go her own way without it.

From our modern viewpoint, Carswell's condemnation of Frieda also seems "antediluvian." Though Frieda could play the Earth Mother, the primal female nurturer of her husband's talent, she refused to surrender her spiritedness for the sake of dissembling an insipid docility. Lawrence had admired that quality in her to begin with, and much as he did not want to "damage" it, he found it less comfortable to live with than to admire—another instance of intrusive reality in conflict with his romantic projections.

In one of Lawrence's notebooks, next to a poem he had written about his own mother, Frieda had scrawled in the margins, in a characteristic overstatement: "I have tried, I have fought, I have nearly killed myself in the battle to get you in connection with myself and other people." The message as inserted in a strategic space, the new mother's words jostling with the old, and it was followed by a cryptic acknowledgment: "I know your secret and your despair, I have seen you ashamed." Was this shame related to Lawrence's awareness that in choosing Frieda he had pursued a reflection of his own mother?

In his *Fantasia of the Unconscious*, Lawrence himself contrib-uted to the oepidal argument, stating that the major difficulty for a man in marriage was the fact that his emotional regard for his mother was deeper than it ever could be for a wife: "This makes him unhappy, for he knows that passional communion is not complete unless it be also sexual. He has a body of sexual passion which he cannot transfer to a wife. He has a profound love for his mother. Shut in between the walls of tortured and increasing passion, he must find some escape, or fall down the pit of insanity or death." What is most interesting about Lawrence's remark is the way in which he presupposes a universality about the oedipal predicament. However, even Freudians would admit that the maternal ties that so impress Lawrence represent a very special condition. Lawrence's emphasis only suggests the extent to which he was indeed subject to it.

Frieda saw Lawrence from the start as a man who needed to depend on her, a man whom she could release from the inhibitions of his culture. Lawrence preferred the company of women, Richard Aldington once observed, because they were trained not to contradict and would never "puncture his assertions with argument and fact." Frieda felt, perhaps starting with Weekley's original remark that a genius was coming to lunch, that Lawrence had a talent that she could nurture and help develop. As she wrote to Lawrence's friend Dorothy Brett, after Lawrence's death, "It was given to me to make him flower." As she got older, Frieda became rather patronizing and proprietary about her role in Lawrence's work, assuring all who would listen that she had been his creative collaborator, not merely his muse. Her faith was undoubtedly crucial, and Lawrence was the type of man who wanted a helpmate, just as originally Jessie Chambers had sent his early poems to Ford Madox Ford for *The English Review*, the act that launched his literary career. As Lawrence once told Murry, he hated the awareness that everyone but Frieda thought him a "queer fish that can write."

What Lawrence wanted most was a confirmation of his masculinity, which on a sexual basis Frieda could sustain. As she recognized herself, Lawrence was the first writer to approach sex religiously, even if with more pagan than Christian overtones. The adoration of religiosity may not carry over from fiction to real life and Frieda may have represented a kind of knowledge which Lawrence could not safety admit. By most accounts, he was priggish, uneasy when talking about sexual matters. Murry asserted that by choosing Frieda, Lawrence was on some buried level trying to resurrect his mother, a woman whose fundamentalist

Christianity would have made her strongly disapprove of his novels. Frieda, the sensual mother, argued in her *Memoirs* that "in his heart of hearts, I think he always dreaded women, felt that in the end they were more powerful than men."

The arrangement of power is the salient factor in any marital relation. Victorian women had been conditioned in their dependence but, in *The Rainbow*, Ursula Brangwen expressed the dissatisfaction of the new woman with Victorian expectations. In marriage with Weekley, Frieda had been trapped in the traditional child-bearer role, a situation that prevented her human evolution, and she had taken the radical step of eloping with Lawrence in order to free herself. While the ideology of liberation and the romantic possibilities it suggested had enormous intellectual appeal for a novelist like Lawrence, it arrived implicitly with certain emotionally threatening potentials as well. On the most gross level, if Frieda had been willing to desert her family once, might she not leave Lawrence for another? And although Frieda seems to have been more jealous than Lawrence (and jealousy is a power lever in marital relationships), he was more reliant on her for emotional support (even as the "devouring mother" or perhaps especially, because this is how he saw her!). Frieda's emotional independence is one reason why she was able to consider and consummate other liaisons while she was with Lawrence.

The "power" that Lawrence insisted on with such fanatical devotion, the cause of so many of the fights with Frieda, was part of his own artistic process, a stoking of his craft. Aldington remembered that Lawrence was capable of speaking novels, and what Lawrence imagined during the hysteria of the war years was an absolute control over idea and expression such as a novelist might have when inventing or manipulating characters. But such control does not usually include the guests in one's living room. Frieda, in her *Memoirs,* admitted that she was verbally maladroit and clumsy; after all, English was her second language. The battle with Frieda was anticipated in the smaller skirmishes with the Murrys, with Forster and Russell, with anyone who could not agree with Lawrence's "spoken novel," his illusory notion that art could be joined to life in the passion of his own enthusiasms. While fiction is subject to artistic control, life itself is too messy. The idea of such a seamless pattern makes Lawrence one of the most ambitiously arrogant of modern writers. It is this exaggerated quest for an impossible control that characterizes the true romantic.

Given his psychic and physiological infirmities, however, Lawrence may have been more victim than agent of his suffering and his illusions. His work may have been therapeutic in that it gave him a vitalizing center as well as a forum for understanding and trying to cure himself, as he claimed in a letter, "One sheds one's sicknesses in books—repeats and presents again one's emotions to become 'master of them.'" And in the novels, such "mastering" becomes a way of organizing and emphasizing, as Rupert Birkin confesses to Ursula in *Women in Love* his longing for companionship with a "few other people." Actually, however, Lawrence repeatedly failed to establish the harmonious relationships that he fantasized about in his novels or in his plan for Rananim.

Shattered Pieces

The tension between Frieda and Lawrence abated after she struck him with the earthenware plate (which was transformed into a piece of lapis lazuli in *Women in Love,* an example of how art improves life or at least makes it more esthetically appealing). Their conflict had been "horrible and agonizing," Lawrence concluded in a letter, but "Frieda and I have finished the long and bloody fight at last, and we are as one." The violent expression of friction is both dangerous and destructive, but for Lawrence and Frieda there was a feeling of release after an outburst of pent-up emotions that drew them closer together. This also seems to have been evident in the aftermath of the fights that Katherine Mansfield had witnessed and found so bewildering and so suspect.

The summer of 1916 had brought terrible news of the war: twenty thousand British soldiers were killed on July 1, the first day of the Battle of the Somme. The war had sickened Lawrence, made him "the enemy of mankind." Writing to Murry at the end of the awful summer of carnage in which 400,000 British soldiers had died, Lawrence claimed he only wanted to be left alone by a world which he found "despicable and contemptible." His own personal retreat, as always, was in his work and in the observation of nature: the wildflowers, the celandine, the heather and the foxgloves, the flaming gorse on the moors, blackberries, mushrooms on the cliffs where the primroses settled like butterflies, and finally the sea, in which he would bathe naked, rapt in the pale green fire of a wave that would burst into a "furious wild incandescence of foam."

Lawrence met a neighboring farmer, a young man named William

Henry Hocking, and developed an intense friendship with him. From Frieda's point of view, it was a "dreadfully unhappy" attempt to discover the male bond that Murry had refused. While Lawrence was wandering in the moors with William Henry, Frieda was often at Bosigran Castle on the Cornish cliffs with a new lover, Cecil Gray, a tall, broad-shouldered young Scotsman who lived there on a small but comfortable allowance.

In *Musical Chairs,* his ponderously dull memoir, Gray remarked on Lawrence's "puny" physical insignificance and his low vitality. Gray presumed that women would not be attracted to Lawrence (although Eleanor Andrews had recently offered herself up to him, without lasting consequence, according to Frieda, who was still jealous), and like John Middleton Murry he argued that Lawrence had probably become impotent. To some extent, Gray's view of a diminished Lawrence was conceived as a rationalization for his own liaison with Frieda.

On one matter, however, Gray was quite perceptive: Lawrence's inclination to "treat his friends and acquaintances as if they were characters in one of his novels." When he failed to manipulate them as he could with a fictional character, he "took his revenge," as Gray put it, by working "his will upon them" in his books. In effect, Gray argues, this makes his fiction a substitution for life, a form of wish-fulfillment, an "imaginary gratification of his desires." Gray's assertion echoes complaints by Forster, Russell and Murry, who all felt to some extent unfairly manipulated by Lawrence. Coleridge, discussing *Hamlet,* once argued that the genuine romantic sees the world as his own reflection. The charge that Lawrence could see his friends as fictional characters suggests a dangerous solipsism, a fascinating instance of the intensity of art, with Lawrence so driven by the process of his own creativity that actual circumstance became secondary to imagined possibility. It is the reason he could so vilify and caricature his friends in his novels. But it provokes a suspicion of the views of modern artists in general, a questioning of the extent to which what they advocate is the result of positions that are much more personal in origin than they are universal in application. Such suspicion confirms the need for a biographical criticism, a perspective which may help determine whether a fictional act exists because of some organic artistic necessity or whether it has been devised to gratify some element of an artist's deepest fantasy.

Gray (who is portrayed as the musician Cyril Scott, fat, with a pince-nez, in Lawrence's novel *Aaron's Rod*) recalled Lawrence's dark power, which he claimed could have made him into a British Hitler. That view echoes Russell's earlier contention that Lawrence was a proto-Nazi, and subsequent critics have argued the fascist implications of later novels like *Aaron's Rod* and *The Plumed Serpent,* his Mexican novel. Lawrence did attack democracy (as Pound, Eliot and Yeats did in the 1930s) because he saw it as a sham, particularly in England, where a landed class had the real power to control the press and formulate policy and used the illusion of egalitarianism to placate the masses, which would be ruthlessly sacrificed if the need arose, as it did in the war. Lawrence's attack on democracy seems the result of an intense romantic idealism gone sour, a messianic fever become embittered.

Lawrence was still concerned with his Rananim, and was now determined to situate his utopian community in the Andes. Gray remembered that Lawrence could be "foolishly lax and indiscreet" when speaking in the company of others, especially when he spoke of a desire to initiate a pacifist, nihilist campaign to end the war. In the fall of 1917, when the Lawrences were spending a few days at Bosigran Castle, their own house was searched and ransacked. The following night, a group of men burst into the castle when Gray and the Lawrences were having dinner, alleging that they were signaling to a German submarine. The accusation was ridiculous, a matter of fluttering curtains causing intermittent light, but the authorities gave the Lawrences three days to pack and depart from Cornwall. For Lawrence the charge of spying in wartime was worse than the public burning of *The Rainbow.* In her *Memoirs,* Frieda remembered that as a result "something changed in Lawrence forever."

Once again, Lawrence was depressed by his lack of prospects. There was no money, all he had to wear was a single pair of patched trousers, and Lady Ottoline's threat to bring suit over her portrayal in *Women in Love* would delay its publication. In fact, there would be no income for Lawrence until 1921, when the publisher Martin Secker agreed to take him on and published *Women in Love.* Lawrence had to depend on charity until then. Richard Aldington's wife, the poet H.D., offered the use of her London studio while she was visiting her husband at training camp. Lady Asquith saw Lawrence and noticed that he looked drained and ill, as if "every nerve in his body has been exposed." Frieda was also unwell, complaining of colitis and neuritis, anxious to find some permanent place in which to live. Aldington felt in Lawrence the animosity of a man alone against the world. He was "satirical," Aldington said, a half-trapped creature, a satyr, desperately trying to free himself of England forever.

Lawrence learned from his friend Murry that Katherine Mansfield was in a hospital with tuberculosis. When Lawrence went to visit, he saw how thin she had become, with Frieda's old wedding ring sliding on her finger. She told him of hearing a man in the next room cough in response to her cough like two roosters calling to each other in a false dawn. Her disease was spiritual in origin, she asserted, a notion that had particular poignancy for Lawrence, who had similarly carried the source of his consumption in his own body for his entire life. The Murrys were no longer a couple, and the Aldingtons were drifting apart as well.

A tall slim woman with a pale oval face, Hilda Doolittle Aldington had a nervous shyness of manner that signaled fragility. Tuned to the slightest vibration, she could be demanding and impetuous as well as volatile and sexually ambivalent. Her husband was bluff and hearty, a beefy man with an athlete's body, who could not understand the ambiguities that for H.D. were second nature. H.D. had been traumatized by an abortion, she had flirted with other men, too fearful to give herself to any of them; Aldington was interested in another woman, whom he would marry after the war. Lawrence had known H.D., whose initials inverted his, and her poems since the beginning of the war that seemed to be shattering all friendships. Her poems were bloodless and disembodied, without the direct emotional urgency of Lawrence's, chiseled images instead of his overt Whitmanesque declarations. Returning to London for a period and sharing the studio with the Lawrences, H.D. sensed distance between them. Lawrence, always theorizing about the need for friendship and community, made suggestions which H.D. misinterpreted. Lawrence had once reflected, connecting H.D. to her work, that she seemed "like a person walking a tightrope: you wonder if she will get across." In her novel *Bid Me to Live*, H.D. describes her overture to Lawrence, though it seems to more jaded sensibilities almost too delicate to qualify, a ripe matter of touching his sleeve and seeing him withdraw his arm "like a hurt animal." She imagined that he was repelled, while Lawrence, obsessed by the continuing horrors of the war, was only ready for spiritual connections. H.D., however, was searching for physical communion, which she would find for a brief period with Cecil Gray, to whom Frieda had introduced her.

The Lawrences would leave for Sicily after the war, England reminding Lawrence of a gray, dreary coffin sinking into the sea. It was the beginning of the final wandering, a decade in which Lawrence would seek a comfortable place and a new subject matter. From Sicily they would sail to Ceylon, where Lawrence felt oppressed by the heat, and then on to Australia where he wrote *Kangaroo,* a fragmented novel of ideas that was more effective in its descriptions of the raw edge of the Australian countryside than anything else.

He had been invited to New Mexico by Mabel Dodge Luhan, a wealthy banker's daughter who had been married three times, and who had lived in Europe and in New York, where she conducted a salon for artists and intellectuals. She had read a book Lawrence had written in Sicily, *Sea and Sardinia,* and offered Lawrence a house on her property in Taos where he could apply his descriptive powers to the New Mexico landscape. A squat, bustling and bossy woman, who believed she was equally irresistible to men and women, Mabel had an Indian boyfriend whom she had married, and she imagined she could stake a proprietary claim to Lawrence. Frieda was immediately hostile, particularly after Mabel informed her that she was not the right woman for Lawrence, in effect repeating Lady Ottoline's assertions. The Lawrences would spend much of the period between 1922 and 1924 in New Mexico, although they found it necessary to avoid their hostess and what Lawrence derisively called "Mabeltown."

In 1923, Frieda returned to Europe to visit her mother in Germany and her children in London. She visited John Middleton Murry to console him for the loss of Katherine Mansfield, who had died six months earlier. Murry had arrived to visit her at the Gurdjieff Institute outside Paris, where she was convalescing from tuberculosis. After an excited day with Mansfield introducing Murry to the other patients, she collapsed after running up a flight of stairs and died during the night. With perhaps inopportune timing, Frieda found a way to remind Murry of their stifled romantic yearnings when they lived as neighbors in Zenmor, seven years earlier, but Murry could still not betray his feelings of friendship for Lawrence.

When Lawrence arrived in England in 1923, he felt a muffled stillness, in a land without resonance. At a dinner that he organized for his friends at the Cafe Royal in London, after too much claret and port, with Koteliansky smashing wineglasses, Murry warned that he would someday betray Lawrence. Murry was referring to

Rananim, which Lawrence now planned to situate in New Mexico or the Rockies in his perennial dream of harmonious community. Called the "last supper" by some of Lawrence's critics, the evening ended in a drunken rout, with Lawrence vomiting and passing out.

Too fragile for the cold winters of New Mexico, the Lawrences traveled to Oaxaca in Mexico in the fall of 1924, where he wrote *The Plumed Serpent* and where he contracted malaria and was also found to be suffering from a recurrence of tuberculosis. Assured of at least a modest income from his writings, Lawrence decided in the winter of 1925 to live on the Italian Riviera, where the weather would be conducive to his health. In Spotorno, he rented a pink villa from an Italian army officer named Angelo Ravagli, to whom Lawrence began to give English lessons. Ravagli accompanied the Lawrences on long walks and became close to them. While Lawrence was in the late stages of his illness, Frieda had an affair with Ravagli, and after Lawrence's death in 1930 she married him.

In Italy, from 1926 to 1928, Lawrence worked on *Lady Chatterley's Lover*, the novel that would cause considerable uproar on several continents. The venomous picture of an immobilized Clifford Chatterley, an aristocratic English landowner who has been crippled during World War I, reflects Lawrence's anguish over his own predicament, the awareness that he would die of tuberculosis as Katherine Mansfield had died. In the novel, Chatterley is occupied by trying to modernize the coal mines on his property. Partly paralyzed and impotent, he is married to Connie, an attractive and robust woman who is having an affair with Mellors, the gamekeeper. An educated son of a coal miner, like Lawrence, Mellors has also been an officer in the war and has been disillusioned to the point that he is happy with the life of a gamekeeper. Quite cynically, Chatterley accepts the affair and the possibility that it could produce a child who would become his heir. However, by the time Connie learns she is pregnant, she has fallen in love with Mellors and demands a divorce.

While the novel presents Lawrence's central theme, the triumph of life forces over sterility and industrialization, it seems also to reflect his own situation, in particular Frieda's affair with Ravagli, as much as it is a parable of England after the war. During Lawrence's last years there were recurrent flarings of the old hostility that had caused him to beat Frieda. Mabel Dodge Luhan remembered black and blue bruises on the "big voluptuous woman," surmising that Lawrence beat her after "he capitulated."

Mabel Dodge Luhan's testimony is a bit suspect. The views of any thwarted or rejected lover are apt to be self-justifying. And to a certain extent the witness offered by many of those who saw Lawrence and Frieda struggle, even the Murrys, is always complicated by their own personal involvements and intentions. But there are too many signs of such a struggle to discount it. Frieda wrote Aldington that once in Italy, while Lawrence was writing *Lady Chatterley's Lover*, he seized her by the throat, fiercely claiming that he was her master. In his rage he was trying to strangle her, but he had insufficient strength. The incident suggests how central the antagonism in their relationship must have been. It also suggests how frightened he was at losing mastery over her and his own body.

Lawrence told his friend Brett (a deaf English painter who had followed the Lawrences to New Mexico, and whom Frieda resented and called the "asparagus stick") that women were rarely "true to themselves: that is why they are not true to others, and that is what makes most of the tragedies of married life. Also women destroy themselves by their obsession to have their own way." The statement indicates that Lawrence had not changed much since the time he so ferociously beat Frieda at Zenmor in 1916. Theoretically, at least, he was ready to abandon the violence, and in a letter criticizing *The Plumed Serpent* he denigrated the leader-follower relationship, predicting a new basis of tender sensitivity between men and women, though ending his letter with an appeal for what he still called "the phallic reality."

At the same time, despite the prolonged quarrel with Frieda, they stayed together. Near the end of his life, in the first sentence of a very direct essay called "We Need One Another," Lawrence bluntly admitted that men and women depended on one another much as a flowing river needed its banks—without them the river would be only a marsh. It was a characteristically organic image, a perception seen through an analogy to nature, and a romanticism recharged by Lawrence's view of the conductive electricity of the male-female relationship.

In his last years, Lawrence seemed unable to decide on a final resting place, moving all over Europe, from Italy to Switzerland to Germany to Spain. Most of the time was spent in Bandol in the south of France, a town that Katherine Mansfield had particularly cherished. His illness became progressively worse. He panted and coughed through the night; he had violent hemorrhages and refused medical attention. He claimed his illness came from "chagrin"—grief in French—and the "absolute frustration of my primeval societal instinct." Emaciated, too weak even to walk, he entered a sanatorium at the end of February 1930, and died in a few days. He was only forty-four.

Five years later Angelo Ravagli was dispatched by Frieda to disinter Lawrence's body and burn it. Lawrence, who always took himself so seriously, would not have appreciated the ensuing farce. Ravagli returned to the ranch in New Mexico after having forgotten the ashes in a railroad station in the confusion of his arrival. Mabel Dodge Luhan, unsuccessful in getting Lawrence in the flesh, now curiously contended for the ashes, but Frieda had them cemented into an altar on the ranch, where she would guard them for another two decades. She may even have been more faithful in death than in life, because she refused a second marriage proposal from Ernest Weekley, who, repudiated once again, still had the fortitude to endure until the age of ninety, dying in his sleep two years before Frieda, in 1952.

Secular Blasphemy

As a young man, struggling with what he saw as the provincial legacy of his mother's Christianity, Lawrence read Nietzsche. This interest was sustained by Frieda. For Lawrence, Nietzsche was the last metaphysician, and the two writers shared clear affinities. Both men were frail from childhood, debilitated by illness, and both were dominated by strong mothers. Later, both would use their writing as a therapeutic form of self-healing, and Lawrence would argue that he could "shed" his sickness in his books. Both began their careers as teachers and ended as self-exiled wanderers searching for health. As a projection for their own failing strength, both imagined an ideal of male power. Near their deaths, both men could sound like shrill polemicists, at times even bombastic or magniloquent. Each could seem grotesque in his attempts to subvert middle-class morality, and in his rebellion from religion, family and state. Nietzsche declared that the Christian God was dead; Lawrence confirmed that in his view the "Almighty has vacated, abdicated, climbed down."

Such sentiments began to be heard during the French Revolution, a time when the term "romantic" was used as an opprobrium to condemn its British sympathizers. In his novels, Lawrence imagined a continuing revolution of manners and spirit, a radical new sensibility that would foster erotic awareness while denying repression for the sake of a more intense, passionate existence. To some, Lawrence represented so dizzying and dangerous an emancipation that his books were censored and burned. If certain of his scenes of lesbian or adulterous love seem less daring now, for his time, as Edmund Wilson observed in his review of *Lady Chatterley's Lover*, Lawrence was the most *vital* of writers, and comes down to us as one of the most influential novelists of our time.

One of Lawrence's central precepts was that westerners were crippled by sexual shame. The battle of love which he fought with Frieda and depicted in his novels was part of his effort to overcome this disability. In *Lady Chatterley's Lover*, his last major novel, perhaps as a way to summon angry energy as his own body was faltering, he employed about a hundred common obscenities, the sexual invectives people have always used in daily life regardless of social class or nationality. In the 1920s, such language was still intolerable to large numbers of people, and considered as a sort of secular blasphemy. Lawrence could only get his book printed in Italy, and for writing it he was called a cesspool in newspaper editorials.

In June of 1929, Lawrence arranged to exhibit a series of the paintings he had attempted while writing *Lady Chatterley's Lover*. During a three-week period, some twelve thousand people crowded into the Warren Gallery in London to view thirteen of Lawrence's expressionistic nudes, painted with what the professional critics would dismiss as crude technique. One of the paintings, called *A Holy Family* and actually Lawrence's first effort, was characteristic of the heretical streak that informed his imagination. The painting parodied traditional views of the infant Christ in the arms of an impassive and adoring Virgin. Lawrence's Mary, almost nude, was being embraced by Joseph and enjoying it.

On the fifth of July, six policemen entered the Warren Gallery and confiscated all the paintings, describing them in their report as "coarse, gross, hideous" representations. The paintings were reviled as pornographic, mostly because Lawrence dared to show pubic hair in some of them. The judge hearing the case against Lawrence threatened to have the paintings destroyed, comparing them to dangerous wild beasts. Lawrence admitted in a letter that he had tried to shock people's "castrated social spirituality" with his paintings, and it would seem that with them, as with so many of his novels, he had exposed and then seared some public nerve, violated some taboo of the community that could not be changed at the time. If as a result Lawrence sacrificed his own immediate fame for contemporary infamy, he managed to help change the very social strictures which he felt so confining. In the late 1950s, after the publication of *Lady Chatterley's Lover* was challenged and then vindicated in the highest courts of the United States and England, some nine million copies were sold in the space of a few years.

In *After Strange Gods,* T. S. Eliot disparaged Lawrence as an inadequately educated man whose work demonstrated an incapacity for clear thinking. Eliot's condescension reveals as much about his own inhibitions and need for propriety as it reflects the bias of modernism, which, particularly in Eliot's case, emphasized the impersonal rendering of emotion over romantic, personal expressiveness—a tendency toward "dehumanization," in Ortega y Gasset's words, as opposed to the "human, all too human" elements inherent in romantic literature. Eliot suspected the expression of raw emotions was a form of crudity.

Lawrence indeed was a fountainhead, the spokesman for the romantic mood in the first half of this century. In an essay on Walt Whitman, one of his sources, whom he called the first "white aboriginal," he stated that the essential function of his art was a passionate morality, engaged, aggressive, eager to provoke the stultifying masses into an awareness of the rigidities that bound them. Lawrence's morality, like Whitman's or Nietzsche's, depended on secularizing the soul, accepting it as a premise within the body, and realizing its validity in the present instead of in an afterlife. So pagan a perspective was bound to conflict with Eliot's high-toned Anglicanism.

In his fiction, Lawrence predicted the sexual wars of our century, but more than any other writer before him, he forces us to face the question of what a woman should and could be. Certain of his more messianic males try to make their women submit and worship—a perennial male fantasy of power—just as Lawrence sought the deepest of attachments with Frieda, but never at the expense of his own fierce independence. Through characters like Birkin in *Women in Love,* he would preach that genuine love depended on the suspension of ego and an ability to deliver oneself "over to the unknown." It is this sense of the unfathomable in human relationships and an ability to marvel at natural wonders that exists as an animating certainty in Lawrence's fiction. It is the view of a writer who saw the world from the perspective of someone who has returned from the brink of death and is grateful for any reprieve.

Scott, Zelda, and their daughter Scotty

✹ 3 ✹

Scott and Zelda

His talent was as natural as the pattern that was made by the dust on a butterfly's wings. At one time he understood it no more than the butterfly did and he did not know when it was brushed or marred. Later he became conscious of his damaged wings and of their construction and he learned to think and could not fly any more because the love of flight was gone and he could only remember when it had been effortless.

Ernest Hemingway, *A Moveable Feast*

America is the story of the moon that never rose.
Fitzgerald letter to Marya Mannes,
October 1925

The Dream Dancer

H E CALLED HIS MOMENT the Jazz Age, and he acknowledged that it "bore him up, flattered him, and gave him more money than he had ever dreamed of simply for telling people that he felt as they did." His moment was as brief as it was dazzling, and ultimately F. Scott Fitzgerald's story is that of the great American writer as failure.

Early success, he reflected later in life, convinced him that life was romantic. Even if he realized intellectually "that things were hopeless," he could act as if "he were determined to make them otherwise," an illusion he sustained with boundless optimism and energy when he was still young. He and his wife, Zelda, exemplified the romantic premium on youth. "You were younger than anyone in the world once," Zelda told him, and he did much as a writer to recapture the magic of being young, "when the unfulfilled future

and the wistful past were mingled in a single gorgeous moment—
when life was literally a dream."

They pursued a headlong pace and glittering style that made
them legendary emblems of romantic recklessness, hedonism and
excess. They approached marriage as though it were the continuation of the fairy tale in which the prince and princess live
happily ever after, unprepared for the realities of clashing wills,
jealousy, conflicting needs, the dull patches of everyday existence.
Marriage was to be an extension of the dance, a wild party at which
they were the celebrated guests. Each moment had to be a
"gorgeous" one, a burst of flame that was finally to consume them.
The legend the Fitzgeralds created persists, more flawed and less
radiant now that we have probed beneath the surface and measured
the depths of its costs, both human and artistic.

As a writer he is said to have invented his age—Gertrude Stein
claimed he did it through his ingenuousness. That same ingenuousness had been identified by Henry James with the American
character, but in Fitzgerald's case it led skeptical critics to chastise
him for his naïveté. Fitzgerald was a dreamer who composed stories
with a natural fluency, one hundred and sixty of them, and four
novels in his short life. One of the novels, *The Great Gatsby*, is
considered an American classic, an almost flawless masterpiece
which crystallizes the moral choices of an era with stunning clarity
and concentrated power.

Part of Fitzgerald's personal dream involved a fascination with
the rich. When Lawrence wrote about the centers of wealth and
power, he wrote as the castigating outsider, the hunter of hypocrisy
and corruption. Fitzgerald was more in sympathy with his subjects. Although Fitzgerald read Lawrence and envied the cosmic
reach of his ability—the expansiveness and scope that included so
broad and sweeping a view of the world—Fitzgerald's own vision
was more exclusive, more focused on the social circumstances of
the privileged. He has been accused of pandering to the rich, of
treating them with the excessive devotion and obsessional interest
of the insider, but such charges, true up to a point, fail to follow the
arc of Fitzgerald's development. Though he was decoyed by his
propensity for flamboyant extravagance, he maintained that he
always had an "abiding distrust" for the wealthy, an animosity that
derived from invariably being the poorest boy in a rich man's club.
The follies of the Jazz Age, epitomized by his own wild preoccupations and the priority he placed on youth, soon began to disgust

him. By the time he finished *The Great Gatsby*, he was ready to condemn his own generation as "shallow, cynical, impatient, turbulent and empty," but not before he and Zelda had exhausted themselves in their relentless pursuit of those follies.

Gatsby was published in 1925, five years after Fitzgerald had burst upon the scene with *This Side of Paradise,* a novel he had begun some time earlier under the half-mocking but apt title *The Romantic Egotist.* It was the novel he was still working on when, in a ballroom in the South, he danced with the beautiful woman whom he pursued, married and made the subject of his future work. He felt Zelda was "a great original" who had "a more intense flame at its highest than I ever had." The penetrating incisiveness of certain of her remarks revealed a brilliant if savage anger. Zelda was also a marvelous dancer, though she aspired to become a professional ballerina too late, after a decade of wasting herself in youthful frolicking with Fitzgerald. Their life became an excessive search for good times and their drinking ruinous. The alcohol put Fitzgerald in the dream state he needed to write, but there was an implicit cost involved.

This "cost" had a paradoxical twist accompanying it. Heavy drinking causes its own particular form of psychosis, and Zelda ended her life in a madhouse. Fitzgerald's last major novel, *Tender Is the Night,* was about the process of his wife's mental breakdown and the extent to which he may have abetted it even as it fascinated him as his subject. It is no idle sentimentality to suggest that sickness, whether caused by consumption in Lawrence's case or alcoholic derangement with the Fitzgeralds, can open an artist to a new perspective. Suffering can take its ritual and redemptive forms, a process through which the artist seems able to absorb the world's pain, to magnify it in the prism of self-consciousness and then release it as a form of exorcism.

In his alcoholism, Fitzgerald stated that he and Zelda had believed they had protected themselves from the consequences of their acts by a "theatrical innocence" in which they delighted in becoming the observed, playing with decadence without fully succumbing to it. The phrase "theatrical innocence" seems oxymoronic, a self-defeating contraction. To be theatrical is to be extremely self-conscious, and that is to deny innocence. The writer's position is usually that of the observer, not the participant, and rarely that of the king's fool. Both Scott and Zelda were able to assume a variety of roles, particularly that of the entertainer, or the daredevil on a high wire. Any role that one assumes leaves its impression. The innocence of the Fitzgeralds was to deny their own impact, to blithely continue their dance on the high wire even after the wire had snapped. On some level they felt destined for celebrity, and they believed that their youthfulness made them invulnerable. In this respect, as in many others, they were deeply, symbiotically similar. Zelda compared herself to the mythical salamander that thought it could live in the fire without being burned by it. She was wrong and she was burned terribly.

Lawrence and Frieda could sometimes seem overeager, even rabid, in the lust of their idealism and the weight of their judgments. Scott and Zelda lived in a lighter, more vertiginous world, and they often seemed more hysterical in their gestures. As young lovers, they made a suicide pact proclaiming that they only needed to live until the age of thirty-five. The pact may have been part of the frivolity of courtship, but on some deep level they respected it and felt its necessity. It was a vow of romantically linked extinction. Instead of suicide, a gesture each failed at several times, they chose slightly more gradual paths to disintegration. Their mutual disability was a crippling inferiority, a lack of self-esteem at the core, while they paraded themselves through the corridors of the swankiest hotels looking like the prince and his princess. Such contradictions, Fitzgerald once observed, are requisites for the first-rate intelligence to which Fitzgerald aspired even as he feared he was constituted of lesser stuff.

This is merely the gloss of one of the saddest American stories, almost a romantic version of a fairy tale in which the good-looking, talented couple get too much too soon and are poisoned in the process. It is a story that encompasses much more than the fate of its two protagonists and exists as American paradigm.

A Southern Belle

It was a warm Saturday night in July of 1918, and the young men of America were preparing to enter the war to end all wars. Some of these young men craved certain delicate attentions and refinements, the sort which were generally provided by women, before embarking for the muddy fields of Europe where a bloody, stalemated war had already dragged on for four years. One of these young men, a twenty-three-year-old, recently commissioned lieutenant, who seemed too pretty to be a man and was a bit too short to suit his own expectations of how high a man should reach, was F. Scott Fitzgerald.

He was eager, so evidently self-conscious in his specially tailored Brooks Brothers uniform, so dashing in his gleaming yellow boots that reached just below his knees. In the southern town of Montgomery, Alabama, his kind was an anomaly, a sign of changing times. Not since the Civil War had so many outsiders crowded into Montgomery, where they were being trained for modern warfare. With its reputation for gracious southern hospitality, the governing board of the Montgomery Country Club had proffered a standing invitation to the officers (one had to draw the line somewhere) at the training camps to attend their social functions. Since there was virtually no other way to meet young women of the right class and standing, and since many of these men were bored by long, dusty marches and endless drills, they were happy to find the opportunity to inhale sweet smells, to feel the brush of smooth skin, to hear the cultivated palaver of warm, soft-voiced women who spoke of memories instead of money.

There is at any ball always one woman who seems to be its radiant cynosure, its *belle,* favored with more grace and beauty than any other. This woman is assured of her power, and her admirers are the testimony of that power. The young officer had intently fixed his gaze on such a wonder on the night in question in Montgomery, a girl (for she was not even eighteen) with very long, very blond hair which was curled and regally piled on her head. She had high cheekbones and a pouting look on her face, the superior and insolent expression of a spoiled princess daring the foreign princes to try for her hand despite impossible odds. Mixed with the hauteur was the play of merriment around her eyes. This girl was enjoying herself heartily on the dance floor.

The young man stared at the girl through several fox-trots as though he were mesmerized by an apparition. Years later he remembered that during those moments and afterward he had the feeling that everything, including himself, had melted and merged. The description verges on cliché, but at the same time it is an archtypal account of the sensations associated with instant love, relying as it does on adjectives that for centuries have signified the lineaments of rhapsodic, ecstatic and orgasmic gratification.

For Fitzgerald, the state expressed a central projection of his artistic self, the innocent adoration—is it a kind of Keatsian awe?—with which he beheld beauty. Had his stare been noticed by one of the more genteel, older southern gentlemen in attendance, it would have been called impolite, and it did seem brash. But in its way that stare so aptly matched the arrogance of her pose, Keats's *belle dame sans merci* transposed from some medieval court to the huddle of officers and former football players who sought to know her on more intimate terms of endearment. Finally, she danced with an officer from Fitzgerald's regiment, giving him the opportunity to request an introduction and a chance of his own.

The couple looked good together on the dance floor. They seemed related, part of a family that prospers because of appearance, that succeeds because of good looks and winning smiles. His hair, parted boyishly in the middle, was as blond as hers, and his skin was as pale. His greenish eyes had long lashes which made the eyes seem dreamy, and his talk was about his dream of becoming a great writer. There was something buoyant in the way he imagined his future, a faith in his own promise that would have made him a great salesman or a successful swindler. Later, she would remember in a prose style every bit as romantic as his that there "seemed to be some heavenly support beneath his shoulder blades that lifted his feet from the ground in ecstatic suspension, as if he secretly enjoyed the ability to fly but walking as a compromise to convention."

The young officer's talk of fame through art intrigued her more than the promises of career and fortune which most of her suitors offered. The girl was named Zelda Sayre, after a gypsy queen in a novel her mother had been reading when she carried her to term. Zelda was an unusual name for Alabama, and names do leave their formative impressions. Its gypsy derivations may have had much to do with her inclination for the unconventional, the occasionally wild incivility of her remarks, and a behavior marked by a desire to shock more for the sake of her own amusement than for any reformist or ideological goal.

Zelda Sayre had been schooled in the mannered courtesies that any young southern lady was expected to perform as if instinctively, but her delight in departing from such niceties (the kind of curtsy that transcends the bending body and informs itself in speech, tonal modulation and the downward cast of an eye) was a refutation of her origins and social class. Zelda was a descendant of a Civil War general and an Alabama Senator, of families that had settled and helped govern the South. Her maternal grandfather had been a lawyer and planter who obstinately refused to permit his daughter Minnie, Zelda's mother, to begin a career as an actress because he was convinced that only loose women could show themselves on a stage.

Minnie, a vivacious woman who cherished her own literary ambitions but managed to write only a few sentimental poems, married Anthony Sayre, a conservative attorney who subscribed with all his soul to the seriousness and sobriety of his profession. Uncommunicative, solitary and unsociable, he maintained a life-long vigil with his law books in a depressive state which, though normal for him, seemed discouraging for others in his family. An epitome of dignified respectability, Sayre was elected to the Alabama House and Senate, and then had a long career as an associate justice in the Alabama Supreme Court. As a profession, the judiciary was more distinguished than remunerative and the Sayres, with six children to raise, had to rent their house and watch their expenses.

Zelda was the last child, born when her parents were in their forties, and she was naturally the most pampered. She would have been the most protected had the Sayres been able to manage her. The judge was always at his courthouse or isolated in his study, and Minnie had become permissive and was by nature indulgent of the faults in others. As a child, Zelda had been attracted to danger, manifesting a peculiar desire to jump from high places, to climb trees, to venture on long walks alone. She could also be mischievous: once, she had called the local fire department and then climbed on her own roof waiting to be rescued. It was an unusual prank for an eight-year-old, a forecast of the more melodramatic appeals for attention she would make in later years.

As a teenager, she was irrepressible in conversation, determined to be the center of attention. Easily bored, she could be willful and obnoxiously defiant, especially when she was told she could not do something she wanted to do. At a time when young women were supposed to cultivate passivity, charm and submissive beauty, when they aspired to sit so straight that their backs would never touch their chairs, she would slouch to reveal a developing bosom or cross her legs instead of her ankles. In high school, she disregarded her academic studies and made a private speciality out of coquetry and flirtation. She never needed to be dared to go further than other girls, dancing cheek to cheek at parties, smoking cigarettes or sipping gin, or even necking in what Fitzgerald called the "mobile privacy" of the automobile. Girls who could be kissed without preliminaries of formal courtship were called "speeds," one of the fugitive terms in an underground language formed to define the manners of a new generation, but a better term to describe Zelda would have been "cyclone." She was known as someone who would do exactly as she pleased no matter what rules governed an occasion. Once, after leading a grand march at a fraternity dance, resplendent in her rose velvet gown and bouquet of roses, she saw a large framed photograph of a boy she had dated in a display window. Jealous that she was not in the window herself, she kicked in the glass and removed the photograph, brandishing it as a trophy.

Some of Zelda's contemporaries were amused by her impetuous delight in the immediate, by her lusty way of taking what she wanted, whether it was as innocuous as the bite of a peach or as serious as asking a man to dance with her. The photograph in the display case suggested a sort of notoriety, a local fame, and Zelda saw the possibilities of her own legend at an early age. What she also sensed and incorporated in her being was the emergence of a new woman who flaunted her beauty with brash sophistication. She would describe this new species, a particularly American breed, as the Flapper, the woman who flirted because it was fun and who wore revealing bathing suits because she had a great figure. The Flapper used cosmetics freely and never worried about sincerity or respectability, the shibboleths of the unmarried girl. She could be silly or slaphappy, but "she was conscious that the things she did were the things she had always wanted to do" and that she did them because they gave her pleasure.

Only a month before meeting Fitzgerald, Zelda had graduated from high school. She was supremely confident of her ability to attract men, and she trusted it would do more for her future than her schoolbooks. She had become a specialist in small talk and boys, and she was being pursued by a legion of them. Several aviators from nearby Fort Taylor performed flips, gyrations and other flying stunts in their planes in the air space above the Sayres' home in an attempt to impress her. The fliers continued their aerial gymnastics until they were chastised by their base commander, but the acts exist as a spectacular tribute to Zelda's enticing powers.

Childhood Is Father to the Man

Fitzgerald was drawn immediately by these powers and began visiting or telephoning daily. The fact of Zelda's popularity would have discouraged most men, but for Fitzgerald it was a clear sign that she was the "top girl." He admitted that though he knew he had no money and that he may have lacked the animal magnetism of a football star, he felt he had sufficient intelligence, bearing and good looks to win the prize. There is a smug innocence in his conviction, especially because he had pursued Ginevra King, a similarly popular girl he had dated as an undergraduate at Princeton. Sharing Ginevra King with a swarm of other admirers, he deceived himself that he had fallen in love for her sake, quite vainly because she realized from the start her expectations were much grander than Fitzgerald's hopes, that he was a humorous interlude, a sort of slumming that could never really fit in with her socialite background and ambitions. As it turned out, Ginevra King was getting married just at the time when Fitzgerald met Zelda, and he pasted a bit of Ginevra's handkerchief in his diary over the caption "The End of a Once Poignant Story." But it may have been more of a prelude than an ending, and Zelda the new version of an unapproachable ideal that he would strive to attain.

Such a posture, the imploring young man facing a disdainfully superior lady, is part of the legacy we acknowledge as traditional romanticism, with the cloying, almost saccharine taste one finds in certain poems by Keats (Fitzgerald's favorite poet) or, in its more demented and exaggerated stages, in the work of Poe. The matter is compounded by a latent narcissism, the impression that Zelda was in certain ways a reflection of Scott, and that such a correspondence went far beyond the superficialities of physical resemblance, though they had them as well—the fair skin, the blond hair, the straight noses, the delicate mouths.

Both Zelda and Scott felt the need to ignore or deny their parents. Zelda saw her father as an archaic relic who upheld the rigid proprieties of an earlier century. Fearless, she could insult him to his face, and Fitzgerald remembered that the first time he was invited to dinner at the Sayres', Zelda so enraged her father with a remark that he chased her around the dining-room table with the proverbial carving knife still in hand. The staid Judge Sayre must have seemed a bit ridiculous in his angry pursuit. Fitzgerald was too young and too smitten at the time to discern any pattern or prophecy in the incident, to see that it suggested something essentially untamable about Zelda, a woman who would not be coerced or manipulated by social forms. In her intractability, Zelda was a more volatile version of Frieda Weekley on the

brink of her elopement with D. H. Lawrence. Both women were
emancipated to the point that no one could dictate to them on the
grounds of propriety or convention. But it took Frieda years to
reach that stage; Zelda seems to have been a natural rebel.

The incident with the carving knife upset Mrs. Sayre, who
succeeded in quieting the judge and getting him to return to his
dinner. After raising six children, she was an accomplished master
at restoring domestic harmony, though Zelda had tried her more
than any of her other children. About her mother, Zelda was usually
patronizing, regarding her as someone who was easily
manipulated.

Fitzgerald was embarrassed by his parents, particularly by his
mother. She was the eldest daughter of a mercantile Irishman who
came to America during the potato famines, settled in St. Paul, and
became a wholesale grocer. He died young but had the good sense
first to earn a considerable amount of money. A plain woman,
round-faced, with some detail of her dress, speech or manners
often askew, people regarded her as a harmless eccentric, perhaps
a bit dense or even daft, someone whose mental parts did not
always cohere. Fitzgerald was able to identify more with his father,
a descendant of a prominent family that had settled in Maryland
early in the seventeenth century and helped to govern it
subsequently.

A small erect man, diffidently handsome, with a dapper air of
patrician breeding, Edward Fitzgerald represented a colonial past
but, incongruously, instead of becoming an attorney or a banker, he
had married into his father-in-law's wholesale grocery operation.
The business failed when Scott was an infant and Edward
Fitzgerald took his family to Buffalo, where he worked as a
salesman for Procter and Gamble. Scott was twelve when his father
was discharged, a shock from which his father never recovered,
leaving him wavering in his judgments, ineffectual, unassertive,
and generally unconcerned with pragmatic realities. The family
returned to St. Paul, now destined to live, always quite carefully, off
Mrs. Fitzgerald's inheritance.

Dowdy and unfashionable, she smothered her son with concern,
perhaps because she had lost her first two children in an epidemic,
perhaps as some sort of secret compensation for her husband's
failures. Fitzgerald seems to have decided at an early age that his
parents were liabilities, that he would have to leave them behind.
He pitied his father but could never really forgive his mother, even

trying to work out his resentments in *The Boy Who Killed His Mother,* a novel about matricide that he struggled with for four years and never completed. Later in his life, he disparaged his father in a notebook as a moron and his mother as a pathologically neurotic worrier who was "half insane." Between them, he conjectured, his parents "did not have the brains of Calvin Coolidge." The rejection of one's parents may be a necessary, though painful part of the education of the artist. Lawrence eulogized his mother's warmth in *Sons and Lovers,* but also criticized her narrowness, and mourned his father's separateness. Fitzgerald unsuccessfully tried to write his parents out of his past, and then seems to have virtually forgotten them. It is a sign of the sort of evasiveness that makes some of Fitzgerald's critics see him as shallow.

The flippant hostility of so dismissive a statement about his parents is suggestive. His mother's social ineptness and his father's social disgrace—he was, after all, unable to support his family—left Fitzgerald with an ambivalent humiliation even as he yearned for social acceptance and success. Instead, he had become a young man with "a two cylinder inferiority complex," which he characterized with a curiously apt humor: "I spent my youth alternately crawling in front of kitchen maids and insulting the great."

In St. Paul, his parents occupied the fringes of acceptability, moving from apartment to apartment on the perimeters of the best neighborhoods. Fitzgerald went to school with the children who lived in the grand homes and was invited to their parties, but was still himself located on the social margins. He could have become a rebel or a reformer, an advocate for a more equal distribution of wealth, but instead was fascinated from the start by the rich. His mother encouraged him by sending him to dancing class, the one form of organized learning he loved, realizing from the start that it was a means of social entry, a way to consort, arm-in-arm, with the forces of grace and power.

Fitzgerald was not an angry boy but blessed with a sunny disposition. Apocryphally or not, he claimed his very first word was "up," which implies a perennial optimism once regarded as characteristically American. There were many words to follow and a clear aptitude for persuasion that manifested itself at school in the spirited debates in which he excelled. He was also becoming an observer. At thirteen, he began writing crude detective stories and intermittently recording some of his first formed thoughts and hopes.

Sent to a small Catholic preparatory school in New Jersey, he immediately tried to make himself the most popular boy in his class. He had the advantages of self-confidence and the ability to charm others to the point of domination. In this sense, he was very much like Zelda. He recognized, years later, that this charm had a double edge, that it could become an unscrupulousness, a source of dishonor. To some of his classmates, that charm just seemed like conceited arrogance, the Machiavellian mask of someone who wanted, most of all, to be admired.

Working on a draft of his first novel, he would reflect on his years at the Newman School and make its autobiographical hero, Amory Blaine, admit that he was without "real courage, perseverance or self-respect." It became a typical pattern for Fitzgerald: enormous surface vanity bordering on boastfulness which was compromised by deep insecurities. The fears were debilitating, and they became evident, for example, in games of sport where his poor athletic abilities and his shortness of stature prevented him from taking a boy's traditional route to heroism. He realized that writing could become a "backdoor way out of facing reality," that in fantasy he could invent for himself a lineage and circumstances that had more appeal than the actual, the fact, for example, that he had less money than his classmates and so had to think more about expenses. He was intrigued by Broadway comedies, only a forty-minute bus ride from his school, but these were jaunts he could rarely afford. So he began writing his own librettos. Once, when he was unfairly criticized for cowardice after a football game, by a coach who despised him anyway because of his fresh retorts, he defended himself with a poem in the school newspaper. Writing seemed a route to recognition.

In his last year at Newman, Fitzgerald met Father Cyril Fay, a Catholic priest who was a trustee of the school and would subsequently become its headmaster. Fitzgerald could not confide in his own father, for whom he had little respect, but Fay's cosmopolitan demeanor impressed him. Attracted by Fitzgerald's good looks, his cocksure bravado and self-assurance, Fay offered a convivial friendship without demands and was quickly accepted by Fitzgerald as a father surrogate. A Roman Catholic convert, a pudgy, smiling cherubic man with a double chin, Fay loved the good life, theater, conversation, food and wine. Fancying himself an esthete, he spoke in epigrams and posed like a rotund dandy, and, if he seemed a bit foolish, his natural affability disguised it. He lived in Washington, D.C., with his wealthy mother and moved in a circle of powerful, influential friends, among them the historian Henry Adams, whom Fitzgerald would meet (and portray as Thornton Hancock in *This Side of Paradise*), and Shane Leslie, an Anglo-Irish novelist who was Winston Churchill's cousin.

The introduction to Shane Leslie would become crucial for Fitzgerald, leading directly to the publication of *This Side of Paradise,* and the understanding that the right connections could make things happen. Fay became a model of genteel gaiety for Fitzgerald, of the ability to take hold of and enjoy life, though as a priest he was also a reminder of rectitude and idealism. Later in his life, when things went wrong for Fitzgerald, he would refer to himself as a "spoiled priest."

All through Fitzgerald's years at Princeton, Fay was to be both confidant and a source of reliable cheer and encouragement. Despite his poor academic record at Newman, Fitzgerald had been admitted to Princeton on the strength of a personal interview in which his glib charms made him seem full of promise. His immediate intention at Princeton, as it had been at Newman, was to be regarded an important figure, the proverbial "big man on campus." He would not accomplish this recognition through any scholarly route. Fitzgerald, like Zelda, was largely indifferent to his studies, and much more interested in making social connections, or in getting his songs and sketches accepted by the Triangle, the Princeton dramatic club. When one of his plays was accepted, he received a little local attention, which he realized made him immediately "swell up like a poison toad."

He was gratified at being accepted by the Cottage, one of the better "eating clubs," where one could take meals with a select group of young men who fancied themselves adventurers and well-dressed philanderers. Posing with such friends, learning to assume the right attitude, the gleeful smirk or the perfect condescension while exhaling cigarette smoke, seemed much more important than papers or exams. Princeton, before the war, as Fitzgerald emphasized in *This Side of Paradise,* specialized in social snobbery and privilege, an unaccredited course which determined its atmosphere. Academically, he foundered, failing courses or just barely passing them, cutting classes extensively. Gregarious, effervescent, full of breathless enthusiasm, he seemed very much the open-hearted prodigal, though his pert brashness and his impetuosity could block prospective friendships. Being personally conspicuous was not tolerated by most Princetonians, who were, after all, being bred to be discreet bankers. Fitzgerald's flair often got in his way.

One friend was Edmund Wilson, who would become the most important American literary critic of his generation. A student of the classics, Wilson was an engrossed intellectual, full of books, ideas and skeptical, belligerent argument. As a sort of foil for the outgoing, socially adept Fitzgerald, Wilson seemed oblivious to social distinctions. Withdrawn to the point of almost being reclusive, he was capable of a pedantic haughtiness, and showed signs of a cool, analytical objectivity. With his high-pitched voice, his red hair and his orange ties, he was regarded as a campus eccentric. Quite naively, Fitzgerald declared to Wilson, who edited the undergraduate journal, *The Nassau Literary Magazine,* that he wanted to be "one of the greatest writers who ever lived," and, rather than discouraging the hope as an example of undergraduate vanity, Wilson responded to the healthy intoxication of the remark.

Fitzgerald contributed lyrics for *The Evil Eye,* a musical comedy that Wilson wrote. In it, Fitzgerald was photographed as a chorus girl, his dress seductively draped over one shoulder, looking out at the camera with a coy, mysterious smile. It was a pretty face, as Hemingway would later observe, with long delicate lips and the mouth of an Irish beauty, a mouth that Hemingway distrusted because it was too precious to be on a man's face.

Another college friend, John Peale Bishop, older, as scholarly and bookish as Wilson, introduced Fitzgerald to the work of Keats and the French Symbolists. He began to read these poets in his junior year when he contracted malaria, an appropriate malady for any young romantic (though perhaps not quite so romantically significant as tuberculosis, which Fitzgerald insisted he had as well). Actually, malaria was then endemic in the Princeton area, which was still quite swampy and infested with mosquitoes. Fitzgerald was forced to take a leave of absence, and used the medical excuse to obscure the fact that he was failing to maintain an acceptable academic record.

The unhappy prospect was that even if he were permitted to return, he would be prevented from participating in extra-curricular activities. By that point, Fitzgerald knew that to succeed in the world he would have to excel as a writer. That perception reveals Fitzgerald's ambivalence about his writing. The desire for the social and material rewards of success seems to have motivated his aspiration to be a writer, and that desire would drive him to produce work that he himself doubted and despaired of. He was always confused about the substance of his writing and the glamour of being a celebrated author. At his best, he did not betray the integrity of his gifts, but the tension created by his vision of himself as the committed artist and as the protagonist of his own legend led in his later life to the "damaged wings" of the flightless writer that Hemingway ascribed to Fitzgerald. He had begun a novel about his own coming of age, which he called *The Romantic Egotist,* and which he showed to Christian Gauss, the Princeton professor whom Wilson most admired. As dean of the college, Gauss was fully aware of Fitzgerald's poor record and, though he genuinely liked him, he had little faith in his abilities. Fitzgerald had also given a copy of his manuscript to Father Fay, who had suggested its original title, and who was far more encouraging. Fay spoke of sending it to his friend, Shane Leslie, but instead left on Vatican business in Europe.

Fitzgerald realized that his manuscript was unformed, mostly a collection of anecdotes about undergraduate life at Princeton. The material seemed conceived in innocence, both of the craft of fiction and of the ways in which the world was changing. In 1917 Fitzgerald was twenty-one. Most of his classmates were aware of the implications of the war in Europe, and the probability that they would have to participate in it instead of beginning their careers. Fitzgerald, however (like his contemporaries Hemingway and Faulkner), *wanted* to be in Europe, despite the strong isolationist mood of his own country and his overdramatized fear that he would be killed in combat. With a writer's sure instincts, he understood that the war would become one of the great stories of his time and that he would need to see it firsthand in order to retell it.

Early in his senior year he received a commission as a second lieutenant in the infantry and left Princeton to begin basic training. At Fort Leavenworth in Kansas, Fitzgerald proved to be as irresponsible a soldier as he had been a student. Once, when hiking with a supposedly full field pack, he was found to have stuffed a piece of stovepipe into his knapsack to disguise the fact that it was empty. Instead of attending to lectures on sniping or comportment in the trenches, he hid his notebook in his copy of *Small Problems for Infantry* and jotted down ideas for his evolving manuscript.

It was not that he was a shirker or a malingerer. He found the process of becoming an officer full of petty pretensions and mostly ridiculous. He had resumed his work on *The Romantic Egotist* on the weekends, working at the officers club, with all the distractions of a noisy, smoky room, and in three months had managed to thoroughly revise and expand his story. With considerable prescience he wrote to Edmund Wilson that he had completed the book and that if it was published, he would "wake up some morning and find that the debutantes have made me famous overnight."

He sent the new version of his novel to Shane Leslie, remembering Father Fay's intention and that Leslie was a published novelist. Leslie liked the book enough to submit it to his American publishers, Scribner's, with the strong recommendation that they should take it because Fitzgerald would probably die in the war, and as compensation would win the sort of literary renown of sacrificed promise that the English poet Rupert Brooke had received. Many of the editors at Scribner's were Princeton graduates and sympathetic to the book. The astute young editor Maxwell Perkins supported it, though he sent it back with suggestions for further revisions. By the time Fitzgerald heard this news he had been promoted to first lieutenant and transferred to Camp Sheridan in Alabama, where he met Zelda.

The Pursuit of the Fairy Princess

In a poem, one of his ultra-romantic mawkish complaints about her elusiveness, Fitzgerald wrote that Zelda's golden hair illuminated the ground and dazzled the blind. He was not going to be dissuaded by rumor or evidence of other admirers. Zelda knew that her popularity would only make her seem more appealing: a week after meeting Fitzgerald, at the next country club dance, she led another surprised escort to an outdoor telephone booth highlighted by an overhanging gas lamp and swarmed him with her lips in the hopes that Fitzgerald would emerge and see them. It was a typically defiant gesture—the man who would really want her would have to be prepared to overcome odds and the competition—like the knights of old. She and Fitzgerald were both susceptible to romantic self-mythologizing.

Fitzgerald sent her a chapter of *The Romantic Egotist*. He boasted of the future fame it would bring him, a confidence matched perfectly by Zelda's assurance in her own beauty. In the parlance of the day, he tried to "rush" her, to play the suitor who so besieges his intended with telephone calls and visits that she begins to perceive him as the center of her universe. They sat in the swing on the front porch of Judge Sayre's rented house, swaying gently, sipping tall fruit drinks, talking about Keats and Swinburne, ensconced in a bower of clematis vines, smelling honeysuckle and magnolia. She told him that she had no expectations of money from her family, that she was unsure of any artist's earning capacity, that he might go off tomorrow and die for the glory of the war anyway. Zelda's father disapproved of the courtship, she added; he was afraid Fitzgerald drank too much. The judge's opposition may have made Fitzgerald seem more attractive, a forbidden suitor, another occasion for Zelda to defy stodgy authority. In her novel, *Save Me the Waltz* (published in 1937), she would call him David Knight, that is, the man who would romantically appear as in some chivalrous tale to save a maiden, in this case from the stultifying conventions of Montgomery and its prospect of attendant boredom. She acted nonchalantly, but she noted, shrewdly, that Fitzgerald seemed to have planned his life as if it were a story. Clearly she was making herself a vital character.

It was a summer courtship. In August, Fitzgerald received the equivocal return of his manuscript from Scribner's and began revision again. By early September he had made little progress, for he was spending all his free time with Zelda, and he noted in his ledger on September 7 that he had irrefutably fallen in love with her. Completion of the book and conquest of the girl may have seemed more precious to Fitzgerald because of the incessant rumors that his division was being shipped overseas imminently. In fact, by the end of October he had received his orders and was preparing to depart for New York with his unit. "Here is my heart" were his final words to Zelda as the train lurched northward, a characteristically dramatic outburst of magniloquence. But Fitzgerald would make a career out of trading on his "heart." As he told a young writer years later, "You've got to sell your heart in order to tell your story."

Fitzgerald was stationed in Camp Mills, Long Island, which was as close to the European front as he would get. He would always regret having missed the opportunity to experience the war. There were two factors preventing his embarkation: first, Germany was ready to collapse and accept terms, and, second, the devastating impact of the influenza epidemic of 1918–19, which took more lives than the war itself. Camp Mills was close enough to New York City for Fitzgerald to be able to meet friends and attend parties. Unfortunately, he was the kind of drinker—like Edgar Allan Poe—

who could become intoxicated after a single drink, as if the idea of release was sufficiently exhilarating to disorient him.

On one occasion he used a friend's room in the Hotel Astor, and was caught in it with a naked woman by the hotel detective. Fitzgerald persuaded him to let them leave for a hundred-dollar bribe and placed a folded dollar bill in his hand, gathered his clothes and left with the girl. He would completely restage the incident in *This Side of Paradise*, making his persona, Amory Blaine, assume responsibility for his friend's indiscretions, another instance of how writing could transform reality for Fitzgerald.

Apparently, he had shared some version of the incident with Zelda. In *Save Me the Waltz*, David confesses it to Alabama, the character based on Zelda, who fudges matters by stating that a person "should only be faithful to another when they felt like it." Not one of Lawrence's characters, outrageous as they sometimes seemed to his contemporaries, would have even imagined such a remark. It belonged to a different social order, a different emotional environment. Lawrence's world, despite its scandalous overtures of profligacy, homosexuality and lesbianism, depended on a fixed moral vision. Zelda's remark about fidelity discounts the present of any permanent moral standard and replaces it with a dangerous, unreliable subjectivity. In a larger sense, Zelda's remark is a sort of touchstone for an idea of marriage which in earlier centuries, particularly the Victorian era, would not have been expressed, at least not by a woman. Indeed, it would have been attacked as a rationalization for profligacy. Maintaining fidelity if and when one feels like it, depending on the compatibility or happiness of any particular marriage, has traditionally been a male prerogative (women have exercised it as well, but perhaps more discreetly). Zelda told Scott that she thought like a man, a sentiment which he found intriguing enough to put into his first novel, and this was a supreme instance of it.

Returned to Montgomery, Fitzgerald found that his courtship was stymied. Both his and Zelda's expectations had been denied, and he was not writing love letters to her from the trenches of France, but instead back in the same situation he had been in previously. There were still some good moments: long walks in the winter woods, outings to the vaudeville theater, embraces and perhaps more in a borrowed car—later Fitzgerald would marvel at Zelda's "sexual recklessness." But there were also spats aggravated by his drinking and the news that Zelda was going out with another man. He had asked her to marry him, but she was still insistent on attending college dances with football stars, or the governor's inaugural ball.

Zelda was dating a young golf pro and one night they got drunk and smashed several dozen Victrola records over their heads. Before the evening ended she had accepted his pin, which she returned the next morning, sending an accompanying note to Fitzgerald accidentally. It was not what he wanted to hear and he wrote to her, in part facetiously, although he would repeat the reflection in subsequent letters, that now he understood why princesses were locked in towers.

The remark must have made a deep impression on her. Later, after her breakdown, she would tell a Swiss psychiatrist that Fitzgerald had locked her in their house for a month to frustrate a love affair she had begun with a Frenchman. It was a gross exaggeration of the circumstances. What was much more likely was that she locked herself in a bathroom for an hour, something she did often. The idea of the "locked-away princess" was, however, a central Fitzgerald fantasy, one that echoes the way men have regarded women since the Crusades when many of them had to leave home for long periods and wanted to imagine women as their exclusive property, sealed off in time and space.

That month, Father Fay died quickly after being stricken with influenza. Fitzgerald was too ill himself with a milder version of the same sickness to attend the funeral, but he felt the loss deeply and anguished over it in a letter to Shane Leslie. He had made little or no progress on revisions of *The Romantic Egotist*, partly because of the expectation of going to Europe, partly because of the unsettled state of his relations with Zelda. When he received his discharge papers, he again took the train to New York, bound for the "land of ambition and success," he exclaimed to Zelda in a telegram, hoping there to find the riches and fame that might make him acceptable in her eyes.

He moved into a drab single room in upper Manhattan and found a job writing slogans for streetcar advertisements in a small agency. Evenings were spent on his short stories, and he completed nineteen of them during the spring of 1919, garnering over a hundred rejections, which he pinned to his wall. Finally, he sold a story he had written while at Princeton to H. L. Mencken's lively magazine, *The Smart Set*. He received thirty dollars, which he promptly invested in a sporty pair of white flannels. Fitzgerald and the characters in his stories so often measure well-being in material terms—Daisy Buchanan cries over the beauty of Gatsby's shirts—but in this case Fitzgerald was trying to boost his spirits.

Another method was alcohol. Fitzgerald had been invited by college friends to a number of parties, which often ended in the drunken bouts familiar to undergraduates. After an all-night Yale fraternity revel, he remembered using a friend's derby hat to mix hash, catsup and eggs in a restaurant for breakfast, then searching for a hotel that would provide them with champagne, and finally smashing the empty bottles along Fifth Avenue. He would use these details in one of his first successful stories, "May Day," which became a record of his feelings of failure and frustration, as well as of the cynicism that he later asserted was a touchstone of the Jazz Age.

Drinking could only temporarily alleviate the despairs of a mediocre, futile existence. He wore shabby suits on the subway to and from the advertising job he hated, and he was receiving daily letters from Zelda in which she would juxtapose her anxieties about their future with her most recent outings with this or that most eligible male. When Fitzgerald wrote about an attractive actress he had just met, Zelda responded as she had when hearing of the escapade with the naked woman and the detective at the Hotel Astor, that if she were "good-looking, and you want to one bit—I know you could and love me just the same." It was a cool sophisticated reply, quite without the jealousy Fitzgerald had intended to arouse.

Fitzgerald had sent her his mother's engagement ring and would make three trips down to Montgomery that spring in the attempt to keep their love alive. He captured the spirit of Zelda's resistant skepticism in a story called "The Sensible Thing": "He seized her in his arms and literally tried to kiss her into a long monologue of self-pity, and ceased only when he saw that he was making himself despicable in her sight. He threatened to leave when he had no intention of leaving, and refused to go when she told him that, after all, it was best that he should."

After his third visit, he returned on the train with his mother's ring in his pocket. He had failed to convince Zelda that she should marry him and the pressures had been enormous. How does a man (who had not even received his degree from Princeton) earn the promise of a fortune in a season? In New York, again at his sloganeering, he began a tumultuous three-week binge which ended only on the first day of Prohibition and which left him in a state of physical and spiritual exhaustion.

The depletion gave him a curious resolve which was connected to Zelda but also beyond her. "I was in love with a whirlwind," he recalled later, and had "to spin a net big enough to catch it." In the creative period that can often occur after great emotion, or in Fitzgerald's case the psychic disorganization caused by alcoholic excess and release, he saw the way to rewrite *The Romantic Egotist.*

Returning to his parents' home in St. Paul, he spent the summer virtually writing a new novel, a "substitute form of dissipation," he called it, about the antics and ideas of a group of Princeton undergraduates. The novel was written according to a schedule pinned to the curtain in front of his desk, a schedule recalling Horatio Alger and the American myth of the self-made man who needed only to discipline his own natural powers to succeed. There is a lot of such enterprise in Fitzgerald, and his later portrayal of Jay Gatsby's youth would reflect more of it.

Now called *This Side of Paradise* (the title drawn from a line in a Rupert Brooke poem), the novel was not only intended as the way to gain Zelda's confidence, it was also patterned on his pursuit of her. Her letters to him and a diary which she had let him borrow all figured in the unhappy affair between Amory Blaine and Rosalind Connage that is central in the novel, and which seems conceived as well as a way for Fitzgerald to reconcile himself to the probable loss of Zelda.

The book was quickly and enthusiastically accepted by Maxwell Perkins, who wrote that he found the new version full of life. Scribner's acceptance gave Fitzgerald a surge of creative ebullience that helped him complete a group of short stories and begin another novel, tentatively called *The Demon Lover.* He acquired a literary agent in New York and saw a number of the stories he had just written sold to leading magazines like *The Saturday Evening Post.* Although he was to receive no advance for the novel, he was beginning to earn what seemed substantial sums with the stories, several of which would be optioned to Hollywood. Full of his literary success, he visited Zelda in Montgomery and resumed his courting, aware, however, that he felt his need for her less intensely than before. When he left, he gave her a manuscript copy of *This Side of Paradise.* After she read it, she wrote to Fitzgerald that "I am thine," confirming his intuition that his novel would be the way to win her heart.

The appeal of *This Side of Paradise* depended on its emphasis on youth, a value that American culture would reinterpret for the world in the 1920s. Suddenly, what had once seemed callow and immature would appear fresh and invigorating. Fitzgerald had found the pulse of a new generation "grown up to find all Gods dead, all wars fought, all faiths in man shaken," as he wrote near the end of the novel. His book is valuable as transmuted biography and social history—he wrote like some impassioned, naive anthropologist, Arthur Mizener, his first biographer, once argued. While certain of his characters, particularly Amory Blaine, may now seem jejune, insipid or even vapid, there is an inspired energy in the writing.

But *This Side of Paradise* is very much an apprentice novel, and its defects seem so glaring that its relative success makes it a curious testament to the vagaries of American literary taste. Fitzgerald reached for a Wildean snobbishness with his Princeton setting, depicting the antics of a group of shallow young men who assumed their superiority and privilege in the world, who partied recklessly and relentlessly, making frivolity more of an occupation than a pastime.

Smug, selfish, arrogantly self-important Amory (the name connotes love and appetite) Blaine is Fitzgerald parading the most conceited aspects of his personality while assuming that he is the avatar of a new generation. He prances through the story quoting Keats, Poe, Browning and Swinburne with a precious, stilted awkwardness that is often unintentionally comical, and his own lurid poems are an embarrassment. Fitzgerald uses Amory as a lens through which he will discover his eventual subject. There are types like the "slickers"—clever social climbers who are determined to win admiration and success no matter what the costs—after the fact that they wore their hair short, parted in the middle, soaked or oiled straight back on their heads. Early in the novel, on a winter afternoon in the Plaza Hotel, Amory watches a group of these men impatiently waiting for their counterparts:

"They strut and fret in the lobby, taking another cocktail, scrupulously attired and waiting. Then the swinging doors revolve and three bundles of fur mince in. The theater comes afterward; then a table at the Midnight Frolic—of course, mother will be along there but she will serve only to make things more secretive and brilliant."

This mother is chaperoning the flappers who become engaged every six months to a new contender, girls who would kiss before being proposed to, who would eat supper after dances at three in the morning in questionable cafés without the protection afforded by an attendant mother. Amory tells us that he finds it fascinating to realize that he could meet one of these girls of an evening, girls who would talk furtively in a half-mocking, half-earnest way, girls whom he is confident he can kiss before midnight. A more liberated age like our own, where premarital sex is taught in high school hygiene classes, will find this emphasis on kissing rather quaint. But Zelda was excited by it, as was Perkins, who saw that the world Fitzgerald chose to explore in his novel was shaped by a new moral and social code.

This new code is brilliantly exemplified in the most interesting section of the novel, a sequence which is written as a drawing room comedy. The scene is set in Rosalind Connage's dressing room as she is preparing for her debutante dance. Rosalind is a spoiled, blond beauty with a voice that Fitzgerald tells us is as musical as a waterfall. She can be cruel to men and despises women, claiming (as Zelda did) that they exist primarily to form a disturbing element among men. Amory somehow blunders into her dressing room before they have even been introduced. Within five minutes he has kissed her and fallen in love. He is displaced by Mrs. Connage, who lectures her daughter on the importance of marrying for money. The dialogue to this point has been crisp and funny (and no one in America except for Hemingway would write dialogue as well as Fitzgerald), but Mrs. Connage is deliberately made to sound inflated and ridiculous.

The next scene occurs in a den where Rosalind is being courted by an appropriately rich young man who blames her for inconstancy, for teasing men and playing with them. He is succeeded by Dawson Ryder, an even richer, more phlegmatic man who is surprised by Rosalind's forwardness, especially when she virtually proposes to him. Amory returns, finds Rosalind alone, and they resume their bantering repartee, clever, epigrammatic, and very Wildean. Finally, Rosalind asks him what sort of work he proposes to do in his life:

ROSALIND: What you going to do?

AMORY: Can't say—run for President, write—

ROSALIND: Greenwich Village?

AMORY: Good heavens, no—I said write—not drink.

ROSALIND: I like business men. Clever men are usually so homely.

AMORY: I feel as if I'd known you for ages.

ROSALIND: Oh, are you going to commence the "pyramid" story?

AMORY: No—I was going to make it French. I was Louis XIV and you were one of my—my— (Changing his tone.) Suppose—we fell in love.

ROSALIND: I've suggested pretending.

AMORY: If we did it would be very big.

ROSALIND: Why?

AMORY: Because selfish people are in a way terribly capable of great loves.

ROSALIND: (Turning her lips up) Pretend. (Very deliberately they kiss.)

The little drama continues until Amory declares his love. Rosalind declares hers, but, with a sharp realism that Amory does not notice, she twice emphasizes its temporality, maintaining that it is for now, for the moment, not forever as in the courtly vows. The scene is typical of Fitzgerald. The opposition of selfishness and love would become central in his life with Zelda. The scene also presents a sharp vignette of his view of female fickleness. As he asserted with a disarming candor in one of his many subsequent interviews, "I married the heroine in one of my stories," but in *This Side of Paradise* Rosalind jilts Amory. They have not been able to marry because Amory, like Fitzgerald, was earning a pittance in an advertising agency, and Mrs. Connage staunchly opposed any such marriage. The realistic Rosalind finally chooses Ryder and his millions and Amory is left in his lover's lurch.

What art might deny, life could provide, although Fitzgerald felt the need to reassure himself and Zelda before the wedding. A number of his friends had advised him against marrying Zelda. He responded to one of them in a letter with a frank admission of her reproachable qualities, her incessant smoking, her glee in telling shocking stories, her frequent declaration, for example, that she had kissed thousands of men and intended to kiss thousands more.

His list of her shortcomings—surface flaws that could have been true of a multitude of headstrong young women at the time—reveals how much he really didn't know about Zelda, or himself for that matter. But Fitzgerald was attuned to a quality that for him distinguished her from the other young women in his circle, though he never would learn how to take its full measure or adjust himself to it: he claimed he had fallen in love with her "flaming self-respect." Perhaps to shore up her respect for him, he sent her a series of curious love declarations by telegram, including in each one an account of his latest story sale. The most cheering news was that *This Side of Paradise* had gone into a second printing.

Zelda had agreed to be married in St. Patrick's Cathedral in New York. Just before she took the train north she wrote him a letter. "Darling Heart," she called him, a phrase Fitzgerald would use as a tentative title for his second novel. In her letter she apologized for all the times that she had been spiteful or mean: "Our fairy tale is almost ended, and we're going to marry and live happily ever afterward just like the princess in the tower who worried you so much."

Zelda was twenty and Fitzgerald was twenty-four when the actual ceremony occurred on April 3, 1920. It may have been one of the quietest events of their married life. Both bride and groom wore suits of dark blue. There were no parents present, but Fitzgerald had one Princeton friend as his best man, and Zelda's three older sisters had come with her. Many years later, Fitzgerald ruefully recalled being married on April Fool's Day, a careless slip perhaps, or an implication that his choice had been his folly. In 1938, two years before he died, he admitted to his daughter that after the wedding he did have immediate regrets.

The King With No Ground Under His Feet

The success of *This Side of Paradise* made Fitzgerald into "a kind of king of American youth," according to novelist Glenway Wescott. The novel went through nine printings in 1920 and was widely reviewed. Fitzgerald was celebrated in gossip columns, was asked to lecture, and was invited to innumerable parties. The Jazz Age had begun and with it America was off on the "greatest, gaudiest spree in its history."

The Fitzgeralds spent their honeymoon in New York at the Hotel Biltmore, from which they were asked to leave because of the late-night parties they threw in their room. It did not help matters that Fitzgerald, trying to entertain the attending dowagers, had performed handstands in the lobby. Both of them were determined to live for the sake of entertainment, their own most of all. Zelda dipped into the fountain at Union Square, and Scott jumped into the Pulitzer fountain across from the Plaza. Dorothy Parker saw them on Fifth Avenue adorning a moving taxi—Fitzgerald on the roof and Zelda perched on a fender.

Zelda danced on dinner tables in restaurants and performed cartwheels in public places, and Scott tried to undress while watching a Broadway play called *Scandals* before he was ejected by the ushers. He was thrown out of College Club at Princeton, and his membership was suspended after he appeared there drunk with a lyre, wings and a halo. The suspension was partly due to Zelda, whom he had introduced as his mistress, and who had poured applejack on breakfast omelets and then lit them. They had plunged pell-mell into the "orgiastic future" Fitzgerald would later describe in *The Great Gatsby*, but at this point they were both confused by the swirl of events. As Fitzgerald recalled later: "We scarcely knew anymore who we were and we hadn't a notion what we were."

But it was new, and fun, and the gaiety made them feel young— "like small children in a great bright unexplored barn." Married, Zelda was as flirtatious as ever, witty, unconventional in her remarks, a "barbarian princess from the South," according to Fitzgerald's friend John Peale Bishop. Zelda flirted with Bishop, telling him that kisses were not to be considered an end, but merely a means. To what she did not say, but enough was implied. Edmund Wilson, working with Bishop at *Vanity Fair* magazine, reported that Zelda would exclaim how hotel bedrooms excited her. If the statement seems a bit silly to us now, even banal, it wasn't for Wilson, who accepted it erotic implications. Inconveniently, Zelda's own bedroom was the Fitzgeralds' only room—they had moved to the staid Hotel Commodore—and it was a bedlam of food, paper and clothing strewn everywhere. Worse than the disorder that made it impossible for Fitzgerald to write were the costs of misadventure. Fitzgerald was extravagant, his editor Maxwell Perkins admitted, but not like Zelda, who wanted anything and everything at once.

Life at the Commodore had become too expensive—Fitzgerald began a lifelong practice of borrowing from publisher and agent—

and the hotel manager had asked them to leave anyway. They packed their belongings into a second-hand roadster and found an old house in Westport, Connecticut, for rent. This would give Zelda the opportunity for summer swimming and Scott the privacy to write. Unlike the other couples in this book who were forced by circumstances to accept catch-as-catch-can living places, the Fitzgeralds tried never to live below their expectations of life's material plenitude. Frieda Lawrence had also created disorder in her living space, but she claimed to have appreciated the simplification of living conditions. That was something Zelda would never willingly accept. The house in Westport was large enough to have weekend guests and lavish parties.

Fitzgerald had begun *The Beautiful and Damned*, a novel about a marriage like his own whose hero becomes ruined by drinking and dissipation. The circumstances of his life with Zelda were reflected everywhere in his book: the laundry she refused to wash left piled in closets, the time she "deintestined" their car by running it over a fire hydrant, the endearing idiosyncrasies of their Japanese house-boy, the parties for weekend arrivals.

Although there were signs that the newlyweds were becoming irritated with each other after only a few months of marriage, they were still in love, resembling Anthony and Gloria Patch in *The Beautiful and Damned:* "of all the things they possessed in common, the greatest of all was their almost uncanny pull at each other's hearts."

The critic H. L. Mencken had called love a state of perceptual amnesia. Like the typical romantic swain, Fitzgerald was fixated by Zelda, scribbling the things she said on scraps of paper, absorbed completely by her personality, both its exuberance and petulance, and appropriating it for his story. Only a few years earlier, while writing *The Rainbow* and *Women in Love*, Lawrence had watched Frieda with an equal fascination, transcribed some of her more explosive comments, and appropriated her as raw material for his fiction. While such creative exploitation seems quite natural among artists, it is not always emotionally accepted by the subject, and Zelda, like Frieda, felt somewhat like the person being photographed who fears a loss of soul in the process. Moreover, being a subject in a book is like having one's photograph pasted in an album, a fixed truth, a perception created by the eye of the beholder. It gives the subject no opportunity to correct the image or present an alternative picture. That was something Zelda, who wanted desperately to be someone in her own right, would find especially galling. Though she had agreed to the arrangement, she also regarded Fitzgerald's free-ranging use of her diaries in his novels as an act of artistic confiscation.

Zelda would complain of being bored in the country, so they made trips back to New York, or they would invite guests to Westport. If they were men, Zelda would almost inevitably flirt with them, not necessarily to make her husband jealous but as a natural expression of her playfulness. Of course, Fitzgerald would be jealous no matter what the explanation, but as he would assert in a facile essay on the difficulties of monogamy, "jealousy is the great proof of and prop to love." But no matter how easily he could make a joke about the limitations of monogamous marriage, he was never really a philandering man. He had just enough sexual confidence for a flirtation which might give him some access into a potential character, but essentially he was himself a monogamist.

Alexander McKaig, a college friend of Fitzgerald's, visited during a weekend party in June and noted in his diary that "Fitz and Zelda fighting like mad—say themselves marriage can't succeed." McKaig visited again later in the summer and there was an even more bitter fight. Zelda, drunk, decided to leave and began walking on the railroad tracks nearby with Fitzgerald in pursuit, a scene he incorporated into his novel, marred somewhat by the portentous speeches of his drunken characters.

There was a formidable amount of drinking that summer, at midnight beach parties, and at the gin mills and roadhouses that flourished because of Prohibition. Once at a party given by a neighboring theatrical producer, Zelda activated a fire alarm. When the firemen arrived and asked where the fire was located, she pointed to her breasts. It is reminiscent of the time Zelda called the Montgomery fire department when she was a child and had them rescue her from the roof of her parents' home. In a story by Hawthorne, the act would have allegorical significance, but here it forms part of a pattern, a desperate cry for attention, for personal significance, and it is as well a reflection of the rivalry she felt with her husband whenever he was lionized or became, as on that night, the center of attention.

Another guest that summer was the incorrigible ladies' man George Jean Nathan, the drama critic and co-editor with H. L. Mencken of *The Smart Set*, the magazine that had published Fitzgerald's first story. Zelda showed Nathan her diaries, which he offered to publish, upsetting Fitzgerald, who had depended on them for both *This Side of Paradise* and *The Beautiful and Damned*. Fitzgerald's relations with Nathan cooled immediately, as they did with a number of other friends in proportion to Zelda's attentiveness to them. For her part, Zelda suspected Fitzgerald of a liaison with Gene Bankhead, the actress Tallulah Bankhead's sister, and later that summer with another actress, Miriam Hopkins. There seemed to be a sort of festering sexual activity in the air around the Fitzgeralds at that time. They both heard of an affair between the poet Edna St. Vincent Millày and Edmund Wilson and John Peale Bishop simultaneously.

In the fall the Fitzgeralds returned to New York City, renting a small flat near the Plaza. Alexander McKaig noted in his diary that the place looked like a pigsty. He felt that Zelda needed something to do, some work to occupy her while Fitzgerald wrote: "If she's there Fitzgerald can't work—she bothers him—if she's not here he can't work—worried of what she might do." During the next few weeks McKaig noticed that Zelda seemed increasingly restless, one time claiming that she simply wanted to be amused, another time that she wanted the life of an "extravagant." Several times McKaig felt Zelda was going beyond her usual level of flirtation and making sexual overtures. He felt too much loyalty to Fitzgerald, however, to pursue the situation even though he was convinced that Zelda was the most beautiful and brilliant woman he had ever met.

Zelda was flamboyant and capable of the most unexpected acts—she had the habit of locking herself into other people's bathrooms and then taking prolonged baths. Once, when they were fighting, Fitzgerald broke down a bathroom door in someone else's home. He seemed, at times, to be playing a part in a bad melodramatic play. When Edna St. Vincent Millay asked him about his story "The Camel's Back," he flippantly claimed to have written it in an evening. Millay decided that Fitzgerald was affecting all the attributes he believed appropriate to genius.

According to McKaig, Fitzgerald got drunk every night through the winter and spring of 1921. Work on *The Beautiful and Damned* was completed, Zelda announced that she was pregnant, and the Fitzgeralds decided to celebrate by going to Europe. *This Side of Paradise* was being published in London and Fitzgerald wanted to be there to help publicize his book. Just before they were to sail, Fitzgerald got terribly drunk in a nightclub, and was asked to leave by a bouncer. When Zelda urged him to get another drink, the bouncer barred his way. Fitzgerald took a feeble swing, and ended up mercilessly beaten and humiliated. He would be in barroom fights for the rest of his life, brawls as a correction to bad manners that always ended in minor disgrace and contrition.

The European trip proved disappointing. During the week they spent in London, Shane Leslie was gracious, and Fitzgerald had lunch with the novelist John Galsworthy, who was as condescending as the reviews of *This Side of Paradise* would be. In France and Italy, the Fitzgeralds were tourists without even the benefits of a common language and their experience was a blur of sightseeing and a botched attempt to meet Anatole France.

Back in America by midsummer, the Fitzgeralds contemplated settling in Montgomery, where they stayed with Zelda's parents. It was too hot for Scott, too confining for Zelda, and too dry for the two of them—Judge Sayre, a stickler for the law, maintained a Prohibition household. From Montgomery, the Fitzgeralds took the train to St. Paul, one birthplace after another, and this was where Zelda had her daughter, Scottie. Fitzgerald was at the bedside. He dutifully noted Zelda's first words as she emerged from anesthesia, words pronouncing her daughter a "beautiful little fool," a phrase that he would give to Daisy Buchanan in *The Great Gatsby*.

Fitzgerald worked on stories, on a play, and on changes for *The Beautiful and Damned*. The novel had been serialized in *Metropolitan Magazine* for a large sum on which Fitzgerald depended, but he was dissatisfied with the way his story had been edited and abridged. He began to discuss the Scribner's proofs with Zelda, concerned particularly about the ironic potential of his ending in which his hero, Anthony Patch, is reduced by alcohol to a mindless incapacitation after inheriting his grandfather's estate. We will never know the full extent of Zelda's role in the making and remaking of *The Beautiful and Damned*, but like Frieda Lawrence, Zelda was a sort of collaborator, a feedback resource as well as the actual model for Gloria Patch.

What is most surprising about *The Beautiful and Damned* is not whatever elements it owes to Zelda or its evident flaws—which mostly derive from Fitzgerald's inability to decide whether he was satirizing Anthony and Gloria Patch or more sympathetically presenting the consequences of their bad choices—but how much Fitzgerald had grown as a writer in the short span since *This Side of Paradise*. Instead of the preciousness of the earlier novel, instead of repeating its subject matter, without the abrupt, often jerky movements of his first book, *The Beautiful and Damned* was written with ease and fluency, with passages of magically animating imagery such as the description of the heat waves from a dry road "quivering faintly like panes of isinglas," or a circling Ferris wheel that is compared to a "trembling mirror catching the reflection of the yellow moon."

Even more than style, *The Beautiful and Damned* provided exactly the kind of emotional depth that was missing in *This Side of Paradise*. The decline of Anthony Patch, the man who waited all his life to inherit his grandfather's millions, the man who cannot make a decision but feels he is too cultivated to waste his time in work, the man who does nothing "for there's nothing I can do that's worth doing," is brought down hard and far and the reader is moved by his fall.

The Beautiful and Damned was published in March 1922 to a mixed reception. One of the more perceptive reviews was written by John Peale Bishop, who pointed out that Fitzgerald seemed most concerned with the ramifications of his own legend. As a writer, Bishop added, Fitzgerald had the rare capacity to experience romantic emotions and then to detach himself satirically.

An even more pointed satire was Zelda's review, called "Friend Husband's Latest" and published in the *New York Tribune*. Flippant, facetious, the piece was a compound of anger and fun, with Zelda remarking—because of the use of her diaries—that Fitzgerald believed that "plagiarism begins at home." On a very deep level Zelda disliked being appropriated as material, even though it might get her the fur coat for which she had relentlessly nagged for two winters. Her review, witty and chic though it was, revealed a reservoir of hostility that was almost full to its brim.

Fitzgerald felt the same hostility, and some of it had been drawn in the more vacuous moments he gave Gloria Patch, the "girl who made her living on her prettiness," who cared exclusively about "having the best time I possibly can" when she was young. Zelda's antic poses and outrageous declarations corroborated that portrayal of her, and she was never quite able to let it go completely. She wanted to hold on to the prettiness, to the hedonism that was part of their pact with life, but the source of her resentment was that she also wanted something more—an aspect of her that neither of them knew how to deal with or foster. He extended his view of Gloria Patch to make her stand for all American women in an interview he gave to a reporter for the *New York Evening World*. In a spirit of inappropriate levity, Fitzgerald was always capable of saying some foolish things in interviews, and he asserted that American women were leeches whose main purpose was domination of the American male.

He was generalizing rapidly but basing his remarks on Gloria Patch, who stood for Zelda. He tried to characterize Zelda's power in a letter he wrote to Edmund Wilson, who was busy writing a critical essay on Fitzgerald's sources. In his letter, he reminded Wilson of Zelda's importance: "The most enormous influence on me in the four and a half years since I met her has been the complete, fine and full-hearted selfishness and chill-mindedness of Zelda."

St. Paul may have been a good enough place to have a daughter and complete a novel, but it just wasn't lively enough for the Fitzgeralds, and they decided to return to New York. In one of her more manic projections, Zelda saw herself as a seeker of "unadulterated gaiety." Such a goal seems the result of some frivolous inspiration, but Zelda was particularly conscious of the brevity of life, that she was only a "transient poignant figure, " and both Zelda and Scott suffered from the dullness of St. Paul. Fitzgerald later told his friend Tom Boyd that moving back there was one of the worst decisions he had made in his life.

While staying at the Plaza in New York, the Fitzgeralds looked for a house to rent in Great Neck, a Long Island suburb about a half-hour train ride from the city. Fitzgerald had gone there with Shane Leslie while he was at Princeton, visiting one of the many great estates in the area like those of the Guggenheims or the Astors. Great Neck had become a center for theatrical people and millionaires who could serve as suitable subjects for Fitzgerald's stories. Zelda and Scott had an air of romantic beauty about them. They were an item in gossip columns, regarded with the scrutiny reserved for movie stars. In fact, there was talk of Scott and Zelda acting in a film version of *This Side of Paradise*. Everyone wanted them at their openings and parties, and they were still eager to entertain.

Fitzgerald arranged a lunch at the Plaza for two writers he admired, Sherwood Anderson and John Dos Passos, whose first novel, *Three Soldiers*, he had favorably reviewed. Dos Passos was persuaded to accompany the Fitzgeralds to Great Neck, attracted by the "golden innocence" of the "hopelessly good looking couple." In a red chauffeur-driven touring car, they spent the afternoon with a real estate agent inspecting houses in Great Neck. Between house visits, Dos Passos tried to engage Fitzgerald in conversation, but except for literature, he felt no common points of reference. According to Dos Passos, Fitzgerald knew little about art, music, food or European culture. Shy, retiring, he was disturbed by Fitzgerald's inordinate curiosity, the insistence of his naively personal questions.

On the way back to the city, they passed a carnival. With childish delight Zelda demanded to ride on the Ferris wheel. Fitzgerald refused to leave the car, sipping from a hip flask in the backseat, so Dos Passos went with Zelda. Elevated and circling in the night air, Zelda said something weird—Dos Passos could not remember exactly what it was but it repelled and frightened him, and he characterized it as "off track." He believed that she was on the edge of madness, that sitting perched alongside her on that rickety wheel was like "peering into a dark abyss."

Settled in Great Neck, Fitzgerald began working on stories to help alleviate his debt. H. L. Mencken had seen the danger of easy sales for Fitzgerald, believing that Zelda formed the pressure on him to try for too much money, too rapidly. Fitzgerald is one of the great short story writers of the modern era, and among Americans, only Hemingway has achieved an equal stature as a short story writer. But many of Fitzgerald's stories, especially the ones sold to the *Saturday Evening Post* for considerable sums, were facile sketches without real substance, sentimental affectations which seem the equivalent of soap opera.

Fitzgerald continued to revise his play *The Vegetable*, a satire of the American dream in which a newsboy becomes President. He had resumed his friendship with George Jean Nathan, who was trying to help find a producer for the play. Edmund Wilson, whose wife was an actress and who consequently had strong theatrical connections, believed that *The Vegetable* was perhaps the funniest play yet written by an American, and he tried to help as well. The play actually found a producer, and it opened in Atlantic City in the fall of 1922, where it immediately failed to attract an audience. Fitzgerald had expected a great success which he hoped would resolve his financial difficulties. *The Beautiful and Damned* had not helped, selling only a modest number of copies.

Fitzgerald used his Great Neck home as the base for an interminable party that sometimes began in nightclubs or in other people's homes and that continued on at his. The drinking accelerated, though Dos Passos pointed out that Fitzgerald often pretended to be more drunk than he really was, possibly as a screen for observing. These observations were the settings for his novels. At that time his purpose, after all, was to invent the details that would emerge as his finest effort, *The Great Gatsby*, his account of the disorderly twenties, the malicious gossip and the blather of cockeyed opinions he heard at parties, the Babel of tongues, as Edmund Wilson put it.

The pandemonium of the constant round of partying was affecting the Fitzgerald marriage. The party noise blared out over the sounds of strain that were beginning to be heard by their friends. Their marriage became a balancing act of inflicting pain and extracting pleasure. Carl Van Vechten used them as characters in his novel *Parties*, in which they "tortured each other because they loved one another so devotedly." Wilson reported to Bishop that they had agreed to go out separately with members of the opposite sex. At first the agreement was more a theoretical accommodation than an actual realization, but it did point to a need to create some kind of space between themselves.

Still, most of the time they could hide behind their mask of total gaiety, accomplices in the disguise of perfectly united lovers. The critic Van Wyck Brooks was at a dinner to which the Fitzgeralds, typically, arrived late. As they were eating the soup they were served, they began to nod and doze, Scott explaining they had been up the two previous nights attending parties. Zelda was placed in a bedroom and Scott lay down on a couch, only suddenly to waken and telephone for two cases of champagne and for taxis to transport all the dinner guests to a nightclub. To Brooks, then known for his negative assessment of American Puritanism, the incident suggested that the Fitzgeralds were the most romantic of couples.

Actually they were living in the aftermath of their rash commitment to living as the most romantic of couples. The problem with burdening any relationship with the demand of perfect love, as the Fitzgeralds burdened theirs and as Sylvia Plath was to do in her marriage to Ted Hughes, is that perfect love can be the enemy of real love and of friendship and companionship in marriage. The romantic ideal of perfection leaves little room for growth, for change, for mutability. The Fitzgeralds tried to retain their disguise well after the fabric of their romantic illusions had worn thin and the threads had frayed. It wasn't that they had fallen out of love. They simply had not anticipated anything but perfection. Long after it sustained them, they continued the round of parties, the heavy drinking, the extravagant self-indulgences. But they were also fighting more, torturing each other more openly, with less control.

On one occasion, Eleanor Browder, a friend of Zelda's from Montgomery, had made a date to meet the Fitzgeralds at the Plaza for afternoon tea. Fitzgerald arrived drunk, a bottle of champagne in one hand and the writer Anita Loos in the other. Refused service because of his disarray, all four of them drove out to Great Neck for cocktails and dinner. As they were eating, a woman who had been pursuing Fitzgerald appeared at the door. When she left, Zelda made a cutting remark to him. Suddenly they were both hurling accusations. Fitzgerald jerked the cloth off the table, sending all the china crashing to the floor.

Fitzgerald would now disappear into the city for consecutive nights. Once, returning at dawn, he was found sleeping on his front lawn. At a party, he drunkenly tried to eat his soup with his fork; at others, he crawled under tables and babbled incoherently. He had become friendly with the sportswriter Ring Lardner, a tall, dark, reticent man who had a severe drinking problem. The two men would drink and converse into the night. Fitzgerald persuaded Lardner to collect his short stories for possible publication. He interested Maxwell Perkins in the book and arranged a lunch at his home so that Perkins might meet Lardner. Driving Perkins back to the city in his second-hand Rolls, Fitzgerald misjudged a curve and ditched his car into a lily pond. Fitzgerald later facetiously explained that he had done it because it seemed more fun than merely staying on the road, but the accident terrified poor Perkins, who was not at all appeased by the incongruity of Scott and Zelda trying to push their Rolls out of the water. The incident is not without its symbolic application to the way the Fitzgeralds would live, always diverging from course, restlessly never able to stay in one place for very long. If it was more "fun" to shift course suddenly, Zelda was Fitzgerald's happy accomplice, even if a sudden turn meant dunking the Rolls.

Another night Fitzgerald heard that the novelist Joseph Conrad was staying at the house of his publisher, Nelson Doubleday, in Oyster Bay, about ten miles from Great Neck. Fitzgerald and Lardner drove there, entered the grounds, and began performing a drunken dance, only to be unceremoniously ejected by the gardener. The attempt to meet Conrad personally was one of many blundering overtures for literary respectability. Had Fitzgerald managed to meet Conrad in his inebriated condition, despite the fund of good cheer which Fitzgerald brought to such occasions, Conrad would have despised him as another illustration of what he believed was the infinitely bad taste of Americans.

The graceless Conrad misadventure was characteristic of the reckless abandon of the year in Great Neck, a period of some desperate attempts to retain a vanishing youth. The humiliations and the excesses of that year were transmuted into *The Great Gatsby*, in which Fitzgerald was no longer writing direct auto- biography but filtering aspects of his own life and Zelda's into those of his characters, particularly in the account of Jay Gatsby's courtship of Daisy while he was an officer at training camp. Fitzgerald's own drinking had gotten out of control and in Lardner he had chosen as his best friend a projection of what he would become. But such a choice is rarely a conscious one, and Fitzgerald may have needed his life to take the form it did so that he could write *Gatsby* at all.

Great Neck had become hectic, making it difficult for Fitzgerald to concentrate, and he proposed that he and Zelda might live more inexpensively in Europe. Zelda, who once exclaimed that she was only happy in a room with an open suitcase on the bed, readily agreed. They set sail for Europe, where Fitzgerald hoped to finish *The Great Gatsby.* In his ledger he noted that 1923 had been a comfortable year—referring to Great Neck—but a "dangerous and deteriorating" time which left him in a marriage with "no ground under our feet."

One Thousand Parties

"We are going to be so happy away from all the things that almost got us but couldn't quite because we were too smart for them," Zelda would write in *Save Me the Waltz*. In Paris the Fitzgeralds met Gerald and Sara Murphy, who would partly inspire the characters of Nicole and Dick Diver in *Tender Is the Night*, Fitzgerald's last completed novel. An American couple who had lived in France on inherited money since 1921, the Murphys had adopted an old Spanish adage—living well is the best revenge—as their personal motto. At art galleries, exhibitions and recitals, they had sought out many of the leading artists of their time. They knew the painters Picasso, Miró, Juan Gris and Braque, and Murphy

painted quite proficiently himself. Both Gerald and Sara had
studied set design with Natalia Goncharova of the Ballet Russe and
in this way they got to know Diaghilev's set designer, Leon Bakst,
and the composer Stravinsky. They were more interested in
Europeans than the expatriate American colony in Paris, but they
had already met Hemingway and knew Dos Passos. More than most
Americans in Paris, as Murphy acknowledged, they were able to
measure the artistic pulse of the city at its zenith and enjoy it:

"There was a tension and an excitement in the air that was
almost physical. Always a new exhibition, or a recital of the new
music of Les Six, or a premiere of a new play or ballet, or one of
Etienne de Beaumont's fantastic 'Soirees de Paris' in Montmartre—
and you'd go to each one and find everybody else there, too. There
was such a passionate interest in everything that was going on, and
it seemed to engender activity."

The Murphys were building a villa at Antibes in the south of
France, and they suggested to the Fitzgeralds that this would be an
ideal area in which to settle because Zelda could swim and Scott
would avoid the distractions of Paris. Close to the beach, secluded
by a terraced rock garden, Fitzgerald spent his days at the villa they
found in St. Raphael working on *The Great Gatsby.*

He knew he was doing his best writing, and he was completely
absorbed in his work. *The Great Gatsby* was a fable for America
caught in the swift process of postwar change. The affluent houses
with their opulent interiors that he had seen in Great Neck, the
fancy cars, the endless though pointless parties, became his
landscape. All through his story he was using the color gray as a
symbol, and words like *confusion* and *groaning.* The novel is
presented from the point of view of an innocent Midwesterner
named Nick Carraway, whose cousin Daisy is married to the rich,
snobbish and stiff Tom Buchanan. Connecting Tom Buchanan's
sordid misalliance with Myrtle Wilson to the gangster, Jay Gatsby's
love for Daisy Buchanan, was a way of revealing that something
shoddy and unpleasant had emerged in America, that the old values
had been sacrificed for lust and greed. Fitzgerald was able to tell all
this without bitterness or diatribe, but with a lyrical poignancy, a
sense of nostalgic regret for the faithlessness of time and a
compensating irony. The result was a lean book with no particles of
fat in it, no dead weight or padding, the sort of work in "which a
vast amount is said by implication," as Perkins realized.

Meantime Zelda had little to do except swim and tan herself. In

June she met a group of young French fliers from the nearby airfield at Fréjus. She joined them frequently at the beach and dancing in the casino at night. One of them, Edouard Jozan, a tall, lithe, bronzed twenty-five-year-old officer, seemed particularly attractive. Only a year older than Zelda, he had the self-assurance that would later make him a natural military leader who would serve France bravely in several wars. Soon they were spending their days as a couple on the beach. According to Sara Murphy, everyone but Fitzgerald was aware that something more than a casual flirtation had begun. At one point Jozan flew a plane close to the tiled roof of the Fitzgerald villa, banking its wings in the same sort of tribute that the Montgomery fliers had made to Zelda's beauty during the war. Of course, Zelda had put him up to it.

While Fitzgerald was flattered by the idea of men becoming enamored of his wife, he felt immediately threatened when he realized he was no longer the center of Zelda's orbit. Sara Murphy observed that Fitzgerald made his writing an organizing principle for his household. Zelda's needs, even those of his child, were less important to him and could be attended to by servants. By mid-July there was some kind of confrontation over Jozan, and Fitzgerald had entered the phrase "The Big Crisis" in his ledger. Like certain of the incidents in the novel he was writing, like Gatsby's origins, there is more rumor than confirmed detail to explain the aftermath of this confrontation: that Zelda may have asked for a separation, that Fitzgerald told a relative that he became enraged and locked her in a room, that Fitzgerald demanded a face-to-face meeting where Jozan would be forced to ask for Zelda. There are conflicting reports as to whether Zelda tried to overdose with barbituates.

Jozan maintained that Fitzgerald had clearly defined notions about the world. Jozan was less sure of how the world worked, but confident that he could use his own personal courage to change it. For him, Zelda was a radiant foreigner overflowing with the desire to partake of whatever life offered but not, at least not at that time and not with him, participating in an infidelity. In her novel, Zelda wrote that "you took what you wanted from life, if you could get it" and the conditional "if" represents a considerable barrier. Nothing is consummated in *Save Me the Waltz*, although in *The Great Gatsby* Fitzgerald was plotting the mutual infidelities of the Buchanan couple. According to Jozan, Fitzgerald needed a marital drama, so he imagined that his wife had taken a lover before it actually occurred. Jozan, of course, may have been gallantly lying to protect Zelda's reputation, but Gerald Murphy supported his contention that there had been nothing more serious than a few passionate embraces.

Jozan could not have known how his presence that summer might have influenced the fictional triangle among Daisy Buchanan, her husband Tom, and Gatsby, her former suitor, who like Fitzgerald felt that some idea of himself had been damaged in love. As with everything else in his life, Fitzgerald dramatized and exaggerated the friendship between his wife and the young French aviator. It is an interesting act of the critical imagination to wonder how Lawrence might have responded to so flagrant an advertisement of Frieda's discontent. While both Lawrence and Fitzgerald used their lives as subject matter, Lawrence would have minimized the incident. Fundamentally, Lawrence was more secure in the power of his attraction to Frieda, aware that it went beyond the physical. Fitzgerald, more dependent on a hedonism he needed to begin his own creative processes, less secure in his craft and his marriage, was also more self-conscious, more alarmed by appearances. By appropriating his wife's flirtation and misinterpreting it, he was projecting his own fears. A tendency to self-dramatization was the exact quality that made him into a writer no matter what distortion it may have caused. Years later, he would tell Sheilah Graham about a duel in which he and Jozan fired shots and missed—an imagined scene that he had written in *Tender Is the Night*. Jozan became another instance of Fitzgerald rewriting his own history into a story, fictionalizing his life and then believing implicitly in his fiction.

Memory, of course, is an unreliable historical indicator, and as memory shifts and blurs with time, any notion of history is modified or enlarged. When we combine this trait, what Fitzgerald once called his "backdoor way out of facing reality," with the delusional capacities of the drunkard, then it becomes easy to see why Fitzgerald became his most logical subject, why his work was so inevitably autobiographical in character. During Zelda's friendship with Jozan, Fitzgerald had been reading biographies of Shelley and Byron. If he twisted a summer flirtation into the stuff of romantic tragedy, and limited his wife's freedom in the process, was it the fuel he needed for his own creativity?

When the critic Gilbert Seldes, honeymooning in France with his new wife, came to stay with the Fitzgeralds a few weeks after the supposed confrontation over Jozan, there was no sign of discord. Many years later Fitzgerald wrote that "something had happened that could never be repaired," but whether he was referring to his marriage or some fissure in Zelda's sanity was left ambiguous. In Rome the following winter, where he and Zelda had moved largely because she was reading about it in Henry James's *Roderick Hudson*, he wrote to his friend John Peale Bishop that though he and Zelda were capable of "terrible four day rows that always start after a drinking party," they were still "enormously in love," the only really happily married people he knew.

With *The Great Gatsby* published, Fitzgerald felt the need for the sort of change that might lead him to new material. In May, 1925, the Fitzgeralds rented an apartment in Paris. Life in France had not proven inexpensive, and Fitzgerald had borrowed against what he expected would be the certain success of his novel. Despite very favorable reviews, the book sold fewer copies than *The Beautiful and Damned*, just enough to repay Scribner's for its advances. Fitzgerald was getting $2500 for every story he could sell to the *Saturday Evening Post*, an unheard-of sum at that time, but new debts had accumulated since he completed *The Great Gatsby*, and would continue to plague Fitzgerald. Zelda, only twenty-five, had developed a chronic case of colitis, due in part to an excess of champagne, and she was also having considerable difficulty with her ovaries, her frequent infections stemming from an operation she had had in Rome to facilitate childbirth. Except when she was painting, a practice she had begun when they started living in Europe, she was often unwell and unhappy.

The disappointing sales of *The Great Gatsby*, at least as far as Fitzgerald's expectations were concerned, also proved a source of anguish, affecting his sense of himself as an important voice in American fiction. Even the wonderful personal testimonials he received from writers like T. S. Eliot—who called the book the "first step American fiction has taken since Henry James"—and Edith Wharton, could not sufficiently cheer him.

When Wharton invited him to her home outside Paris for tea, Fitzgerald arrived drunk, having stopped at a number of bistros along the way to bolster his confidence. He tried to shock Wharton, the elegant socialite, and her guests with an off-color story about arriving in Paris with Zelda and checking into a bordello which they assumed was a hotel for three days. Fitzgerald was typically nervous and insecure when with recognized writers and often resorted to the shocking in a desperate reach for credibility. Once, in Paris, when he met James Joyce, he offered to throw himself out of a window to show his appreciation, an offer Joyce naturally dismissed as crazy. Wharton, with a novelist's eye for detail, actually found the situation of Fitzgerald and his wife in a brothel interesting, and asked Fitzgerald to fill the story out with more specific details that Fitzgerald was too drunk to provide. The result was awkward and strained.

Paris was "one thousand parties and no work" he confided to his ledger, a place where he could go on a drinking binge for a week and then find himself alone in a hotel room in Brussels without remembering how he had gotten there. In one of the bars in Paris, he met Ernest Hemingway. He had already read some of Hemingway's stories and had recommended Hemingway as a new talent to Perkins. Hemingway had developed a tremendous concision in his writing, a natural ease and a total avoidance of sentimentality, affectation and superfluous language. He had worked as a reporter and a foreign correspondent, and had been an ambulance driver during the war. A burly young man with an earthy immediacy, he exuded health, vigor and masculinity.

In *A Moveable Feast*, his jaded and sometimes fictionalized memoir of his Paris years, Hemingway described his first meeting with Fitzgerald. As the two writers drank champagne, Fitzgerald asked a series of blunt personal questions, the kind he had asked Dos Passos—whether Hemingway had slept with his wife before marriage, for example. Suddenly, Fitzgerald's face drained of color and he passed out. For Hemingway, this was an act of fatal disgrace. In his code, a man always could hold his alcohol and his talk.

In the two chapters of *A Moveable Feast* that center on Fitzgerald, Hemingway presented a picture of a man who had lost such control. The most incriminating details occur on a trip to Lyons to retrieve a car that the Fitzgeralds had left there for repairs. The car was a Renault whose top had been cut away to satisfy Zelda's whim for an open vehicle, and both Fitzgerald and Hemingway were soaked by rain as they drove back to Paris. Putting up in a hotel overnight, Fitzgerald complained that he had caught pneumonia, a "confession" Hemingway ruthlessly satirized in his book, making Fitzgerald look like a whining, hypochondriacal weakling.

Fitzgerald told Hemingway about Zelda's romance with the French aviator, reciting variant versions on different occasions, and Hemingway believed he was trying to invent a story around it. Hemingway's wife Hadley heard the story with the absurd melo-dramatic twist of Jozan's suicide. Hadley believed that Zelda was frivolous, the sort of woman who took life as a prolonged festivity, using the Jozan story as a way to give herself some romantic status. Zelda accepted Hadley but disliked the way she seemed to cater to Hemingway, despite the fact that it was her small income that the Hemingways depended on in Paris. Zelda had a bitter, sharp wit, and she hated pretensions in others, much as she loved flaunting her own. When Fitzgerald brought her to Gertrude Stein's salon, she dismissed Stein's famous conversation as "sententious gib-berish." When the Fitzgeralds visited London to see the publisher who would bring out *The Great Gatsby*, they saw Tallulah Bank-head in a hit play. Zelda wrote that they had gone to London to see a fog and "saw Tallulah Bankhead, which was, perhaps, about the same effect."

Zelda was equally hard on Hemingway, whom she regarded as a fraud. She detested the cynical edge she heard in Hemingway's tone, a domineering, swaggering machismo. Hadley explained that Zelda could not accept his male self-assurance (though her own self-assurance was shattered a year later, when Hemingway left Hadley and their son for Pauline Pfeiffer, an independently wealthy American who worked for *Vogue* in Paris).

According to Hemingway, Fitzgerald was psychically damaged by Zelda—castrated is his implicit image for a woman he saw as hawkish—but then Hemingway's view of women was clearly biased: in a story he wrote at this time, one of his characters declared that once a man married he was "bitched." His view was reinforced by an apologetic letter that Fitzgerald sent him after he and Zelda visited the Hemingways at home. The visit had gone sour, and Fitzgerald tried to blame Zelda, who suffered, he admitted, from a nervous hysteria that could only be treated by doctors and mor-phine. Fitzgerald was only half-serious about the morphine, but Hemingway thought that Zelda was unbalanced, and he told this to Fitzgerald as well as to others.

Hemingway claimed that Zelda would encourage Fitzgerald to drink because she knew it would prevent him from writing, and most of all she was jealous of Fitzgerald's accomplishments as a writer. In one sense, though Hemingway did not know this, the jealousy may have been augmented because Zelda had contributed so systematically to Fitzgerald's craft. Hemingway argued that whenever Fitzgerald was working well, Zelda would complain of boredom, and call him a "killjoy" if he balked at going to a party or a nightclub. Inevitably he would go and drink and then become, in Hemingway's term, "soft": "He dissolved at the least touch of alcohol." The alcohol was beginning to make him experience bouts of impotence, and Zelda complained about his inadequacy. Again according to Hemingway, who may have been expressing his dislike for Zelda, she told him that his penis was too small to satisfy a woman.

The little vignette Hemingway offers in *A Moveable Feast* of penile measurements over the urinal in the men's toilet may be an act of brutal caricature, but it seems to fit into the context of the Fitzgeralds' relationship. They spent the summer of 1925 in Antibes, drawn again to the warmth of southern France because "one could get away with more" there, Fitzgerald wrote, and by the Murphys, whose orchestrated social gatherings and civilized gaieties fascinated Fitzgerald. The Murphys and the backdrop of relaxed indolence and opulence were being filtered as material in Fitzgerald's story about a young American who murders his mother (variously called *The World's Fair, The Boy Who Killed His Mother*, and *Our Type*), which he would work on for four years without its cohering as a novel. Both he and Zelda liked the Murphys, and they all got on well with each other, although the unpredictable antics of the Fitzgeralds could test the limits of even so suave a pair as the Murphys.

When Gerald Murphy excluded Fitzgerald from one of his parties—and Fitzgerald had already been asked not to enter certain local bars and casinos—he stood outside a garden wall and threw the contents of a garbage pail over it at the Murphys' guests. Fitzgerald was drunk, of course, but the incident suggests a critical though infantile rage, with Fitzgerald being separated from his natural subject matter and then using the garbage as a commentary. The act is typical, as well, of how easily Fitzgerald would choose the most shocking possibility to outrage his own natural constituency. This was a trait that he shared with Zelda, and neither of them ever needed any lessons from the Dadaists or the Surrealists in Paris during the twenties.

The Murphys wanted no part of Fitzgerald for three weeks, but in a forgiving mood they decided to invite the Fitzgeralds to dinner, at a small inn located in the mountains behind Nice with a steep drop into a valley below it. The view was panoramic and breathtaking.

The Murphys and the Fitzgeralds were seated on a terrace next to a flight of stone steps, and Murphy recognized the controversial dancer Isadora Duncan at another table. Forty-six, overweight, with gaudy dyed red hair and three sycophants at her table, she was no longer very attractive. Kneeling at her feet like some troubadour from the past, Fitzgerald began reciting his compliments with Isadora beaming, at one point calling him her centurion. Zelda, seated with the Murphys, was watching this performance when suddenly, without warning, she leaped across their table past the Murphys and plunged down the stone stairs. For a moment, it looked as if she had disappeared into the valley below. Though her knees were scraped, she was not seriously injured, only frightened by what she had tried. Zelda's act seems all the more suggestive because it was provoked by a famous dancer, a woman who expressed her power as a function of grace in movement, which was exactly Zelda's goal, a goal that in some deep center of her being she must have known it was too late to try to attain. Her husband was on his knees apparently worshiping a goddess of the dance, unaware that most of all his wife longed to become that goddess. This must have been too much for Zelda to witness, so she attempted one of her symbolic suicides as a warning.

The Murphys had had enough, returning to Antibes in their own car, feeling that Scott and Zelda were each trying to outdo the other, and that they would attempt during the remainder of the evening to accomplish something even more sensational than Zelda's reckless plunge. Fitzgerald followed in his Renault, but at a point near Antibes where the road converged with a trolley trestle, Fitzgerald turned his car onto the tracks. There it stalled. Both the Fitzgeralds had been drinking all day, and they fell asleep in their car on the tracks, though they must have known that the trolley came around a sharp curve at that point. Early the next morning a farmer in his ox-cart taking his vegetables to market saw them and woke them and persuaded them to leave the car.

At this point legend proliferates: one report states that the car was decimated by the trolley fifteen minutes later; another argues that it was pulled off the tracks by the farmer and his ox. The real point, however, is that the Fitzgeralds had decided to situate themselves on a dangerously marginal edge, no matter what the risk to life or safety. The choice seemed inspired by an insatiable need for excitement, for the kind of unpremeditated action that would leave people amazed and speechless. Such drastic action could be as foolish as throwing garbage at a party or threatening to jump out of a window, but to the Fitzgeralds it was usually an energizing catalyst.

In the fall both the Fitzgeralds and the Murphys returned to Paris, but the friendship had become strained. One night Fitzgerald slept on the Murphys' lawn in St. Cloud, and on another night, sharing a taxi in Paris, Fitzgerald began chewing some hundred-franc notes and spitting them out the window. When the cabdriver stopped to retrieve some of the money, Fitzgerald seized the wheel and tried to ditch the cab in the Seine. The hysteria was beginning to seem forced, and Fitzgerald observed that the Paris parties had begun to tire him. Zelda was frequently ill with colitis, miserable in the interminable winter drizzle and rain of Paris, and cooped up in a stale, crowded apartment. The only good news for Fitzgerald was that *The Great Gatsby* had been successfully dramatized and was on the stage. There were additional royalties when Hollywood bought the novel, a bonanza that sent the Fitzgeralds for a two-month rest cure to a resort in the Pyrenees, and then to Juan-les-Pins on the Riviera in the spring.

Once again social life would rotate around the axis of the Murphys, who were now very interested in Hemingway. Fitzgerald had considerable respect for Hemingway's potential and his talent, and he had tried to boost his reputation, but he felt displaced, no longer admired by the Murphys. At a lavish casino dinner arranged by Gerald Murphy to honor Hemingway, Fitzgerald sophomorically began flipping ashtrays and salt shakers. At another party given by the Murphys, he tossed a ripe fig into the dress of a French countess, and when she ignored it, he hurled several precious Venetian glasses over the garden wall.

Zelda's behavior was even more extravagant. Most of the time she seemed taciturn, brooding, aloof and remote, as disengaged as Nicole Diver in *Tender Is the Night*, with very few words for anyone. When she did speak, she was capable of astonishing lucidity, Gerald Murphy recalled. One afternoon, when the group around the Murphys were toasting the departure of one of their company for America, Zelda shouted that words were completely inadequate. She rose on her chair and deftly removed her under-pants, offering them as a parting gift. Another night in the casino, she lifted her dress high and danced around the ballroom while exposing everything below her waist. The men in the casino were as entranced as Zelda, who was entirely absorbed in her dance,

gliding like one of the enchanted Wilies in *Giselle*. The act was
exhibitionist, but also Zelda's ultimate statement as a dancer, the
occasion when concept and movement were so perfectly modulated
that the dancer in some Yeatsian formula becomes indistinguish-
able from her dance.

There were other occasions when her actions seemed more
suicidal. During a fight with Fitzgerald, she placed herself under the
car wheels and dared him to drive over her. Sara Murphy remembered the morning when Zelda dove into the sea from some
precipitously high rocks with no apparent concern for her safety,
and then repeated the dive again and again.

Such acts were grandly theatrical, but much of the time Zelda
was quite ill. In addition to suffering from colitis, she had her
appendix removed in June and she needed much of the summer to
recuperate. Fitzgerald would often leave her alone at night. There
were mornings when he had not returned and others when Zelda
woke to a house full of strangers. Fitzgerald was introducing
himself very politely as an alcoholic, and demonstrating that
capacity every night. The source of his displeasure was his
inability to progress with his novel. He was only twenty-nine but he
felt he was deteriorating as a writer, unable even to complete short
stories. Mockingly, he had often announced that he only wanted to
live till thirty. Now he declared this in a letter to Perkins, with no
humorous intent. All the extra income from the theatrical and film
versions of *The Great Gatsby* had been dissipated. Disheartened,
Fitzgerald decided to return to America, sailing from Genoa with
Zelda, who was suffering severe asthmatic seizures. In his ledger,
he noted that they were returning "further apart than ever before."

The Battle of Dogs and Cats

Fitzgerald was faced with the perennial problem of money, one of
the disagreeable realities he had previously been able to circum-
vent by writing another facile story for the *Saturday Evening Post*.
But this sort of writing was becoming more and more difficult for
him. Luckily, it seemed, he received an offer from United Artists to
write a screenplay for a film about college youth. Leaving their
daughter with his parents in Washington, D.C., the Fitzgeralds took
the train for the West Coast. Passing through New Mexico, he
suffered severe abdominal cramps and left the train convinced that

he had appendicitis. He was wrong; the pain had been caused by the pressure he felt about writing for film.

The Fitzgeralds spent two months in Hollywood, living in a bungalow on the grounds of the exclusive Hotel Ambassador, with John Barrymore and Pola Negri as neighbors. There was a new set of parties to attend, bigger and more lavish than in Paris, where the women seemed even more beautiful. Scott and Zelda were still full of their puckish pranks, appearing at one party in their pajamas, barking like dogs at another, boiling a stew of watches and the ingredients they found in ladies' handbags at a third. The desperate silliness may have been provoked by the larger shadow of celluloid celebrity, the instant fame of motion-picture stardom. As Fitzgerald would later observe in *The Last Tycoon*, his uncompleted Hollywood novel, film writers were only a marginal means to a more glamorous end.

At one of these parties Fitzgerald met a seventeen-year-old actress named Lois Moran, a blond, blue-eyed beauty who was carefully chaperoned by her mother, who also managed her. In *The Beautiful and Damned*, Fitzgerald had written that "any girl who made a living on her prettiness interested him enormously" and there was a mutual attraction and fascination. Lois immediately suggested fictional possibilities to Fitzgerald as a heroine in a Hollywood setting. In the spirit of naive honesty that runs through so much of his fiction, he could have confessed this to Zelda, who would have felt terrible about being cast aside or possibly replaced. One evening, when Fitzgerald was preparing to go out to dinner with Lois and her mother, he had a heated argument with Zelda, who was staying behind. Zelda was devastated when Fitzgerald shouted that Lois Moran was a woman who was doing something with her talents and beauty.

It is the kind of remark an enraged spouse throws out more to wound than to shout the truth. In this case, Fitzgerald's aim was deadly accurate. He had hit not only on the rivalry Zelda felt with the attractive Moran, but on her deeper rivalry with his talent. After he left, Zelda, stinging from the wound, went into a frenzy. She burned some of her clothing in the bathtub. She had designed the clothes, and she loved her baths, but now she was less in love with herself. Only twenty-six, but terrified of aging, she thought her skin had coarsened and that her face was more angular than it had been. The conflagration in the bathtub was a warning that she could not tolerate the pain of being neglected while her husband cavorted with a younger, and perhaps more realized, version of herself.

In *The Beautiful and Damned*, Fitzgerald had imagined the possibility that Gloria Patch could become a film actress, a possibility that only succeeded in making Anthony Patch terribly jealous. But now the situation was reversed and Lois said she wanted Fitzgerald to play her next leading man and arranged for him to have a screen test, though nothing would ever come of it.

Zelda was aware that Fitzgerald was now using Lois Moran as a figure for his stories, and that she would become the actress Rosemary Hoyt in *Tender Is the Night*, who has an infatuation and then a brief affair with Dick Diver. In stories of her own, which she began writing at the time, Zelda imagined heroines with a desperate need for recognition, one that would be based more on accomplishment than beauty. Zelda thought that Lois Moran had no real presence as an actress, "only an ebullient hysteria about romance," but she represented what Zelda saw as her husband's major reproach against her—that Zelda had never done anything professionally.

Before her marriage she had joked that she hoped she "would never get ambitious enough to try anything," and in her southern world women were expected to be dynastic queens who would look beautiful, supervise home and children and never do anything. Now she felt that Fitzgerald regarded her as lazy, and his attachment to Lois Moran, which never got past the stage of innocent flirtation, became grounds for a deeper resentment. When *Lipstick*, the screenplay Fitzgerald wrote, was rejected, Fitzgerald was stunned, fearing he had lost his magical power with words. On the train heading east they fought again over Lois Moran. Enraged, Zelda threw a diamond watch Fitzgerald had given her during their engagement out of the window. Despite his swaggering, Fitzgerald was a particularly vulnerable man. The rejection of *Lipstick* made him question his powers, and Lois Moran was the sort of bauble a faltering man dangles to appear more potent. On some deep level, Zelda's outrage may have reminded him of his mother's dominance and his father's ineffectuality.

The Fitzgeralds moved to Ellerslie, a Greek Revival mansion near Wilmington, ostensibly so that Fitzgerald could continue to work on *Tender Is the Night*, the novel that for years he had been promising to Perkins. With its columned portico facing the Delaware River, Ellerslie was a grand estate and Fitzgerald wanted to play lord of the manor, inviting old friends to wild parties. When Edmund Wilson came, he sensed the delirium and the oncoming debacle. John Peale Bishop was offended by the disorganization, complaining that no meals ever seemed to be served. Both Zelda and Fitzgerald drank heavily, Fitzgerald for an inspiration that seemed blocked, out of reach no matter how many cocktails he consumed. It was as though he was feeding on himself in desperation for material. When Maxwell Perkins visited, he found Fitzgerald exceedingly nervous and, he thought, on the verge of a nervous breakdown.

The Fitzgeralds fought with frequency, and Fitzgerald termed the two-year period at Ellerslie an "organized dog and cat fight." One night Zelda had to be relieved with morphine, a drastic remedy that had been used once previously on the Riviera. On another evening, when Zelda's sister Rosalind Smith had come to visit, the Fitzgeralds fought and Fitzgerald flung Zelda's favorite vase into a fireplace and slapped her across the face. Such hostilities had curious creative repercussions. Fitzgerald told his friend H. L. Mencken that he was working on a novel about a woman who sought to destroy her husband because she was jealous of his achievements. The woman would first damage herself by drinking, by sleeping with other men, by alienating friends. Except for the promiscuity (which Fitzgerald could only fantasize) these were more Fitzgerald's actions than Zelda's, and he did not write such a novel, although elements of it figure in the struggle between Dick and Nicole Diver at the end of *Tender Is the Night*.

The rivalry and its explosive expressions in physical violence has clear parallels to those of Lawrence and Frieda, but there are differences of temperament and circumstance as well. While both Frieda and Zelda managed to cause conflicts—arising from deviations in taste or ideology or from jealousy—with their husband's friends as a way of asserting themselves, Frieda insisted on recognition as a contributor to her husband's genius; Zelda sought to be recognized for her own achievements. She was also more capable than Frieda artistically. She had a story to tell and the means to tell it.

In her story "The Millionaire's Girl," the heroine decides on a movie career because "everything I do or that happens to me has seemed because of him." Though Ellerslie was hardly the best place to launch such a career, Zelda began ballet classes, going to

Philadelphia three times a week for training, and practicing obsessively in front of a large mirror at Ellerslie for eight hours or more a day. She had always been a graceful dancer and had often passed herself off as one. Fitzgerald had originally been captivated by her movement on the dance floor at the country club in Montgomery. At twenty-seven, she seemed determined to become another Pavlova without the benefits of apprenticeship and with the strength and grace of her youth behind her. Now she was doing things, writing stories and articles and dancing incessantly, but there were long periods of unbroken silence, and she developed a chronic case of eczema, a very visible sign of her anxiety and the pressure to become somebody.

Unable to please himself with his novel, Fitzgerald wanted to return to Paris for the summer of 1928. Zelda was eager to go, believing that in Paris she would find a higher quality of instruction than she had found in Philadelphia. Gerald Murphy introduced her to Madame Egorova, once a leading ballerina with the Ballet Russe, and Zelda began a rigorous campaign of morning classes and afternoon practice. Murphy's daughter also studied with Madame Egorova, and once when he was waiting to pick her up, he watched Zelda. Usually sympathetic to her, he found her dancing a grotesque attempt to retain her youth.

Fitzgerald behaved as though her attempt to become a dancer was a form of vendetta, Zelda's vengeance for a life in which she was made to feel less important than he. Zelda was convinced that he was deliberately trying to violate her concentration so that she could not manage to dance at all. This time they were in Paris for five months, a period during which Zelda recalled they never had sex, mostly because Fitzgerald was drunk the entire time. He was jailed twice because of bar fights, and he spent his time getting drunk with a procession of visiting friends, all part of his implicit belief that intense experiences would lead to creativity. No matter how much alcohol he consumed, he was not able to progress with his novel. As he confided in his ledger, he wrecked himself that summer with dozens of friends. It was an "ominous" time, a word he underlined three times. Yet he had no real insight into what was happening and no control over it—only a sense of dark presentiment.

The Fitzgeralds returned to Ellerslie and Zelda to her hectic schedule of dancing. Fitzgerald had brought back a French chauffeur whom Zelda despised, a sort of drinking companion with whom he got arrested several times under embarrassing circumstances in the winter of 1929. The drinking and the inability to write had darkened the cavalier insouciance of his vision, made it more pessimistic and full of foreboding. He summarized the shift in his own perspective in an essay which was posthumously collected by Edmund Wilson in *The Crack-Up*:

"By this time contemporaries of mine had begun to disappear into the dark maw of violence. A classmate killed his wife and himself on Long Island, another tumbled 'accidently' from a skyscraper in Philadelphia, another purposely from a skyscraper in New York. One was killed in a speak-easy in Chicago; another was beaten to death in a speak-easy in New York and crawled home to the Princeton club to die; still another had his skull crushed by a maniac's axe in an insane asylum where he was confined. These are not catastrophes that I went out of my way to look for—these were my friends; moreover, these things happened not during the depression but during the boom."

The lease on Ellerslie expired in the spring of 1929 and the Fitzgerald family, practically out of habit, sailed to Europe. In Paris, Zelda was concerned only with her dancing, and Fitzgerald mostly with carousing. In a letter to Hemingway he admitted that when he drank he made his friends "pay and pay and pay." He also confessed that he thought he had no real friends, and did not himself really care for anyone, including Zelda. He might have added that drinking gave him the ability to relate, to please people, to overcome his own inhibitions to the point where he could draw people out with the sort of direct questions that they invariably regarded as invasions. The drinking also filled him with self-pity and prevented the flow of his writing rather than abetting it. He had trained himself to drink quantities of alcohol, mostly gin and wine, in a way that was analogous to Baudelaire's description of Poe's drinking habits, which he saw as barbarously American, accomplished with homicidal speed, as if Poe had to poison or feed some inner turning worm.

Zelda drank as well, and she could always consume more than Fitzgerald. She was moody and hypersensitive. Barely eating, she had lost fifteen pounds. She was writing a series of stories about bored and beautiful but adventurous women for an American magazine, most of which were co-signed by Fitzgerald, and which she claimed she wrote to defray the cost of her ballet lessons. The stories rely more on description than they demonstrate the ability to develop characters and make them seem real; they are more competent than convincing. When the Canadian novelist Morley Callaghan visited the Fitzgeralds, Zelda presented herself with great insistence as a writer. On two occasions, Callaghan remembered, she dominated conversations about books and writing until Fitzgerald suggested that it was time for her to go to sleep so that she could be ready the next morning for her ballet classes. Like a good little girl, she obeyed each time.

It is hard to know just what she was trying to establish by these thrusts into writing and literary opinion. She was intelligent and she was talented up to a point, but she may also have been trying to present a counter to her physical and emotional deterioration, which grew more pronounced with the passing days.

Paris was suffocated by an invasion of Americans, so the Fitzgeralds retreated to the Riviera. These "fantastic Neanderthals," as Fitzgerald called them, followed, and even the Murphys' beach at Antibes was overrun. Gerald Murphy remembered a new and disconcerting quality in Zelda's laughter which seemed to him a mixture of unhinged delight and terror. Sometimes, eerily, there were unprovoked fits of wild laughter.

Zelda danced in Cannes and Nice in the summer of 1929, small roles perhaps, but a sign that she was more than a student. She even received an offer to join a company in Naples, which she refused. It must have been an agonizing choice. In *Save Me the Waltz*, Zelda's autobiographical heroine accepts the Naples invitation to dance in *Faust*. During the course of her engagement, she injures herself and contracts blood poisoning in her foot and is forced to give up her dancing as a consequence. On an apparent level, and in terms of what one expects to see in most fiction, this sounds like the price paid for a Faustian bargain, but on a deeper level it suggests a fear of exposure as a dancer with more nerve than talent, a young spirit parading in a body too old already for the task. The fear of failure is connected to Zelda's dependence on Scott, which was always excessive, as she would realize later when she was institutionalized.

As the belle of Montgomery, Zelda had been taught to find a strong man to care for all her needs. Her story is about the rebellion against such expectations, but the cruel suspicion is that it was a rebellion more of surfaces, more of manners than of substance, and that her artistic efforts might have been richer had her rebellion been more realized and sincere. She was twenty-nine, but hardly capable of leaving her husband and daughter in order to dance alone in Naples, and it is unlikely that she could have persuaded Fitzgerald to accompany her. He did not like Italy and felt bound to the Americans in Paris and on the Riviera because he knew they were his subject matter.

For the first time in three years, Fitzgerald had been able to work successfully on his novel. He had changed its focus and now concentrated on the character of Dick Diver, fusing in him the social sophistication he admired in Murphy and his own awareness of how he was disintegrating as a writer and as a man. While the progress on his novel pleased him, the Naples offer remained in Zelda's mind, torturing her as a missed opportunity. She expressed her frustration in another bizarre suicidal gesture. While Fitzgerald was driving his family back to Paris through the mountainous region of the Grande Corniche, Zelda seized the steering wheel and tried to turn their car over a cliff. Fitzgerald managed to retain control of the car, but he made the mistake of accepting Zelda's action as part of the general pandemonium of their existence. All along, they shared the ability to deny the other's pain, the raw facts of their existence. When a similar incident occurs near the end of *Tender Is the Night*, Nicole Diver laughs hilariously and looks defiant. In the Grande Corniche, Fitzgerald pushed aside Zelda's mad attempt and kept driving.

In Paris the writing seemed harder and the distractions were necessary. Zelda returned to her fanatical program and generally ignored Fitzgerald except for an attack when she accused Fitzgerald of a homosexual liaison with Hemingway—an improbability because neither writer had any such proclivities and because relations between the two writers had cooled considerably anyway. Zelda idolized her teacher, Madame Egorova, and only wanted to discuss the ballet. Skeptical about her future as a ballerina, Fitzgerald resented the time she spent practicing. Zelda felt she was ready for a place in the dance world and expected an offer from the Diaghilev company in Paris. The offer never came. Instead, someone from the Folies-Bergère asked her to perform a coarse version of a belly dance for tourists, an invitation that demoralized her.

By the spring of 1930, Zelda was discouraged but paradoxically all the more committed to her strenuous regime. She had accompanied Fitzgerald to Algeria for an end-of-winter holiday and returned gaunt, hunched and pale, strained in the face with deep lines around her mouth and dark shadows around her eyes. During a luncheon at their apartment, she panicked about getting to her dance studio in time for her afternoon rehearsal. She seemed particularly nervous, and she had been drinking—she thought alcohol stimulated her to dance just as Fitzgerald thought it could help him to write. One of Fitzgerald's friends went with her in a taxi, where she decided to change into her ballet outfit to save time. When the taxi was impeded by traffic, she jumped out in her tutu and began running in between the cars in the direction of the studio. It was an absurd moment, Zelda's final dance of hysteria, all the implied delicacy and grace of ballet pirouetting to the music of horns and motors in an atmosphere of putrid fumes. Zelda reached her studio too agitated to dance. The friend, alarmed, called Fitzgerald, who left his guests and came to calm her.

What followed were the hallucinations and savage accusations of a nervous breakdown. Fitzgerald took Zelda to a hospital on the outskirts of Paris. During the ten days she spent there, she was still full of tremendous energy, writing three stories and the libretto for a ballet. Against the advice of the doctors, she returned to Paris and immediately resumed her dancing. As she remembered later, in a startlingly poignant statement, if she was not able to excel at something, life was not worth continuing: dance was all "I had in the world at the time."

And it was too much. She had terrible nightmares, she heard voices, fainted, and took barbiturates one night. This time Fitzgerald took her to Prangins, a fancy psychiatric clinic in Switzerland, where she was diagnosed as schizophrenic, and where she would spend fifteen months. Over the years, despite her forays into charting a somewhat independent course for herself, despite her rivalry with Fitzgerald, she had never relinquished the desire to have him want and need her. The revolt of the flapper generation hadn't changed what still seemed at the time the "natural order of things": that women were there to take care of men. Suddenly the grounds of the order of their relationship radically shifted. From now on, Zelda would be the one who required tending and care, the permanent invalid. It was a role many middle-class Victorian women had learned how to play as an equalizer in the domestic power struggle with their husbands. But Zelda was too genuinely sick, too tortured by her demons, to take comfort in her illness.

Zelda's letters from Prangins are full of the sad torment of her suffering. At first, she complained that she only wanted to leave Prangins so that she could continue dancing, that her body was getting flabby, that every day it became more difficult to think coherently. She saw that she was caught in a process that could only serve to break her spirit and humiliate her, "wasting the dregs of me" in a landscape of "devastating bitterness." She developed a horrible case of eczema, so debilitating that it was not relieved by morphine, which only abated when she was hypnotized. Her letters show signs of her former wit and intelligence, an ability to see her own demands and delusions, and they voice plaintive hopes for a more temperate future. First she blamed Fitzgerald for his drinking, and then she absolved him, explaining that the problem was that there was no real place for her in his life except as a playmate. She had put her finger on a sore spot. They were both now too old, too life-weary for acting as nothing more than playmates. The dance was over long before the dancers, like marionettes pulled along on the strings of their own fantasies, had stopped their frenetic two-step. But faced with the reality of being the danceless dancer, both figuratively and literally, she had felt disoriented and subordinated.

At Prangins, she had been placed under the care of an eminent psychiatrist, Dr. Oscar Forel, who had quickly perceived that Zelda's anger was directed at Fitzgerald. Gradually, tentatively, she began to respond to his treatment. Fitzgerald was allowed to visit at first and then, later, to take her on short outings to a museum, to lunch at a café, and finally for a few days' stay with the Murphys, who were then living in the Austrian Tyrol.

Zelda was released in the fall of 1931, according to the psychiatrists a case of what they called deceptive ambitions that were invented as a compensation for her feeling of inferiority. The labels seem stark and somewhat misdirected, as if all efforts that didn't end well were the sign of some aberration, some fugitive disguise for human failure. Nowhere did they recognize the thwarted "flaming self-respect" Fitzgerald had so admired in her. Thirty-one and stiffened by her ordeal, no longer the gay flapper of her youth, she sailed back to America with her husband and her daughter.

"Zelda in Hell"

Zelda found no sustained reprieve for her torments. By the beginning of 1932 she was in the care of doctors, this time at the Phipps clinic in Baltimore, the psychiatric wing of Johns Hopkins. Fitzgerald had spent the preceding fall working on another botched screenplay in Hollywood while Zelda remained in Montgomery. She had resumed her painting and writing—plaintively wishing in a letter that Fitzgerald could teach her to write. In his absence, she was scouring his stories for lessons in style and subject matter, virtually apprenticing herself to the products of his imagination.

During this period, Zelda's father died. This meant she had to spend lots of time with her family, an exacerbating situation, for she had always seen herself as a brigand within the family. Her eczema recurred, followed by the asthma. When Fitzgerald returned, he took her to Florida, hoping that a change might alleviate her condition, but it only got worse, and she began to blame dark external forces that were controlling her. When Zelda and Fitzgerald returned to Montgomery she suffered another breakdown and was placed in Phipps.

Fitzgerald found a rambling and somewhat ramshackle large Victorian house called La Paix on the Bayard Trumball estate on the outskirts of Baltimore so that he could be near her. During her first six weeks at Phipps, Zelda wrote the novel, *Save Me the Waltz*, her thinly disguised version of the Scott and Zelda story, which she sent on her own directly to Maxwell Perkins at Scribner's.

Years earlier she had remarked that Fitzgerald tried to conceive of his life as if it were a story. In truth, they had both participated in living their lives self-consciously, joint conspirators in their own legend. He had told friends visiting La Paix that at times he was unsure of whether "Zelda and I are real or whether we are characters in one of my novels." His statement is provocative. Either he had captured the action of their lives so perfectly, or the emotional intensity of his life had caused a blurring between what was real and what was imagined.

Fitzgerald assumed that their mutual history was exclusively his story to tell—an assumption common enough among writers—and he did not take easily to her sharing the same material. When he read her manuscript, which Perkins had sent him, he was outraged at seeing how Zelda had resorted to their lives as subject matter. She had even used Amory Blaine, from *This Side of Paradise*, as the name of the character who represented Fitzgerald in her novel. Fitzgerald wrote Perkins, demanding changes in Zelda's manuscript. He had tried to make Zelda into a legend in his books, he argued, while she had done her best to make him a nonentity in hers.

In *Tender Is the Night*, the novel he was still working on at the time, the relationship between Nicole Diver as invalid and Dick Diver as guardian is his depiction of what he saw as the inescapable circumstance of their marriage: "Her problem was one they had together for good now." Nicole suffers from Zelda's mental illness, and Dick Diver is portrayed as the doctor who nurtures and cares for her. Though certain components are invented, and Nicole's schizophrenia is the result of incest with her father, the novel is another illustration of the extent to which he drew directly on his and Zelda's lives for his material. *Tender Is the Night* also afforded him a vehicle for expressing his feelings about the price he has paid for concentrating all his energies on his role as Zelda's caretaker: Dick Diver's emotional resources are depleted, his work undermined, his self-possession snapped. He is at the end totally diminished and exhausted before his life's work has realized its full potential, as though the self-confident and untested assurance of youth has given way too late to achieve the promise of artistic maturity.

Fitzgerald's fury over *Save Me the Waltz* brought to the surface all the underlying resentments in their marriage. Meeting with Dr. Thomas Rennie and a secretary with a Dictaphone, the Fitzgeralds amassed a 114-page transcript of their grievances. Fitzgerald believed that as the family provider, the story of their lives belonged to him. He was incapable of conceding that the romance or despair of their existence together was mutually available to each as inspiration or subject matter. He told Dr. Rennie that he resented having to write stories and films to pay Zelda's medical bills, because that work prevented him from completing his novel. Zelda's writing, he argued disparagingly, was third-rate because she had essentially nothing to say.

Zelda agreed to revise her manuscript, though her changes would not really assuage the resentments. When Dr. Rennie raised the possibility of separation, Fitzgerald admitted that Zelda's affair with Jozan (which he now had convinced himself had been consummated) and his own revenge with Lois Moran had shaken the foundations of their marriage, but they could not be expected to "go on paying and paying forever." Separation or divorce was not his intention, Fitzgerald told the psychiatrist: "our mutual front is less a romance," he admitted in a letter, "than a categorical imperative." Zelda's recovery and their continuation was more important to him than anything else. To reject Zelda would be to cast her into a hostile world. At the same time, he could not permit her to build a dubious career on "living matter chipped from my mind." While he would play the martyr, he would claim that he and Zelda had never been as in love. "Goofo," a nickname with a particularly ironic context, "please love me," Zelda implored in a letter.

After three months at Phipps, Zelda's condition had improved to the point where she was able to live at La Paix and return for morning psychiatric consultations or for longer stays whenever she felt the possibility of relapse. Fitzgerald now assumed complete control of the domestic order at La Paix (which Zelda was never very good at maintaining anyway), which allowed him to exert the kind of authority she had resisted in the first place. Such authority seemed important to Fitzgerald, perhaps because of the powers he was attributing to Dick Diver, but also because basically he saw women as social satellites, entertaining or serving him to help relieve his creative burdens. A woman's most important place, he once said in an interview with Zelda at his side, was to encourage her husband, keep their love alive and maintain her beauty and her house to that end. It was not a view that could persuade either the flapper or the feminist, and it implied something infinitely disparaging about the superficiality of women. "When I like women," he confided to his *Notebooks*, "I want to own them, to dominate them, to have them admire me." The statement sounds similar to Lawrence's contention that women have to "yield some sort of precedence" to men. The implication is that women are genetically predisposed to being dominated on some level because of the physiology of the sex act.

At La Paix in 1932, Fitzgerald worked on *Tender Is the Night*. Zelda swam, sat in the sun, played tennis and rode horses. She was frequently reclusive, spending hours writing, dancing and painting in her third-floor study, but her former wit had not deserted her. She wrote Perkins that she enjoyed riding horses, but she did it as noncommittally as possible so as not to annoy the horse. Anyway, because of Fitzgerald's recent interest in Marxist theory, she was no longer sure whether she should ride the horse or be ridden by it. Fitzgerald took up boxing and developed a swagger in his walk. He was thirty-six and especially apprehensive about *Tender Is the Night*, afraid that his work might no longer relate to an audience during the Depression years, that they would prefer the social realism of a Dos Passos. Scribner's had accepted *Save Me the Waltz*, and Zelda was trying to write a play, *Scandalabra*, and beginning another novel, *Caesar's Things*. This new story was about insanity and psychoanalysis, and in some ways may have been influenced by sections she had read of the manuscript of *Tender Is the Night*.

Again, Fitzgerald became incensed, demanding that Zelda stop writing fiction. He was particularly irritated because she had quoted things that he had said that she had found perceptive—a device he had used himself to deepen his authenticity, using her letters and diaries in all his fiction. The Phipps psychiatrists pointed out that his stand was unreasonable, and Dr. Rennie advised Fitzgerald that he too needed psychoanalysis, especially because of his drinking. It was the same advice he had received earlier from Dr. Forel, Zelda's physician in Switzerland. He had declared to Forel that he could not abstain from alcohol because it animated him to write and made life seem less like a "hopeless grind," and his position had not changed.

Locked into the old resentments and rivalry, their fights began to intensify. "Family quarrels are bitter things," Fitzgerald acknowledged in his *Notebooks*. "They don't go according to any rules. They're not like aches or wounds; they're more like splits in the skin that won't heal." Zelda was again silent for long periods, and her face sometimes twisted into a peculiar smile for no apparent reason. She decided to burn some of her old clothes in a disused fireplace in her study and caused a serious fire that threatened to consume La Paix. Like the time she set fire to her clothes in her Hollywood bathtub when Fitzgerald went for dinner with Lois Moran, it was a signal of sorts. When the critic Malcolm Cowley visited La Paix shortly after the fire, Zelda seemed emaciated, unraveled, her mouth etched by deep lines, her face twitching. She had special cause to appear so unnerved: one of her brothers had suffered a nervous breakdown and jumped to his death from his hospital window.

Cowley saw Zelda's paintings and was both impressed and frightened by them. In one, she had portrayed herself as the victim in a crucifixion scene, and in another she had imagined dancers with gross, deformed feet. Fitzgerald persuaded a friend associated with a New York art gallery to exhibit Zelda's work. In January, 1934, Zelda was returned to Phipps. She was unhappy about the poor sales of *Save Me the Waltz*, the fact that no one wanted her play, and that Fitzgerald had tried to prevent her from continuing to write *Caesar's Things*. At Phipps she read the serialized version of *Tender Is the Night*, which was appearing in *Scribner's Magazine*, and recognized the extent to which Fitzgerald had used their life on the Riviera and in Paris during the late 1920s and drawn on the letters she had written to him during her initial breakdown in Switzerland. Although she praised the novel, she must have inwardly raged at Fitzgerald's presentation of Nicole Diver as an emotional parasite who relies on her illness as a control device, uses her husband until he is depleted, and then abandons him for a French lover.

Unresponsive to treatment at Phipps, Zelda was taken by Fitzgerald to another psychiatric hospital in Beacon, New York. Escorted by a nurse, she was allowed out to meet him in New York City to see the exhibition of her paintings. Zelda was ambivalent about her paintings. The exhibit failed in any way to boost her spirits and she was transferred to the Shepherd Pratt hospital in Baltimore in May, a month after the publication of *Tender Is the Night*. Fitzgerald noted in his ledger that she was in a catatonic state, her face was listless and without any expression—"Zelda in Hell," he bluntly wrote.

That summer, when Fitzgerald took her for a walk on the hospital grounds, she ran from him toward a railroad track and tried to throw herself under a passing train. She spoke of suicide frequently to her doctors in the following weeks and admitted that her condition was hopeless. In letters to Fitzgerald she painfully apologized for the way in which she had ruined their life together. There was no chance at any resumption, Fitzgerald realized, all hope, he observed bitterly, having been left on the various roads leading to Zelda's sanatoriums.

"The Crack-Up"

Tender Is the Night, the novel on which Fitzgerald had labored for so long and at such emotional cost, received a poor reception at the hands of the critics and its sales were mediocre. The novel lacked the focus of *The Great Gatsby* and some of its plot seemed contrived. Fitzgerald was particularly dismayed when Hemingway—the writer he most respected, the "stick hardened in the fire," as he called him in a letter—wrote saying he disliked the novel, that the dishonest mistake of fusing the Fitzgeralds and the Murphys as models for the Divers had only resulted in "faked case histories."

Fitzgerald's confidence in himself as a writer was damaged and, like Dick Diver, his morale had begun to crack. With the hospital expenses for Zelda and his daughter's boarding school, he was more deeply in debt than ever. Depressed, guiltily pondering the extent of his responsibility for Zelda's breakdowns, his own health began to falter, with an episode of liver disease and another of tuberculosis that left him with a spot on his lung. He felt like a piece of "cracked crockery," he told a friend, and he was in and out of hospitals. When he began to feel better, he broke his shoulder badly while diving, showing off for a young woman. The shoulder took months to heal, and then it turned arthritic. Worst of all, his agent was unable to sell his stories, and he found it even more difficult than ever to write. The love stories which he had sold for so much money depended on a certain ebulliency about frivolous matters which he could no longer muster. He managed a few sketches about what he called his own "emotional bankruptcy" for *Esquire*, pieces like "The Crack-Up," in which he tried to account for his "disintegration of personality."

In the spring of 1935, Fitzgerald moved Zelda to Highlands, a facility for the insane where she would spend much of the rest of her life. Highlands was in Asheville, North Carolina, the town Thomas Wolfe described in *Look Homeward, Angel* and known as a place where one could recover from tuberculosis. In fact, that was where Fitzgerald had gone when he discovered he had tuberculosis, and now he lived in a hotel in Asheville so as to be near Zelda. He hired a secretary to help him with his writing, but it did not go well. He needed gin to work and sedatives to sleep.

And Zelda's condition seemed worse. She was convinced she was a messenger of God destined to preach the coming apocalypse. She was still capable of periods of lucidity, which made everything more pathetic. She knew, as she revealed to him in a letter, that she was now only an "empty shell" with not even the "smallest relic" of the love and beauty with which they had begun. Yet, the old antagonisms, like the recurring torments of myth, would not disappear no matter how reduced her condition. When she visited him at his hotel for a weekend, they quarreled and she walked out. Fitzgerald began shredding the clothes she had left behind in the carrying case on his bed while she wandered to the railroad station, penniless, waiting for a train and reading her Bible. Another afternoon, he took her to visit friends in Asheville and somehow she managed to consume a glass of wine, which affected her badly. Fitzgerald took her into a corner and began a fairy tale in which she was a princess in a tower. The story relieved her anxieties, but in one sense she was now the princess locked in a tower that Fitzgerald in a joke had once proposed to her as a model for courtship and marriage.

There were other blows to his self-esteem. *This Side of Paradise* was out of print, and there were virtually no royalties from his past work because his other story collections and novels, including *The Great Gatsby*, were unavailable and Scribner's showed no interest in bringing out new editions. Hemingway, in a story published in the summer of 1936, "The Snows of Kilimanjaro," slurred him by naming him as a writer who had been wrecked by his subject matter and by the discovery that the rich were not romantic at all. Fitzgerald felt betrayed. Ironically, he needed the rich more than ever and there was nothing romantic about it. Desperate for funds, his mother loaned him some, and so did Gerald Murphy. He was at a low point but still eager for publicity, and he made the mistake of granting an interview on his fortieth birthday to a young reporter for the *New York Post*. The result was a vulgar travesty that provoked Fitzgerald to swallow a vial of morphine in an unsuccessful attempt at suicide.

The rest was like a cruel coda. Hollywood seemed to offer some temporary relief from his financial worries, and he got a contract to write screenplays for Metro-Goldwyn-Mayer. Ruefully, he had noted in *The Crack-Up* that film as a medium would probably replace fiction, but his heart was not in film work. He had difficulty with its collaborative nature, and he often clashed with producers. It was the "last tired effort of a man who once did something finer," he wrote to his daughter, and it seemed that it was mostly for her benefit that he continued.

During his first week in Hollywood he met Sheilah Graham, a twenty-eight-year-old journalist who had been raised in London's slums. She was blond, witty and intelligent; Fitzgerald felt she resembled Zelda, and she was charmed by him. Their love was attenuated by Fitzgerald's own declining energies and his recurrent drinking, which caused several terrible fights, one of which ended with Fitzgerald threatening Graham with a gun. Graham called the police after one of their melodramatic battles. The next day Fitzgerald flew to Asheville and arranged to take a vacation in Cuba with Zelda. That was equally disastrous and ended with Fitzgerald being badly beaten when he tried to stop a cockfight. Fitzgerald had always had his own pugilistic cockiness, but the beating landed him in a hospital with tubes in his arms. It was the last time he saw Zelda.

Fitzgerald depleted himself by drinking excessively, an abuse his diseased liver could no longer take, and he had to be hospitalized and nourished intravenously several times in Hollywood. In all this, Graham stood by him with considerable devotion. Most of the time Fitzgerald seemed subdued, drained and gray. Friends observed that he drove his car as slowly as an old man.

There was still some life left to his mind, however. He had compiled a notebook of observations on Hollywood and the film industry, which he found slack, corrupt, indifferent to talent and capable of sacrificing it ruthlessly. He had begun *The Last Tycoon*, the novel he would only half-complete, using the people he met in Hollywood and his own disappointments as the basis for his story. The manuscript he left, posthumously edited by Edmund Wilson, is taut and compelling. Fitzgerald had eliminated the philosophical rambling that had marred *Tender Is the Night* and was working again at the very height of his powers.

In November of 1940, he went to a drugstore to purchase some cigarettes and felt everything start to fade. His doctor told him it was a cardiac spasm. A month later, taking Sheilah Graham to a farce, *This Thing Called Love*, he felt a similar loss of strength and almost fainted. On the following day, eating a chocolate bar after lunch, he rose abruptly from an armchair, grasped at a mantelpiece, and then fell down gasping. His heart had given out at forty-four.

For a year prior to his death, Zelda and her mother had been pressuring Fitzgerald to arrange her release from Highlands. It was once again the story of the princess locked in the tower. Fitzgerald had been suspicious of any plan to free Zelda, but since her condition seemed to have improved, she was permitted to live with her mother. She spent most of the next six years in Montgomery, gardening, painting and continuing the writing of *Caesar's Things*, which was now complicated by her persistent messianic delusions.

In the fall of 1946 she began to feel unwell again and wanted to return to Highlands. She received insulin shock therapy; her condition, always cyclical, improved somewhat, and she was planning to return to Montgomery. On March 11, 1947, there was a terrible fire at Highlands, which started in a kitchen and traveled up to the top floor where Zelda had been sedated for the night. Only forty-seven, she was consumed in that fire.

As horrible a death as it must have been, there was a certain grim logic to it. She was always associated with fire. Fitzgerald used its imagery when he said he was originally attracted to her because of her "flaming self-respect." She had first called the firemen in a false alarm when she was eight for her own amusement; she had called them another time at a party to liven things up; she had burned her clothes in her bathtub in Hollywood, and burned them again and almost destroyed La Paix. During the twenties, she and Fitzgerald had been the hot coals igniting a generation. They had been the most famous couple of their era, though few at the time realized how disputatious their love had been. A consuming inner fire had led Fitzgerald to an early death and her to madness. She was placed beside him in a grave in Maryland, where they shared a common, unmarked headstone.

Generational Spokesmen

Every so often a writer appears who so aptly captures the music of a moment, the attitudes and aspirations of an era, that the writer becomes recognized as the voice of a generation. Both D. H. Lawrence, around the time of the First World War, and F. Scott Fitzgerald, in the 1920s, were such figures.

Lawrence's vision of the antagonism between the sexes was drawn, in part, from his own conflicts with Frieda, although what he wrote may have been more diagnostic than curative or redemptive. As the bohemian outsider, taken to be a spy in Germany just before the war and again in England near its conclusion, Lawrence was the dissident artist of causes, plunging his fiction into volatile social circumstances, which he sought to improve. Like Shelley, he could be impatient, intolerant, even obsessive in the pursuit of his vision. His novels were panoramic in scope, surging oceanic accounts of emotional conflicts that had no solution or resolution except in age or death. Like Whitman a rhapsodist intoxicated by his own rhythms and language, he could have drawn his motto from "Song of Myself": "Urge, urge and urge / Always the procreant urge of the word." Again like Whitman and like most other romantics, Lawrence could be deluded by such a rush of energy, mistaking the momentum of his own words for a permanent impression on the world. Proselytizing for his impossible vision of harmony between the sexes, Lawrence sometimes seems like an archetypal Romantic overreacher, ranting over the disappointment of sacrificed ideals. It is reductive, and perhaps cynical as well, to belittle Lawrence, to patronize him with the charge that his fictions now seem dated and irrelevant; at his best, his novels give us a sort of barricade of memory, a monument to the way things were and might have been.

Fitzgerald was more of a Keatsian miniaturist, though like Lawrence he drew directly on his life for his subject matter. More the esthetician of romance, he projected an aristocratic fantasy of prince and princess in an affluent kingdom, which he then tried to sell to a world muddied by middle-class virtues. Where Lawrence outraged his audience, Fitzgerald attempted to entertain his with a precise stiletto view of the insincerities and machinations of the wealthy and privileged. Boastful, vain, only a swollen, poisoned toad, as he once remarked about himself at Princeton, he was at the same time desperately insecure.

He began, as Hemingway observed, with a great effortlessly natural talent that soon became crippled by a sort of Flaubertian anxiety, a monumental concern with language and story that blocked his ability to write. Like Lawrence, he used his fictions as a vicarious means of self-gratification and projection, fashioning a romantic image of himself with the sort of absolute disregard of the actual that seems like impunity but often licenses great creative expressions. In his voracious desire to make himself and to succeed, he seems particularly American. You have to "sell your heart," he once told a young writer, and that seems to be a characteristic, though cold and perhaps even meretricious, statement. What he sold was his depiction of the smug superiority of slickers, flappers and other narcissists, whose primary concerns were pleasure and the fluctuations of the stock market, all of which seems so emblematically American now. To a large extent, Fitzgerald was a part of what he pilloried, having from the start chosen to sell himself in a mad race to live ostentatiously, to enjoy the good life. In so doing, he gave us a model of living beyond one's means, which Americans have emulated in a rejection of their past heritage.

Like Lawrence, Fitzgerald fell in love with a woman who would become the subject of his fiction, but who fought against and resented being regarded as a subject in his life. Both Frieda Weekley and Zelda Sayre fell in love with the allure of the writer, his power and potential. Both women had an aggressive sense of their own capacities which, perhaps presumptuously, they equated with the creative abilities of their mates. Frieda had been swept away at a point in her life when her marriage to her first husband seemed a stale disappointment; Zelda had been groomed to seek the highest bidder, and because Fitzgerald's father did not own a bank, he seemed an unlikely suitor. While Frieda was intellectually emancipated, she had little tradition to draw on. Zelda may have been less free because she thought of women in terms of men. Zelda believed that women existed primarily to disturb their mates, to excite them, to rouse them from routine and the lethargy of small dreams and security.

Like the courtly lovers of the late Middle Ages, Fitzgerald felt he had been damaged in love and in marriage, and the deterioration of his art after *Gatsby* reflects his own spiritual decline. What is most astonishing about Fitzgerald is that living beyond his means, in a frenetic race with bankruptcy, he was able to reach deep down beyond the depletion of his resources into psychic recesses of which he was only dimly aware to give us a work like *Tender Is the Night.*

For both Lawrence and Fitzgerald, theirs was a generation in conflict. First of all, the war changed everything, even relations between the sexes. The war made Lawrence into an "enemy of mankind," he acknowledged in a letter, and he loathed its senseless slaughter. It is always difficult to imagine romantic possibilities in wartime, and much of Lawrence's rage was fueled by the war. The ultimate cost for him was that the war made him lose faith in the future, bringing him closer to Nietzsche's nihilism. What complicates Lawrence's vision is that personal sex was war's female face. Such an analogy—or is it a confusion—has its linguistic derivation, and terms like assault, penetration, surrender and conquest have their military application just as they form part of the language of love. As Bertrand Russell observed, sex with Frieda—in fact all aspects of his life with her—was a perpetual struggle for Lawrence, though it is likely that much of the energy he needed for his fiction was derived from that conflict. Such a view puts Lawrence into that category of artist who is consumed by life rather than in control of it—itself a quintessential romantic formulation.

Fitzgerald was no less self-consuming, though his anger was less a function of the war—a war that never scarred the consciousness of America as it did Europe—than the result of sodden mornings when the spirit is still paralyzed from the excesses of the night before. Fitzgerald saw the war as a field for knights who could rise in honor by participating in it. In training camp, he shirked his duties, mocked the pomp, worked on his first novel and courted Zelda. She was his equal in self-centeredness, though ultimately she baffled him, and his drunken glee was an ineffective disguise for a questionable potency. Though perhaps less cosmically romantic, and certainly without Lawrence's embracing view of the world, Fitzgerald's strength as a writer was, at its best, the ability to portray insistently and in a detached manner a romantic dream of which he was both a harbinger and a casualty.

© Abraham Shuman Fund–Abraham Shuman Collection.
Courtesy, Museum of Fine-Arts, Boston.

Anaïs Nin

Henry Miller

✪ 4 ✪

Henry and June and Anaïs

I will give you Horatio Alger as he looks the day after the
Apocalypse when all the stink has cleared away.

Tropic of Cancer

And when you show me a man who expresses himself
perfectly I will not say that he is not great, but I will say that I
am unattracted . . . I miss the cloying qualities. When I
reflect that the task which the artist implicitly sets himself is
to overthrow existing values, to make of the chaos about him
an order which is his own, to sow strife and ferment so that by
the emotional release those who are dead may be restored to
life, then it is that I run with joy to the great and imperfect
ones, their confusion nourishes me, their stuttering is like
divine music to my ears.

Tropic of Cancer

The Surrealist Don Juan

HISTORY IS FULL of giant lacunae, but it is tempting to wonder
whether Zelda and Scott Fitzgerald, careering from bar to bar
in Manhattan during the heyday of the fabulous twenties, might
have tripped into a basement speakeasy on Perry Street in Greenwich Village—a tenement area inhabited mostly by Irish longshore-
men and their teeming families. As upper-middle-class success
stories in the making, the Fitzgeralds aspired to the most glittering
social echelons, but they would feel occasionally revitalized by
such visits, condescendingly referred to as "slumming."

The Perry Street speakeasy had no sign or real name, but
businessmen as well as tourists knew it as a place where they might
obtain a prohibited libation, and maybe even an affectionate

143

squeeze from the buxom proprietress who served the drinks. She had a series of names, June Smith or Mona Mansfield some of the time, but she could change her name to suit her convenience or her customer. Enticing, exotic in appearance though not conventionally beautiful, she was dark, with a sultry, almost gypsy allure. She might have tried to explain her occupation as a provisional means of supporting herself while she tried to write. She might have even tried to sell a poem or a sketch printed as a broadside, the way it had been done in the seventeenth century when the technology of printing was still rudimentary.

In a cramped kitchen area set off behind a heavy damask curtain was an ordinary-looking, plain-featured, balding man who prepared drinks, rinsed glasses and read desultorily when he could. This man was her husband, although June (or Mona if you prefer) never advertised their marriage and always seemed to suggest that she could be available for some kind of nefarious fun. It was a bizarre union, in which this woman and that man would turn upside down all of the conventional rules of hierarchy and dominion in marriage. Actually, the man in the kitchen had written the poems and sketches she sometimes was able to peddle, although he was so unknown as a writer that his fellow Americans would only hear about him forty years later. His name was Henry Miller.

Miller is the hidden, dark, dirty secret deep in the American cultural closet. He wrote *Tropic of Cancer,* his major novel, in the early 1930s. Europeans have regarded him as an important writer for decades, but his reputation in his own country is still ambivalent at best. He has been fiercely attacked as the archetypal misogynist by feminists and eagerly defended by Norman Mailer as a man with an iron phallus and an "incomparable relentless freedom in his heart." Mailer also asserted that Miller's two best novels, *Tropic of Cancer* and *Tropic of Capricorn,* qualify him as a genius. But many critics have regarded him more as a cultural force than as a major writer.

He presents difficulties in that he was determined not to be what he regarded as "literary"—which to him meant being structured or artificial. Instead, he wrote as spontaneously as he could in a surge of emotional anarchism that released everything in an uncensored sweeping rush. "Learning crushes the spirit," he wrote in one of his eccentric pamphlets, while "belief opens one up."

Miller is another Nietzschean romantic. His purpose is to sow disorder because the existing system offers only palliatives. The goal of his disorder is the possibility of an emotional release that will wake us to the miracle of life. He was always willing to shake up the ground beneath him, to stand traditional morality on its head. Lawrence had seen sex as an animating cosmic force that would redeem the world. Miller had no such transcendental purpose, but he was no less messianic an advocate of his own views. He told a lover that his intention as a writer was to "leave a scar on the world." In his blunt and unrestrained descriptions of sexual adventures, he demystified sex, reducing it to its carnal elements. He relished sexual gratification shamelessly, and he expected women to do the same. He became the American Grand Master of the bed and the bordello, the recorder of phenomenal fornications that many still find obscene.

Miller never cared much for what the critics believed. He even reveled in his obscurity, his reputation as a con-man gangster who lived by his wits, content that at the end of World War II American GIs were reading his novels and smuggling them home in their duffel bags. He enjoyed being a writer whose contraband books often passed surreptitiously from hand to hand, were subverting American morality from underground. A spiritual exile who chose to write in Paris, he abused America in his novels as a "cesspool of the spirit," a "black curse on the world." And not just America—the whole world was out of kilter, he proclaimed, screaming in pain and madness.

In *Tropic of Capricorn,* he admitted to being a fanatic with a crucifixion complex. He called himself a "megalopolitan maniac," a "schizerino" and finally a "traitor to the human race." At turns blissful and sordid, rejoicing ebulliently and then becoming savagely bilious, he paraded a dozen different masks: enthusiast, lyrical rhapsodist, full of warmth and Whitmanesque effusiveness, the gullible clown or the bumptious tourist, quixotic, contradictory, maniacally voluble, or a braggart full of vehement intensity and meanness. A sort of rabid Mark Twain, he was capable of a scabrously vitriolic humor that used sex as its vehicle in the tradition of Petronius, Boccaccio and Rabelais.

Iconoclastic, unpredictable, his voice ringing with a strident urgency, "he shows us how much of a great monster a great writer must be," as Mailer put it in *Genius and Lust,* his tribute to Miller. In a book of essays called *The Wisdom of the Heart,* Miller argued that monsters can be heroic because they are born without fear and they have developed an immunity to pain and suffering. And

Miller's life, particularly his seven-year marriage to June, is the record of just how much suffering he could endure.

June and Miller abused and vilified each other much the way Miller's protagonists abuse and vilify his women characters to a scandalous degree, although with less vindictiveness and more mutual pleasure than we associate with the Marquis de Sade. De Sade's ancestor, ironically, was the Laura of Petrarch's sonnets, one of the sources of Romanticism. However, the Marquis transgressed against the women in his life, torturing and defiling them, and was put into prison as a consequence. Miller's "transgressions" are entirely fictitious. His fictions have often been taken by critics as an exact equivalent of reality because they seem so uncontrived, so natural, and his confessional ardor has allowed his stories to be used as biographical evidence. But there is a difference between the actual and the imagined, and to see Miller merely as a vicious pornographer is to simplify.

Miller is the sexual surrealist who proposes that love itself is one of our supreme fictions. Unlike Lawrence, who regarded sex as a sacred communion, or Fitzgerald, who draped it in a wistful nostalgia and could never bring himself to describe it in his fiction, Miller used sex with a malicious ferocity as the occasion for comedy. It was the best vehicle he knew to expose male vanities and fantasies. With his anarchist distrust of official truth, with Zoroastrian proposals on the unity of God and the Devil, Miller will try to leave his readers astonished and outraged. When their rage matches his, he will have accomplished what he set out to do.

Like Lawrence in *The Rainbow* and *Women in Love,* and Fitzgerald in each of his novels, Miller's subject was his marriage. Lawrence used his life with Frieda to chart the new independence of women strong enough to reject Victorian models of subservience. Fitzgerald delighted in Zelda's flapper sensibility, her slaphappy hedonism and puckishness in the face of serious conventions. Both Lawrence's and Fitzgerald's were difficult marriages, but Miller raged within an even more brutal marital vortex. Initially, June Miller supported him so that he would be free to write. Soon he discovered that she was betraying him with other men and women. Her cavalier abandon crushed him to the point where he could no longer even believe in his own writing. Used, humiliated, he went to Paris and fell in love with another writer, Anaïs Nin. At the same time he began to invent a new manner of writing that would result in *Tropic of Cancer* and *Tropic of*

Capricorn, the novels in which he would describe his life with June in New York and his struggle to find himself in Paris.

Miller found his own powers as a novelist only after an arduous twenty-year apprenticeship. He was over forty when he discovered his own literary voice and published his first novel. If he is a great writer, he stands alone in his uniqueness, the case of the anonymous master who perseveres without income, encouragement or success because his writing is his only desperate release and he is absolutely driven to do it.

Brooklyn

Social scientists, occupied with the broad elements of breakdown in this century, have not begun to chart the circumstances that lead to either the pariah or the prophet. That is the true province of the novelist anyway, and more a question of psychology and inner compulsion than social structure. To magnify the alienation that has been so pronounced in Western consciousness since Marx, to emphasize one's separation rather than groping for accommodation within the group, implies origins that would have to be imagined by a Dickens or a Dostoyevsky.

Miller's childhood was neither deprived nor turbulent. His grandparents had arrived in America early in the nineteenth century amid the waves of German immigrants trying to avoid military conscription. His parents spoke German at home and with their friends. He spoke it as well, which left him with the impression after he began school, where only English was spoken, that his family derived from a culture older than America's, and that they were suspiciously different.

He was born in 1891 in Yorkville, the German enclave on the Upper East Side of Manhattan, but the family soon moved to the Williamsburg section of Brooklyn, a tenement area crowded with Eastern European Jews. Miller's parents disliked the area because of its Jewish inhabitants; his parents despised Jews and contributed to a strain of anti-Semitism evident in Miller as a young man. The household centered on Henry's mother, a cold, humorless disciplinarian, a dour woman who criticized and scolded husband and children, who groaned through the day and lamented her luck. In a piece called "Childhood in Brooklyn," Miller remembered a particularly humiliating instance of his mother's tyranny. He had received a Christmas gift of socks and mittens from his kindergarten teacher, but had returned the gift, asking that it go to the poorest member of the class. Furious, his mother slapped him and dragged him back to school to reclaim his gifts, leaving Miller confused about his own intentions, and convinced of his mother's cruelty. The incident typified an essential quality in Miller, a disregard for material things that he continued to manifest by giving away his childhood toys or his birthday presents. His mother regarded such generosity as madness. He hated her frugality, her Lutheran strictures, her obsession with cleanliness and order, and the ways in which she mistreated his younger, retarded sister. She taught her children to distrust any departure from the routine and the regulated, any new idea or variant approach. Miller would spend the rest of his life repudiating her lessons.

Anaïs Nin conjectured at one time that his attitude toward women was formed by the duality of his feelings for his mother. As with Lawrence and Fitzgerald, Miller's rebellion began at home, directed against a maternal order that stressed caution and conservatism. In each case, the father was absent or less than potent in family matters and often easily humiliated by his wife.

Miller had felt a certain kinship with his father, a genial, gregarious man who used the barroom and the racetrack to escape from wife and work. A tailor, he opened a shop on lower Fifth Avenue in Manhattan. He dressed fastidiously to impress his genteel customers, though most of them were "Broadway" types, actors like John Barrymore, gamblers, assorted European nobility and pretenders, salesmen and stockbrokers.

Henry was an unexceptional boy. He went to public school and did well in his studies. Frail, blond, slightly deaf in one ear and needing glasses, he seemed a delicate child. One afternoon a week he had his piano lessons, at which he excelled. On another afternoon his mother would leave him at the tailor shop where Henry would read to his grandfather, who had taught him to cut out his first pair of pants at the age of five. Occasionally, he was allowed to play in the street, and later he fondly remembered a little friend named Jenny Maine, whom the older boys would undress, rubbing their genitals over hers in a prepubescent anticipation of their future pleasures.

Jenny remained fixed in his mind even after his family moved to Bushwick, another section of Brooklyn as yet unaffected by the Jewish immigration that Miller's parents deplored. When Miller was sixteen he found his way to a whorehouse and contracted gonorrhea. It evidently was not to be either traumatic or inhibiting, for he would frequent prostitutes for another half a century. By this time he was in high school, an extremely healthy boy who had outgrown his frailty and was now an accomplished bicyclist and gymnast. Uncomfortable at home, he became irritated by what he felt were the addled inanities of his parents' conversations, and also by their incessant squabbles. His father would return in the evening tipsy or inebriated, which would provoke an attack by his mother that left Henry nervously gagging on his food. He withdrew to what had become a major occupation, an inveterate and omnivorous appetite for books. Once he brought home a copy of Balzac's *The Wild Ass Skin,* which his father decided must be pornographic and which he forbade in his house.

Actually, his thoughts had turned to desire and love for a high school classmate. Cora Seward wore her golden hair swirled like a conch on her head. She had limpid blue eyes and an icy demeanor, imperiously intimidating. For the next five years Miller would clumsily court her, too afraid even to declare his feelings. There was a dance where he trembled and stumbled, a teenage party where they managed to kiss, but it was mostly stammering frustration. He would walk past her house several times a day in the hope of seeing her, but when he did, he was tongue-tied.

In high school, Henry thought he would become a professional clown, but Cora made him feel like an oaf. Cora had become his goddess. His fatuous pining for her, he remembered later, had turned him into "the ridiculous man, the lonely soul, the wanderer, the restless frustrated artist, the man in love with love, always in search of the absolute, always seeking the unattainable."

On the other hand, he developed an inordinate attraction to women who could descend with him into the subterranean hollows of his being, prostitutes and con artists like June. If, as he himself admitted, he placed certain women above him, out of reach, it is impossible to see June as a figure on a pedestal. Yet, if she was not beyond his reach, she did always elude his grasp. Thus in some subtle and odd way she may have bridged the disparate aspects of his need to worship and to descend. Later, he would see both Cora and June, each in her way, as a wound from which he never recovered. Cora had become a projection of his fear that, like his mother, women would be indifferent to him. He complained that his mother had always been so distant, that she had never been affectionate, that she did not hold or kiss him.

If Miller was starving for mother love, he would find it while he
was still a high school boy. Another blond, but this time cleverly
peroxided, Pauline Chouteau was the proverbial older woman who
eagerly indoctrinates a young man in love, the "hot" widow. Pauline
had a seventeen-year-old tubercular son, Henry's age, whom they
would hear coughing in the next room as they made love. That
cough disconcerted Henry, who feared possible contamination.
With Pauline he entered a world of torrential lusts that made any
risk worthwhile. Soon he became obsessed with her and kept a
calendar of their trysts. He moved in with the widow and her
coughing son (her place was only a mile away from his parents'
home) and got a menial job with a cement company. After a
summer of endless monumental couplings, he began to feel
depleted.

His father was ailing and needed help in their tailor shop, and
Henry used that excuse to move back home. He liked the shop
loiterers who came in to gossip and pass the time. It helped him to
see the endearing quality in failures, he said, something he would
specialize in as a novelist. His parents, however, were alarmed
because he did not seem capable enough to take over the business.
He was too easygoing, too friendly with the employees and customers, too ready to console or just listen. It was a singular talent
that would make him a writer, but never a businessman. He felt
confined in the shop, trapped in a routine he found idiotic. Full of
ideas and the books he had been reading—lots of Nietzsche,
Dostoyevsky, Dreiser and Knut Hamsun—he was occupied with his
own plans for stories. In the early morning he would walk to the
tailor shop, crossing through the Williamsburg section of Brooklyn
and over the bridge to Manhattan, inventing dialogues with imaginary characters as he went along. In the shop he taught himself to
type and began setting down some of these dialogues, instead of
sewing or trying to collect unpaid bills.

He was still seeing Pauline, who had become pregnant by him in
the spring of 1912. Another girl, Frances Hunter, had fallen in love
with him. That gave him a confidence that grew into a haughty
superciliousness touched with youthful arrogance. Despite the fact
that he now had women in his life, he felt a brooding irritability, a
discontent with things as they were. Life had to offer more than
books and sex to make it worthwhile. He was twenty-one and the
work he was doing (or evading) in the tailor shop was not what he
wanted to do.

He knew he was at loose ends and was disturbed about it. He had no fixed purpose, no plan for the future. For the next year, his course was haphazard: a trip to California at the suggestion of a theosophist friend, Robert Challacombe, to seek out believers in mysticism and the occult; a stint picking oranges and working on a cattle ranch; an encounter with a Wobbly, a member of the International Workers of the World, one of the most radical unions on the West Coast, who stimulated Miller's interest in socialist thought; a meeting with Emma Goldman, one of the leading anarchist orators in America, who gave him a book by Nietzsche. All of these experiences influenced his outlook on life but gave him no clear sense of direction.

Back home in New York, he continued to mark time for the next three years, even drifting into marriage. A patron of the tailor shop had given him a series of tickets to Carnegie Hall in lieu of payment, and Miller considered the possibilities of becoming a concert pianist. He began taking lessons again from a young teacher named Beatrice Wickens. Diminutive, slender, she had learned to play the piano in a convent and was full of puritanical inhibitions that made her all the more tantalizing to Miller. In the summer of 1917 he was required to register for military service. He was almost twenty-six, an age at which Lawrence had already written his first novel and gotten noticed in London. At that moment, in a military training camp in Alabama, Fitzgerald, then twenty-one, was revising the novel that would propel him to fame. Unknown, unaware that he even had a story to tell, Miller sought a deferment on the grounds that he was responsible for his sick parents, and then he persuaded Beatrice to marry him as insurance against conscription.

There were immediate matrimonial difficulties. Beatrice expected the man she had married to be her provider, but he preferred to spend his time reading and trying to write, which he knew was what he wanted to do. For Beatrice, as for Miller's mother, this was mere idling. During the war years work was plentiful, but Miller was unmotivated by any sort of regular employment. When the tailor shop finally failed, he began working at a series of jobs that lasted for brief intervals: garbage collector, bartender, bellhop, typist, streetcar conductor. He taught in a gym, filed in a library, worked in a gas station and an advertising agency, but none of these jobs lasted very long either. Miller's attitude toward work was that it provided a provisional means for him to write. He had retrieved his father's oversized desk from the tailor shop and had it moved to the center of his living room, where it dominated, bare and unused. He wanted Beatrice to get regular work good enough to support them both and maintained this stance until she got pregnant.

During one of his uninterminable jaunts, Miller had encountered Emil Schnellock, an elementary school classmate who was already a successful commercial artist. Schnellock interested him in the history of painting, lending him Elie Faure's monumental history of art and Walter Pater's essays on Renaissance art, and urging him to take himself seriously as a writer. Schnellock's advice was timely: Miller glimpsed his potential as a writer when a small subscription magazine, *The Black Cat,* took several brief essays in which he deplored the disillusioning hazards of marital existence.

The intimate difficulties with Beatrice had given him the material for the essays. She was very much the proper married woman who, in a throwback to the Victorian period, thought sex was for procreation, not pleasure; but Miller had more experimental notions. They bickered and fought and began to sleep in separate rooms. When they visited Beatrice's mother in her bungalow in Delaware, Miller, never much intimidated by taboos, found a way to initiate a summer liaison with his mother-in-law. She reminded him of Pauline, free and easy in matters of sexuality, quite the opposite of her prim daughter.

This was the sort of transgression that neither Lawrence, oedipally tied to his own mother and sexually initiated by Mrs. Wix, a surrogate mother, nor Fitzgerald could have even imagined in their fiction. The violation, not of his mother-in-law but of his wife's trust, suggests that Miller, in terms of his sensibility and scruples, was of a different, more dissident order than Lawrence and certainly Fitzgerald.

Beatrice, who discovered that her husband was sexually cavorting with her mother, was too shocked to confront him. Instead, when they returned to Brooklyn, she criticized Miller constantly, intensifying the hostility between them. If she hoped her reprimands would change him or make him feel guilty, she was wrong. The transgression with Beatrice's mother seems to have opened the Pandora's box in Miller's sexuality. He found numerous opportunities to betray Beatrice, even using his infant daughter in her perambulator as a screen for his assignations.

Later, he acknowledged that his treatment of Beatrice had been abominable, but that he had felt powerless to change it. In a fictionalized sketch called "The Tailor Shop," he brings home a syphilitic older man who pretends to be a baron and asks Beatrice to let him live with them. She is horrified, both by the man and the disease. The old man begins to cry uncontrollably, one of Miller's abject failures begging for pity, the kind of character who appeared frequently in his fiction.

Beatrice gave birth to a daughter in the fall of 1919. Though Miller was now a father, he still kept shifting from one menial job to the next. Early in 1920, as another temporary measure to pay some bills, he applied for work as a Western Union messenger, the kind of position available even for drunks and the simpleminded. Miller was rejected as overqualified. He had listed a Columbia Ph.D. in philosophy as one of his attainments, an early example of his hyperbolic daring. When Miller complained to officials at Western Union, he was so persuasive in his appeal that a vice president, worried about the problem of careless messengers, hired Miller to investigate the company's hiring practices. Soon Miller was managing a Western Union employment office near city hall.

The result was the hilarious pandemonium at the Cosmodemonic Telegraph Company that Miller described in *Tropic of Capricorn.* His duties involved interviewing a procession of undesirables, wanderers, criminals, broken-down disillusioned men pleading for work, and sending those he had hired to the various branches of the company so that they would be manned at full capacity. The time he spent with these men gave him some of the material he would use for the heartbreaking, grotesquely humorous anecdotes of his later fiction. But contact with these unfortunates also diminished his sense of his own superiority and helped him to realize that whatever personal suffering he had experienced was only a minuscule fraction of the suffering that existed in the world. Work at Western Union reawakened his socialistic inclinations. He began to question the authority of institutions, and to extend what he had accepted as his own failure into one which was perpetuated and generalized by the social system.

To avoid Beatrice, he returned home as late as possible, going to burlesque theaters after work, attending lectures, drinking and dining with some of his fellow workers. Often he would spend an entire evening with one or another prospective employee, fascinated by their stories and taking notes for future use. Neglected, virtually abandoned, Beatrice moved with their daughter to a rooming house in Rochester, New York. Miller began writing her long, nostalgic letters, but when he visited her, he realized that all that he really wanted now out of the relationship was the power to make her succumb to him, and that wasn't enough to keep them together.

His statement, taken at face value, sounds like a characterization of typical male dominance, but he may have been responding to subtle impulses that he himself was unaware of. Beatrice did not mother him, but she was the one woman in his life who was most like his mother, and he may still not have reconciled his conflicting desires for her approval and for revenge on her. Certainly, his relationship with June was very different: he was the one who succumbed to her over and over again. Despite his protestations and his awareness that the marriage with Beatrice had already ended for him, he wasn't quite ready to let go. During her absence in Rochester, he had moved into the studio of one of his assistants at Western Union, a man named Joe O'Regan, and together they had turned it into a kind of freewheeling bordello. Yet when Beatrice sought a reconciliation, he moved back to their apartment.

In the spring of 1922, during a three-week vacation from Western Union, he planned a novel based on the lives of the messengers. Inspired by his reading of *Crime and Punishment* and Dreiser's *Twelve Men,* a dozen portraits of men Dreiser had met, which Miller believed he could use as a model, he deliberately sat himself down with his typewriter and wrote, he told his friend Emil Schnellock, an enormous five-thousand-word segment on his first day. He had been evaluating his experiences at Western Union in a large looseleaf journal, and he incorporated much of this material. Regarding his subjects, the messengers, as fallen angels, he decided to call his book *Clipped Wings*. The book was a medley of other voices, a library of the novelists whose techniques Miller had been studying. For years he had dredged through the work of other writers, Walter Pater and Henry James for style, for example, searching for beautiful phrases. He was fascinated and repelled by James's novels, "didactic monstrosities," he would call them, full of "artificial distillations, lucubrations, and menstruations." He knew that he needed to imagine a more "blatant phallic desecration" in his own writing, but was still too attached to the accepted manner. As a result *Clipped Wings* was merely imitative and derivative, often forced, awkward and mostly turgid. His own language was stilted, inflated, self-consciously formal and overwrought. He sent the finished manuscript to Macmillan, where it was quickly rejected, causing Miller to lose faith in what he had done.

During the year after the completion of *Clipped Wings*, Miller continued to work at Western Union and to write—sketches, essays, stories. Except for a fragment of *Clipped Wings* that appeared in W. E. B. Dubois's little magazine *The Crisis*, there was no sign that the world would accept him as a writer. He was thirty-two years old and convinced that he was a failure. He had become discouraged, fatigued by his own strenuous literary efforts, bored with his job and burdened by life with Beatrice, but the mundane routine of his existence was about to end.

Narcissists in Love

One evening late in the summer of 1923, Miller went to a dance hall on Broadway near Times Square. Wilson's was a place for lonely men, mostly tourists and sailors, who were willing to spend a nickel for the favor and fragrance of female company in a fox-trot, a waltz or some speedier number. The women were called "taxi dancers," and they cruised the hall looking for customers. Many of them were aspiring showgirls; some were prostitutes who needed a reprieve from the demands of their profession. As a group the taxi dancers had the reputation of being easy and open to solicitation.

Miller was approached by a stylish and poised, full-bodied twenty-year-old woman, whose dark bluish-black hair was fine and straight and parted on the side like a man's. Her blue eyes were accentuated by her tailored blue suit. She was a bit taller than Miller, and her legs seemed especially long. Introducing herself as June Mansfield, she said she had overheard Miller mentioning the playwright Strindberg while dancing with one of the other girls, and she wanted to talk to him about Strindberg. She suggested that they could dance while they spoke.

What she said and the way she said it, in her deep, guttural, thrilling voice, astonished and fascinated Miller. She began by asking him whether he had seen Strindberg's play *Miss Julie,* saying that she identified with a character in it who personified evil. Frenetic, racing her words practically into a jumble, she moved with random illogical leaps from philosophical questions to literary preferences to graphic sexual confessions.

Miller felt the shock of recognition that one narcissist must feel when he encounters another. Usually, he was the indefatigable marathon conversationalist, and this was the power he employed to attract women. Now June was the one whose talk seemed oceanic, intoxicating and galvanizing. It was like talking to someone in a dream, he said. She moved from reverie to raving with one heated, uncompleted sentence after another, a pell-mell chaos of language all carried by a spurting rhythm of digressive plunges. The effect mystified him. In some deep recess of his being, Miller may have glimpsed in her talk the writer he wanted to become, and he wanted avidly to pursue all of her digressions. At Wilson's he discovered a subject which would take him three decades to exhaust.

When the dance hall closed, he went on listening to her in a Chinese restaurant. Just before dawn, they embraced in a cab in Brooklyn. Miller was amazed. In his experience, women were not supposed to be brilliant—he had never met one so bursting with ideas and the ability to discourse on them. After all, he was a writer, committed to words, and here was a woman who made words malleable and bent them to her will. He had fallen effortlessly into marriage with a woman who he felt was as small-spirited as his mother and had wandered into bed with a good number of other women, but none had challenged him. In June he detected something as disturbing as it was compelling, an excitement that went beyond sex. He was as immediately mesmerized as later he would be obsessed. Furthermore, he learned that June was Jewish, and he realized how this fact alone would shock his own parents even more than the eventual desertion of his wife and child.

Their meeting had the gritty aspects of bohemian romance, a nightclub or dance-hall pickup that led to a passionate exchange of ideas and an instant attraction. Miller sensed a raw vitality in June, an energy closer to the street than to the museum. In her way, she was a projection of Miller's love of burlesque, with a brazen recklessness he admired. He told her he was a writer, and that had special appeal to her. Traditionally, women have sought men as protectors who could provide financial security. Certain other women have been drawn to men with the ability to praise beauty. Both Frieda and Zelda had been attracted to men who were writers capable of great impact on their times. Fame is the headiest of aphrodisiacs, though given her essentially mercenary intentions, it may be surprising that June succumbed to it.

Miller, fascinated by June's feverish, compulsive conversation, wondered now how much of what she said about her past was fabricated—because of the contradictions in her stories of pursuing lovers and her propensity for playing the role of the wholesome innocent. Interspersed in her tales were furtive hints of drugs, rape and sadism, as well as an account of a demanding landlord to whom she had to barter her virginity so that her family could have a place to live. She invented the most intricate stories about her past, claiming her mother had been a Romanian gypsy and her father an English engineer who had lost all his money on the horses.

Actually her parents were impoverished Romanian Jews named Smerth (which means "death" in Romanian) and her father sold used clothes. Her father had brutally beaten Julia, which was her given name, until she fled from her home before finishing high school. Miller was willing to accept what he sensed were June's fantasies, intrigued by her manner of presenting her confabulations. He would ask meticulous questions about details and her feelings, which she precisely answered, even when she was describing her former lovers. Soon she epitomized Miller's view of women, practically a stock archetype of sentimental fiction, the angelic celestial who is in fact promiscuously lax.

June offered to provide Miller with the freedom to write. They moved to a furnished, roach-infested room in the Bronx after being discovered by Beatrice in her own marital bed. Beatrice had pretended to leave on a trip and returned early the next morning with witnesses. Then she initiated proceedings for a divorce.

An Undeclared Marriage

In June of 1924, after his divorce was final, Miller reluctantly agreed to marry June. He was thirty-three, twelve years older than June. They had been staying with friends in the Village, pretending to be married, and June was eager to conform matters legally. Miller's parents had opposed his divorce, feeling that their grandchild was being abandoned by their son, and June's mother was uninterested in whomever she married. The actual ceremony, performed by a justice in Hoboken, was improvised and parodistic—Miller had hired two drifters as witnesses, as though he were mocking not only the solemnity of the wedding ceremony but marriage itself. Afterward, the newlyweds went to a bar and, as a randy rejoinder to propriety, spent their first evening as a married couple in a burlesque theater.

June had found an apartment in elegant Brooklyn Heights, with inlaid floors, paneled walls, molded ceilings and stained-glass windows. It was spacious, grand and expensive, and June thought

Miller would be inspired to write there. She tried to persuade him to leave his job at Western Union. Miller had been even more annoyed than usual because a team of efficiency experts had decided that his indiscriminate hiring of criminals and foreigners and the chaotic way in which he ran the employment office had hurt the company. Early one Monday morning, Miller just walked away from his desk without notifying anyone that he did not intend to return. He had been inspired by Sherwood Anderson, who was supposed to have similarly abandoned the paint factory in Ohio that he managed for his father-in-law.

June was now the sole provider. Months earlier, she had left the dance hall, stating that she had been accepted by the Theatre Guild and was working as an actress. After staying out most of the night, she would return with large sums of money which she explained as gifts from older men who admired her and wanted her dinner company. She was also hostessing in speakeasies, working very late at night for a percentage of whatever her customers would drink. What she could earn was insufficient to pay the rent on the Brooklyn Heights apartment, and they began to move into a series of more affordable flats.

Miller was supposed to be writing at his leisure, but he was blocked and found it difficult to interest himself in writing. He reworked *Clipped Wings* but realized it was still unsatisfactory and could think of no new story he wanted to tell. June had conceived of the idea of her selling sketches, poems and brief stories that could be contained on a single piece of colored cardboard to some of her customers in the speakeasies. Miller called these "mezzo-tints," and with them June could always rationalize her mysterious extra dividends while pretending that she had actually written the sketches. The idea that she was a writer delighted her particularly, and she was attracted to Miller primarily because she knew that through him she could find a way to satisfy this fantasy. In this regard, she is very different from either Frieda Lawrence, who wanted to be her husband's inspiration and collaborator, or Zelda Fitzgerald, who wanted to re-ignite her appeal for her husband and at the same time rival his work. June was in a sense slyly undermining Miller's singularity, subsuming him into herself, ex-propriating his talent to create a false identity that coincided with her delusions. But the charade also appealed to the con woman in her. She was always looking for a new game to play, a new opportunity to make her way in the world.

June had the idea of opening her own speakeasy. During 1924 she had worked in so many different ones that she felt confident about managing her own. A friend told her about a basement flat on Perry Street in the Village, which she rented and decorated, arranging for a supply of liquor with a bootlegger. In order to obtain money, she had resorted to various petty swindles, mostly trying to fleece male admirers, and now she had her own arena in which to operate.

Henry, however, represented a problem, since they had to live in the speakeasy. As bartender, short-order cook and dishwasher, Henry had to pretend that he was not her husband, a role he grudgingly accepted. What this really meant was that he would have to be willing to deny what was now obvious, that June was entertaining her admirers in their bedroom for cash gifts, in short, that she was a hooker supporting him with the sex she could sell.

To shut out the reality of his wife's prostitution, Miller began consuming the alcohol stock and burst into several violent rages, breaking dishes and furniture. Despite June's strenuous efforts, she had to struggle to earn enough money to afford the Perry Street speakeasy, and they were always on the verge of eviction.

Miller decided that he would resolve their financial problems by going to Florida, where he hoped to profit in a real estate boom. How he hoped to manage it without any investment capital is unclear, and his lack of a plan is another sign of the dream world he inhabited and the desperation he must have felt at this time.

Leaving New York on Thanksgiving Day of 1925, he hitchhiked down to Florida, where he immediately realized that any alleged prosperity was invisible—all he saw was groups of unemployed men begging for handouts on corners. Miller joined these men in a week of vagrancy, something like what Jack London had experienced earlier with Coxey's Army of unemployed converging on Washington, but without London's sense of social mission. Miller felt more aimless vacancy and bafflement. Unable to reach June, penniless, humiliated and exhausted, he managed to contact his parents, who wired him train fare. He returned to Brooklyn on Christmas Day, just in time for the beginning of his thirty-fifth year. June had been forced to vacate the speakeasy and had sought refuge with her mother. Depressed and confused, Miller made a similar choice and remained with his parents until he could decide what to do with his future.

At home with his parents, Miller had to accept an atmosphere of piously mournful condescension. To his parents, he was the prodigal son who had ruined his life, the lazy boy who had walked out on a solid position so that he could continue his scribbling. On several occasions when his mother's friends came to visit, she asked him to take his typewriter and hide with it in a closet.

Though his parents were ashamed of him, Miller had returned to his writing. For years he had been fascinated by exotic words; his idea of great writing was that it depended on the use of strange, mysterious language. Usually, he had long lists of such words posted above his bed. He sent his friend Emil Schnellock a short list and it suffices as an example of his preoccupations: gallipots, neumes, rath, fortalice, verjuice, dingle, thurible, mullioned, spume and whorls, a jumble of arcane words he would incorporate into his own writing, often more for the sake of using esoteric language than for communicating.

One afternoon, after studying his Funk and Wagnalls dictionary for hours, he sauntered out for a short walk and suddenly began composing sentences in his head. Rushing home, he started transcribing dovetailed sentences that sifted through his mind like "sawdust spilling through a hole," he remembered. He liked what he had produced even though it didn't make much sense. A certain inner door controlling a reservoir of material had been opened, even if only slightly, and even if he would have to wait several years until he could open that door more fully, it was still a positive sign. What he had written was an example of "automatic writing," although he was entirely unfamiliar with any such term at the time. He called his piece "The Diary of a Futurist," and he sent it to H. L. Mencken at the *American Mercury*, but was not discouraged even when it was returned with a form note addressed to "Miss Miller."

In a rush of inspiration he spent hours at his typewriter and sent articles to *Colliers*, the *Saturday Evening Post* and several newspapers. He received some encouragement but nothing definite until he sent some sketches to an editor at *Liberty Magazine* who liked them, and asked him to write an article on language based on the new Funk and Wagnalls. Excited, he sent *Liberty* a piece that was three times the assigned length. It was never used, but he did receive a kill fee of $250, enough to rent a furnished room in Brooklyn that he could share with June.

Still posing as a writer, June had persuaded one of her elderly admirers to accept, print and pay for a series of stories that Miller wrote under her name. She played the same trick with the editor of a magazine called *Snappy Stories,* but Miller so loathed the magazine that he simply obtained a number of back issues and changed the characters' names and places in previously published stories and resubmitted them. These efforts perfectly corresponded to the magazine's tastes, and none of its editors were sharp enough to notice the plagiarism, but after placing a dozen stories, Miller became bored with the duplicity. In fact, he was bored not only with the duplicity; he was feeling restless about his life. He was still infatuated with June and allowed her to do as she pleased, but he was aware that he was spinning in her orbit. Perhaps to get her away from her natural habitat, the seedy side of New York, and to neutralize her power, he persuaded her to accompany him to Asheville, North Carolina, in the spring of 1926. He wanted to go there as a stopping-off place, to take advantage of its reputed real estate boom, and then continue on to Taos, New Mexico, to be near D. H. Lawrence, whose novels he had read and admired. He didn't know Lawrence had already left and settled in Italy.

The opportunities in real estate in Asheville were open only to insiders. June and Henry were once again flat broke, and though June concocted a scheme for beginning a fine hosiery business for ladies and touring the South with her wares, there was no practical solution to their financial straits.

The problem was money, and how to get it. The formula for writing successful pulp fiction still eluded him, and his heart wasn't in it, anyhow. They ran up debts for rent and food in Asheville that they had no way of paying. At the end of the summer, like stealthy thieves, they hitchhiked out of Asheville in the dark of night.

A Miraculous Wound

Only twenty-one, June had already lost much of the freshness of youth. She was a night lady who would never rise before noon, and then only to preen for hours while she painted herself with cosmetics. She found another squeezed flat in Brooklyn and another nightclub where she could charm male admirers into lending her sums of money which she had no intention of repaying. Sometimes, she would bring admirers home, and Miller would be forced to wait outside at 2:00 A.M. for the right moment to return, pretending to be dropping in himself for a visit. He was totally dependent on her, although he halfheartedly had tried to sell encyclopedias and newspapers. June had a predilection for con games, but she never seemed to have enough money to instill any sense of security. Theoretically, June was Miller's patron and protector, but her pursuit of males and her odd nocturnal habits made him feel more like a rejected lover. In effect, in their bohemian experimentation, June and Henry had totally reversed the usual male-female dominance relationship so that Henry would be free to write, but nothing that he set down on paper had any value for him.

Finally, June disappeared for three days in October of 1926 and then returned without any explanation, carrying a cadaverous-looking puppet named Count Bruga, which had violet silk hair, purple eyes, a flaccid, depraved mouth and hollow cheeks. Count Bruga signified the decadent turn that June had taken. She carried him about like some talisman, and he emphasized the more bizarre and even demonic aspects of her character. The puppet had been a gift from Jean Kronski, who had become June's lover. A sculptor, painter of skulls and serpents, an ambitious poet who had been an inmate in mental institutions, Jean was June's age. She identified with the French poet Rimbaud, and if she lacked his talent, she shared his self-destructive capacities. Extremely neurotic, she had learned a great deal about psychoanalytic theory, and professed the importance of total frankness, of absolute declaration of all intentions, while characteristically hiding as much as she could.

June found a small two-bedroom basement flat on Henry Street in Brooklyn, and the two women took one of the bedrooms. Miller was still under June's injunction not to reveal that they were married, but now he had also to accept the fact that his wife was sharing her bed with a woman as well as accepting sundry males for money. The two women conspired to humiliate him at every turn, complaining about his ineffectuality, his inability to earn a living or to take charge of matters. Still, he didn't walk out; nor do we know whether he was even considering that as an option. He was so completely dominated by her and her will, it was as though he had none of his own left. Things would get worse.

Under Jean's influence, that winter was a period of hysterical arguments and long confessional sessions, with each account seeming more distorted, brazen and twisted than the last. June would try to better Jean's revelations of her past sexual exploits with a story of her own, how she had fleeced or hoodwinked some poor fool like Miller for his money, and Miller felt he was living in a nest of pathological lies, which were told, perversely, as a sort of entertainment. The arrangement of their rooms reflected the internal disorder of the situation: sheets were soiled, dirty shirts were used as towels, dishes were washed in the greasy bathtub because the kitchen sink was usually stopped, and the floor was littered with cigarette butts, old newspapers, books, garbage, burned pots. The atmosphere was somber and dim, the stained shades perpetually drawn to disguise filthy windows, and everything had a mournful aspect to it.

Both Frieda and Zelda had disdained housekeeping, both rebelling against the expectation that women were responsible for domestic order. Frieda was self-indulgent and lazy, and Zelda expected that servants would clear her mess, but the disarray of the Henry Street flat was disastrous and suggested an almost pathological aversion to order. But the disorder was much more painful for Henry that it was for June. Miller was fundamentally much less of a bohemian than June and always dependent on middle-class comforts. In his fiction, however, he would reverse these characteristics, making his hero flamboyantly unconcerned with whatever was proper and conventional.

In the midst of this chaos, Jean decided to teach Miller to draw and to use watercolors. He had enjoyed the advantage of an informal training in drawing from his friend Emil Schnellock, but as a commercial artist Emil's bias was toward realism. Jean criticized Miller's efforts as lifeless and encouraged him in more figurative directions. His first lesson was to copy a human skull juxtaposed with a bunch of violets. The result was a sepulchral and surreal expression of Miller's mood and the ambiance of the Henry Street dwelling. Cheerless, cold in heart as well as body, Miller began to sign his letters as "The Failure," and he burned a pile of manuscript as well as furniture to keep warm. One day he obtained a supply of barbiturates from a friend and took what he thought was a lethal dose, which only resulted in an opiated twelve-hour sleep, as his friend had substituted a milder sedative for the barbiturate.

In the spring of 1927, Jean began describing the beauties of Paris and the stimulations which that feminine city afforded for artists. Without informing Miller, the two women suddenly embarked by boat for Europe. At first Miller felt devastated, abandoned, left in a void. No matter how temperamental or eccentric June had been, despite the frequently of her betrayals and his ability to blot them out of his mind, despite the relentless quarreling and hysteria and the despotism of her quickly changing moods, he had felt a kind of urgent love with her that he had never previously felt. He knew, also, that it had been a hopeless desperate love—in *Tropic of Capricorn* he would use the image of two maniacs groping for each other through an iron grate.

Enraged, Miller attacked the Henry Street apartment, breaking the furniture, smashing the dishes, tearing down the shades, ripping letters and papers. Then he left it, returning again as the prodigal son to his parents' house in Brooklyn. Psychically communicating to himself the end of his dependence on June, he began outlining a book about his life with June. This was the beginning of the story he would later tell in the *Tropics* novels, although he still had not found either the form or the voice with which to tell it.

Almost as soon as she had departed, Miller received telegrams from June pleading for money, which he sent. Returning in midsummer, June was overflowing with stories of her Parisian adventures, claims that artists like Picasso had pursued her, and the news that she was no longer infatuated with Jean Kronski, who had gone off to North Africa with a man named Alfred Perlès. June became intoxicated by Paris, and intent on going back with Henry. Immediately, she resumed a friendship with one of her former admirers, an older man whom she had nicknamed "Pop." June had already convinced him that she was a struggling writer, and she had shown him the sketches and stories that Henry had written under her name. She told him she had begun a novel in Paris and needed to return to complete it. Generously, "Pop" agreed to subsidize the novel and the trip to Paris, but he wanted to see what she had already written.

Miller spent the next five months writing the story of Dion Moloch, a Western Union employment manager. Essentially, he was still reworking the material from *Clipped Wings,* using the focusing filter of a central consciousness to organize perspective. The work was arduous, full of hesitations and faltering starts, and Miller was dissatisfied with what he was doing, aware that it was clumsy, inadequate and artificial. He had been telling the story from his male point of view when he realized that "Pop" expected something written from June's. Her admirer and newfound patron was either not sophisticated enough in literary matters or he was too distracted by June's amorous attentions to notice. He approved of what he had read and agreed to supply the cash.

Without fully realizing it, Miller once again had allowed himself to become dependent on June. It is an indication of how demoralized he was that he was still acquiescing in the deception about the authorship of his work. In the spring of 1928, they sailed for Liverpool, went to London, and then straight on to Paris. Excited, June tried to show Miller all she had seen a year earlier with Jean, and her excitement and the new setting allowed him to forget her former betrayals and to see their trip as a new honeymoon. June wanted to visit her parents' hometown in Romania, so they traveled by train through Germany and Poland and Eastern Europe. Miller was overwhelmed by a barrage of details that he could not fully assimilate: the sense of the past he felt in Roman ruins and medieval castles, ancient churches with jeweled ornaments and peasants fervently praying on their knees in the pews, the slower pace of the old world with its continuities, its own customs and conventions, fragments of which seemed familiar from Brooklyn, where he realized he had seen the final appearances of certain of these traditions.

After two months in Eastern Europe, they returned to Paris, where June wanted only to sleep away the day and spend the nights talking in cafés, the Select, the Dôme, the Deux Magots, the Wepler. The cafés of Paris were as much a medium for intellectual and artistic life as the literary magazines and art galleries: they were the place to meet, to debate, to write or draw or just ponder, the natural living room of exiles and expatriates and the sign of their metropolitanism. June introduced Miller to some of the artists she had met on her earlier trip, German painters Hans Reichel and Oscar Kokoschka, and a sculptor named Zadkine, but Miller was dissatisfied with conversations about art in cafés, partly because he expected more, and partly because of a new ambivalence about June. In the cafés of Paris he was made uneasy by her flirtatiousness.

In the interests of seeking what was authentically French, he persuaded June to take a bicycle tour to the South, even though she had never been on a bicycle before. Starting just outside Paris, they slowly made their way to Lyons, with frequent stops because June was unable to continue for long without losing her wind or her courage. For a woman who shunned daylight, cycling was a peculiar adventure, and she did not enjoy it. Most of the time she was irritated, completely out of her element, uninterested in the historical sites that fascinated Miller, anxious only to reach some comfortable destination. In Nice, with characteristic improvidence, they ran out of money and had to sell their bicycles. It was

the familiar situation of being stranded and appealing with telegrams to friends and "Pop" for assistance, and then frequenting the
American Express office in the hope of a favorable reply.

Finally, the American consul gave June a train ticket to Paris,
where she was able to raise the money for Miller's ticket. In Paris,
June appealed to "Pop" for money to get home, and he agreed to
send it. While they lingered, waiting for the money, Miller's
uneasiness recurred. June again expected to spend each night in
the cafés, drinking and talking till dawn. He felt disgusted that he
had not written anything, and disappointed that he had not seen
enough outside of cafés during the nine months he had been in
Europe. It had been a period of constant oscillation between
violent fighting and ardent reconciliations, a parading of emotions
that June seemed to enjoy and that Miller, perhaps more masochistically, could not avoid. He knew the distance between June
and himself had become insurmountable, yet he did not have the
courage to let go.

It would be simplistic to place Miller's situation with June
exclusively within a dominance/submission framework. Certainly,
his marriage suggests such a conclusion, but it is also true that he
was floundering inwardly, that he had not yet found his real voice
as a writer, and that he was suffering from a crisis of identity. It was
not completely out of character for Miller to hang on in a relationship long after it had worn him out. He had remained married to
Beatrice out of inertia. June, on the other hand, was a stinging
presence, and the pain she inflicted was one way of knowing he was
still alive. In the end, he would find the pain he endured had been a
"miraculous wound," and in cauterizing it he would discover the
lifeblood of his inspiration as a writer.

On the night prior to their departure for New York, they went to a
dance hall with Zadkine to celebrate. Miller had suspected that
June had been Zadkine's lover and he began to flirt with a striking
blond. Drunk and aroused, he went to the bathroom where he
encountered her. Equally drunk, after a few minutes of touching in
the toilet, she was ready to consummate matters right in a stall.
Either they were too inebriated or not sufficiently prone, but when
they couldn't accomplish the act, they began to waltz in the
bathroom. Hilariously happy, Miller lost control and ejaculated all
over her gown, staining it indelibly. Furious, the woman stalked off,
but Miller could not forget the sense of irrepressible release of that
moment. The ejaculation incident appealed to him for its irrespon-

sibility and spontaneity, and he would use the scene almost verbatim in *Tropic of Cancer* to launch the mad antics of that novel. It can be linked in a sense to the artistic giddiness Fitzgerald experienced in Paris and on the Riviera, cut loose from the restrictions he felt at home in America. Miller's delight in the sheer vulgarity of the incident is characteristic, and he drew on such moments to revitalize his art.

June and Henry returned to New York in January of 1929 to discover that Jean had preceded them, had been recommitted and had killed herself. Beatrice, Henry's first wife, had also remarried to a much older man with money, so crucial elements of the past seemed settled and in order. The past would become Miller's central preoccupation for the next year as he began the novel about June that he had conceived prior to leaving for Europe. The idea for the book had come in a rush of despair and loss, and writing seemed a way to relieve those feelings, but now June was at his side, exhorting him to write a book that would praise and deify her.

Miller was aware that he was writing more to please June than himself and that she was now trying to control him through his writing. One of her admirers was an editor on a Hearst newspaper who paid her for a daily fifteen-hundred-word column on the city, which Henry wrote so that June would get a regular reporter's job. To do the column, Miller spent hours prowling the streets of Brooklyn and Manhattan, getting the feel of the city again. Usually he had no money, and he occasionally began to panhandle, along with hundreds of other destitute victims of the economic depression that had already begun.

His major concern was the story about June in which a character whom he named Tony Bring would represent Miller himself. June had always expressed great interest in anything he wrote, and usually admiration and support, but now she was full of commentary and clarification, full of the desire to explicate the mysteries of her past, which Henry was trying to set down on paper, and especially concerned about the way in which she was made to appear. Miller was convinced that she was simply embroidering old lies with new deceptions and that the story he was writing, and she was making him rewrite according to her prescriptions, was a tissue of fabrications. By Thanksgiving Day of 1929, the Tony Bring manuscript had grown to over four hundred pages, with almost twice as many pages of notes and material that had been excised by June. Tony Bring had been so deemphasized by June's changes that he was now merely a narrator, a mouthpiece for June's actions, and Miller felt ashamed of the result because it seemed so far from any real truth he could remember.

June had confessed to "Pop" that she was not an author, but that Henry had written everything she had shown him. "Pop" was not surprised or very concerned; it was June he was after, not her art. He agreed to provide a steamship ticket for Henry to return to Europe and finish the novel about June, hoping that with Henry removed, he would have unobstructed access to June.

Depressed, numbed by June's intricate machinations, unable to imagine for himself a future course of action with June in New York, he agreed. He saw himself as merely a ventriloquist's dummy manipulated by a woman whom he would later, in *Capricorn*, visualize as a Mithraic bull with an acetylene torch in her womb. June, he calculated, had accepted forty-two male and sixteen female lovers that he knew of during the seven years of their marriage.

The number of lovers he cites is interesting: if these were the ones that Miller knew about, and if June was as deceptive as Miller claimed, then how many more lovers actually existed? Of course, the accounting is complicated by Miller's reputation as a myth-maker, which is to say a writer who distorts and exaggerates reality to create a more powerful picture than the actual can provide.

Parity between the sexes may begin in the bedroom. The swaggering male personae of the *Tropics* novels, who seduce new women in practically every chapter, can be seen as Miller's displaced fictional equivalent of June's sexual betrayals. As a liberated woman, June magnifies Frieda's occasional infidelities. More than a difference of scale, June is the professional who indulges in sex outside marriage to secure her livelihood. Frieda is merely an amateur of pleasure. The act of infidelity, however, gives both women an added power, a freedom that previously had been associated with men.

The question of June's lovers exists also as a test case for biography. Miller's point of view is expressed in the thousands of letters he wrote to June and to friends like Emil Schnellock. Letters, however, can seem much more objective or truthful than their authors. And Miller's letters incorporate the same elements of fabrication as his fictions; they exist to justify himself. Perhaps this is why Miller, like Fitzgerald, felt that biography was impossible.

Before Miller's departure, Schnellock sketched him in charcoal, his forehead prominent because he had already lost most of his hair, his green eyes hidden behind round horn-rimmed spectacles, his face averted, his lower lip especially full, almost pouting, emphasizing the sensitivity of his pursed mouth. It was a portrait of a man who had been hurt, pensive, softened in thought, looking apprehensively off to the side.

Miller sailed for Europe in February. All that he had besides his clothes, manuscripts and a copy of Whitman's *Leaves of Grass* was a ten-dollar bill he had borrowed from Emil.

The Broken Twig

"As quietly and naturally as a twig falling into the Mississippi," he reflected in *Black Spring,* "I dropped out of the stream of American life." The comment was made in retrospect. He would not have known, when he arrived in Paris and found an attic maid's room for twenty dollars a month, that he had crossed a dividing line in his life. The ocean that separated him from June imposed an uneasy truce on their relationship, a moratorium in their private daily war. Not free of her, but free of her presence, he irresolutely, without any conscious willingness to make a break in his marriage, experienced a liberation from her that proved to be the turning point in his writing.

In Paris he had intended to revise and polish his novel about June, but the manuscript could not hold his interest at the moment. Instead, he decided to describe Paris in the first person. That would justify his presence there and motivate him to learn all he could about the city.

Free of June, though still longing for her, he made the city of Paris his mistress, the object of his copious devotion. For Miller, the cosmopolitan streets of Paris sang with history and romance. He responded to what he felt was the city's aptitudes for pleasure, happiness and vitality. As his French improved, he was beginning to hear the seductive mellifluousness of the French language, the swing and sonority of its measured cadence. It was part of the rhythms of the city whose chimerical beauty kept him gasping and on the verge of tears, he confessed. His letters to June and especially to Emil (who was under instructions to circulate them among Miller's other friends, forming a select audience) would become a record of his explorations. Using a book on literary Paris and Francis Carco's *Bohemia,* he mapped out a series of long walks.

That was the way he had trained himself to observe Brooklyn and Manhattan, composing in his head as he proceeded on foot, stopping only to make notes.

His eye was fixed on the quotidian: the pushcart peddlers on the rue Saint Antoine in the Marais selling peeled oranges, skinned rabbits, wooden shoes and country mushrooms, the omnipresent flower stalls and tiny art galleries, the horse butchers with their giant carcasses, the police who could smoke on their beats or converse over a drink in a bar, a whore with a swollen face and eyes swimming like big onions in a bowl of soup, another one with skin so delicate it appeared as blue as skimmed milk, and also on the streets the dwarfs of Velázquez and Chagall's simpering idiots. Illuminating all was the soft, mellow light that seemed to glow off the grayish walls of the ancient buildings.

He saturated himself with the specifics of each quarter: the animated elegance of the Champs Elysées, "sterilized, cauterized, and polished like a piece of old silver"; the working-class pigments of the vegetable market at Les Halles with its aromas of leek, cheese and fish; the Italian girls with smoldering eyes set in enameled faces near the Place d'Italie. Running through Paris like some twisting intestine was the Seine, a dirty river in a picturesque setting, which he compared to an old woman squatting in the gutter while urinating.

Before long, he had no money left and could not remain in his rented room. He was still dependent on remittances from June, but he heard nothing from her and was not even certain of where she was living, writing to her in care of the club where she worked. He soon learned to sustain himself through luck, charm and nerve. He stayed one night with an immigrant Russian family, dismayed by their squalor. He remembered how it felt to be completely without resources in a foreign country and later would use the incident in *Tropic of Cancer.* Miller's gregariousness was more than a means of survival: it was a form of social research, the way he could collect material to use in his writing.

If he had one capability, it was his ability to talk about his experiences, interest and memories, to expatiate in rollicking sentences with enormous enthusiasm. In this gusto for talking, talking, talking, he was like D. H. Lawrence, an indefatigable conversationalist. As he told his friend Emil Schnellock, others saw him as a romantic figure embroiled in adventures and willing to confess them. By interacting with him, those who met him often felt they were somehow enriched by the contact with a man who seemed to epitomize the unknown artist, the man who was making the sort of sacrifices they could imagine but never personally sustain.

As a result, simply in exchange for his spirit and conversation, because with him around life would seem less conventional and boring, Miller was often able to find people in Paris who would feed or house him. Among them was Alfred Perlès, the Austrian writer with whom Jean Kronski had run off after she and June quarreled in Paris three years earlier. Miller was drinking at the Dôme, without money to pay for his drinks, when he encountered Perlès and tried to work up the courage to confess that he couldn't cover his tab. Instead, he launched into a long monologue about America, the poverty he had endured, his father's tailor shop, the women he had slept with, his job at Western Union, his favorite reading. He immediately felt a common bond with Perlès, an aspiring novelist with a furtive, conspiratorial air that made him look like an illegal psychoanalyst, Miller thought.

Generously, Perlès put Miller up at his hotel, loaned him money and then introduced him to an editor who was practically a namesake: Henri Müller could read English, and he advised Miller to submit the Moloch manuscript to a publisher in Berlin, and also cautioned him to write less realistically in the future. It was potent advice, which encouraged Miller to pursue object lessons among the Surrealists, who had existed as a force in Paris since they had succeeded the Dadaists some five years earlier. Stressing the potential for ambiguous and sometimes contradictory messages, the Surrealists made ambiguity, irrationality and free association ends in themselves and suggested to Miller numerous ways to de-emphasize realistic depiction.

Perlès, earning a living as a proofreader for the American newspaper in Paris, the *Herald Tribune,* and writing an occasional article, was willing to help. But he did not have enough himself to support Miller, who was learning how to live marginally, eating three bowls of oatmeal a day as an inexpensive way to stay alive. Miller sold some of his clothes, the finely tailored suits that his father had made, and then pawned his wedding band. At the Dôme, he met a Hindu pearl dealer whom he had known when working for Western Union, and moved into the dealer's flat, where he occupied a corner, sleeping there on the floor in exchange for sweeping dirty carpets and washing dishes. He had virtually stopped writing, and his real work was haunting American Express, expecting news and money from June. There were cables promising money, and some small amounts actually did come, but no letter, causing Miller to worry and to imagine her intrigues.

Suddenly, at the end of September in 1930, he did receive a letter in which June announced her imminent arrival. When she appeared a month later, it was without much money, and they spent a month together in miserable hotel rooms, frugally measuring their resources. Ironically, June believed that she was in Paris to begin a career as a film actress. It is true that Miller had spoken of new connections in this field, which fed her fantasy. The penurious reality of Miller's life was a harsh contrast to such a notion, and much of their time was spent quarreling. They had been apart for seven months, a period during which Miller had longed for June, but had already distanced himself from her obsessions. Her criticisms of Paris provoked him to attack New York, and when she left to return to America, he knew that he would be on his own.

Miller was concerned about the conditions of his own survival and he remembered that even when he had depended on June, there were many days when he had gone hungry. Thirty-nine years old, he had no regular job or expectation of employment, and, besides, he considered that his work was his project to describe Paris and the manuscript about June, which he now called *Crazy Cock* and was revising. With nothing to lose, and armed with the Surrealist injunction of *lâcher-tout,* the notion that anything— values, friends, even family—should be abandoned for the sake of self-expression, Miller trusted in his providence. "Always merry and bright" was his motto, and he continued to rely on what seemed an innate joyousness and gaiety no matter how desperate his circumstances.

There were several American painters whom Miller had met who listened to his talk and fed him, gave him some money, or allowed him to sleep on a studio floor. Brassai, a Hungarian photographer, posed him erotically and sold the pictures to tourists. He would treat Miller to a meal and then take him to Pigalle, the area where the prostitutes paraded and catered to the most perverse demands. Another reliable resource for a meal or a few francs was Wambly Bald, who wrote a gossip column for the *Tribune* on bohemian life in Paris and would pay for information or for a column if Miller would write it.

Through one of his painter friends, Miller met Richard Osborn, a graduate of Yale Law School who was administering the legal matters of the Paris branch of an American bank. Loud, convivial, Osborn wanted to be a writer and chose to live in Paris and enjoy himself while he searched for material. Although he had a stream of visiting women friends, most of whom were French, Osborn was eager for American companionship, and he invited Miller to share his ample lodgings. Suddenly, Miller had a comfortable place in which to work, as Osborn would be at the bank until evening and often would go out after work. Generously, he would leave Miller a little pocket money near his typewriter in the morning and would be willing to hear whatever section of *Crazy Cock* Miller had revised or completed. He was interested and encouraging, although he complained that Miller's style was old-fashioned. He preferred what Miller was doing with his first-person Paris sketches in which a new persona was gradually emerging, that of the anomalous misfit, the buffoon, martyr, monster, who would later dominate the *Tropics* novels.

Years later, Miller would express outrage when critics refused to believe that this persona was not a literal replica of Henry Miller. Actually, it was a fabricated exaggeration, a projection, a fantastic version of the virility and abandon to which Miller aspired. Miller was far more charming and much less aggressive and daring than the vagabond hero of the *Tropics* novels. If he was with a prostitute, he scrupulously employed a prophylactic. He was always meticulously dressed in the suits his father had made for him, those he had not pawned or sold. Usually, his gastronomic tastes were monastically simple, because he suffered from hemorrhoids. He was considerate of others, realizing that he might have to ask them for money someday. A fastidious sense of order was reflected in his housekeeping, which was one reason why people like Osborn appreciated his presence. Neat and clean, he made sure everything was in its place, a sort of Dutch houseboy, Norman Mailer observed. The bohemian disorder he claimed for himself, like the personal chaos and the sexual excess, was more imagined than lived. It was June who had a special genius for chaos and personal disarray.

Part Surrealist, part anarchist, this new persona Miller was forging owed something also to Perlès, who had shown Miller how to exist on the margins with the tough irresponsibility of the exile. Perlès also got Miller assignments early in 1931 to write feature articles on the circus and the six-day bicycle race for the Sunday *Tribune*. Comfortably ensconced in Osborn's apartment, Miller set about reorganizing his Paris notebooks, placing sections as feature pieces in the *Tribune* under the names of different staff writers. He also found other small writing jobs to help sustain himself—a bit of promotional copy for a new brothel that catered to Americans, and articles about Jews in Paris that would be published in various Jewish papers under the name of a retired furrier he had met. When Osborn was forced to give up his sublet for two months, Miller moved in with a graduate student in psychology at the Sorbonne whom he was helping write a thesis on mental retardation.

He was overspilling with material, he wrote Emil Schnellock, with ideas that came to him in telephone booths, on the Metro, in his sleep and on the toilet. He constructed oversize wall charts and complex diagrams to lay out the Paris notebooks, which he realized were more interesting as material than anything in his other three manuscripts, *Clipped Wings, Moloch,* or *Crazy Cock.* Also, he was reading D. H. Lawrence and felt that Lawrence had been limited by the boundaries of his orthodox forms. His own earlier work, he informed Emil Schnellock, dissatisfied him because it was too plotted out, too painstakingly structured, so that he felt claustrophobically "cramped, walled in, suffocated." He wanted most as a writer to explode, to discard all formal properties, and he felt the possibility for that lay somewhere within the Paris material. He soon met someone whose advice helped him to discover his unique voice.

Walter Lowenfels, a poet Miller had gotten to know, who was writing an extended elegy on the death (in 1930) of D. H. Lawrence and who believed that Western civilization was caught in a kind of deathly sleep, introduced Miller to his mentor in the philosophy of death. Michael Fraenkel, a Jew of Russian origin who had left New York with enough money to retire to Paris, had published one of Lowenfels's books of poetry. A tiny, pale man with a staccato delivery and words that pierced like stilettos, Fraenkel fascinated Miller as the genuine intellectual he had previously never met. Miller spent many rapt hours listening to Fraenkel and Lowenfels discuss the implications of their death theories in a language that Miller compared to a sort of higher mathematics: "weird, ghostly, ghoulishly abstract." Fraenkel was a born metaphysician of language who pursued every nuance of meaning with a relentless intensity of inquiry that Miller appreciated. Miller soon became Fraenkel's ideal audience and then his partner in philosophical pursuits. First, he spent hours listening to Fraenkel and Lowenfels discuss the implication of their death theories. With Fraenkel,

Miller was exposed to a Nietzschean intellectual nihilism that prepared him for the death of his former self, that denied the need for security or the very ambition that he could be a writer. Before long Miller moved in with Fraenkel, who became his provider while he absorbed himself in Fraenkel's talk for the next two months.

He was particularly inspired by a remark Fraenkel had made when dismissing *Crazy Cock,* that Miller should write as he spoke, spontaneously, without thinking of revision or what would qualify as literature. Suddenly, as if an impassable barrier had been lifted or dissolved, Miller found the voice he would use in his best fiction: raw, manic, natural, uninhibited and so purely, inimitably, himself. He felt excited by the prospects of what he could write, and by his life in Paris, in the way he supposed all vagabond artists must have felt: "absolutely reckless, childish, irresponsible, unscrupulous and overflowing with carnal vitality, vigor, ginger."

Anaïs

He was ready to begin *Tropic of Cancer* and knew that he would have to reserve much of his energy for it. In order to save the time he wasted searching for food, he drew up a list of fourteen friends who could be counted on to feed him a meal, contacted each of them, and organized a convenient rotation. If a friend proved insufficiently stimulating, he would find another as a replacement.

Perlès came to his aid again by putting him up in his hotel room and by helping him get a night job as a proofreader on the stock exchange pages of the *Tribune.* The job was conveniently mindless, and the nighttime hours freed Miller for his own work. Before beginning *Cancer,* he made one final attempt at the revision of *Crazy Cock,* virtually cutting away half his manuscript and submitting his new version to Edward Titus, who published books under the imprint of the Black Manikin Press. He began what he called an album of his Paris life, a collage of his impressions drawn from his Paris notebooks in which he would mix watercolors, remembering the freedom D. H. Lawrence had discovered when at forty he had begun painting. Miller was also forty. He did not yet know it, but when he began writing *Tropic of Cancer,* he had finally found the way to tell his story.

One of the keys to that story was June and how she had affected his view of women. As if in response to his thoughts, in the fall of 1931, he received a cable from her announcing her imminent arrival. He was shocked when he saw her in the Dôme. Although only twenty-eight, she looked like one of the walking dead that Fraenkel had described. Her whitened face looked bleached, cadaverous. She had lost weight and moved as if in a trance; her speech was incomprehensible, slurred. All her former voluptuousness had faded. She had been using hashish, cocaine and opium and looked emaciated, consumed, spectral.

As long as they were separated and he was writing about her, he exercised control. Aware that her presence and her demands could upset and distract him, he tried to maintain his routine of proofreading at night, writing by day and keeping his regular rotation of appointed meals with friends.

At one of those meals with Osborn, he read an essay on D. H. Lawrence written by a young woman whose husband, Hugo Guiler, was Osborn's superior at the bank. Although he had developed reservations about Lawrence's formal restrictions, Miller liked the essay.

Mrs. Guiler had extended the essay to book-length and had invited Osborn to lunch to discuss the contract offered her by Black Manikin Press for *An Unprofessional Study*. He asked Miller to join him as a sort of comic relief. He felt Miller's ranting against Lawrence would enliven the afternoon, and he knew that Miller always appreciated a good lunch. Mrs. Guiler wrote under her maiden name, Anaïs Nin.

Nin had been attracted to Lawrence as an opposite: the scorned liberationist relied on emotion and intuition, on a "blood-consciousness" that repudiated reason, order and "civilization." These qualities appealed to her as a woman, closeted in a domesticity that seemed too protectively reassuring. In a sense, she had written her book on Lawrence to chart the route she wanted her future to take.

By the middle of lunch, while they were all discussing books, Nin was overwhelmed by Miller's laughter. She recognized a man inebriated by life, a gust of tremendous enthusiasm. She was twenty-seven and had been married since she was twenty, cloistered within her husband's stuffy world of bank and golf course, talk of trusts and investments. She had servants, a chauffeur and what the French call *ennui*—the sort of boredom that comes with breeding and a good deal of money, the sort that creates wanderlust. She resented her husband's work, the long hours he spent at his bank, and at times even abhorred it. Hugo seemed listless, anemic. Their marriage had become stale. To rejuvenate their sexual appetites, he suggested that they attend an orgy or watch others make love, which they did, meeting two women in a cabaret on the rue Blondel, who later performed for them with hot tongues and a pink dildo in a room upstairs.

Miller and Nin formed the immediate bond of two writers who each had a first book submitted to the same house. He had already written the first pages of *Tropic of Cancer* and was full of the tremendous energy an artist feels when he knows he has caught the full rhythm of his work. Nin gave Miller a copy of her Lawrence manuscript, and Miller sent her some of *Crazy Cock*. She was stunned by the brutal vehemence of his prose, Miller's stylistic avalanche different from the mannered, almost precious icy precision of her own work.

To Miller, Nin looked like a poised lady holding lilies in a painting by Watteau. Pensive and serious, she was thin, with fragile bones and chiseled features, a veiled, misty look in her eyes and an extraordinary liquidity in her movements. Nin would costume herself: a black turban, a rose dress full at the bottom, a lace collar, lacing over her breasts, a little black velvet jacket, a coral necklace, a turquoise ring. She changed from the coy ingenue to the seductive sophisticate from minute to minute. Actually, she had once been an artist's model, and she seemed perpetually in search of someone who could admire her.

When Miller described his new acquaintance to June, she was immediately curious, perhaps even a bit jealous since Nin was the writer she had fantasized herself becoming. When Nin invited Miller and June to spend an evening at her home in Louveciennes, a suburb of Paris, to meet her husband, June eagerly accepted. Walking from the dark garden and into the warm pink glow radiating from a bronze Moorish lamp, June seemed like a demonic annunciation to Nin. She felt June was the most beautiful woman she had ever seen. She was mesmerized by the darkness of June's eyes, with their suggestions of infinite abysses, and the phosphorescent pallor of her skin. Nin may have seen her own reflection in June: the posturing, the exaggeration, the theatricality, the enormous ego. But where Nin was an exotic, June was bizarre.

June now saw herself as a Byzantine *femme fatale,* capable of evil and cruelty. She still had the ghoulish purple manikin, Court Bruga, that Jean Kronski had made for her. She brought it along like a talisman, a darkened projection of her power, on her first visit alone to Louveciennes. She asked Anaïs for her perfume, for her stockings, her gloves, even her undergarments, though June usually dispensed with such impediments.

They first saw each other's bodies when trying on clothes; soon they were touching, and then Anaïs marveled in her journal over the soft and subtle penetrations of their union. Miller had already left Paris for the winter, for a job at a lycée in Dijon that he later mercilessly caricatured in *Cancer*. Nin fell infatuated with June, who was so much like the characters in her own stories, so trapped by their fantasies, so drugged by their dreams, so caught in a self-annihilating vortex. June's interminable stories about her life, fragmented, disjointed, contradictory, hinged by transparent fabrications, products of an intense self-consciousness and an enormous though shallow pride, fascinated and repelled Nin. Like Miller, Nin was bewitched by the primal storyteller in June—the untempered narcissism, the parade of sheer ego—and both were terrified by these qualities as well.

Impulsively, June decided she had had enough of Paris, that she disliked the French, that she needed to return to New York. Characteristically, she had used her affair with Nin as a means of support, and part of her power and charm was her ability to extort money. Nin supplied her fare home. Miller, chastened by the dreary routines of academia, returned to Paris. Once again, his friend Perlès came to his aid. Perlès found a two-bedroom flat in Clichy, cheap enough so that by sharing it, they could economize and survive even if only one of them was working. After three years of rooming houses and substandard hotels, of hall bathrooms and cold-water showers, of dampness, bedbugs and distracting noises, Miller finally had his own space in which to write.

He had been working on *Tropic of Cancer* and he had shown some of it to June, who disliked the frank way in which she was portrayed. He also gave some of what he had written to Nin, who in turn let him read some of the stories she was writing. They met in her studio at Louveciennes to discuss their mutual literary efforts. The room was warm and inviting—burnished mahogany paneling, stained-glass windows, inlaid tables, glowing lanterns, burning incense. They sat on a low silk couch with silk cushions. Miller gazed into Nin's oval face, admiring the lustrous gleam of her hair, staring into eyes that seemed to smolder.

Nin's home was part of the former estate of Madame DuBarry, and Nin had decorated it as an extension of the exotic image she wished to project: apricot and peach walls covered with astrological charts, a pervasive scent of jasmine, open fireplaces in which she burned tree roots and apple wood, carved black wooden bookcases, indigo lamps, collections of curious stones and crystals. She showed him her diary entries on June and talked about making June the subject of one of her stories, "Alraune." They discussed Dostoyevsky, Proust and Gide, French prostitutes and American women. He showed her his watercolors; she described her dreams, including a particularly suggestive one of crawling on her stomach through tunnels.

Nin would spend years with psychoanalysts trying to understand what she interpreted as her father's desertion when she was eleven. Egotistic and exacting, Joaquin Nin was a Spanish pianist and composer who had married Nin's mother, an opera singer, in Cuba. Raised in Europe and Cuba, Nin moved with her mother to New York City after the collapse of her parents' marriage, and she began a diary in English which she addressed to her father. She would be left with a lingering suspicion of the disloyalty of men. In Hugo, she had found a surrogate father, a man who represented stability, consideration and security. She realized that she had only been attracted to timorous, genteel, overrefined men like Hugo. While her husband had detested June, he tolerated Henry. Hugo was sedate, dignified, even a bit pompous; Henry was a celebrant, eager for the next glass of wine. Miller was also capable of as much coarseness as sensitivity, and Nin feared he was capable of a ferocious sensuality.

First, they connected on the literary plane. He warned her against abstractions but was fascinated by the obscurities in her prose. There was something malleable, ductile, susceptible about her that was reflected in her writing, and he offered the most deft and delicate observations. Her diaries had enthralled him. In a letter he told her that they contained immortal passages of hallucinated, magical prose and they confirmed his belief that his own actual experiences could figure as the matter of his own fiction. His talk was extravagant, eloquent, exultant, and his imagination powerful enough to win her over. On his part, he was attracted to her as an opposite, a woman of exotic sensuality with none of the predatory bird-of-prey qualities of June. He was charmed by her European accent, excited by her feline movements, and incomprehensibly attracted to her because she had known June.

He sent her a declaration of love, which she answered with a visit to his room. The first thing she noticed was a photograph of June on the mantelpiece, which she found transfixing. Lying on a coarse blanket spread over an iron cot, covered with an old overcoat, they came together. She was amazed at his tenderness, the deliberation of his penetration, the way he slowly drew in and out of her, savoring every second. She compared the pauses and twists of his lovemaking to sinking in warm blood.

Hugo went on a trip for the bank, and the lovers met in Louveciennes; Hugo returned, and they found a hotel room or used Henry's room with its single small window. Henry taught her to encircle him with her legs; he coaxed her to bite him, to lie on top of him, to turn in positions of which she had only dreamed. He made her bones crack and her soul groan with pleasure, she confided in her diary. In a letter, he promised to open her very groins. She was caught in the great passion of her life—they were articulating it in hundreds of letters—but she still realized that if she had to choose between Henry and her husband, she would choose Hugo. Such a choice was a pragmatic qualification of Nin's own romantic tendencies. Hugo represented safety. Instead of burdening her with children, he was her patron and comforter. Clearly, Henry was far more destabilizing.

Cancer

Late in the spring of 1932 Nin was startled to hear Henry telling her that he did not find her beautiful. He complained to her that with his whores he had no need for love letters or courtship. It seemed a turning point. But she realized that being with Henry had transformed her. It exposed Hugo's limitations. She lay fraternally in bed with Hugo, writing in her red journal about Henry. She saw that Henry had liberated her, had opened a secret door of her being. She went to a hotel with Edouardo Sanchez, a cousin who had pursued her for thirteen years, and offered herself to him. It was a way of measuring differences and confirming her seductiveness. Edouardo introduced her to his psychoanalyst, Dr. René Allendy, whom she began to visit regularly. There were days when she flirted with Allendy, and had sex with Henry, Edouardo and Hugo, in turn. By the summer of 1932, Henry was fantasizing about marriage, though he still wrote love letters to June, and he showed some of them to Anaïs. In turn, she showed him her story about June. She also began to give him money to free him to complete *Tropic of Cancer.*

The book inspired him as no writing had previously; it obsessed him, and filled him with an energy that Nin felt was magnetically transmitted to her. In turn, her diaries had taught him that one could be unapologetically confessional and autobiographical. Years later, in an essay in *The Cosmological Eye,* he claimed that even if *Cancer* seemed to be the work of a supremely confident, self-assertive writer, it had been written practically as an act of desperation, on the reverse side of an early version of his *Crazy Cock* manuscript. The fate of that manuscript seemed emblematic: Edward Titus, the publisher of the Black Manikin Press, had lost the manuscript without ever having remembered whether he had read it. Miller had spent a year revising it, and it was a blow, even though he realized that Titus was not especially committed to good writing and that Black Manikin was more of a social than a literary venture, subsidized by Titus's wife, Helena Rubinstein, and her fragrance fortune. Undaunted, indomitable in his way, Miller was "so great an optimist that he saw hope even in hopelessness," his friend Perlès observed.

The story Miller wanted to tell in *Tropic of Cancer* was not so much different in content from the unpublished manuscripts of his apprentice efforts as it was different in form and point of view. Typing very rapidly and composing directly on the machine with little or no revision, he devised a savage and giddy protagonist without money, resources or hope, who was at the same time "the happiest man alive." Finally, Miller had found an authentic voice, the sound of his own natural speech, a manic and angry whiplash suitable for a world which he saw as depleted and insane.

In *Cancer,* his impoverished protagonist uses his wit and rancor to connive an existence in Paris. The book is organized as a series of encounters with women, most of whom are prostitutes, and the men who become Miller's hosts, providing him with food or lodging. Clearly based on his Paris friends, men like Perlès, Osborne and Fraenkel, the book had a *roman à clef* element that Miller transcended with a calculated, systematic distortion of the actual.

A surrealistic Whitman with the rancor of a Swift or a Céline, Miller castigated bourgeois complacency and genteel culture from the perspective of the alienated and outraged pariah who felt that Western civilization was doomed, destined for some apocalyptic termination. His interest was neither sociological, in the sense of a Dickens or a Dreiser charting the clashes inherent in class structures, nor was it literary. Nothing had been written in several hundred years, he wrote his friend Emil, that was as savage, brutal and frank as *Cancer,* and his only fear was possible expulsion from France as an undesirable alien. Such a possibility would be catastrophic, Miller felt, because his flight to France had been like Van Gogh's to Arles or Gauguin's to Tahiti, that of the voluntary exile who was at home nowhere except where there was some glimmer of romantic possibility. Such self-imposed exile requires a permanent disguise, and it is in its way an extreme form of self-protection. No wonder, then, that the sexual buccaneer that Miller created in *Cancer* was part of his disguise, an alter-ego projection that existed primarily as fantasy. In later years, when James Laughlin, who would publish Miller's essays, met Miller, he was astonished to discover how ascetic, considerate, mild-mannered and temperate he was.

Tropic of Cancer was like an old leather suitcase that could expand or collapse and could contain anything, he wrote Emil. His intention, a magnification of what Lawrence had first attempted in *Lady Chatterley's Lover,* was to include exactly what had been consistently omitted from novels on the grounds of taste or propriety. Taste, Miller believed, was not a moral matter but merely a euphemism for inhibition, the fears which limit human potential and growth. If he stressed the cruel, the ugly and the immoral, if he took such special delight in his prostitutes and orgies, it was because he regarded his work as a sort of tonic that might immunize his readers against what he regarded as the world's real poisons. In a harsh and sometimes hysterical voice, he could project himself as an utterly unscrupulous, sex-obsessed monster, the man who could ejaculate on a woman's fine gown in a toilet and exult in what had been soiled, the man who would filch the money he had paid a prostitute while she was assisting her ailing mother downstairs, the man who would steal his friend's money given the chance.

The episodes of *Cancer,* with their rhythmic release, their chaotic digressions, their vitriolic caricature and burlesque, seem true because of the apparent sincerity of a narrator who repeats his conviction that nothing mattered in the end anyway, that he had lost everything and would sacrifice anything without regret, that he had absolutely no concern with the way others saw him. The ensuing monster was an exaggeration, a distortion, a summoning of the power Miller needed to tell his story.

In one of the final episodes of *Cancer,* a character named Fillmore (modeled on Richard Osborn, the attorney who introduced Miller to Nin) becomes engaged to a Frenchwoman whom he can no longer stand. Bound by his honor, he feels he must go through with the marriage. Miller advises him to board the next ship in denial of his obligation. Guilty, Fillmore gives Miller a sum of money which he hopes will placate his intended, but the Miller hero pockets the francs as another of his shameless survival tactics. The incident is typical of Miller's fiction, particularly of the way he will twist conventional values to a more rakish end. Even more significant, however, is the way Miller rewrote what actually happened. Osborn, after a mental breakdown (an event Miller omitted from his narrative), did give Miller such a sum, which Miller in fact honorably delivered, though he kept part of it as a commission.

The moment Miller sat down to write, his friend Michael Fraenkel cogently observed in a letter, everything changed drastically:

> He'll twist, distort, deform, beg, borrow, steal, cheat, lie, hoodwink, do anything and everything, he is absolutely irresponsible, in the grip of a mania over which he has no control whatsoever. He is the artist then. A species of artist whose effectiveness as artist is in direct proportion to his irresponsibility.

Miller's view of his own fabricating imagination was more sanguine. His writing had finally helped clarify the past to himself, and was acting to open in him an exfoliation of spirit and outlook. If he had begun *Cancer* as a means of discovering his own salvation, it was becoming a way to liberate himself for a higher purpose. If he falsified in the process, he wrote to his friend Emil, it was because he was interested in the discovery of an implicit truth that art as well as life traditionally concealed. And if the world ended by calling him a liar, he was sure that he was at the same time its most creative and sincere liar.

In the fall of 1932, Miller heard from June in New York that she was returning to France. He had consistently dangled the delusion that somehow they could once again live together compatibly. It was an impossible delusion, the sign of a residual romanticism in his soul that even June's multiple betrayals could not expunge. When he was writing letters to June in America, the delusion could be sustained. He had been intimate with several other women in the year since he had last seen her. At the same time he was totally enamored of Nin. He told Emil Schnellock that his experience with her was the richest he had ever had, that he could discuss books and ideas with her because she was his equal in every way. Since meeting Nin, he had been able to work effortlessly, and his life in Paris had become almost a dream. Most important, she was his unquestioning support in the matter of his writing, and had even offered to pawn her fur coat to help get *Cancer* published.

Fortunately, an American literary agent named William Aspen-wall Bradley managed to interest Jack Kahane in publishing *Cancer.* An Irish Jew who specialized in books on the borderline between the erotic and the pornographic, he had established Obelisk Press in Paris on the success of several randy novels which he had written himself under various pseudonyms. Kahane felt obligated to search for and publish a certain number of distinguished writers such as Frank Harris and Cyril Connolly, the editor of *Horizon,* and he responded favorably to *Cancer.*

June's reaction, when she arrived at the end of October, was less receptive. Even as Miller felt he was coming into his own as a writer, his life was still complicated by his unresolved relationship with her. Previously, she had tried to manipulate and control his writing. Now she was openly hostile. She hated the way she was depicted in *Tropic of Cancer,* remembering that she had shaped her role in *Crazy Cock,* and she threatened legal repercussions should *Cancer* appear. At the same time, she had supreme confidence in his attachment to her. She had installed herself in a hotel for which she could not pay, but demanded that Miller come up with the money, though he was living off the generosity of Nin and his roommate Perlès.

The "internecine war" had begun again, Miller wrote Emil—heated spats and awful declarations, complicated by June's renewed pursuit of Nin and the fact that both Nin and Miller had hidden their affair from June. By the end of November, when Paris had turned damp and raw, June decided to return to America. She managed to bend him to her will once again. Nin had given Miller money for a trip to London, mostly so that he could escape June. Just before his departure, thirsting like some psychic succubus, June appeared and provoked a melodramatic final encounter during the course of which she persuaded Miller to give her all his money, which had already been changed to English currency. Having established her superiority as a con artist, June took the money and left him a note scribbled on toilet paper asking for a divorce. Insisting that Miller follow through on his projected trip to England, Perlès got an advance on his salary and Miller took the boat train for London, only to be rudely turned back by British customs as a potential vagrant.

Free finally of June, he told Emil Schnellock that emotionally he had been enslaved and mercilessly bound. The result was a crippling wound that would never heal. If Miller couldn't understand the tidal ebb and flow of his responses to June, Nin was able to offer some insight. She had finished her analysis with Allendy and begun regular sessions with Otto Rank, a disciple of Freud's who specialized in the sensitivities of the artist and believed in the redeeming and therapeutic capacities of art. Soon Miller and Nin were reading Rank's *Art and Artist* and discussing his theories whenever they met. Rank proposed that neurosis could become a successful catalyst for art if the artist squarely confronted and examined it. The ideal arena was the world of dreams, and Miller began to keep a dream notebook. Interpreting one of the dreams, Nin speculated that Miller's attitude to women had been largely formed by the duality with which he regarded his mother, that while he was able to blindly worship women, he always suspected that they were capable of treacherous cruelty. Based on nothing more than his dream, Nin's insight may seem facile. But she was remarkably attuned to Miller, and she was aware of his seesaw relationship with June, his painful and unresolved emotional bond.

Miller saw Nin several times a week, more often when Hugo was away, and she continued to help him with money. He had resumed his work on *Cancer*, revising it and trying to imagine a powerful conclusion. Kahane had suggested that in order to achieve some degree of literary respectability, given the incendiary sexual nature of *Cancer*, Miller should write an essay on D. H. Lawrence, which he would publish before *Cancer*. Miller spent much of 1922 floundering in what he called the "genital banquet" of Lawrence's world, compiling a mass of notes while frequently shifting his own point of view, from negation to complete devotion. Lawrence was entirely a man of ideas, Miller later told George Wickes, who interviewed him for *The Paris Review*, and what Lawrence wrote depended on those ideas. Certain of these ideas, especially on the struggle for communion between the sexes, influenced Miller. Though Miller wrestled with his Lawrence project, it never really cohered, and only served to distract him from more important work. Immersed in Lawrence, he told Emil that he was planning separate essays on Joyce and Proust. Like some possessed version of Benjamin Franklin and Horatio Alger, he had work schedules and charts covering the walls of his room, and he had begun two other projects, *Black Spring,* his episodic autobiographical sketches, and *Tropic of Capricorn,* the novel about his Brooklyn childhood, the Western Union experience and June.

The Villa Seurat

By the beginning of 1934, with *Cancer* completed after going through four different versions, Miller felt radiant with a sense of inner content and accomplishment. He wrote Emil that some raging part of his earlier self, the clowning sentimental part of him that had been so tormented by June, had died. He sensed that he was ranting less in his writing, partly as a result of his study of Lawrence, partly because he was reading Chinese philosophy. Matters in the outside world were not quite so peaceful, however. The franc was fluctuating erratically and France was caught in the full force of economic depression. There were riots on the streets of Paris, armed conflicts between militant communists and fascists.

The political instability caused Kahane to hedge on his decision to publish *Cancer,* claiming that he needed help with printing costs. Nin raised the money Kahane sought, mostly from her unsuspecting husband and Otto Rank, and so subsidized the most incendiary fiction written by an American in our time. The book appeared in the fall and Miller moved out of Perlès's place into an apartment in the Villa Seurat that had been vacated by the mad French writer, Antonin Artaud. Miller heard that June had obtained a Mexican divorce, and he began to press Anaïs about marriage. She was still apprehensive: because of June, she feared Miller would always see women as destroyers. Nin understood that the affair had served as a release for the poisons in her marriage, but she also felt that Miller was incapable of sustaining any relationship; his obsessiveness with his own writing precluded genuine commitment. Miller had also tried quite consciously to subordinate the romantic impulses of his own early fiction. As an extension of this Miller believed that the artist had to conquer the romantic impulses in his own life. In the Rabelaisian moments of *Cancer* and in frank accounts of his relations with other women, particularly prostitutes, he had revealed to Nin a gritty, rough crudity that had both attracted and repelled her.

More important than any of these reasons, however, was that Nin had become pregnant without knowing whether the child she carried had been fathered by Miller or her husband. When it was delivered stillborn, she was shocked and decided she had to change her life. Her writing had not brought her any success or recognition, and she realized she needed a way to support herself if she wanted to be independent. She had had considerable experience with psychoanalysis and thought she could help others with Rank's assistance. Just at this time, in the winter of 1934–35, Rank had decided to move his psychoanalytic practice to New York. His writing had brought him some renown, but there were too few French patients and they were not willing to pay as much as Americans would. Nin followed Rank to New York and soon began seeing patients recommended by him.

Miller had received letters of praise for *Tropic of Cancer* from Ezra Pound and T. S. Eliot, but his novel had not made any great impression on the world. He had completed *Black Spring*, but was having difficulty with *Tropic of Capricorn*, feeling he needed to revisit the streets of his childhood in Brooklyn. He also missed Nin.

He arrived in New York early in the spring of 1935, and soon he was seeing four patients a day referred by Nin. His only qualification was that he was a consummate conversationalist with a large reservoir of sympathy. At first, psychoanalysis seemed like the answer to his perennial inability to earn a living, but the process of citing homilies from the transcendentalists or the Buddhists to assuage the tensions of his patients disgusted him. He knew the temporary relief he was able to provide was the ultimate confidence game, but his intuition warned him it would not work, that his patients would depend on a process which in itself could offer no real cure.

Much of his disillusionment had to do with Nin. He had followed her to America on a romantic premise she no longer shared. For her, the energy of their affair had dissipated. "We don't see things as they are," she wrote in her diary, "we see them as we are." Miller's disappointment was more profound than Nin's, and the denial of his romantic urges had caused him to show her a rancorous, bitter edge. Nin still needed the security afforded by Hugo and the freedom to enjoy illicit adventures. Ultimately, she was more interested in middle-class comforts than in a vicarious bohemianism. Her real signature was in the stories she was writing, which were composed with a precious and often stilted quality, as if they had been translated awkwardly from another language. Gothic, obscure, enigmatic, introverted and excessively prismatic, with less action than mood, these tales often fail to communicate. Highly contrived, self-consciously striving for "art," Nin's stories are entirely different from Miller's work, so different, in fact, that one wonders how they remained spiritually compatible for so long.

By May, Nin decided to return to Paris to be with Hugo, and Miller realized that she would never leave her husband. This shattered Miller's hopes and left him unsure of where he wanted to live, and how. The city had changed and many of the locations he had wanted to visit for *Capricorn* had already been demolished and rebuilt. He was too hurt to continue working on *Capricorn* anyway, and none of the publishing contacts he tried to make were interested in publication of *Cancer*.

As an expatriate in Paris, even as an unpublished writer, he had shared in a literary community which seemed impossible in New York. The literary scene was extremely politicized by writers advocating social reform from either the left or the right. Miller's more anarchistic voice, which denied the value of the system altogether, struck a discordant note. He met a few other writers—James T. Farrell, Nathanael West and William Saroyan—but, other than Saroyan, they seemed too caught up in their own interests for genuine communication. He was earning some money as an analyst, but was spending it as quickly as he earned it. At the end of the summer he had just enough for a return ticket to Paris.

Back in his apartment in the Villa Seurat by the end of October of 1935, Miller began a sustained letter-writing campaign in the hope of gaining the recognition he felt he deserved because of *Cancer*. He also wrote two extremely long letters on behalf of Alfred Perlès, whom he considered his first real benefactor in Paris. He had already described Perlès's writing in a letter to Emil in ways that served to describe some of his own imaginative flights: "He blows gently on the object and it floats, it breathes, assumes infinitudes of form. I think of soap bubbles when they are still glued to the pipe bowl, when they are refracted, bent, when they quiver and succeed almost in breaking away, when they become elongated and the colors inside change violently and all that is mirrored dances in a freakish deformity so outrageously pleasing to the senses."

Nin's cousin Edouardo and Fraenkel decided to pay the printing costs of Miller's extended pieces on Perlès, *What Are You Going to Do About Alf?* and *Aller Retour New York,* and published them in pamphlet form. Miller had also initiated a series of epistolary exchanges with Fraenkel, which began as critical discussions of Shakespeare's *Hamlet* but quickly digressed into discussions of their own histories and ideas, a correspondence that would later emerge as the *Hamlet* letters. Miller had also received a letter from a Harvard undergraduate named James Laughlin requesting permission to reprint part of *Aller Retour New York* in the *Harvard Advocate*—which the Boston police subsequently seized and destroyed. Laughlin would become a crucial American connection for Miller, publishing most of his nonfiction at New Directions, the publishing firm Laughlin would begin just before the war.

During the Villa Seurat period, Miller worked on *Tropic of Capricorn*. He realized that he had to abandon the realistic approach of his earlier attempts to depict June, which had been a vain effort to subdue June in print as he never had in life. Inspired by the flat declaration of castration in Abelard's *Historia calamitatum*, Miller was able to detach himself from the memory of the actual June, aware that he had ceased to love her and he could no longer even relate to the concept of love. A spiritual and psychological automaton, Miller's hero in *Capricorn* observed the absurd lunacies of the world from his perch in Western Union, roused only to feel life through brazenly unromantic sexual ecstasy. Full of bitter burlesque and angry parody, applied to the hero's sexual excess as well as to the foibles of his world, *Capricorn* was completed in 1938. It gives us the past of Miller's buccaneering persona, his American origins and his revolt against middle-class conditioning. Along with *Cancer* and *Black Spring,* it would form the most powerful part of his work.

At the Villa Seurat, Miller had become the nucleus of a circle of mostly unknown artists, among them Hans Reichel, who painted miniatures and who, twice a week, gave lessons to Nin's husband. During these lessons, Nin would visit Miller, who lived across the street, primarily to discuss what they had been writing. She had purchased a houseboat on the Seine, which she used as a private retreat for her writing, and the members of Miller's circle occasionally met there to dine, drink and converse.

Another member of the circle was a young American named David Edgar, who intended to paint but never did. He had some inherited money and would often discuss Hindu or Zen philosophy with Miller, who was entertained by a quality of comic helplessness in Edgar. Betty Ryan, a painter and an heiress who lived on the floor just below Miller, often threw parties for the Villa Seurat group. Miller thought he was in love with Betty Ryan, but so did Perlès and several other members of the group. Apparently she encouraged them all.

One person who influenced Miller among the Villa Seurat circle was an astrologer named Conrad Moricand, an impoverished dandy whose wealthy Swiss family had lost their money in the Depression. With Moricand, Miller became fascinated by astrological interpretation as one way to deny the supposedly rational system that had brought the world once again to the brink of disaster.

George Orwell was an early visitor to Villa Seurat, and he would write an important essay praising Miller, calling him a remarkable writer, "the only imaginative prose writer of the slightest value" to have published in English in recent years. Skeptical, disillusioned, Orwell saw everything in political terms, and tried to enlist Miller's support for the Republican cause in the Spanish Civil War. All Miller could give him was an old corduroy jacket. Miller had no faith that organized political action would stem a crisis that he sensed was much more far-reaching than the civil war in Spain. Two French novelists, Raymond Queneau and Blaise Cendrars, became engaged members of the Villa Seurat circle, and Cendrars also wrote in praise of *Cancer.*

Another novelist who would join Miller's circle and become an acolyte was Lawrence Durrell. Raised in India, twenty-five, boyish and blond, he had written a slick, commercially successful novel under a pseudonym, and *The Black Book,* a more serious novel than Obelisk would print. Durrell had been living in Greece and talked constantly about his experiences there, intriguing Miller with his tales of Mediterranean freedom.

Big Sur

On Bastille Day, 1939, as Europe was bracing for war, Miller left France by boat for Corfu in Greece, where he planned to visit Durrell. After spending a decade in France, he was forty-seven years old and all he had to show for it was an underground reputation.

In Greece, Miller was overwhelmed by the warmth he felt, both climatically and among the inhabitants, and fascinated by the ruins he visited, which set him to thinking about the origin of things and the autochthonous gods. Durrell introduced Miller to the translator, novelist and editor Katsimbalis, whose ebullient spirits and gargantuan appetite for words made him a sort of Greek reflection of Miller.

Intoxicated by Greece, Miller was also subdued by the news of Axis military advances. At the end of 1939, when Americans were advised to leave Greece, Miller sailed home. In New York he visited his parents, who were old and ailing, especially his father, who was dying of cancer. He saw Nin as being unhappy about the distance that had developed between them because of her decision not to leave her husband. They still had their common interest in writing, though Nin was discouraged by her lack of acceptance or success. When a collector of erotica asked Miller to write conventional pornography for a dollar a page, Miller tried because he needed money but found that he could not do it. He asked Nin to try, and she was able to please the collector.

Miller had begun writing his book about Greece and several shorter pieces, "The World of Sex" and "Quiet Days in Clichy." With his small income from Obelisk Press cut off by the war, he was as usual practically destitute and dependent on the assistance of friends like Nin and Caresse Crosby, a wealthy American who had published books in Paris. Miller's idea was to write a travel book about America which he would call *The Air-Conditioned Nightmare,* and he secured a modest advance from Doubleday Doran. He spent 1941 touring the country in an old Buick he bought for a hundred dollars, living in cheap motels and eating in diners. The essays he wrote about revisiting a more technological America lacked the joy of discovery of his book about Greece and the intensity, the vividness and density of his *Tropic* novels.

He had turned fifty and did not know where he wanted to live or how to sustain himself. In his travels in America he had been most impressed by California; he had met John Steinbeck and Aldous Huxley, and both novelists had encouraged him to settle there. When two young painters invited him to share their cottage in Los Angeles, he accepted, writing to his friend Emil that in California he would "ventilate" his soul. Living with painters inspired him to begin painting again himself, some of which he was able to sell. He received small amounts of money from various friends and wrote many letters asking for more, including letters to the *New Republic* publicly appealing for donations and another to Frieda Lawrence in Taos, who responded, noting Miller's affinity with Lawrence.

Another painter, Jean Varda, showed Miller the area around Big

Sur, north of Los Angeles, and the dramatic coast with its soaring cliffs and panoramic views of the Pacific. Big Sur was still undeveloped; there was no electricity, no telephone lines, only an untouched paradise of huge redwood, oak and eucalyptus trees. Miller was offered a cabin on Partington Ridge and lived there very minimally, collecting wood for cooking and warmth during the periods of dense coastal fog, hauling supplies on a rickety cart from the grocery depot two miles down the hill.

His intention had been to work on *The Rosy Crucifixion,* the trilogy he had elected to write to expand the story of June that he had begun in *Capricorn,* but his creative flow had halted, and he no longer had the discipline to sit at his desk for hours on end accumulating words. Part of the problem may have been that Miller was repeating material that he had already used in the most forceful manner imaginable, and the repetition made the spontaneity and joyous recklessness of his style difficult to sustain. Separated from Nin and Paris, he had lost the antinomian energy that had animated his best writing, an energy that he would never regain. Instead, he would work for years on the various sections of *The Rosy Crucifixion—Sexus, Nexus* and *Plexus*—but they would be flat and mostly uninspired. He would also write a series of essays that Laughlin would publish under such intriguing titles as *Stand Still Like the Hummingbird* and *Remember to Remember,* but the quality of his thought seemed homiletic, preachy, a package of correct sentiments presented without much substance.

Miller had fallen in love a few times since his return to America but none of the relationships lasted until he met Janine Lepska, a twenty-year-old Polish refugee who was studying philosophy. He had been visiting his ailing mother in Brooklyn when he met her—attracted by a Slavic quality that he later said reminded him of June—and he saw her again at Yale, where she had begun graduate studies and he had been invited to show his watercolors.

Despite an enormous difference in ages—more than thirty years—Lepska agreed to marry Miller, perhaps as a way of escaping graduate school. From the start there were temperamental differences that separated them. Lepska insisted on a domestic order which she used as a control device to make herself feel secure. Miller rented an even more austere cabin in Big Sur, which once had been inhabited by a convict and had only a wood stove for cooking. Lepska claimed she stressed routine and regularity to free Miller for his writing—she discouraged his friends from visiting whenever they felt like it, and in many petty matters reminded Miller of his own mother's tyranny. But Miller had become much less interested in his writing and welcomed interruptions, responsive to the more casual and carefree Californian manner. When Lepska gave birth to a daughter and then a son, there was constant conflict over how they should be raised. Lepska was in complete disagreement with Miller's Rousseauistic notions of freedom and spontaneity.

Problems with Lepska were compounded by a lack of regular income, though the outlook was improving for Miller because of the phenomenal success of his books in France. There had been a literary row, his books had been castigated as pornographic, and the royalties mounted. Unfortunately for Miller, this money could not easily be taken out of France, but he managed to accumulate enough of it to purchase a house in Big Sur. Just when matters with Lepska seemed to be improving or at least becoming tolerable, Miller allowed his old friend, the astrologer Conrad Moricand, to visit. Moricand behaved like a caricature of the French, criticizing everything and complaining constantly. Instead of leaving, he declared himself dependent on Miller. The pressures of what had become so unwelcome a visitor were an added strain on Miller's marriage. In the summer of 1951, Lepska fell in love with a biophysicist and left Miller. He was now sixty. His marriage to Lepska had lasted seven years, as long as his marriage to June.

Only a few months after the dissolution of his marriage, Miller received a letter of admiration from another young woman, Eve McClure. Twenty-eight, an aspiring actress, beautiful and graciously accommodating, McClure was drawn to older men and soon agreed to marry Miller. They lived together for eight years in Big Sur, a period during which Miller was distracted by an increasing flow of visitors and correspondence, both of which Eve facilitated. Eve helped in other ways as well. When Miller's mother was dying, she accepted the responsibility of nursing her during her final three months (while Miller did his evasive best to avoid his mother), and she also cared for Lepska's children whenever they came, for months on end, to visit their father. While Eve was able to give generously of herself, she resented increasingly having the roles of caretaker and secretary. When she realized that Miller was seeing other women, she turned to alcohol, which rendered her incapable and depressed. In 1960, amicably, they agreed to a divorce.

At this time Miller's situation in the publishing world was about to change. Barney Rosset had published D. H. Lawrence's *Lady Chatterley's Lover* at his Grove Press and won the legal contests that ensued. Rosset wanted to publish the *Tropic* novels and was willing to assume the costs of any consequent legal action. In fact, there would be over sixty local legal contentions, with cases going to five state supreme courts and the United States Supreme Court. At first Miller had balked, happy with his reputation as an outlaw author whose novels were smuggled into the country by returning soldiers. He agreed only when he realized that unlicensed "pirated" editions of his work were beginning to appear. When the Grove Press edition was published in 1961, it broke all records for fiction in America, selling over 100,000 hardcover copies in the first month of publication, and then more than a million paperbacks.

Though the success of the book brought Miller money, it seemed to pass through his hands as soon as it arrived. He had seen June in New York. She had been begging him for assistance for years, and he had tried to help her with small amounts. She had barely supported herself as a social worker in Queens. Now she was emaciated, her teeth were gone, she was living in a furnished room and old beyond her years, and he wanted to help her. There was also his sister, whom he had moved to a nursing home in Los Angeles after his mother's death, as she could not care for herself. Furthermore, there were huge tax bills, various alimony and child-support payments, and requests from friends who needed help.

Despite his increasing age and its consequent debilities, Miller was still intent on pursuing women. At the age of seventy-five, he met a twenty-seven-year-old Japanese jazz singer who specialized in sentimental love songs. He courted her for a year, and she only relented when American immigration authorities informed her that she had to leave. The marriage lasted for two years, with Miller frequently jealous, since her work, like June's, kept her in clubs till dawn. If Miller had never been really able to communicate with his Japanese wife because of differences in age and language, he was still an undeterred romantic, acting as if only women could be the fuel for his fires.

At the age of eighty-five, despite circulatory problems and a stroke that had left him blind in one eye and partially paralyzed, he was courting another woman, a dancer and bit-part film actress named Brenda Venus. Though this courtship did not result in marriage, and though it was primarily epistolary, Miller did conduct it with the verve and exuberance of a man half his age. At one point Miller proposed that he and Brenda exchange a blood vow. She pricked her wrist with a penknife but when Miller used the knife on his wrist he cut too deeply and the blood would not stop flowing. He found the incident extremely romantic, and the little cameo suggests all the zeal and enthusiasm that is so characteristically Miller's. The world seemed mad for sex, he wrote Brenda, though it had forgotten love. It was a world that his *Tropic* novels had helped to envisage, if not create.

At the end, frail, shuffling, painting a watercolor or playing Ping-Pong, Miller was still thinking about those whom he had loved excessively, insufficiently or inadequately, or in a delusion of his own making. Brenda Venus was only the latest instance in a history of misplaced loves, at a historical moment when romantic love itself seemed suspect, foolish, insincere. His critics would accuse him of the heresy of self-love, seeing his fictions as enormous gratifications of his own ego. Miller had an answer for such critics, however. Would any man who loved himself present himself so monstrously? Near the end of *Cancer* he had declared himself a "plenipotentiary from the realm of free spirits," here primarily to create fever and ferment. When he died in 1980 he had lived practically through the twentieth century, almost ninety years. His essential message was that life itself, not God or any possible afterlife, is the only miracle, and in a despairing age this may seem like the ultimate romantic expression.

A Brutal Romantic

Clear, unaffected, always natural as a storyteller in the *Tropics*, Miller is a romantic conundrum. He insisted that the modern writer needed to transcend the romantic elements in his life, and to accomplish such an end he resorted to the savage voice of the parodist, the vision of the caricaturist. At turns both unbelievably coarse and exquisitely tender, bilious one moment and lyrical the next in his fiction, he could walk out of the only responsible job he had ever held, his four-year stint at Western Union, and disappear into the blue without giving notice or telling anyone that he was leaving, or he could connive a liaison with his first wife's mother. Even in marriage, he did not conform to any established pattern. Though they lived their lives unconventionally, D. H. and Frieda Lawrence and Scott and Zelda Fitzgerald followed the conventional hierarchical shape of most marriages of their day, in which the wife was expected to be, and was, the secondary figure. June and Miller reversed the pyramid. The configuration of Lawrence's and Fitzgerald's writing was present before they met the women who became their subject matter, who provided models for the realization of their work. Miller had to discover his form and language as he went along, he had to dig down into himself and his life to find them. June was more than his subject matter; she was a powerful tool in the process by which he quarried the distinctive building stones of his genius.

Unlike Lawrence or Fitzgerald, he was unable to romanticize sex in his fiction; he could not fog it with euphemistic evasions or cooing sentiments. For sex he needed the microscope, and like a tailor threading a very fine needle, he rendered it more meticulously than anyone had before. Like Lawrence, he was a liberationist—and the romantic ambition is freedom from conditioning and social control—but what Lawrence saw as theoretical was for Miller a matter of practical accommodation. Orwell liked him because Miller was plebeian to his core; Miller could never have played Lord Byron, though he would always take the opportunity to toy with Don's Juan's affectations. If his encounters with his legion of adulteresses and prostitutes seem a bit too sordid for romance—with Miller acting the transcendental fool waving his phallic wand more for the sake of a locker-room laugh than sensation—then he seems by contrast masochistically romantic when he describes June, the angel-whore tormentor for whom he will endure any defilement, dishonor, repudiation. For Miller, June's allure is a function of the power women have to attract men—innate, immutable, instinctual. Though he knows her soul is so thin he could turn it inside out like his sleeve, he worships her into his ultimate subject.

Miller is another Nietzschean romantic. As his pal Fraenkel observed, his effectiveness is in direct proportion to his excess, his exaggeration, his irresponsibility. His first priority, as he declares so emphatically in *Tropic of Cancer,* is the overthrowing of all existing values. Unlike Nietzsche, Miller refuses to despair over the value vacuum that so nihilistic an imperative causes. Instead, he veers madly in a Dionysian direction, choosing the path of rejoicing, of revel, even in the face of annihilation. In the tradition of the vagabond artist, he inhabits Baudelaire's "Fleurs du mal," because on the depraved, indifferent street he has nothing material to lose.

For Miller, the artist exists merely as a medium of consciousness and should never be admired as an idol. Lawrence and Fitzgerald had more inflated and elitist expectations of where the artist should stand. As seer, Lawrence rose above his audience; as dissecting surgeon, Fitzgerald anatomized the Jazz Age but could not separate himself from his need to be its brightest and most celestial body. Miller proposed no such illusions. He was a demotic romantic, one of Whitman's rowdies, an egalitarian lounging in your doorway with a swagger in his posture, a leer on his lips and a rasping sound in his voice.

If Lawrence and Fitzgerald could still believe in heroes, Miller could not: his world was all hard-boiled absurdity. Compared to Lawrence, Miller looks like a novelist without compassion, a quality that can make his moments of passion seem mechanical, more the willed result of his rhetoric than of his imagination. And unlike Fitzgerald, Miller is a messy novelist, haphazard, disparaging artistic means and contrivances. Anaïs Nin, with all her linguistic veils, is far more conventionally romantic and coy, and like Poe, shuns the real because it is boring. Miller finds nothing boring, not even repetitive sex. His brazen descriptions separate him from most romantics, who prefer subtle hints and omissions. But Miller may be the first writer to have accepted at face value the romantic credo on language formulated by Wordsworth and Coleridge in their preface to the *Lyrical Ballads:* to use the actual language of ordinary men. The implications of avoiding a precious or inflated style and speaking directly, without the need for a literary super-ego, can indeed make Miller seem threatening. No wonder his honesty still makes us uncomfortable.

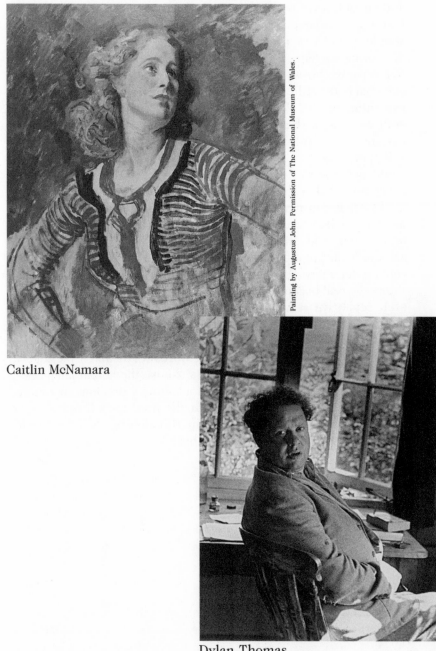

Painting by Augustus John. Permission of The National Museum of Wales.

Caitlin McNamara

Dylan Thomas

✿ 5 ✿

Dylan and Caitlin

I hold a beast, an angel and a madman in me, and my inquiry
is as to their working, and my problem is their subjugation
and victory, downthrow and upheaval, and my effort is their
self-expression.

From a letter to Henry Treece

Oh, let me midlife mourn by the shrined
   And druid herons' vows
The voyage to ruin I must run,
   Dawn ships clouted aground,
Yet, though I cry with tumbledown tongue,
   Count my blessings aloud:
               From "Poem on His Birthday"

DYLAN THOMAS was the rhapsodic poet of this century, the great lyrical voice of his time. The lyric poet relies more on the ability to summon feeling than intellect, and Thomas did this essentially through the sound of his own voice. His poems were heated, violently introspective, charged with dark melancholy and a morbid self-awareness. Declamatory, especially percussive, full of clangorous dissonance, the poems used a twisting, baroque language to create swirling energies.

In an age when poetry was largely dominated by the antiromantic sensibilities of T. S. Eliot, Thomas seemed like a throwback to a more ancient, romantic oral tradition. With his gregariousness, his reckless drinking, his scandalous overtures to women, he became the image for our time of the Dionysian self-destructive bard, the dying genius who consumes himself in the flame of his art.

199

He projected a powerful kind of desperate, romantic enthusiasm. His language was brilliantly rich and reverberant, lavish at times to the point of gaudiness. The poet Robert Graves claimed that Thomas was drunk with melody, implying that he was less concerned with the sense of his words than with their sheer sensual impact. He read his poems with immense flourish and range, with a boastful truculence that sometimes approached hysteria, yet in other moments seemed infinitely gentle and composed. It was a voice that sounded incantatory, vehement, ominous and forebodingly apocalyptic, while still capable of finding bursts of exuberant joy. The asthmatic Welshman who became the most compelling and famous reader of poetry in this century delivered his poems in a booming, breathless, throaty voice which women claimed had an aphrodisiacal appeal. In poems full of grand elation and enormous anguish, he enthralled large audiences, particularly in America in the early 1950s, during the final years of his brief life.

Before he died of what his doctors termed a "severe alcoholic insult to the brain," Thomas made three epic tours of the United States, where he declaimed his poems to overflowing crowds. There are still survivors of those audiences who remember Thomas's impassioned readings as the literary high-water mark of their lives. The critic Elizabeth Hardwick observed, in an essay published in the *Partisan Review*, that Thomas was *adored* in America, not just admired. That adoration was in large part a response to the extent to which Thomas, more than any other poet of his time, fit the image of the *poète maudit*, doomed and damned, "undeniably suffering and living in the extremest reaches of experience," Hardwick wrote.

This reaching for the extreme was not lived only at his own expense. As a very young poet with a few books already published, Thomas met and married Caitlin Macnamara, a hot-tempered, outspoken Irishwoman who was utterly indifferent to the opinions of others. They had children and lived together on the seacoast of Wales, mostly in impoverished conditions, for seventeen years. An unusually difficult and perplexing man, Thomas was cared for by his wife but also berated by her. Their life together was like "raw, red bleeding meat," she once wrote in a characterizing image almost as powerful as those in his poems: but when his life ended so prematurely in America, she tried to commit suicide. She had resented his American trips, perhaps with a premonition of the danger of flattery for an artist like Thomas from what she called the "multitudinous, scavenging spawn" of America.

Frieda Lawrence, Zelda Fitzgerald and June Miller were centralizing figures in their husbands' work. Caitlin Thomas is harder to fit into that pattern. Her presence doesn't force itself on the reader's consciousness: it is possible to read the content of Dylan Thomas's writing without a cross-reference to her or awareness of any direct linkage between Thomas's wife and his work. Instead, Thomas's life with Caitlin represents a tormented paradigm of the romantic agony, a contest of accelerating costs and demands. On a plane of surpassing intensities of hostility, their life together depended on psychic as well as physical laceration and pain. Yet, vulnerable as he was to the myth of the womanizing poet and to the adoration he elicited from women in their fervent response to his easy and self-defeating charm, he always turned again, like a child reclaiming his nurturer, to Caitlin.

A number of critics suspected Thomas of simply celebrating the instinctive life or narcissistically hurling himself back into childhood. Together, Thomas and Caitlin were all instinct, unprotected by the accommodations and civilities that shelter most relationships. Their marriage was as jagged and unsparing as the cliffs of Wales he had grown up beside, a sustaining reminder of the hard realities of his formative outer and inner landscape. In that odd way, the marriage both stimulated and nurtured him.

The Love Swoon

They met in the spring of 1936 in a London Soho pub, an appropriate enough location for a man who would become one of the most intemperate drinkers of his generation. They were both in the full flush of youth: he was only twenty-two, she was a year older. It was in one sense an inconspicuous occasion, since Thomas usually spent his days drinking beer after beer while telling stories to his friends. On that afternoon he had lined up ten steins on the bar in front of him, imbibing from each in its turn. Caitlin Macnamara, blond, blue-eyed, with a glowing complexion, was wearing a white, flowered dress she had borrowed from her older sister. She said it made her feel enticing. Thomas wore his usual worn tweed jacket and baggy corduroy trousers. With his large, soft, caramel-colored eyes, full lips, and curly dark gold hair, he looked cherubic, almost effeminate. What she remembered about him first was a sense of his vulnerability despite the barrage of his words—a small man, only five feet and a few inches high—her height—tiny and light, she remarked, with the most delicate hands.

At the time they were both perfunctorily occupied with other lovers—Dylan with a woman whose bed he occasionally shared when he was stranded in London; Caitlin with a much older man, the painter Augustus John, who had already described Dylan to Caitlin as a "bright young spark." Caitlin thought of herself as a dancer and she had modeled for John, who assumed as a matter of course that his models would become his mistresses. His portrait of Caitlin depicts a fine-featured beauty who seems to be thrusting forward with vitality, especially open, as sensitive as she is strong.

Dylan was discoursing, engrossed in his conversation, "an endless jabber," as she put it, in the middle of a swarm of other poets and painters whom he was entertaining with a tale that seemed to have no end. She sat on an adjacent stool. Suddenly, without interrupting the flow of his talk, he leaned over low and placed his head in her lap, cradling it between her legs. It was a sort of swoon, an obeisance, but at the same time it was a territorial invasion, a violation of her most intimate center. Unoffended, Caitlin accepted the gesture as a natural inclination, an expression of the spontaneity artists sometimes feel. Uninsulted, unthreatened, she remembered that the movement filled her with a deep maternal feeling, a special closeness that gratified her and made her happy. Bent over in this extraordinary position, looking up at Caitlin's face, the young poet told her that he loved her. It was the first time she had heard such a declaration, and she heard it repeated while he continued to talk with his friends, who seemed disinclined to notice anything unusual.

To escape the crowd, they found another pub where they could talk and drink alone. Caitlin knew of a fancy restaurant in the vicinity, the Eiffel Tower, that had private bedrooms on its top floor for secret liaisons. One of Augustus John's daughters occasionally booked a room there and charged it to her father, and Caitlin proposed that they do the same. Thomas agreed immediately, as though it were the natural next step for them to take, without surprise or shock. The small larceny of charging expenses to Augustus John seemed appropriate to Thomas, who initially had resented the older painter's proprietary manner. For its sheer spontaneity and impulsive rush toward sex, the scene could have been invented by Henry Miller, who also would have applauded the petty fleecing of John.

A man can tell a woman he has just met that he likes her, even that he loves her; she accepts it as part of the assertiveness of the male, though she may disbelieve him, may accept whatever he says as part of his "line," the story he needs to spin to seduce her. Thomas's declaration to Caitlin that he loved her, his explicit avowal of love at first sight, could have been taken as a staking of a sexual claim, the kind of rutting artists are popularly believed to indulge in while they rouse their spirits. But such a role was hardly Dylan's—though his own legend would ironically superimpose it on him during his last years.

The two lovers spent four nights in the Eiffel Tower, but they did more talking and drinking than caressing or cavorting. The episode at the Eiffel Tower, less sexually exploratory than comradely, defines aspects of the relationship between Thomas and Caitlin. Her guileless consent to his gesture of putting his head in her lap indicates that surely some connection had been established between them that did not need language. They had intuitively accepted that connection, and once it had come into existence, neither of them could ever unjoin it.

The Trickster Poet

Dylan Thomas's initial meeting with Caitlin Macnamara reveals a man with the spontaneously fluid imagination of the actor, a man who could play for the grandstand, who realized the value of the bold, grand gesture, a man who could bend his sensibility to fit the circumstances just as he bent his body into Caitlin's waiting lap. As a Welshman and a poet, Thomas took quite naturally to a variety of roles. Subordinated by the English for a thousand years, the Welsh take pride in their cunning evasiveness, their ability to mask themselves in enigmatic mystery and picturesque effrontery. Such qualities suit the notion of the poet as the thespian who both shapes and directs his own part and who, like Dylan Thomas, thrives on indirection, on elliptical commentary while grieving for his place in the general order of things.

Was it in accord with some deep intuition that Thomas understood at an early age that poetry would become the chief vehicle for creating his identity, that poetry would trumpet his rage at the transience of life? He said that he began to write poetry because he fell in love with words, with what he called their colors, and their sheer, sensuous sound. When he was twelve years old, he sent a poem called "His Requiem" to a local newspaper, which published it.

The title and the sentiments of the poem were entirely consonant with Dylan's later work and its preoccupation with death, but the problem was that this poem was not Dylan Thomas's at all; he had found it in an old magazine and simply appropriated it as his own. While borrowing among poets is not uncommon—T. S. Eliot both apologized for it and made an aesthetic principle of it—outright plagiarism is another matter. What had made Thomas do it—boyish high jinks, a tropism toward theatrical self-aggrandizement or impatience to acquire the reputation of a poet? He had been writing poems from the age of nine, and with his friend Daniel Jones would invent intricate word games, fabricate radio broadcasts and write the alternating lines of poems they composed jointly.

His chief model was familial: a nineteenth-century granduncle had been a poet. The granduncle, Gwilym Marles Thomas, was the most notable figure in the Thomas family myth—a minister and a schoolmaster who was known more for his advocacy of the rights of small tenant farmers, sheep-herders in a hilly region of South Wales, than for his poems. He had taken as his middle name the name of a neighboring river, the Marlais. Dylan Thomas was given the name as well as a sign of continuity.

His father was a more problematic influence, a man who had wanted to write but instead became a small-town schoolmaster. Honorably, he had married Florence Williams when he believed he had gotten her pregnant, and he found himself with a vivaciously sunny woman, talkative, enthusiastic, basically very sweet in disposition, but someone with whom he was intellectually incompatible. Where she was sweet, he was sour. At the Swansea Grammar School, D. J. Thomas was known as the teacher with the caustic tongue. His subject was English literature, which he loved and idealized, one of those teachers who could never understand why his students did not similarly appreciate what he considered great writing. He was particularly effective when reading aloud, able through the power of his voice to transfix his students, an ability he may have passed on to his son. Withdrawn, acidulous, pessimistic, a heavy drinker, an outspoken atheist who was reading

D. H. Lawrence when Dylan was a boy, D. J. Thomas was surely one of the more despondent and brooding inhabitants of Swansea.

The name Thomas is common in Wales, and although D. J. was an exceedingly proud man, actually despising his students, his was an ordinary lineage, the same toiling-class origins as D. H. Lawrence's. His father, like his wife's father, worked for the railroad—an indication of a yeoman small-farmer class shifting from the stony hills to the towns. When Florence Williams met D. J. Thomas, she was working as a seamstress in a drapery store. Her parents had been first cousins, a marriage practice that was accepted in Wales as a way to consolidate family money, though in the Williamses' case the marriage may have been due more to remoteness from the nearest village than family fortune. Later, when Florence had children, each birth was accompanied by a pronounced fear of retardation or insanity. That, too, was part of family legend. Florence's father had been the deacon of his church—Wales was fundamentalist, hell-fearing country—and her religious belief and church attendance were among the factors that alienated her husband.

Sprawling around a horseshoe-curved coast—the "mussel pooled and the heron priested shore," Thomas described it in "Poem to October"—Swansea was a large, hilly town with over one hundred thousand inhabitants at the time of Dylan's birth on October 27, 1914. Nancy Thomas, born eight years before Dylan, was often recruited to care for her brother. Florence Thomas doted on her son, obsessively fearing the possibility of tuberculosis, turning every childhood cold into cause for alarm. Given to theatrics and emotional outbursts, she also had a capacity for exaggeration that proved to be a much more formative influence on her son than his father's arrogant rationalism. Much like D. H. Lawrence's father, D. J. Thomas was fundamentally estranged from his family and from the world he inhabited. But Dylan was still a much-loved child. He spent the first year of his life on a cot in his parents' bedroom where his father would read Shakespeare to him in place of lullaby.

As a child in Swansea, Thomas was surrounded everywhere by the rolling constancy of the sea. The name "Dylan" itself is a Welsh noun signifying the sea (though he claimed in a letter that in the *Mabinogion*, a formative collection of medieval Welsh tales, it stood for the prince of darkness). A boy could wander the beaches of Swansea throwing stones into the sea, listening to some raving evangelical preacher on a soapbox in the sand, watching the tankers and tugs and banana boats, walking the docks and piers of the fishing section with its salted white cottages and retired sea captains. In Wales, after the sea, there is the weather (in a sense, an extension of the sea), which is the wettest in Europe, subject to frequent drizzly rain or mist, an omnipresent dampness amid the dank sweet smells of bracken, peat, mushroom and marsh.

Swansea was undeveloped enough during the years of Dylan's childhood so that he could hear sheep coughing in a field opposite his house, owls hooting in the woods, the calls of gulls, herons and swans. For further distraction there were the slaughterhouse, the gasworks, the blackened monuments, the museum so ancient it looked as if it belonged in a museum itself. Everywhere, but especially in the hills above Swansea, there were mysterious stone formations, reminders of druidical worship and legends of human sacrifice.

The Thomases lived with just enough money to be considered respectable, though Dylan wore hand-me-downs and D. J. had to teach Welsh a subject to which he was indifferent if not hostile, in the evenings to help make ends meet. His son's education was important to him. From the age of seven, Dylan was sent to private school. From the start he was disobedient, a rebellious joker full of fresh retorts, a boy who had swallowed a dictionary as he described himself. Once, urinating on a wall behind the schoolhouse, he claimed he had inscribed "God Save the King" with his own urine, an invisible graffito but shocking to his teachers; another time he was given a fig to taste, and he said it was like eating a woman's sex, hardly what one would expect from an eleven-year-old. At the same age, still in his short pants, he was caught smoking a cigar in a movie theater and seen dressed in his sister's clothing, loitering on a street corner and staring down the passing boys. In one of his stories, "The Peaches," Thomas recounts how he had once cut his knee and showed his mother his bloodied handkerchief, claiming that the blood came from his ear. He was clever, naughty and pampered, an "absolute tartar," according to his sister's best friend.

Thomas's boredom and audacity were part of a deeper rebelliousness and defiance that remained with him all his life and that was expressed in the grand gesture, in rambunctious escapades and in pushing the image of the self-indulgent poet to the limits. His mischievous devilry was in direct contrast to his ability to look angelic, his face framed by his burnished golden curls. Despite his weak chin, a certain slackness about his mouth and eyes that seem hooded, countless photographs capture the face of a cherub, though in later years a bloated and dissipated cherub.

The devilish boy was frail, small-shouldered and thin, asthmatic and anemic, a sickly child with weak hemorrhaging lungs, fragile bones and an ailing liver. As a result, there were a hundred excuses for missing school and instead reading in his father's library, where his real education took place. Sometimes he would spend a few days of recuperation and much of the summertime at Fern Hill, his aunt's ramshackle farm, a square of mud and rubbish and falling stones with a few scratching chickens, where he observed the animals and nature that would figure in his poems.

At thirteen he was registered at Swansea Grammar School, where his father taught. By then he had fallen into the role of an awful student, strolling in or out of classes according to his own timetable, contemptuous of the curriculum and of his teachers. He performed with consistent mediocrity or worse in all subjects except for English literature. He had already begun smoking and drinking seriously, part of a tough image he needed to compensate for his small stature. He would probably have been expelled if not for the protection of his father's position. Like many of the other boys, but even more so, he could be devious, disrespectful, disorderly. He would rattle his desk, hide in the coatroom during algebra, scuffle during prayers, or find himself stuffed upside-down into a wastepaper basket before French class.

Obsessed by his tiny height, he tried cross-country running and did manage to win a one-mile handicapped race when he was twelve, but he was basically too weak for that sort of exertion and so took his refuge in reading: the Bible, Shakespeare and Marlowe, Blake and Keats, Poe and D. H. Lawrence. He read prodigiously, with his eyes "hanging out on stalks" as he "bulldozed" his way through books, tearing into what once he called in a radio talk the "babbling dead like a tank with a memory." He had a few poems published in his school magazine, the uncertain, ungainly efforts of his early years, but by the age of fifteen he was entering his poems in a private notebook, which by the end of his high school year had almost two hundred entries. He wrote laboriously, sometimes managing only two lines in an hour, he told Pamela Hansford Johnson. The poems accumulated, despite or perhaps because of an academic record so deficient that there was no talk or possibility of attending a university, which was a bitter disappointment for his father.

By then he had chosen his course in life—the refractory poet free from the constraints of ordinary expectations and responsibilities. A picture of the disordered romantic "trembling on the verge of disease," as he put it, this chimerical young poet with an ability to reinvent and re-create himself to suit an internal imperative was in process of formulating his own code for concealing the poet behind a disguise of the poetic persona: "No one can deny that the most attractive figures in literature are always those around whom a world of lies and legends has been woven, those half mythical artists whose real characters become cloaked forever under a veil of the bizarre." Thomas did not always distinguish the real character from the veiled one, the poseur from the man. Relentlessly pursuing the image he had created of the doomed, self-destructive poet, he became a victim of his own legend.

A Provincial Rhythm

Although Thomas left school in the summer of 1931, he would continue to live at home. His older sister, Nancy, was at home as well. Elegant, attractive, Nancy was either indifferent to her little brother or hostile, regarding him as a slovenly burden and a source of embarrassment. The responsibility of caring for children who showed no indication of leaving home was a source of continual anxiety for D. J. Thomas. Wales was suffering because of the international depression, factories and mines were shutting down or laying off workers, and though he had the small security of the schoolteacher, the severe economic climate was enough to make him apprehensive and fearful of the expenditure of any extra money.

D. J. was relieved when Dylan found a job, even if it paid very little, at the local newspaper. In one of his radio broadcasts, "Return Journey," Dylan Thomas described himself at this time as a bombastic seventeen-year-old bohemian, an exhibitionist adolescent who was provincial without knowing it, loquacious, ambitious, pretentious and a bit affected—wearing his sister's scarf as a thickly knotted tie. With his perpetually dangling cigarette, his bulging eyes, one broken front tooth and his blubber lips, he posed as a journalistic tough guy on the prowl for a story. What he covered for the *South Wales Daily Post* as a cub reporter—mostly a dreary round of weddings, deaths, concerts, church auctions and sporting

events, some of which he described without bothering to attend—
was too trivial and routine to warrant the pose.

He lasted only fifteen months at his newspaper position, although he continued as a free-lance contributor afterward. Dismissal, he rationalized, meant salvation from mediocrity and freedom
to write the poems he was compiling in his notebooks.

Actually, the years 1933 and 1934 were to become his most
productive period as a poet, and almost half the poems he published in his first two books, as well as some twenty-five stories,
were begun then. Without his newspaper salary, however, he was
once again dependent on his father for spending money, and this
increased family tensions. It was a nervous and quarrelsome family
situation at best, which was exacerbated by Dylan rising at noon,
suffering from a hangover and demanding to be left alone so that he
could work on his poems. The poems, of course, would bring him
no income, and Thomas was not above purloining small sums from
his sister or his mother. He exhibited a reckless disregard for
earning money and had begun a lifetime habit of borrowing from
friends. He had, in fact, set the pattern of his future behavior that
would not change even when he assumed the responsibilities of
marriage and children. In his insistence that Caitlin accommodate
herself to his self-indulgences and to the imperatives of his work, a
source of constant friction between them, he was asserting pre-
rogatives that he had already established in his parental home.

Most often, then and later, his petty borrowing was for the beer
he loved, and which he drank as his father did in defiance of a
tradition of Welsh fundamentalism that preached temperance and
saw beer in particular as the devil's own brew. In "Old Garbo," one
of his stories, he described his fondness for it in the lush splendor of
language by which he could transform the commonplace into a
sensual perception: "...its live, white lather, its brass-bright
depths, its sudden world through the wet-brown walls of the glass,
the tilted rush to the lips and the slow swallowing down to the
lapping belly, the salt on the tongue, the foam at the corners."

On Wednesday evenings, some of his Swansea friends would
assemble to hear his poems or recite theirs in his father's study or
in his bedroom, its walls lined with the cardboard shirt-stiffeners
on which he wrote his stories. Another place for poetry gatherings
was Bert Trick's grocery store. Trick was fifteen years older than
Thomas, a family man with pronounced Marxist notions. Trick's

political sympathies did not find direct expression in Thomas's poetry—in contrast to the expressed political anxieties in the work of W. H. Auden and his circle—but Trick did encourage Thomas's sympathies for the poor and oppressed and his antipathy for the rich and the smug.

Trick had written a poem using the refrain "For Death is not the end," a lachrymose effort that inspired Thomas to write one of his great early poems, "Death Shall Have No Dominion." In place of Trick's sentimentality, Thomas's poem is hardened by a series of paradoxical turns, in the manner of John Donne, as madness becomes sanity, lost love is restored, and all animal and human life experience violent rebirth into nature—"hammer through daisies"—a graphic rendering of an analogy between the human body and the earth.

For Thomas, any idea could be translated into bodily terms, and what he once called his "small bonebound island" often provided images that seemed quite baffling. The field of action in "Death Shall Have No Dominion" is both grand and pathetic, an unequal struggle between humans who must die and vast, implacably consuming forces. The inequality of the contest is somehow ameliorated, balanced almost, by the undaunted defiance of the refrain adapted from the Bible for Thomas's own purposes, "And death shall have no dominion." That pealing affirmation, which occupies seven of the poem's twenty-eight lines, is also reminiscent of Donne, in particular the harrowing, thunderous line "Death be not proud."

It was a Romantic convention, expressed in countless poems by Shelley, Keats and other poets, to summon and embrace illness, sorrow and death. To Thomas, who had spent his childhood as a sickly boy with early premonitions of fatality, death has no such soft appeal. Instead he urges us, in one of his most compelling poems, to "rage, rage against the dying of the light." It is the cry of a man who always lived at risk, at the very edge of death's dominion, and his daring admonition may have been an act of bravado. For a man who railed at death, he gave little thought to how he would live, rejecting all obligations other than his holy devotion to making his poems. In his relationships with women, including his wife, in his destructive spiral of drinking and carousing, in his indifference to earning money, he was heedless of consequences, though he was always somewhat querulously dissatisfied with the circumstances of his life.

Just as Nottingham became unendurable for the young D. H. Lawrence, Wales suddenly seemed to Thomas a narrow, confining and isolated place, where he complained he would have to walk three miles to buy a pack of cigarettes and where the chief subject of conversation was likely to be the proper way to snare a rabbit. Besides what he termed in a letter the "eternal ugliness" of the Welsh, what was most depressing was the squalor of the industrial sectors, festering sores full of diseased miners and vulgar though pretty young women in cheap berets staring into shop windows, all "breast and bottom."

In a letter he entitled "Night and Day: A Provincial Rhythm," he outlined the course of his dissatisfaction. It began with a slow uncertain rising from bed, then perusing the newspaper while smoking a few cigarettes prior to reading in front of a fire till noon. Then down the hill for several pints of beer at the Uplands Hotel, lunch at home and more reading in his room, which smelled of bad tobacco, with his own pastel drawing of a syphilitic Christ and a green-bearded Moses hung on a wall looking like some evil omen. After working on a poem or story, he might walk to the desolate cliffs before tea, and then continue his haphazard reading. The evening was reserved for the pubs—the Marine, the Antelope, the Mermaid—and metaphysical arguments inspired by beer. Finally, home to supper and what he considered the pettiness of his mother, and more reading.

Publication of "Death Shall Have No Dominion" in the *New English Weekly* caused him to look to London as the logical place to further his poetic aspirations, and the fact that his sister had married and was living in a houseboat on the Thames on the southwest edge of London was an additional inducement. In the summer of 1933, he boarded the train to London and began a series of literary visits, to A. R. Orage, who took a story for the *New English Weekly*; to Sir Richard Rees, who accepted a poem for the *Adelphi*; to a phlegmatic, cautious and condescending T. S. Eliot, who as editor of the *Criterion* and an editor at the publishing house of Faber & Faber was in a position to substantially assist any young poet. Eliot, however, was not particularly encouraging, seemingly more interested in discussing cures for rheumatism than poetry.

When Thomas returned to Swansea in the fall, he began to submit work to the magazines that took poetry seriously. The process, particularly waiting for a response, made him especially tense and he complained of insomnia. The tension was only temporarily relieved when one of his poems was accepted by the *Sunday Referee*, a newspaper that had achieved some literary standing because it published essays by writers like George Bernard Shaw and Bertrand Russell. The *Referee* had what it called a "Poets' Corner," which received some notice, particularly among poets. Thomas's poem, imitating the desolate mood of Eliot's early work, was admired by a young woman named Pamela Hansford Johnson, who worked in an office, lived with her mother and had published several poems in the "Poets' Corner" herself. She wrote Thomas a letter of appreciation, initiating a voluminous correspondence in which Thomas began to practice wearing the "veil of the bizarre," assuming his persona of the doomed, damned, dissolute poet who suggested he was possibly afflicted with consumption or diabetes (because of his incessant craving for sweets) and who had a limited time to live.

Thomas's childhood premonitions of an early death were quickened by the news that his father had a cancer in his throat. Early detection and immediate treatment with radium needles saved D. J. Thomas for another two decades, but in the fall of 1933 Dylan was particularly morbid and despairing. He was also unhappy because his father had claimed that his poems were too difficult to understand. Furthermore, Dylan received a letter from Richard Rees, the editor of the *Adelphi*, returning a group of poems as being too insubstantial, too dreamy, too like the automatic trance writing of the Surrealists to please him. Just a few weeks later, another of his poems, "Light breaks from where no sun shines," was published in the B.B.C. magazine, the *Listener*, causing a furor amid charges of obscenity. The enigmatic poem, not one of Thomas's better efforts, was about conception, and the offending images of an unwrinkling phallus and a hairy candle filing through flesh seem quite innocuous today. The controversy spread Thomas's name around London, though it had its unpleasant associations.

In his letters to Pamela Hansford Johnson, Thomas described himself as an odd and little man with a damaged lung and a persistent cough. The cough was due to excessive smoking, and like the young Scott Fitzgerald he seemed to be wishing for tuberculosis, as if he had to invent the illness to satisfy some romantic expectation or to rationalize the rejection he imagined he would receive as a poet. When he actually arrived in London near the end of February in 1934 to stay with Pamela for a week, he had been preceded by the barrage of his letters. Both poets fully expected to fall in love. Thomas, who was then only nineteen (though he had lied about his age and added a few years for Pamela's benefit, since she was twenty-one), was in all probability still a virgin. He had managed no close relationship with a woman, and, unless he had been with a prostitute, had only a secondary knowledge of sex.

Pamela Hansford Johnson was certainly still a virgin, determined to remain one until she married, a factor that complicated their friendship. She was short and pretty—"nice" and "round" are Thomas's adjectives. Her initial impression was of his "rich, fruity, port-wine" organ voice, and luminous, hypnotic eyes. In her memoir, *Important to Me*, she remembered Thomas appearing at tea time in an oversized raincoat, pockets bulging with manuscripts and a small bottle of brandy. He looked like a diminutive but brilliantly audacious fourteen-year-old schoolboy. Even though he had criticized her poems in his letters with an "astringent and not infrequently hilarious" tone, she was prepared to like him. The two young people talked about art late into the night, with Thomas engaging in "stupendous bluffing" on any subject other than poetry.

As soon as he was back in Swansea, he wrote her that he loved her, with much the same rash thoughtlessness with which he would later declare his love to Caitlin, not bothering to reflect on what his words might mean to Pamela, who might easily have believed they signaled a deeper commitment. He romanticized love as a swift rush of feeling, quickly conveyed and to be enjoyed for its momentary flashing elation. Impetuously romantic, in his relations with women he gave little consideration to the reality that his feelings ran fast rather than deep.

At Easter, he returned to London for a much longer stay, six weeks this time, an interval during which he seemed to draw closer to Pamela. He arrived with a sense of heightened excitement about himself and his work. He was beginning to be celebrated. Another of his poems, "The Force That Through the Green Fuse Drives the Flower," had appeared in the *Referee*, and it had excited literary London as the sign of a new young prodigy. The poem's tremendous rhythm was animated by a language that was both desiccating (blasted tree roots and dried streams) and volatile (the driving force of nature, the whirling water and blowing wind) and a paradoxical energy that was apparent in the poem's opening lines:

> The force that through the green fuse drives the flower
> Drives my green age; that blasts the roots of trees

Is my destroyer.
And I am dumb to tell the crooked rose
My youth is bent by the same wintry fever.

Like so many of Thomas's subsequent poems, this one is full of
the anguish of mutability, the fact that life is measured by time,
what in another poem he brilliantly defined as a "running grave,"
an awareness that for Thomas always tempered joy. On an even
deeper level, the poem contains another perennial theme of
Thomas's, the interconnections of life and death, presented here in
the comparison of the bloodstream of the infant Dylan to the
natural system of sea, clouds and rain by which water circulates on
the planet.

Pamela Hansford Johnson claimed that they were "deliriously
happy" during this period and talked of marriage, though there
were some disconcerting signs. Once, emerging from a pub with
Pamela, he met someone he knew and pretended to be drunk. This
was a protective device, one Fitzgerald had also been accused of
using. Dylan would continue to feign drunkenness, but it frightened
Pamela. On three occasions, he returned very late and quite drunk.
Several times, when Thomas would see another writer he knew, he
would leave Pamela abruptly to talk, without introducing her.
Thomas could not have been so self-absorbed as not to realize that
he was snubbing the woman to whom he had practically proposed.
The prospect of marriage may have frightened Thomas more than
he realized, and especially the expectation of having to support a
family. During his extended Easter visit, part of his purpose had
been to search for a suitable position, which never materialized,
neither at that time nor at any later date in Thomas's life.

In a letter, perhaps intending to frighten Pamela off, he related a
weekend escapade with a "lank red mouthed girl" in a bungalow.
The story he told was sordid, tempestuous and compulsive—he had
accompanied another couple to the bungalow, there had been a
good deal of alcohol, and the woman had flung herself at him.
Thomas was contrite and puritanically self-condemning when he
described the incident, not boastful, but there is the possibility
that the incident was invented, a nightmare he later objectified as
factual. The letter did succeed in making Pamela suspicious of
Thomas's stability. The end of the unconsummated affair, an
epistolary romance centered more on poetry than emotions,
occurred when Pamela and her mother, who genuinely liked

Thomas and found him well-behaved, came to Swansea late that summer for a visit that Dylan dreaded, and he chose to sulk.

By then Thomas had learned that he had been selected in the Sunday *Referee's* "Poets' Corner" contest for publication of a first volume of his poems. The prize had been initiated the year before, and the award then had gone to Pamela Hansford Johnson.

Although the rivalry between Dylan and Pamela was understated, she was aware of it and once remarked that "like Scott Fitzgerald, I don't think he wanted another writer in the family." She was prescient. Caitlin would become his beleagured antagonist, not his rival or would-be collaborator. Later, Johnson married the novelist C. P. Snow, and she herself turned to fiction.

City of the Restless Dead

In November of 1934, Thomas left for London with the intention of staying. His father had retired on his pension, but Thomas's parents still set aside a weekly pound for their son's expenses. Except for beer, these were minimal. He shared a large room and later a three-room flat with several painters, friends from Wales all studying at the Royal College of Art. He slept on a mattress on the floor and was not expected to contribute to the rent. The place was a shambles, basically a dormitory for sleeping. But that meant little to Thomas, who felt he was now living the bohemian life of an artist, in keeping with his romantic self-image. He would wake, reach for a cigarette, begin the day with his wracking coughing spell, sip his teacup of beer and entertain his roommates with tales of his previous night in the bars.

During the day he would often read at Partons near Red Lion Square, a small left-wing bookshop whose owner had agreed, in conjunction with the *Referee*, to publish his poems. Across the street was Meg's Café, where he could mingle with an assorted group of revolutionaries, poets and runaways, Thomas appearing among them like some grubby Chatterton in a dirty, green wool scarf, talking endlessly. Later, tea, a ham sandwich and a cheap lager could be taken at the Royal on Regent Street, an enormous room with the atmosphere of a Parisian café. In the evening, around Fitzroy Square in Soho, there were a variety of small, off-hour drinking clubs or the pubs, the Fitzroy Tavern, where writers and artists habitually gathered, or the Wheatsheaf, a long narrow wood-paneled bar with a special Scotch ale and a more working-class clientele. He met the sculptor Henry Moore and the novelist and painter Wyndham Lewis, who had been Pound's Vorticist collaborator. The young writer Kay Boyle met him at the Fitzroy Tavern and immediately connected him in her mind to D. H. Lawrence, imagining him as a coal miner's son, impressed by the mixture of tenderness and savagery she felt in his gaze. His own poems were appearing in an influential magazine, *New Verse* (four of them that fall), and another in the *Criterion*, perhaps the most important of the London magazines. He had done several reviews for the *Adelphi*, and just before Christmas his first book, *Eighteen Poems*, had appeared in a modest edition of 250 copies, to generally favorable reviews.

Thomas was shuttling back and forth between Wales and London, staying with his painter friends in the city or wherever he could find an amiable host, preferably female, with a spare couch. His social circle was enlarging, though it still revolved around pubs, which would always remain centers of easy conviviality for him. The critic and editor Cyril Connolly invited him to a dinner attended by several other writers. One of them, Evelyn Waugh, left as soon as he realized the extent of Thomas's drunkenness. He met an advertising copywriter named Norman Cameron, who also wrote poems and who introduced him to the historian A. J. P. Taylor and his wife, Margaret. They invited Thomas to spend a few weeks with them in the country.

Margaret Taylor observed that Thomas was always ready to drink, "up for the cups," as she put it, especially in London. Associated with the drinking was the changing group of friends whom he would invariably try to entertain with his conversation. Much the way Henry Miller had, Thomas partly supported himself, at least in the pubs, with his expansive, hilarious, renegade talk. He could disparage himself by telling the story of how, bored at a luncheon, he had eaten a bowl of chrysanthemums, or how he had fallen off his sister's houseboat in the drunken night and had to be fished out of the Thames with a boat hook. More iconoclastically and scatologically, he could recite limericks like the one about God, the old bugger, who had gotten "a virgin in pod."

Sometimes his remarks were as odd as certain of the lines in his poems, saying that he slept "with a fetus" instead of "in the fetal position," or asserting that he was the "short world's shroud" and that he expected to be dead in two years. A story could last for half an hour or more, as Thomas embellished, brocaded and fabricated.

He might describe a group of Welsh miners in a Lawrentian way, bathing after work before a huge kitchen fire. Using innumerable details peculiar to Welsh life, he could build the scene to a point approaching communal orgy, which of course was quite unlikely, given the strict fundamentalism prevalent in Wales. He would not hesitate to distort or lie if he felt that in that way he could interest his listeners or deepen some imagined bond.

At times, the intended bond was sexual, and in one of his characteristic exaggerations he claimed that his first years in London were "sardined with women." Undoubtedly there were a few, though basically he was sexually timid and inhibited. He would drift into bed, almost as an afterthought, usually with older or especially solicitous women who could help him feel secure. In general, he was much less of a Don Juan than a clown, trying to fondle his friend Norman Cameron's wife in her pantry while she was preparing dinner, and then pinching the maid on her backside as she served it. Geoffrey Grigson, who had published some of Thomas's poems in *New Verse*, wondered whether any woman would want a man he regarded as sexually unattractive, shabbily dressed, emitting an air of unwashed squalor. Grigson would later call Thomas the "little runt." Other friends called him "Ditch" or "The Ugly Suckling." It is curious to note, in this connection, that rarely in the poems or the stories does Thomas describe or even suggest a successful sexual act.

London, he wrote his friend Vernon Watkins, meant too much to drink, too much talk, too many women. He complained of difficulty with his writing, uninspired by the "flat and unpunctuated" landscape of the city. Hoping to rescue Thomas from the pubs, Grigson proposed that they take a trip to Ireland, where he knew of a remote farm in Donegal near enormous cliffs and the Atlantic. He helped Thomas move into an old donkey shed perched on a hill half a mile from the sea, which had been converted into a studio by the American painter Rockwell Kent. Two weeks later Grigson left and Thomas had no one to talk to except a deaf farmer and his illiterate wife, who fed him hearty meals and buttermilk.

Without even a clock, Thomas felt himself in the presence of a vast, lonely silence relieved only by the incessant rain. Miles from any village or pub, he would walk to the cliff to watch the seals on the beach below. He worked on a novel loosely based on *Pilgrim's Progress*, which he discontinued, and on his most elliptical poems. After a month, without bothering to inform or pay the farmer, he walked ten miles to a town where he found a bus and set off for London. Thankless and thoughtless, the act was typical of a certain impulsive irresponsibility that was close to the center of Thomas's nature. He had come back from Ireland fatter than before—Dylan said it was all the buttermilk—and even less concerned with his own appearance. When Grigson heard that Thomas had absconded, he was enraged and offended, and stopped accepting Thomas's poems for *New Verse*. Other friends noticed a subtle hardening of sorts in Thomas, a greater willingness to turn inward and ignore obligations to the outside world.

A "Lunatic Course"

Back in Wales in the fall of 1939, Thomas turned twenty-one and wrote his sister that he had bought a new tweed suit with colored spots with the money she had sent him, but he had no hopes. Typically self-pitying, he failed to reveal that Richard Church, an editor at Dent's, a respectable house that issued the Everyman's Library, was interested in a second book of poems. Many of his poems were being accepted by magazines, and he was earning a little money by reviewing mysteries for the *Morning Post*.

Dame Edith Sitwell, a member of an eccentric but well-known literary family, had written a very encouraging notice of his work in a little magazine, the *London Mercury*. The only disquieting news was that Richard Church wrote that winter to say he found the poems too surrealistic, too labored by the "private eccentricity" of "dissociated symbolism," which he could not understand and so was reluctant to publish them. Later, the critic Donald Davie and other reviewers would make a similar observation, accusing Thomas of fabricating a sort of pseudo-syntax, tumbling things together without an articulated structure. Tactfully, Thomas admitted to Church that his poems could seem muddled, overweighted with imagery, and offered to show Church others that were less densely textured.

It would take six months for Church to be persuaded, a period in which Thomas most avoided London, except for the trip he made in March, during which he met Caitlin Macnamara at the Wheatsheaf Tavern and went off with her to the Eiffel Tower. Exhausted from the few days with Caitlin, he immediately retreated to Cornwall in Wales, where he found it difficult to work on his poems and was distracted by heavy rounds of drinking with friends visiting from

London. Interestingly enough, for a man who had instantly declared his love, he did not attempt to correspond with or see Caitlin again for several months.

In June, he was back in London to attend the opening of the International Surrealist Exhibition at the New Burlington Galleries, a crowded circus of arch spectators, art speculators and artists assuming the most extreme poses, including Salvador Dali wearing a diver's suit and nearly suffocating as a result. The opening had a carnival feeling. Thomas had the misfortune to go home with a young lady whose head was allegorically hidden by a wire contraption supporting dozens of roses, an encounter from which he emerged with a case of gonorrhea. In an era before antibiotics, weeks of treatment were required and alcohol was forbidden, which, coupled with his difficulty working, destroyed whatever gain the fun and excitement of the exhibition might have provided.

Though he hadn't attempted to see or communicate with Caitlin when he arrived in London, he chose the moment of his departure for Wales to write to her, telling her how much he had missed her in the intervening months since their days and nights at the Eiffel Tower, and once again declaring his love. He did not reveal that he had contracted gonorrhea. Instead, he used as his excuse for returning to Wales a serious case of bronchitis he had developed.

Neither did he reveal that he had gonorrhea to his mother, who tended to his bronchitis in Wales. His father was morose and bitter, preoccupied with death even though he had been cured of his cancer. The atmosphere at home must have been unpleasant.

Partly to escape such depressing circumstances, partly because of his swift recuperative powers, and in the hope of again seeing Caitlin, Thomas planned to attend a poetry and painting festival at Fishguard in Wales. Caitlin had told him that Augustus John was judging the art entries and that she would accompany him. Fred Janes, one of the Welsh artists whose flat Thomas had shared in London, had entered his work and was driving to Fishguard.

Uninvited, Thomas and Janes appeared at the home of the novelist Richard Hughes in Laugharne, which was where Caitlin and John were staying. Hughes had already met Thomas and liked him, and so allowed him and Janes to join the others for lunch. Caitlin remembered that Thomas's presence visibly upset John. Tall, bearded, handsome, John was a man who was used to being in control, especially where his women were concerned. Men like

Thomas, outspoken and with a disdain for obeisance, provoked him. Years earlier, D. H. Lawrence had visited his studio while John was working on a painting of Lady Cynthia Asquith. Quite perversely, Lawrence challenged John to reveal her disagreeable qualities in his portrait. As far as Lawrence was concerned, John could never do it; he was merely a "drowned corpse," who would only seek to please his audience, no matter what the cost to artistic truth.

After the lunch, John drove Caitlin to Fishguard in his powerful six-cylinder car while Janes and Thomas followed in their smaller, less reliable vehicle. John was sixty, worried about the possibility of waning virility, though another one of his mistresses had recently given birth to his son. Caitlin's youthful presence seemed like an antidote to his fears about aging. When Janes's old car broke down that evening, Dylan joined Caitlin in the backseat of John's car. John drove furiously and recklessly, agitated because Caitlin and Dylan were fondling each other and kissing in the back. They had all been drinking heavily. When John stopped the car for another libation, angry words erupted between the two men. John knocked Dylan down immediately and drove off with Caitlin, leaving Thomas stranded in the road.

Thomas would return to Wales, spending his final summer at his childhood home. Working on the proof's of *Twenty-five Poems*, he would not see Caitlin again that summer, although he would continue to profess his love in his letters. The fact that she was still in Augustus John's orbit was no real impediment. John was more of a surrogate father than a lover. Caitlin's actual father, Francis Macnamara, had left his wife and four children when Caitlin was eight.

Fastidious, descending from an old family, a man with grand airs, a great talker who thought he could change the world with words, Francis Macnamara lived in London on his small allowance and wrote poetry. He moved in artistic circles and Augustus John was a close friend. When Francis Macnamara left his wife, she moved to Hampshire, close to where John lived with his dozen legitimate and illegitimate offspring, and the two families saw each other often during Caitlin's childhood. John had decidedly bohemian inclinations, presiding over an extended family with wife and mistresses and assorted children, all raised in a carefree atmosphere of sexual license and wine. In the evening, there would be communal dinners with guests like Bertrand Russell or T. E. Lawrence. Caitlin was fifteen when she had her first infatuation with Caspar John, one of Augustus's seven sons, thirty years old, a navy man and extremely handsome. Caitlin fell absolutely in love and always maintained that Caspar was her image of the perfect man. The relationship never proceeded very far, as Caitlin's mother secretly interceded.

Uninhibited, graceful but also considered hard, capricious and arrogant, Caitlin had a striking, beautifully proportioned body that she exhibited as a chorus girl in the London Palladium. Her ideal as a dancer was Isadora Duncan and her highly interpretive, expressionistic, improvisatory dance. Caitlin had danced in Paris and Ireland at small social gatherings and though she had made no spectacular success, she had, like Zelda Fitzgerald, the air of an original. The first time she posed for Augustus John, he overpowered her and assaulted her sexually. She continued to sit for her portrait, and each session ended with a primal violation without tenderness or concern. She said she never spoke about it to anyone because she rationalized the sexuality as an exchange for the sophistication of joining John's circle—even if it made her bitter, contemptuous and distrustful toward men.

Caitlin told Michael Holyrod, John's biographer, that she only slept with John as a form of tribute, a sign of respect, a way for him to maintain his own Casanova illusions. This explanation does not sound at all convincing. It is clear that the incident in which John knocked Thomas down was the turning point in a relationship that had already lost its significance for Caitlin. When her father asked her to come to Ireland to help him with the estate he had inherited and which he had turned into a hotel, she agreed. She spent the fall of 1936 working as a barmaid in a hotel that seemed destined to fail, and did.

That same fall *Twenty-five Poems* was finally published. It received its share of hostile reviews. The critic in the *New Statesman* complained of "eerie bombast" and the *New English Weekly* of "chaotic rhetoric." The anonymous reviewer in the *Times Literary Supplement* admitted that he could not understand many of the poems and advised readers not to try. The most malicious review was written by Grigson, who called the poems "psychopathological nonsense put down with a remarkable ineptness of technique." These critics were uncomfortable with poems that lacked defined narrative lines, that clustered images instead of focusing on a central image. The attacks, however, were more than offset for Thomas by Edith Sitwell's review in the Sunday *Times*, a large-circulation newspaper. She called him the most promising poet of the new generation. Her glowing praise gave his reputation an enormous boost.

Sitwell's article caused the small initial printing to sell out immediately. The book was reprinted three more times, but each printing was cautiously small, as Richard Church at Dent's had little faith that any large audience would welcome work as obscure as Thomas's. The royalties were not substantial—enough perhaps for Thomas to live on for a footloose and freeloading year, but hardly enough to propose marriage to Caitlin.

As far as money was concerned, Thomas was improvident and careless. Much the way Henry Miller had, he assumed there would always be a friend to help him. At the same time he felt a deep need for the emotional security that marriage represented. The fact that his parents were finally leaving his childhood home intensified his need.

Whatever sense of dislocation he may have felt in his life, Thomas had always been able to go home again. His parents had been his caretakers. Now that role was threatened by circumstances and he needed someone to fill it. Difficult as it might be to see Caitlin as a mother-substitute—she could be as elemental and as forceful as a sea squall—she had exhibited an easygoing acceptance of him and his low-keyed sexuality. She was a good companion, a partner in drink, a carouser like him, and, most comforting of all for a man who masked himself behind his poetic persona, she had few illusions about him.

For Caitlin, marriage was certainly preferable to returning to her mother. Her father had abandoned poetry for the hotel business, but poets retained a special attraction for her. Now she had found one who was being acknowledged in literary circles and whose spoken and written language was compelling. "Taken by the light in her arms," Thomas wrote in a poem called "Love in the Asylum," he might "suffer the first vision that set fire to the stars." For Thomas, women were the catalysts for his creative urges, and many women would have responded to so deeply romantic an appeal, despite its dangers.

Words were her weakness, Caitlin acknowledged in *Leftover Life to Kill*, one of the three books she wrote after her husband's death. Frieda Weekley, too, had been swept away by D. H. Lawrence's use of words, the magnetic power of his language. The memoir she worked on after Lawrence's death was an attempt to consecrate their relationship. Caitlin Thomas's books were, instead, an attempt to explain herself. Both women, so attracted by their husbands' words, felt inept in their own use of words, blocked and unable to express themselves. Part of Caitlin's feeling of inadequacy about language had to do with the rather haphazard nature of her education, which had been at home under the tutelage of a French governess who knew little about English grammar. But her father's aspirations had led her to admire poetry and Caitlin fell in love with Dylan's words, the way he used language, and with the actual sound of his voice. It was most certainly not with his prowess as a lover. Thomas was not ardent, as she explained in her book *Caitlin*: he was inhibited, shy, prudish about sexual matters. At night he always wore an extra-long undershirt covering him down to his mid-thighs. It made him look comical, and he insisted on keeping it on through the night. As a lover, he was timid and clinging, and Caitlin described him as "childlike."

Dylan and Caitlin spent the month of May in a borrowed cottage in a fishing village near Mousehole in Wales. When they decided to marry, Thomas informed his parents of what he admitted was his irresponsible plan, his "mad scheme." Regretting that they would not be present, he inquired whether they could send him his green suit and other items of clothing. For D. J. Thomas, the idea of Dylan's marriage was disastrous, a "lunatic course" he called it. He told Hadyn Taylor, Nancy's husband, what he thought and Taylor tried to persuade Caitlin's mother that the match was ill-advised.

Broad-minded, involved for years in a lesbian relationship, she had always expected that Caitlin was spirited and beautiful enough to marry someone with money, and she objected to the fact that Thomas had none. But the lovers could not be dissuaded. Thomas asked Taylor for a loan when describing his "eccentric" plan, certain that Caitlin did not care about material matters and that she was ready to share a life of genuine poverty.

Thomas had once told Pamela Hansford Johnson that the institution of marriage was dead and that rigid monogamy was a restriction of individuality. The artist needed to be a law unto himself, he declared, making Pamela all the more unsure of Thomas as a possible husband. Caitlin had no such qualms. She has stated that she believed in free love and was happy to continue living with Dylan without the benefit of a legal tie. While she liked the idea of marriage, she felt it had no particular point.

The wedding was casual, an event the couple drifted through in an alcoholic haze. Two previous dates for the ceremony had been canceled because they had spent all their money in pubs and could not afford the license fee. Finally, Wyn Henderson, a friend of Thomas's who had helped him previously paid for it. The simple ceremony, conducted in a bare registry office, took only two minutes, without relatives or friends present. The only romantically incongruent note in the modest affair was struck by Caitlin, who had adorned herself for the occasion; Thomas asserted that she resembled an ornamental princess on top of a Christmas tree. Blithely unaware of the responsibilities marriage might entail, he told a friend that though they had no money or prospect of it, they were completely happy about what they had done.

Impoverished Love

Wyn Henderson ran a guest house in Mousehole. Her business partner, a painter named Max Chapman, had a studio over a fish market in the nearby village of Newlyn, which he agreed to let the newlyweds occupy. The "honeymoon" was celebrated in pubs. Alone at night, Dylan read Dickens, Hardy and D. H. Lawrence to Caitlin.

Caitlin had no illusions about Thomas, but that didn't mean she was completely prepared for just how difficult life with him, stripped of its precipitous romanticism, would be. He was jealous, he was manipulative, and despite his embracing of bohemian values, he demanded that she at least cloak herself in the proper robes of wifely respectability. He had a jealous fit when he saw her walking, innocently enough even if flirtatiously, arm-in-arm with Chapman. His unwarranted jealousy was exacerbated when Augustus John came to Newlyn for a visit.

If he hadn't been so eager to marry and so capable of romantic self-delusion, he would have realized that he admired and wanted Caitlin precisely because she was unconventional, untamed, the perfect playmate for his escapades, not the conformist to his will he now insisted she be. They were in open conflict, secret sharers of a hidden agenda of hostility and contention, which always threatened to split them asunder but that somehow bound them together for the duration of their lives, the way so many couples who appear to be tearing each other apart are perplexingly bound by the threads of the invisible web they have spun and inhabit together.

Thomas's poem "I Make This in a Warring Absence," one of his more complex and indecipherable efforts, was written for Caitlin. He spent almost a year fashioning the poem, which some critics assume is based on the jealousy he felt; others see in it the possibility that Caitlin may have wanted to leave him. Caitlin is projected as a sailing vessel and the tensions of heading for ocean or anchoring in a harbor are sexual in origin, though unclear as they function in the poem. Thomas's anger takes the form of a donkey's jawbone, with which he threatens to "topple sundown" and breach Caitlin's "sped heart." Somehow, tensions are ameliorated so that in a "forgiving presence" he can make her his poem. Clotted, coagulated by conflicting images and murky circumstances, the poem suggests that marriage had its confusing, if not terrifying, implications, and that for two free spirits trying to live together there was more hazard than opportunity.

In *Leftover Life to Kill*, Caitlin criticized Thomas for his controlling ploys, his insistence that she dress in a certain way for market, that she speak in another way in a pub. Such pressure for her to conform to what he considered respectability may have been a suppressed motive for his marriage—a version of the model provided by his parents—but Caitlin resisted from the start.

What little money they had, and the indulgence of friends like Wyn Henderson, kept them in Newlyn and the surrounding area through the summer of 1937. In the fall, they visited Thomas's parents, who had moved to a small semidetached house in Bishopston, a suburb of Swansea. They were unprepared for Caitlin, who dressed in bright colors, spontaneously putting together outfits whose parts never matched. When they gave her money to buy suitable clothes, she and Thomas promptly drank it away. Caitlin found the Thomas family smothered in respectability. She thought that D. J. Thomas was the unhappiest man she had ever met, frozen in his reserve, hypochondriacal, and drinking to relieve the dullness in his life. Florence Thomas seemed obsessed with domestic order, babbling banalities most of the time.

Since Caitlin and Dylan were still without money, they spent the winter of 1937–38, a six-month period, with Caitlin's mother. Mrs. Macnamara found her son-in-law difficult and strange, and disliked his frequent requests for small loans. Reviews and the sale of a story or a poem brought in small amounts, but only enough to meet pub costs. Disciplined all his life only about his writing, Dylan was pleased to have a room in which to work. Afternoons, they went for long walks, invariably finding their way to a pub, and then returned to their room to eat sweets and read to each other, both happy in the spirit of their fundamentally childish innocence.

That spring they returned to Bishopston, and then for two months were guests of Richard Hughes in Laugharne until they found a small fisherman's cottage, four damp-stained rooms at a minimal rent. A small, quaint village on the edge of the sea, Laugharne was a cluster of whitewashed houses around the ruins of a twelfth-century castle covered with ivy; it faced beaches, marsh and a shallow bay with fishing boats, cormorants, herons, gulls, geese and curlews. Laugharne had no industry and many of its eccentric inhabitants received government support. A timeless spot with seven pubs, its citizens could be seen wandering the streets, Dylan once observed, like dazed opium-eaters. Florence Thomas's family, the Williamses, owned Brown's Hotel and the local buses and taxi, and Thomas had enjoyed many idyllic summer visits to his aunt's farm at Fern Hill only a few miles away.

After two months they were able to rent a larger house, lit only by candles, from the Williamses. Caitlin's pregnancy calmed her and made her more domestic. She soon realized that what her husband needed to do his best work was a regulated existence. She took greater pains to provide wholesome meals, hearty stews and mussels collected on the beach. They purchased a bed on the installment plan, approaching the purchase with the same careless disregard of how they would pay for it that characterized their lives. The bed was repossessed, but the immediate problem of furnishings was resolved when Caitlin's aunt died and Caitlin's mother sent down all the aunt's furniture. The perennial problem of money remained. Both their families sent them some, but there never seemed to be enough.

Thomas, the pampered boy who could never have endured the lower-depths, hand-to-mouth existence of Henry Miller, was not above living by his wits and cadging money wherever and in whatever way he could. He was constantly writing letters to friends, to rich acquaintances, to his agent and publishers begging for assistance. He even asked certain friends to recommend potential supporters, for whom he could write a "sponger's song." He called these theoretical donors the soft white silly ravens whom he trusted would always appear to somehow bail him out of crisis. The "ravens" provided a collective patronage which trickled tokens of support through the years. Whether or not the Thomases had money, their credit at Brown's Hotel, because of the family connection, was always good, and they managed to spend a lot of time in pubs. Dylan once facetiously remarked that he had never written a line of poetry while the pubs were open, but it is certain that at Brown's he would listen carefully to the local gossip, which he would later use so skillfully in his play *Under Milk Wood*.

There were visits from Vernon Watkins and a young man named Henry Treece, who intended to write a book about Thomas's poetry. Treece's analytical questions irritated Thomas, who disliked any intellectual approach to poetry. He was working on the stories that would become *Portrait of the Artist as a Young Dog*, a collection which Richard Church at Dent's rejected because of what he thickly saw as its potential for prosecution for obscenity. Thomas felt Church had a mind like the Sunday newspaper, too cautious and conservative to reach for anything that was unusual. The stories, influenced by Joyce, were not nearly as surrealistic as Thomas's earlier efforts, and they took a more narrative form. James Laughlin, who was beginning to organize New Directions in America, wrote expressing interest and sent a small advance.

With the baby expected and money in very short supply, Thomas and Caitlin decided in the fall of 1938 to spend the winter with her mother. He had written very little poetry during the year at Laugharne, but before leaving he would finish one of his most brilliant lyrics, "Twenty-four Years":

Twenty-four years remind the tears of my eyes.
(Bury the dead for fear that they walk to the grave in labour.)
In the groin of the natural doorway I crouched like a tailor
Sewing a shroud for a journey
By the light of the meat-eating sun.
Dressed to die, the sensual strut begun,
With my red veins full of money
In the final direction of the elementary town
I advance for as long as forever is.

The poem is like an abrupt telegram announcing Thomas's central preoccupation with a death that he believed was imminent. Frequently, he told Caitlin that he never expected to see forty, so a birthday was an occasion to record. Death may be the mother of beauty, as Wallace Stevens observed, but the poem is characteristic of the rigorous refusal to sentimentalize death. Crouching or strutting, the movement is all advance, accepting and unafraid.

Without the bunching of images that confused many earlier poems, "Twenty-four Years" has a logical clarity and the strong, inevitable "pulling," the sort of oppositional tension that Thomas once argued makes a poem an event. Much of the rest of Thomas's work would be dedicated to remembering the imagined paradisiacal dimensions of his youth in Wales, but he also brought to many of his poems an awareness of the inevitability of death as a way of making life seem more holy, or, as he formulated it with such Yeatsian grandeur in another poem:

> Time held me green and dying
> Though I sang in my chains like the sea.

Death-haunted, often feeling chained by the demands of his existence, Thomas always seemed to believe that singing "like the sea" took precedence over finding a way out of his morass. However irresponsible he was about supporting his family, however much he squandered himself on drink and other excesses, he was never reckless toward his gifts. Like Villon, Thomas has been seen as a wild man of poetry who created works of genius automatically, without knowing how he had done it, but such a characterization ignores the other side of Thomas: the poet who made painstaking efforts to fashion a poem so that it would work for him, his stringency in picking over images and words till they satisfied him, no matter who else might find them difficult to follow, the willingness sometimes to spend months on the same poem till he felt he had gotten it right.

Dylan and Caitlin spent the winter of 1938–39 with Mrs. Macnamara, a five-month visit which Thomas found confining, complaining in letters of a houseful of women in a land of narrow vowels and an uninspiring flat countryside. Just before Christmas, Lawrence Durrell sent him money to come to London to meet Henry Miller, a writer for whom Thomas had enormous admiration. Already much heavier, ruffled and tousled, Thomas looked as if he had slept in a haystack, according to Durrell, who remembered the visit in *Encounter*. The three writers talked and drank late into the night. They met again the next evening, Thomas reciting some of his poems and Miller presenting him with a copy of *Tropic of Cancer*. Miller was a "dear, mad, mild man," Thomas told Vernon Watkins, with great enthusiasm for ordinary things. The affinity between the two men was immediate, as if they had known each other all their lives. Both were spontaneous, irreverent, unpretentious, and Miller could listen as brilliantly as he could talk.

At the end of January, Caitlin gave birth to their son Llewelyn. The birth was particularly difficult, but Thomas was not present, as he would not be at the two subsequent births. Caitlin was convinced that he spent the night with an ostentatious, tall and glamorous woman with whom she had once attended dancing classes, and that he continued to see her in London in the future because he was especially drawn to tall women. Caitlin realized that Thomas was regularly unfaithful when he went to London, a place he needed for stimulation even though he could not write poetry there.

According to Caitlin, Thomas's liaisons began with the birth of his children, because he was jealous of the attention they received. Later she would find other men when her husband was away. In *Caitlin* she confesses to never having reached orgasm with her husband because he was what she called either childish or physically insufficient, but she admits that she did not reach orgasm with any of the other men she found for sex either.

By May the family was back in Laugharne. There was some money from an American poetry prize, and an advance from Dent's, which had decided to publish *The Map of Love*, a collection of sixteen poems and seven stories. Thomas knew the money would not last long, especially because some of it was needed to repay previous debts in Laugharne. After the Royal Literary Society denied him assistance, he tried to establish a fund for his own support which would be donated to by several wealthy contributors who would each put aside a small amount for his support on a weekly basis. The idea was sensible but it needed the organizing zeal and persistence of an Ezra Pound, who had once proposed such a plan for T. S. Eliot's benefit. At best, Thomas was the recipient of a few incidental gifts, but no permanent funding.

The War Years

The Map of Love appeared at the most unpropitious moment, September, 1939, just when the Germans invaded Poland and began the second great conflagration of the century. The book was largely ignored because of the war hysteria and few copies were sold. A similar fate was in store for *Portrait of the Artist as a Young Dog*, the story collection that would be published a year later. All the

young men of Thomas's generation were facing military conscription. A few writers, like Auden and Christopher Isherwood,
found their way to America instead. Thomas had no intention of
serving; he was basically apolitical, except for a very vague
attachment to the working-class poor. Much like Henry Miller, he
was suspicious of any organized effort, particularly if it was state-
organized. His initial reaction to the war was to resent it, as it made
his already precarious existence all the more precarious. He wrote
Henry Treece that he was prepared to let his country rot before he
would help it with a bayonet; he admitted to another friend he was
an "antisocial softie."

With virtually no income, the Thomases shuttled back and forth
between his and her parents. The winter months were spent, once
again, with Caitlin's mother. To help them, Stephen Spender raised
a substantial sum, even though Thomas had unfavorably reviewed
one of his books as communist propaganda that foundered as
poetry. Other friends like Vernon Watkins continued to send the
occasional sum. Thomas once thanked Watkins for a timely gift,
writing that he had heard the money singing in its envelope. On a
subsequent occasion he was less cheery. His son was with his
parents, he told Watkins, and he and Caitlin were in a room in
London feeling like prisoners in a melodrama.

It was a period of extreme hardship, and conflict between the
poet and the woman he usually called "Cat" increased. Arguments
often led to physical assaults, although it was mainly Caitlin who
would strike her husband. Caitlin's rage was provoked whenever
their possessions were pawned, sold or repossessed by a finance
company or left behind in one of their frequent moves. The couple
that seemed at the time of their marriage prepared to accept a
future of bohemian poverty found it as inconvenient or difficult as
anyone does to live without means. It was even harder for Thomas
than for Caitlin. He depended on certain comforts, like the radio
broadcast of the cricket matches he loved, to feel secure. As he told
his friend Margaret Taylor, he was as "domestic as a slipper."
Actually, he was more like a child who wants to have it both ways—
the freedom to range unfettered and the reassurance of having
comforts provided.

The impractical and virtually indigent couple was temporarily
rescued by another friend, John Davenport, who invited them to
Maltings, an artist's colony of sorts that he had established in his
home. A critic who had inherited some money, Davenport had

purchased a large manor house in Gloucestershire, about a hundred miles from London. A fat, hearty man, gregarious and quite generous, Davenport opened his house to a number of painters, writers and musicians, among them the composer Benjamin Britten. While at Maltings, Thomas would collaborate with Davenport, mostly in a local pub, on a novelistic parody of some of the artists and poets they knew (posthumously published as *The King's Canary* in 1976).

The air of sexual liberation at Maltings was encouraged by the war and fears of imminent invasion, but Thomas was upset by what he regarded as Caitlin's excessive flirtatiousness. In *Caitlin*, she describes her abortive affair with the critic and pianist William Glock. Caitlin was dancing again, and Glock would sometimes serenade her with Schubert and Mozart. When she thought she was falling in love with Glock, she arranged to go to Swansea on the pretext of selling some furniture, and managed to meet him in a hotel for a night of passion. Caitlin remembers that they were each too timid or petrified to make the first advances, and they spent the night looking at shadows on the ceiling. When Thomas found out about Caitlin's adventure, he threw a knife at her—missing by several feet.

That fall, Caitlin took her son to stay with Thomas's parents in Bishopston. Thomas had heard of a possible position as a screenwriter for a film company that specialized in documentaries, run by a man named Donald Taylor, who wanted good writers working on his projects. Taylor hired Thomas, allowing him to work in Wales, though he was expected to appear in London for meetings. Thomas began traveling back and forth, a cold, uncomfortable train ride that could take from six to twelve hours each time.

After central Swansea was destroyed in a series of vicious air raids, his parents decided to leave Bishopston. Dylan and Caitlin found a small cottage inland, one that was less vulnerable to air attack, but it had to be shared with another woman and her child. In London, now being blitzed by German bombs, Thomas had no place to stay except with friends. While the scripts he worked on provided his first regular source of income since his newspaper days when he was sixteen, he felt a certain dissatisfaction with what was essentially a collaborative group effort. Another discouraging aspect was the fact that little of his contribution was ever realized on screen. He wrote part of a film about the Nazi leadership, another about Britain's defense forces, and a sentimentally patriotic film called *Our Country*. The time demanded by his work for Strand Films interfered with his absorption in his poetry and he would write very few poems during the war. The meetings kept him in London too often as well, which made Caitlin uneasy, especially because she was afraid Thomas would leave her.

Unable to concentrate on poetry, he was working on another collection of his stories, the unfinished *Adventures in the Skin Trade*, but he never felt that writing stories was as important to him as his poems. Both fiction and film were simply ways to earn money through writing. The war-related documentaries produced by Donald Taylor had the additional advantage of helping to keep Thomas out of the army or from being forced to work in a factory for the war effort. He was as feeble with his hands as a penguin, Caitlin remembered, and he dreaded the possibility of having to work in a factory almost as much as he dreaded the army. D. H. Lawrence had had a similar dread of serving in World War I, and had felt soiled and humiliated during his preconscription physical examination. Thomas went him one better, arriving for the army physical in such bad shape that it was as though he had figuratively soiled and humiliated himself. The night before he was called for his physical examination, he consumed quantities of whiskey, gin, sherry, and beer chasers, appearing the next morning with hives, shaking and coughing terribly. His condition was caused as much by his fear as by excessive drinking, but it served his purpose.

In the fall of 1941, Thomas found a large, sparsely furnished room in Chelsea. Caitlin, pregnant again, joined him, but Llewelyn was sent to live with her mother because of the air raids. The room was available for very little money because no one else wanted it. It had a glass roof that leaked when it rained, which, given the weather in London, meant that the plaster was always peeling or falling. The room was furnished with a single table, a primitive stove hidden behind a curtain, and a fireplace, but there was no private space for Dylan to work. A daughter, Aeron, was born that spring. Named after a river in Wales, she slept in a bassinet covered with its own umbrella.

Thomas was still working for Strand Films, now spending much of his day in their offices in Soho, where he had a small room in which to write. At night he would frequent the pubs where he could talk and play darts—mostly the Eight Bells in Chelsea, which drew an artist crowd because it was not modernized. The only alcohol was beer, and even that was not always available. Certain of his drinking companions were cynical about the war, but on occasion he would meet old friends like Daniel Jones or Vernon Watkins who were active participants and in uniform. In the pubs, full of robust effrontery, Thomas was as entertaining as he had been when he first arrived in London, only more seasoned as a raconteur, capable of a more malicious clowning and pretense.

As Donald Taylor, his boss at Strand Films, observed, he was a complete chameleon who could adapt himself to any company and play any role—the Welsh country gentleman, the B.B.C. actor, the erudite professor, the drunken poet. This last role seemed the most natural, and once he was seen drinking beer from his shoe, ostensibly to impress some woman he had picked up. Another time he was seen slicing someone's tie with a razor blade. The American writer William Saroyan met Thomas in a pub before noon and found him "swollen by sleeplessness, nervousness, boredom, bad eating and general poor health."

Thomas believed there was a relationship between illness and creativity—most literature is the work of men who are ill, he observed in a letter. According to Caitlin, there was always something physically wrong with him. Saroyan felt that Thomas smelled unwell, that he needed to bathe and change his clothes. He spoke in a "wild, funny and grim" monologue about "the war, the weather, art, poetry, other writers...the whole thing seemed to be some kind of rhapsodic throw-away poem."

Often he was drunk and could seem intolerably gross, like the time he chose to urinate on his very proper sister-in-law's living room wall. He explained to his fellow scriptwriter, Ivan Moffat (who had originally introduced him to Donald Taylor), that he drank to correct the imbalance between the order he felt in his being and the disorder all around him, a convenient apology that could very well stand as the motto of a generation of drinking writers like Thomas Wolfe, Fitzgerald, Hemingway and Faulkner. The more he drank, the more he fabricated. Caitlin claimed that although he was a congenital and often perverse liar, he lied mostly as a way to hone his imagination. His friends put up with him because he made them laugh, but also because he was capable of expressing a deep and immediate sympathy.

The sympathy may have been a pose, part of his facade. He once confessed a lack of interest in any other person's emotions, and he realized that was exactly the quality that made him a poet instead of a fiction writer. His impersonations were frequent and contrib-

uted to the legend of the irresponsible poet. His personal appearance added to the notion of him as the Rimbaud of Soho, the
literary outlaw who was unconcerned with propriety. He was
forever losing articles of clothing, or borrowing shirts and jackets
from friends, which were never returned. Sometimes the "borrowed" object—a fur coat, precious silver, someone's gramophone
or sewing machine—was pawned by him, an act of clear theft.

All his life Thomas behaved like a self-indulgent child who
refused to bring an adult perspective to his actions. He could steal
from his friends without shame or guilt, as a matter of entitlement.
His childishness was also expressed in his love of sweets, of bread
soaked in milk whenever he was feeling unwell, in his exaggerated
fear of mice, in his boyish avidity for science-fiction films and the
more slapstick elements of the humor of Harpo Marx and Charlie
Chaplin. But that childishness was also a critical ingredient of his
imagination, an aspect of the kind of naive vision so admired by
artists. Though his poems were often encumbered by dense
pockets of enigmatic surrealist imagery that made their meanings
impenetrable and obscure and that worked against the accessibility
of the lyricism, he never lost the direct fusion of the self with
objects and nature that characterizes the early child's adaptation to
the world. The immediacy with which he responded to objects and
to nature produced in his work at its best a riot of unexpected and
breathtaking images, and a marvelous richness of language.

Caitlin was rarely with him in the pubs now. She was home
instead, caring for their infant, occupying the space her husband
had meanly identified as the perfect place for a woman—in bed or
in the kitchen. She resented the turn their lives had taken: for the
first time her husband was able to support his family, but now he
was drinking most of his pay away. Bitter, she felt he had been
corrupted by his film associates, that he was regularly sleeping
with other women whenever he had the opportunity or if she left
London because of the air raids.

One night after a fight with Caitlin, in a fit of self-pity, Thomas
tore up the manuscript of a poem on which he had been working.
But it was merely another dramatic gesture; he had another copy.
During this period, near the end of the war, Thomas grew heavier,
lumpier and more flabby, looking more and more debauched, like
the image of the unmade bed he often used to describe how he felt.

When the Germans began bombing London with rockets, early
in 1944, the Thomases found a cottage in Sussex. He kept his room
in London and continued to divide his time between city and

country because of his film work. That spring the Thomases lived
with Donald Taylor in a suburb west of London, where the rich
played bridge like ferrets, Thomas told Vernon Watkins. Collaborat-
ing with Taylor, Thomas wrote *The Doctor and the Devils*, a
filmscript which was later published though not produced until
recently. Summer was spent with his parents in Wales, until he and
Caitlin found a bungalow in New Quay, on the coast of Car-
diganshire, which they rented for a year.

He was writing again, poems more simple and direct than before:
"A Refusal to Mourn," "Ceremony After a Fire Raid," "Fern Hill"
and "In My Craft and Sullen Art," which are regarded as the
masterpieces of his maturity. Many of these poems appeared in
Cyril Connolly's magazine, *Horizon*. Thomas was also speaking
about his Welsh childhood on the radio, talks that were recorded
and later published as *Quite Early One Morning*. The dislocations
of the war years were drawing to a close, as was his peripatetic
alternation between country cottage and London film work, and
even though he was beginning to write poems he liked again, he
was still disoriented and ready to be the buffoon. When his friend
Vernon Watkins asked him to be the best man at his wedding,
Thomas accepted but failed to appear. He claimed he had forgotten
the name of the church and was racing around London in a taxi
trying to find it, but Caitlin conjectured that he was probably
drunk in some pub.

In New Quay, where Thomas spent most of the summer of 1945,
he did a lot of drinking at night. Caitlin often drank with him in the
pubs, but she found it difficult to accept the way her husband was
now being lionized by those whom he ordinarily despised—tourists, transients, retired middle-class people and military personnel
on leave, who cared nothing about poetry, but were aware of his
growing fame.

One of these military people was a commando captain whose
wife lived in a cottage adjacent to the Thomases and who had
returned from guerrilla combat in Greece in a state of nervous
prostration. His wife, who had known Thomas in Swansea as a
child, became especially friendly, and the captain was inordinately
suspicious. Thomas was late with a filmscript and Donald Taylor
had sent a Russian-born Jewish secretary whom Thomas liked to
help him finish it. In a pub she attacked the captain when she
thought he had made some anti-Semitic slur. Thomas, who had
engaged in pub fights with several soldiers, scuffled with the burly
captain. The captain was ejected from the pub, but later that night,

quite drunk, he appeared before the Thomas cottage and fired a
submachine gun into it. The cottage was a primitive wooden shed
with paper-thin asbestos sheeting for walls, an altogether insubstantial affair. Caitlin and a visiting friend hid their children in the
brick fireplace, as the captain burst through the door threatening
them all with a hand grenade. Thomas remained calm and managed to placate him until the police arrived, but the incident
brought all the madness of the war home to Thomas with full fury.

"Hiraeth"

The Thomas family returned to London in the fall and stayed with
various friends. Thomas had no intention of settling permanently
in London, a draining place for him, which he proved quickly by
breaking down and spending four days in a hospital, suffering from
alcoholic gastritis and hypertension. The breakdown had much to
do with the imminent publication of *Deaths and Entrances*, which
Dent's released in February to the accompaniment of excellent
reviews and sales—the book went through several editions and
Thomas's reputation as a poet seemed secure. Thomas hoped to be
able to emigrate to the United States, which he always regarded as
the place where poets could transform their words into gold. He
wrote to James Laughlin, who was preparing a book of Thomas's
selected poems and essays for publication by New Directions,
asking for help in finding some kind of regular employment with
Time or as a lecturer at Harvard, but nothing came of it.

Christmas was spent with A. J. P. Taylor and his wife in Oxford,
where Taylor was a don. Margaret Taylor had always been partial to
Thomas; she thought he was a genius and had helped him in the
past. Now she had inherited money and she offered a summerhouse
on the Taylor property, a "stunted bathing house," Thomas called
it, a damp place situated on the river Cherwell. If the problem of
accommodations was temporarily resolved, even if unsatisfactorily,
Thomas still needed money. Donald Taylor had gone bankrupt and
films did not seem an avenue for any immediate employment.

In 1946, the year that the Thomases lived in the Taylors'
summerhouse, income was provided by the B.B.C., which offered
Thomas fifty-three different on-the-air engagements reading poetry or discussing it on panels, an opportunity to act in radio
dramas and to write scripts. With his acting ability and rich voice,
radio was the perfect medium for Thomas. The actor Richard

Burton, who played with Thomas in several B.B.C. productions, remembered Thomas's unusual ability to project his voice when a director asked him to scream: "Dylan, short, bandy, prime, obese, and famous among the bars, screamed as I have never heard, but sometimes imagined a scream, and we were all appalled, our pencils silent above the crossword puzzles, and invisible centuries-gone atavistic hair rose on our backs. And there was a funny silence and Dylan said that he'd bet I couldn't do that scream like that with a cigarette in my mouth and I shook off the centuries, stopped staring, smiled a little, noted that he had indeed monu-mentally screamed with a cigarette in his mouth and went stunned back to my crossword."

Burton's account, amusing as it is as an anecdote, does capture the show-off side of Thomas, the boy who had inscribed "God Save the King" on a schoolhouse wall with his urine, the man who would outdrink everyone else, the "actor" who had to outscream the professional actors. It was a characteristic moment, revealing his boyish pride in his own antics.

The problem with the B.B.C. readings, especially as Caitlin saw it, was that Thomas invariably disappeared for three or four days on a trip to London to earn money, and returned without any, but with a hangover. Much of the B.B.C. work was negotiated in pubs, and after a performance there was usually some sort of pub celebration. In baggy corduroys, a worn and stained tweed jacket, bloated, uncombed, his face flushed, his cigarette dangling from his lips till it went out, Thomas could be seen surrounded by his auditors, whom he would exuberantly entertain in a variety of accents, or rudely attack if he found them pretentious. The critic G. S. Fraser remembered standing near Thomas in a pub close to the B.B.C. Broadcasting House. Thomas told an "immensely long and enor-mously funny" story about a wartime train journey in the dark in a carriage crammed with Canadian soldiers, and his embarrassment at opening an untidy parcel of sandwiches in front of the hungry soldiers, then choking on the sandwiches, and repacking them.

In his pub monologues he provided previews of the eccentric Welsh types he would later portray in his radio play *Under Milk Wood*: a woman with a gooseberry birthmark who lay with dogs, a farm worker convinced that the stream running near his house was the Jordan, a lay preacher who believed the war was begun only to sell newspapers, another man who hung his pony to save a bullet when the pony could no longer work, a woman who screamed "cancer" whenever anyone passed her open door. Thomas's pub encounters were beginning to have a savage, almost sinister edge, such as the one he described with a man who blamed the fact that he had been shot in the groin during the war on the Jews, who then painfully detailed the best way to boil lobsters, and then told Thomas how he had gotten a six-year-old drunk.

When the pubs closed, Thomas often went home with whatever woman he could find who would put up with him, though what he wanted was primarily to be comforted and held. On the next day, his pub rounds began at eleven in the morning. Once Caitlin and Thomas were taken by friends to Ireland, where Thomas was supposed to write a commissioned article about a fair. During this particular fair the pubs were allowed to remain open without closing at all, and Thomas and a friend vowed to stand at the bar and continue drinking Guinness stout on tap. He lasted forty-eight hours, then collapsed speechless—another example of boyish show-ing off.

In Oxford, A. J. P. Taylor was growing severe and distant, tired of the noisy, brawling Thomas family, of Thomas's requests for loans, of Thomas arriving home drunk from London, sixty miles away, sometimes in a taxi for which he could not pay. Margaret Taylor, an intellectual who painted and wrote mediocre poetry, showed her poems to Thomas. Caitlin resented Margaret's proprietary attitude, hated taking her charity, and was suspicious when she found a letter in which Margaret exclaimed that sleeping with Thomas would be like sleeping with a god. Her own marriage was faltering, and later she would propose that Thomas and she elope, but he was never attracted to her, and was interested only in her patronage.

In the spring of 1947, Edith Sitwell, concerned over Thomas's apparent physical deterioration, managed to get him a traveling grant from the Author's Society. The Thomas family went to Italy, settling in a beautiful villa outside Florence with terraces, a pool, a rose garden and a vineyard, cypresses and olive trees. Thomas began writing again, the last poems of "In Country Sleep," which he once described as poems in praise of God's world, written by a man who didn't believe in God, but only in the impending awareness of his own death and the possible death of the planet as a result of the atom-bombing of Hiroshima. The villa was idyllic and Thomas was able to write there, but he hated Italy. Since he did not speak Italian, he could talk to few people. When he was invited to dinner by Eugenio Montale, the Italian poet, he stuffed his own bottles of beer into his pockets because no good beer was available in Italy. He began drinking quickly, shocking his sedate, formal host.

Thomas found the Italian heat intolerable, his own screaming children impossible. He had once written Lawrence Durrell that the "highest hymns of the sun are written in the dark." He had what Caitlin called, using a Welsh term, "hiraeth," or what in English would roughly translate as "hearth," a deep longing for the damp grayness of Wales. The trip to Italy had begun with Thomas putting the luggage on the wrong train. On their return to England, there was another note of the comical disaster that often surrounded Dylan. A friend in London had invited them to stay but was away on holiday, and when Thomas tried to enter through a window, he fell and broke an arm, one of what Caitlin dubbed his chicken bones because they were always breaking. The news that Margaret Taylor had bought a house that she would rent to them for a nominal amount was some consolation. Near Oxford, in the rustic country village of South Leigh, the Manor House, as it was too grandly called, was a small, simple, whitewashed farmhouse in a field. It had no bathroom, only a tin-bucket outhouse, and there was no electricity, it had to be lit with oil lamps, and it was near a German prisoner-of-war camp full of dejected detainees.

Thomas resumed his broadcasts for the B.B.C., and he found some more film work, but money was still a problem. No matter how much he had, no matter what windfall would occur, it seemed mysteriously and quickly to disappear, and there was never enough for necessities or even the rent. In the accumulation of debts, the race against the creditors, and the alcoholic carousing that was in part an effort to forget the debts and the creditors, Thomas seems related to Fitzgerald, cousins in embarrassment, although Fitzgerald's profligacy was conducted on a grander scale. Thomas would borrow from acquaintances, larger sums now, which he had no intention of ever repaying. The financial burden was compounded by the Department of Inland Revenue, which had discovered that Thomas had never filed an income tax statement. He was terrified by the prospect of an investigation, but fortunately an accommodation of sorts was arranged whereby a large portion of his future earnings would be deducted in advance. This arrangement had the unfortunate consequence, however, of insuring that he would never have enough money in the future.

A more serious burden, emotional as well as financial, was the desperate condition of Thomas's parents. His mother had fallen and broken a knee and so could no longer care for D.J., who was a semi-invalid. Harried, trembling, moaning and despairing, D.J. was also losing his eyesight, though all that didn't prevent him from trotting off to the nearest pub. Thomas visited his parents in Wales and impulsively decided he had to bring them back with him to South Leigh by ambulance.

Caitlin was indignant that she was never consulted. For a long time she and Dylan had led separate lives, and he would absent himself from the house as much as possible, though they continued to live together and were still inextricably entwined. The presence of his parents caused Thomas to stay away from the Manor House more than ever, leaving Caitlin to deal with the children and her in-laws as best as she could. Thomas had impulsively responded to his parents' plight—the child-savior—but, characteristically, had never thought of the consequences.

Another complication, which added to their "rows," to use Caitlin's term, was Margaret Taylor, who had given Thomas a trailer to work in, which she felt free to visit whenever it pleased her. Since she had helped and would continue to help, Thomas felt obligated to tolerate her, even perhaps to sustain some romantic fantasy. To a journalist preparing an article on him, Thomas claimed he was only "an impermanent, oscillating, rag-bag" of a man, given to sullen glooms and melancholy, with an atrocious temper and a morbidly obsessive fear of death.

Worried about money, perplexed by film projects and B.B.C. assignments, battling with Caitlin and pursued by Margaret Taylor, whom he did not want, and weary of all the trips to London, he felt he needed an escape, and he imagined that everything would be better if he could only find his way back to Laugharne. With that in mind, Margaret Taylor purchased the Boat House in Laugharne.

The Voyage to Ruin

The Thomases hired a van to drive their furniture down to Laugharne—for the first time in their many moves, they had not had to sell or discard familiar objects. The Boat House was the site they had dreamed of without ever really hoping to be able to take possession of it. Perched on the cliff over the estuary, it stood on stilts just at the high tide line. Reached by an overgrown walk along the cliff edge, it was secluded, with views of the estuary and the hundreds of birds that fed in its muddy flats during low tide. Their living conditions were fairly primitive—a three-story house with six small rooms, an outside well for water, and a lavatory visited almost daily by a one-armed exterminator for what Thomas called tittering rats. But the house had its magical qualities as well, with the high tide reflecting its shimmering light on the ceilings and walls, and the feeling on the second-floor balcony of being at sea. In high tide Caitlin could dive off the garden wall into the estuary, which would in its turn flood the lower part of the garden in fall and spring. Thomas's parents were in another house, more centrally located across from Brown's Hotel, where Thomas liked to drink.

When they moved in May of 1949, Caitlin was seven months pregnant, and she would give birth to another boy that summer, her husband absent as usual. She claimed he seemed happier than ever, spending the morning visiting his parents and occasionally doing a crossword puzzle with his father, having a pint or two at Brown's, listening to the local gossip, then returning to the Boat House for lunch after the children had been fed. He worked in the afternoons, usually from two to seven, as disciplined about his poetry as he had always been. His work space was an old green wooden shed up the walk and away from the house. Small, with two windows facing hills and the sea, the space was cluttered with piles of manuscript, letters, magazines and tradesmen's bills.

Over Thomas's desk was a curled and faded photograph of Walt Whitman, and there were photographs of Hardy and D. H. Lawrence as well, icons of sorts who looked down at Thomas "scribbling, muttering, whispering, intoning, bellowing and juggling" his words, as Caitlin has put it. He had begun a new poem, "Over St. John's Hill," some of its words spurting out without him having any conscious recall of their origins.

He wanted all his time for his poems—he had spent three weeks on the first line of "In the white giant's thigh," he told Vernon Watkins—but there was always the need for money. When Caitlin had Colm, Thomas wrote his friend John Davenport that there was no money for milk or coal, and that on top of everything his father had a bad case of pneumonia. Harassed by the lack of what most of us take for granted, Thomas had a particularly harrowing dream, descending into a deep mountain cave to find his own skeleton hanging.

He did very few radio broadcasts and so needed to make only a few trips to London, but he reneged on several radio and film scripts that he had promised and for which he had already accepted partial payment. This, of course, compromised his credibility with two of the former sources of most of his income, the B.B.C. and the film world. He was earning some money by accepting engagements to read his poems or speak, but these often turned into fiascoes— for example, when he failed to appear at the Swansea branch of the British Medical Association. Instead, he was dead drunk in Bristol, being read to sleep by a childhood friend.

Such lost opportunities could hardly support him, but his hopes rose when he received an invitation to read his poems from John Malcolm Brinnin, Director of the Young Men's and Young Women's Hebrew Association in New York. The "Y," as it was known, was the most prestigious forum for poetry in America, the place where the most prominent poets wanted to read. Thomas had been dreaming of America as the solution to his problems and suggested that he would like to come for three months for an extensive reading tour if Brinnin could arrange it. Arriving at the end of February, 1950, Thomas was bundled in a rough woolen loden coat for an unusually harsh New York winter. He had suffered through a seventeen-hour flight, hung over badly from a giant going-off party to which Caitlin had accompanied him in London. When John Malcolm Brinnin met him at the airport, Thomas looked awful, pallid, with several broken and discolored teeth, his nose swollen, his body bloated. Brinnin was a fan, having discovered Thomas's poems fifteen years earlier. Part bar companion, part secretary, and part nursemaid (the part he didn't like), Brinnin saw more of Thomas than any other American. What he saw was not always easy to take, though Thomas could be sweet and gracious much of the time. On their first evening together, at a dinner for a group of academics whom Thomas despised, Thomas was rude, lewd, aggressive and scatological. After the dinner there was to be a party given by the *New York Times* critic who had interviewed Thomas that morning. As soon as he reached the address, Thomas fell asleep for an hour in Brinnin's car. He had already had too much to drink. That afternoon he had visited the Third Avenue bars, which he observed were all owned by Irishmen.

He would fall asleep in the middle of occasions many times during his three-month tour, or just pass out at parties. This particular party included some of New York's literati: W. H. Auden, who had already warned Brinnin about Thomas's wayward reputation for booze, Lionel and Diana Trilling, and James Agee. Katherine Anne Porter was also there. Fifty-nine years old, old enough perhaps for Thomas to flirt with since he could always be drawn to older women, she was too old for him to seize and lift in the air like some trophy of conquest to which Thomas felt entitled.

Thomas's hotel room was on the thirtieth floor of the Beekman Tower—until the management asked him to leave because of his drinking—in the center of what he described to Caitlin as the nightmare of New York City, a "cancerous Babylon" of huge phallic towers and wailing "banshee sirens" of interminable noise. He could not understand how the inhabitants could tolerate such cacophony, or why they all seemed to be incessantly talking on the telephone—it was like breathing, Thomas observed.

On the morning of his reading, Brinnin found him in a Third Avenue bar, morosely drinking beer and complaining that he felt like "death itself." His face was sepulchral and resigned, his body sagging, but then he revived just prior to going onstage and read brilliantly his own poems and some by Yeats, Hardy and Lawrence. The audience of about a thousand people, a capacity crowd, gave him a tremendous ovation, which was repeated when he read again on the next evening to the same kind of overflow crowd. After each reading, Brinnin noticed, Thomas had uncontrollable fits of coughing, and had to flee to the nearest bar as soon as possible and would then continue bar-hopping in Greenwich Village.

The one person Thomas had wanted to meet in America was the poet Theodore Roethke, who came to New York for this purpose. A big bear of a man with a boyish face, self-doubting and insecure, but like Thomas searching for a universal vision in poems that depended on direct apprehension and recording of the natural world, Roethke believed that illness was a way to break through ordinary perceptions to a supreme reality. Thomas shared this belief. The two men sat in a bar drinking Guinness, talking about poetry, about Dashiell Hammett and Nelson Algren's *The Man With the Golden Arm*, which Thomas especially admired. Then they wandered through some of the bookshops on lower Fourth Avenue and saw a Marx Brothers movie.

Thomas had a particular need to shock his American audiences, behaving much more outrageously than he ever had in London, resembling some of the raunchier male characters in Henry Miller's *Tropic* novels. When he was asked at a party what his poem "The Ballad of a Long Legged Fly" meant, he retorted that it was about a "gigantic fuck." When an aspiring young woman asked him how she might expect to earn a living through poetry, he advised her to consider prostitution. At a meeting with a group of male professors, he wished out loud that everyone present were hermaphroditic so that they could each screw themselves. At Yale, he spoke obscenely about the royal family. When visiting the critic Stanley Edgar Hyman for dinner, Thomas made a concerted pass at his wife, novelist Shirley Jackson, who had to evade him by running through her house. At Mount Holyoke, the oldest women's college in America, the chairman of the English Department remarked that Thomas "read like an angel," but found his performance miraculous because Thomas had drunk so much before it. At a party after his reading, Thomas flirted quite indiscriminately with women faculty and professors' wives, singing his dirty limericks, pinching a few behinds, declaring his need to touch a warm bosom. Then he passed out on the coffee table.

All this contributed to the developing legend of the Pan-poet deflowering the Holyoke maidens. While it is unlikely that Thomas even got to hold anyone's hand at Mount Holyoke, and while the tales of his sexual conquests were surely exaggerated, Brinnin claims that he slept with at least three women in New York: an avant-garde poet, a married fashion model, and a woman Caitlin called Pearl, a journalist he met at *Harper's Bazaar*, the magazine to which he sold a version of his radio broadcast of "A Child's Christmas in Wales."

On tour, Thomas's speech was not always sequential, and he was capable of sudden incoherent digressions. With interviewers he was witty or evasive. When asked what he had been working on before he came to the United States, he replied that for six months he had been staring at the sea and birdwatching, or rather letting the birds watch him. Merely a "voice on wheels," he wrote Caitlin that he was always on the move to his next destination. Occasionally, he would miss his train or bus because he could not stop playing pinball in some bar. At Bryn Mawr, he told British literary critic David Daiches that he thought he was finished as a poet, and that he expected to die soon.

In his letters home, his love for Caitlin and his children increased proportionately the farther west he traveled. He found San Francisco especially beautiful and tried to obtain a teaching position at Berkeley, which never materialized because of his reputation for drinking. He went down to Big Sur to visit Henry Miller, his third wife, Lepska, and their two small children, who lived six thousand feet above the "blinding blue Pacific," he told

Caitlin. Perhaps ironically, Miller seemed "gentle and mellow and gay" to Thomas, who had been experiencing in his travels the kind of inebriated delirium that Miller had once so buoyantly described. The visit was brief, and it had its weird dimensions, as if a fictional character were meeting its maker. For Thomas, Miller's happy domesticity (which in fact was quite unhappy) was only a reminder of what he wanted but now knew was unobtainable.

After three months in America and more than forty readings, Thomas should have been able to save a few thousand dollars, but his money seemed to dissipate almost as soon as he received it. Secretly, Brinnin put eight hundred dollars in a leather handbag he had bought for Caitlin, and packed the bag with Thomas's clothes. This was to be the net profit from his first American tour. With impending taxes and accumulated debts, this sum would hardly suffice. Thomas returned to Laugharne, Caitlin's recriminations and the specter of insomniac worries about money.

Another serious problem was Pearl—the American journalist with whom he had enjoyed a liaison in New York. She was in London during the summer of 1950 and Thomas met her there, using the pretext of meeting John Malcolm Brinnin to talk about another American tour. All three took a boat outing on the Thames and Thomas confided to Brinnin that he was in love with Pearl and with Caitlin but did not know which way to turn. He went with Pearl on a weekend to Brighton, but his mind may have been decided by the more forceful Caitlin, who found in his pocket a letter from Pearl asking him to join her in the south of France. Margaret Taylor, anxious about losing Thomas herself, also told Caitlin that she had seen the lovers together in London, adding to Caitlin's resentment.

In her memoir, Caitlin wrote that she had wanted to leave her husband several times, but felt incapacitated by the children and the fact that there was no money. Caitlin's anger was expressed in an increasing series of intense encounters that began with shouting and often ended with Caitlin pummeling Thomas, pulling his hair and, on one occasion in the presence of Brinnin, pounding his head on the kitchen floor.

There was a respite from the tensions when Thomas went to Iran to work on a filmscript for a documentary on oil. Absence, as the cliché has it, made him miss her and worked to make him want to salvage the marriage. Thomas was always able to be a more ardent lover in his imagination than in reality, and now, sitting far removed in Iran, he could remember that he loved Caitlin and that nothing seemed worth salvaging more than his marriage. He sent Caitlin several imploring letters, declaring both his love and his need to remain with her, which she left unanswered until she finally wrote listing her grievances, a letter that he said made him "want to die." For all her anger, she had taken no actual steps toward ending the marriage. Instead, she seemed less to want to leave him than to secure his repentance—a common enough means of reconciliation between husbands and wives. Reconciliation did not mean peace between them—merely a recognition that they needed and wanted each other.

When Brinnin visited Laugharne in the summer of 1951 to continue the discussions of another American tour, Thomas met him at the train station in a new tweed suit. In a hired car driven by a distant cousin of Thomas's, they proceeded three hundred yards to a pub, and then spent the next two hours driving the thirteen miles to Laugharne, stopping at another half-dozen pubs along the way. Brinnin met Caitlin on their last stop, in Brown's Hotel in Laugharne, and he was struck by the exquisite, fine-boned sharpness of her face. On the next day she questioned him about Pearl. When he balked at answering, she made him the object of all her suspicions about America, the place where her husband would escape his responsibilities and indulge in drunken sex with pursuing women, while she remained in the "moist, smothering, lost boghole" of Wales with children and ailing in-laws.

Caitlin had been picking up men in pubs when her husband was in London, and she had become pregnant again. In her sixth month, with money provided by Marged Howard-Stepney, another of Thomas's patrons, she had an abortion. She hardened toward her husband once more, and found it impossible to either forgive him or accept him as he was. As she tried to explain in her memoir, they each expected a fidelity that would not fit the circumstances they had created—victims of their romantic illusions.

Despite the domestic rancor and turbulence, Thomas was writing poetry again, his final efforts, as it turned out. He had begun "Under Milk Wood," the "Poem on His Birthday," and a villanelle, "Do Not Go Gentle Into That Good Night," inspired by his father's steady disintegration. In the fall of 1952, the Thomas family moved into a basement flat in a run-down London house owned by Margaret Taylor, so that Thomas could earn some B.B.C. money. Caitlin and the children accompanied him because she no longer trusted him alone in London, and because she intended to go to America with him on his projected trip.

Thomas and Caitlin arrived in New York on the *Queen Mary* at the end of January. Brinnin met them and was immediately forced to advance them money because they had brought none, even though Thomas had received an advance for a projected book of his American impressions. Brinnin observed that Caitlin was either sullenly withdrawn or belligerent. She would contradict Thomas at any opportunity with her version of his stories. Brinnin concluded that their marriage had reached a state of open rivalry, which would be displayed that spring during the forty readings that Thomas gave, in a series of public spats and a continuing spectacle of smashed glasses and overturned party tables. When novelist Nelson Algren met them at a party, Algren wrote a friend to say how sorry he felt for them and how enormous their desperation must be for them to have consumed so much liquor. No longer satisfied with beer, both Thomas and Caitlin were downing double whiskies, unlimited quantities of rye and bourbon.

They were also always in need of money. After a lifetime of deprivation, Caitlin began accumulating clothing and gifts for herself and her children. With all the improvidential spending, Thomas forgot to send a check to his son Llewelyn's school and as a result the boy was dismissed, a fact that caused a particularly intense attack by Caitlin in San Francisco. Generally, the American trip was an opportunity for a revenge that she could not control. Deliberately antagonistic, often cruel, she had felt ignored and pushed to the sidelines too long. She saw all American women as sexual hunters, and she had some reason to feel justified on this account when she discovered a cache of love letters in different hands in her husband's briefcase.

During the summer and fall of 1952, Thomas was in Laugharne working very slowly on *Under Milk Wood*, his brilliant comic account of twenty-four hours in the life of a seaside Welsh town like Laugharne. When Brinnin met him in London after one of Thomas's trips to read for the B.B.C., he looked harried, his hair was knotted, his eyes bloodshot and yellow, his complexion blotched. He had been ill with a bronchial complaint that later turned into pleurisy and pneumonia. He was again worried about money; the "nervous hag" that rode him, "biting and scratching into insomnia, nightmare, and the long anxious daylight," as he melodramatically put it in a letter.

There were problems with the payment of back taxes and health insurance premiums. The publisher who had advanced funds for Thomas's American impressions now wanted his money back since nothing had been written. Margaret Taylor was short of money, threatening to have to sell the Boat House unless she received rent. Marged Howard-Stepney, the new patron, committed suicide before she could help buy the house. In the middle of it all, Caitlin announced that she was three months pregnant, unsure of which man had helped her conceive, and she wanted an abortion. Finally, the greatest shock for Thomas was that his father died, and then a few months later his sister Nancy died of cancer in India, where she had gone to live with her second husband. Thomas had never been close to his sister, but his concern for his father had been one of his strongest bonds and in some deep way related to his need to write poetry.

The ability to continue to write poems at all was Thomas's deepest personal concern after his father's death. It had been a gathering worry ever since the beginning of the Second World War, and he had always dreaded any sapping of creativity. Whenever he could not write successfully, he would still struggle with the process, still force himself to face the paper and set down what he could even if he tore it up afterward. His poetry was always deliberately crafted; there were often pages of manuscript for the variant versions of a single line of one of his poems. The poems were hewn, they did not flow from a fount of inspiration. He spent his last year arduously trying to write a verse prologue for his *Collected Poems*, a poem with a very intricate rhyme scheme, but it dissatisfied him and he called it a tangled and sentimental effort.

What depressed him most of all was the gnawing fear that he had depleted his talent, that he would no longer be able to write poems that mattered. Even the great acclaim that accompanied the publication by Dent's of his *Collected Poems: 1934–52* failed to lift his spirits. Poetry, he said, was merely a series of "statements made on the way to the grave." The critics saw his work more enthusiastically. Phillip Toynbee declared him England's greatest living poet in the *Observer*. In the *Sunday Times*, Cyril Connolly said that his uniqueness lay in a lyricism that defied analysis. Stephen Spender called him the incarnate romantic because so much of his work was beyond paraphrase, making it the embodiment of Keats's ideal of a poetry of sensation without discourse.

An Iron Band Around the Skull

Though Caitlin opposed it, Thomas was drawn back to America by Brinnin and the publication of his *Collected Poems* by New Directions. More latently, he was searching for a public energy that he thought he could tap through his readings, a communal knowing he had come closest to demonstrating in the work he had almost completed, *Under Milk Wood*, and the new form of radio drama he hoped it would help forge.

Early in May, he read an unfinished version of *Under Milk Wood* at Harvard, and then, nervously chain-smoking, met with Igor Stravinsky, who wanted him to write a libretto for an opera about a couple who had survived a nuclear catastrophe. Thomas liked Stravinsky and was excited when he was invited to stay at Stravinsky's home in California while writing the libretto.

In New York, where Thomas and five actors would read *Under Milk Wood* at its premiere at the Y, Brinnin found him quieter than on his previous trips, more mellowed. Scribbling additions and revisions on scraps of paper, Thomas was anxious about completing his play, and the pressure of not being able to do that satisfactorily until minutes before its opening was considerable. Some of that pressure may have been relieved by Thomas's liaison with Liz Reitell, Brinnin's assistant at the Y, a tall Bennington graduate who had taken over as nursemaid and confidante. *Under Milk Wood* was a rousing success, and Thomas received another great ovation from the Y audience. But he had been drinking heavily before the premiere, he had suffered several instances of alcoholic gastritis and painful gout, and then had fallen down a flight of stairs after a dinner party and broken his arm. Dr. Milton Feltenstein, the physician who treated him, warned him about his drinking and advised that some course of rehabilitation was imperative.

In Laugharne in the summer of 1953, Thomas listlessly worked on revisions of *Under Milk Wood*, and on an elegy for his father that he could not complete. He spoke of writing a stage play, and did read a story on television, which he finished only minutes before he was scheduled to appear, but he read poorly. He did several B.B.C. broadcasts, and after one of them lost the original manuscript of *Under Milk Wood* in a pub. He was having difficulty writing letters, he spoke of his impending death, and he fainted or suffered blackouts on several occasions.

As usual, he felt the pressure of financial obligations that he could not meet—his children's education, the income tax bills. Quite predictably, he saw America as the way to resolve these pressures though that had not proved true on his previous trips. When he arrived in New York in late October for another series of readings of his poems and *Under Milk Wood*, Brinnin thought his face was flaccid and the color of lime, his lips twisted, his skin blotched and his eyes dull. Thomas told Liz Reitell, who was still willing to help him but now afraid of continuing their liaison, that he felt a pressure like an iron band around his skull.

Although the readings ultimately went well, Thomas was distraught and strained when rehearsing the *Milk Wood* reading at the Y. There were a series of parties at which he got drunk, days when he ate nothing because of anxiety and only drank beer and raw eggs at the White Horse Tavern. At night he took sleeping pills to get some rest and amphetamines to awaken in the morning. On at least two occasions, after vomiting caused by gastritis and a consequent loss of energy, he was visited by Dr. Feltenstein and injected with ACTH, a cortisone drug, which revived him. Two weeks after his arrival in New York, after a day of social engagements and the drinking that inevitably went along with such visits, Liz Reitell brought him back to his room at the Chelsea and stayed with him. At 2:00 A.M. he woke and said he had to go to a bar. He returned an hour and a half later, claiming he had consumed eighteen whiskies. Probably he exaggerated the number, but the next morning he vomited profusely and then suffered an episode of delirium tremens, imagining a procession of triangles, squares and circles. Dr. Feltenstein gave him another cortisone shot, and then was called a second and then a third time during the day. On his third visit to quiet the raving Thomas, he administered a large dose of morphine. Thomas fell asleep immediately but never revived, slipping instead into a coma that would persist for the next four days.

He was taken to St. Vincent's Hospital in the Village, very near the White Horse Tavern, which had been his favorite American drinking haunt. With an oxygen mask and various tubes in his nose, throat and arms, he remained insensate. Brinnin, Liz Reitell and a changing stream of visitors, including the poets e.e. cummings and John Berryman, gathered in a corridor outside the room. When Caitlin arrived, she was in an alcoholic haze. She had written Brinnin that she felt her marriage was at its end and had bitterly opposed the trip. In one of his last powerful poems, Thomas had written to his dying father that he should not die gently but ragingly, fighting with all possible resources till the end. But it was Caitlin who fought, striking her head against a window in his room, breaking a crucifix on the wall, biting an orderly until she had to be restrained with a straitjacket and brought to a private sanatorium for treatment. Later, she futilely attempted suicide several times, attempts which she recognized as alcoholic appeals for help.

Just before he died, ironically enough, Thomas had signed a lucrative lecture contract, and after his death the sales of his poems and the Caedmon recordings of his readings brought an income he had never seen in his lifetime. Caitlin took his body back to Wales on a ship; still riotous she smashed up the ship's bar after drinking five double-whiskies and then did a series of splits and cartwheels in the wreckage.

After Thomas's burial in Laugharne, the rumors began to feed the legend. John Middleton Murray, D. H. Lawrence's friend, wrote to Frieda Lawrence that he found something "appallingly ignoble" about Thomas's death. John Davenport, another friend, observed that the ultimate tragedy for Thomas was that when his lyric gift faltered, he was left only with a public personality that he himself despised. T. S. Eliot observed that as a poet, Thomas either wrote a great poem or "something approaching nonsense," and that his audience should have accepted both. Cyril Connolly said that he had come to America to seek money for those poems, but instead was "mobbed to death," like Orpheus by the Thracian women. For Theodore Roethke, Thomas was the poet who drank his own blood and ate his own marrow to get at his material and deliver it. It was a dance that Roethke knew something about, an expression of what Thomas once called the "burning and crested act" of making poems.

A Romantic Inebriate

Dylan Thomas was a man who lived for the rhythm of words singing in his soul. Like Lawrence, he fought with his wife when she reminded him of his obligations in the world. A romantic, acting on impulses and flashes of feelings that he could easily mistake for the real thing, he was not prepared for the long-range consequences of his actions. Just as he had invited his parents when they were facing hardships to live with him and Caitlin at the Manor House and then disappeared, he felt a charge of emotional well-being from the mere fact of offering love or support that he was unable to sustain in his behavior. He had the generosity of a child who refused to be held accountable. He put Caitlin through hell, and he knew it, but he was powerless to change. And she, who could assault him verbally and physically, was powerless to help herself dissolve the marriage. In fact, neither of them wanted to finish it. Each touched raw nerves in the other, and those exposed nerve endings were a way of feeling alive. It was not merely hyperbole that caused her to title her memoir *Leftover Life to Kill.*

Caitlin Thomas did not have for her husband the Earth Mother dimensions of Frieda Lawrence or the starlit radiance of Zelda Fitzgerald. Nor did she have June Miller's sinister ability to inflict the wound that her husband found so "miraculous." In terms of the effect on Thomas's work, the marriage of Caitlin and Dylan Thomas is more prosaic and familiar, but perhaps more than anything else, Caitlin Thomas's vigor and her untamed fury kept Thomas at the boil that prevented him from slipping into an utterly nihilistic existence. In reality, Thomas needed no outside stimulus to incite his imagination. But he did need her, as he realized when he was away from her in Iran. She saw through him pitilessly and without illusion—the man who wanted to hide behind the veil of a poetic persona but who also needed a cloak of respectability and constancy. For all her volatility, she was a fixed point in a chaotic life that often threatened to overwhelm him.

He lived in a murmuring, mumbling, chaotic cauldron of language, a sort of witch doctor of the word, whose psychic medicine was alcohol. His dependence resembles Fitzgerald's, especially as it is related to deep insecurities about whether he could continue to create. Much of Thomas's work seems to have been written in a preconscious metalinguistic state in which he was only partly aware of what he was transmitting. His voice emerged from an even more deeply unconscious state than with most poetry; it seemed connected somehow to his very blood. Lawrence spoke about "blood-consciousness," but he himself was voluble and intellectual, not as primal an exponent of his own principle as Thomas.

Thomas's emotional life raged loudly at the expense of any restraining intellect or premeditation. Like Lawrence, Thomas responded to the wonders of nature, often more interested in his poems in nonhuman spectacles than in the sort of reasoned articulation that would appeal to an Eliot or an Auden. Like Lawrence, Thomas expressed a pantheistic vitalism which venerated anything he associated with life. Both saw sex in terms of the life-force and knew that when it was powerful, it was capable of a spiritual dimension that could make one healthy and whole. For both Lawrence and Thomas, sex was more an envisaged route to completion than an actual journey they could take. Lawrence saw sex as part of his messianic mission and proselytized for it. Thomas rarely alluded to sex in his poems, and he pursued women blindly and desperately, an infant-ogre groping for maternal comfort.

Thomas was obsessed by death, but in his poems he strenuously proclaimed the miracle of life. His driving awareness was of its brevity. Like Keats, he wrote many of his poems before he was twenty-one. Stumbling and confused in the world of work and career, he stands as the romantic delinquent of our century, our Rimbaud or Villon, acting as a complete irresponsible in matters of family or state. No wonder he could identify with *Tropic of Cancer*, whose hero defiles the idea of community at every turn. Like Miller he is apolitical, not avoiding his taxes because of any ideological stance but because he needed what little money he could earn or cadge for his beer. Besieged, the outlaw artist often seems both ignoble in his desperation, his cunning or conning, and heroic in his defiance, the obstinacy of his choice to live for creation despite the squalor, the odds, the probable defeat. Thomas's prodigal improvidence, his sponging, his petty thievery, gave him a pathetic edge that helped some people forgive him some of the time. Charming, incorrigible, a fabricating taleteller, he was a man for whom action had less significance than language. The poems he could write and then read aloud in his magical voice were astonishing enough to make most of those whom he betrayed rationalize his weaknesses.

His reputation became transmogrified into legend in post–World War II America, a time when Eliot's influence on poetry was preeminent. As a reader aloud of his own work, Eliot was dry, as distant as the wasteland he evoked. Instead of invoking the lacerating aridity of Eliot, Thomas was the impassioned whirlwind of sheer sound and sensuous image, which overwhelmed emotionally more than it signified. Such momentum can disturb order and risk unintelligibility, dangerous possibilities for any poet. In a historical moment when totalitarian order had almost crushed Europe, Thomas raised his voice to speak from the heart's blood. The urgency, despair and lyricism of his voice had its anachronistic quality, but most would agree that it was a phenomenally romantic cry.

Sylvia Plath and Ted Hughes

♔ 6 ♔

Sylvia and Ted

Oh, only left to myself, what
a poet I will flay myself into.
Journals, May 11, 1958

Dying
Is an art, like everything else.
I do it exceptionally well.

I do it so it feels like hell.
I do it so it feels real.
I guess you could say I've got a call
From "Lady Lazarus"

Possession

"THE BLOOD JET is poetry," Sylvia Plath once exclaimed in a poem. "There is no stopping it." In the winter of 1962–63, the last four months of her abbreviated life, she would wake herself at 4:00 A.M. from a drugged sleep to write poetry before her children rose and the drudgery of the day began. Using a hallucinated voice—like writing in a "train tunnel" or in "God's intestines," she told a friend—she wrote a series of poems of brutal and hypnotic power that shocked the literary world in England and America. These grim predictions of her own doom were posthumously published as *Ariel*. Joyce Carol Oates proclaimed her our last Romantic, especially because of her self-pitying solipsism. Others called her the most ruthlessly original poet of her generation. The novelist Doris Lessing met her in the last month of her eerie writing surge and later spoke of an "incandescent desperation" that drove her.

Her husband, the poet Ted Hughes, from whom she was separated in those terrible final months before she took her own life,

255

insisted on a shamanistic dimension to her last poems, comparing them to visitations from a spirit world, saying that they were written with a "free and controlled access to depths formerly reserved to primitive ecstatic priests." He also suggested that she was without the "usual guards" most people invent to shield themselves from their own reality—in other words, that she may have been too sensitive to her own pain, and that she too readily took on the world's pain without a capacity for rationalizing anodynes.

The woman who had sought all of her life a perfect, "smashing" love that in some magical way would safeguard her sanity and protect her life, the love that "casteth out fear," had at the end of her life no protective resources left. When her marriage collapsed, she announced in her journals that she had a violence in her "as hot as death's blood" and she began to use that violence in the anguished last poems, poems like "Lady Lazarus" or "Daddy," which portrayed an ill, abused, betrayed woman using her art as her only vengeance. Her friend A. Alvarez, the editor and critic, proposed that she was possessed—in effect that she existed primarily for the shaping and expression of a vision that may have been as demonic as it was transcendent. In *The Savage God,* his book on suicide, he suggested that the intensity of the last poems in some way prepared Plath for her death, opening an emotional door through which she would pass more easily because of what she had released in her poems. The circumstances surrounding the composition of these poems, their urgent self-loathing intensities, their paroxysms of rage in a medium of almost poisonous clarity, their gallows humor and dreadful foreknowledge of death, make them seem more like telepathic messages.

Plath's poems presume an anger so great that it seems to reach beyond her own personal dissatisfactions to embrace the centuries of subordination, servitude and denial that we associate with the female experience. In her journals, she saw herself as a "vessel of tragic experience." As a young woman attending an outstanding college, brilliant in her accomplishments and extremely ambitious for herself, imbued even then with an overwhelming sense of pain and fear, she had tried to kill herself with pills and would have succeeded had she not been heard moaning in a crawl space two days later. Institutionalized, she was treated with electric shock, which terrified her and caused a "fire under her skin." Much of her subsequent writing would refer to such trauma. She said her first book of poems, *The Colossus,* was a book about being "broken and mended." Her novel, *The Bell Jar*, was a fictionalized version of her breakdown and recovery. Writing that novel, she forged a protective voice, wry, brazen, arrogantly cutting and clever; it was a voice that gave her some measure of control over the experience, an authentic vessel to contain and seal in the terrors that were always close to the surface.

Her poems were influenced by Hughes, who was her pivotal, immediate audience, but in some mysteriously brooding way she felt relegated to his shadow, less significant than her husband, whose reputation and contacts were larger than her own. She used the harmonies and abrasions of her marriage as a subject, without relinquishing her belief in the redemptive powers of perfect love and perfect marriage. At the same time, she resisted being totally subsumed by her image of romantic love. A central concern for her was her fear that marriage might sap her creative powers and diminish her.

Sylvia Plath's marriage to Ted Hughes exposes and highlights many of the issues faced by the couples in this book. Frieda Lawrence, Zelda Fitzgerald and Caitlin Thomas were engaged in struggles for leverage against the dominance of their husbands. All these women had pronounced but unrealized creative drives that caused them to both admire and become jealous of their husbands. Like them, Plath was assertive, combative and unsubmissive, but in her case, the struggle was complicated by the fact that she and Hughes were both poets of passionate intensity and commitment. Her battle to claim her own identity, the anguish of the last months of her marriage and the incendiary nature of the *Ariel* poems served to make her an issue beyond the ordinary concerns of poetry and aesthetics. While the marriage is central to any consideration of Plath's art, it is complicated by the psychological predispositions she brought to it. When she met Ted Hughes, married him and had children—all the roles a young woman at the time (the mid-1950s) was expected to fulfull—she seemed on the surface as radiantly smiling as ever, as involved in domestic affairs as in her work. Essentially Plath's life is a testament to the unreliability of appearances—itself, perhaps, the most fundamental of literary motifs.

Daddy

Born quite coincidentally on Dylan Thomas's eighteenth birthday, on October 27, 1932, Sylvia Plath was an especially precocious child who had her first simple poem published in a Boston newspaper when she was eight. Bright children are usually the most impressionable, and she began forming sentences before she could walk. While it has become commonplace to assume that parents influence their children, that children often become their parents' projections, Sylvia was unusually affected by Otto and Aurelia Plath.

A scholarly entomologist who taught at Boston University, Otto Plath had written a standard text on bumblebees, a subject that began to fascinate him when as a young boy in Germany he habitually stole honey from field hives because there was no money for sweets. In her novel, *The Bell Jar*, Plath wrote that her father was born in some "manic-depressive hamlet in the black heart of Prussia." Otto Plath once told his wife that his mother and a sister had suffered from depression. His grandparents had already settled in Wisconsin, and they paid his fare to New York City, where he spent a year learning English by auditing elementary school classes; he had so pronounced a gift for languages that he learned to speak English without an accent. His grandparents offered to subsidize his college education, hoping that he would become a minister—the Plaths were strict Lutherans. Instead, he studied classical languages, decided to become a teacher and broke with his family altogether. For a period of eighteen years, after a brief first marriage, he pursued graduate studies in zoology while supporting himself by teaching German and biology.

Aurelia Schober, Sylvia's mother, was a student in a graduate class in Middle High German that Otto Plath was teaching at Boston University. Aurelia's family had emigrated from Austria; though she was born in America, she spoke only German until she began school. Imbued with the profound respect for education shared by many European immigrants after the turn of the century, she fully subscribed to the notion that through sustained effort one could improve one's condition in life. She read widely, believed Horatio Alger's stories about effort leading to opportunity, worked in a public library during high school, and as a typist and secretary. When she met Otto Plath she had already been teaching German and English in a high school for a year, and she brought the missionary zeal of the young to her work. When she married, she agreed to stay home and care for her children, one of many compromises.

In her introduction to *Letters Home*, a collection of her daughter's letters, which she edited after Sylvia Plath's death, Aurelia admitted that she had subordinated her own inclinations for the sake of domestic harmony. But it is also true that her husband was much older, that as her teacher he was a figure of authority and that he often seemed autocratic. One year after her marriage, she had Sylvia; two and a half years later, a son named Warren. Like many college professors, Otto was home most of the time. Aurelia assisted him in his research and writing as secretary and collaborator, remembering in *Letters Home* how he had insisted on spreading his material over the dining room table, where it remained for months. Occasionally, on the evening that Otto taught a night class, she would invite someone for dinner and have to make a map so that everything could be returned to its proper place. Otto Plath was devoted to work and accomplishment and he dominated his household, even to the point of doing the marketing because he believed he could purchase food more economically than his wife.

Though a loving father, surely not the fascist with the *Mein Kampf* look Sylvia would later invent for him in her poem "Daddy," Otto left his children to his wife's care and retreated to his study. Sylvia was eager for his approval and especially competitive with her younger brother, whose appearance she had initially resented. In a radio talk which she prepared shortly before her death, "Ocean 1212W," she remembered in a classic instance of sibling rivalry how Warren's birth had "wrenched" the axis of her little world, leaving her with a "polar chill" and a well-defined sense of her own separateness. By this point the Plaths had moved to Winthrop, Massachusetts, a shore town within commuting distance of Boston. Aurelia's parents lived there, in a house on Point Shirley facing an Atlantic bay, with Aurelia's younger sister and a brother who was only thirteen years older than Sylvia. The opportunity to be with her extended family was fortunate for Aurelia because Otto was not a social person. When he fell ill and suspected that he had cancer, though stubbornly refusing to see a doctor, the Point Shirley house became a place to send Sylvia. Warren was also frail; suffering from bronchial problems and asthma, he remained at home so that at Point Shirley Sylvia was again the lone child, often the center of everyone's attention. As she reveals in "Ocean 1212W," she had the sea as perpetual playmate.

Believing that he could cure himself through the force of indomitable will, Otto Plath would become enraged at the slightest suggestion that he needed medical attention. He developed a chronic cough and sinusitis, his formerly ruddy complexion paled, he lost weight and he withdrew even more into the world of his study. He needed his wife's help to prepare his lectures, and when he would return from Boston, he was invariably exhausted. Evenings, for only a half hour, the children were permitted their visit, to sing a rhyme, to show a drawing or to perform a little dance for their father's affection. A natural pedagogue, Otto encouraged his children's precociousness, teaching them the Latin names of insects and then testing them on their knowledge. Aurelia was also a teacher at heart, and she would urge Sylvia to play the piano, or would read poetry to her. In "Ocean 1212W," Sylvia remembered how her flesh quivered when she first heard Matthew Arnold's "Foresaken Merman," which confirmed for her a belief in the mythical creatures of the sea.

In the summer of 1940, when Sylvia was eight, Otto Plath stubbed a toe before leaving for Boston. When he returned that evening, his foot was black, with red streaks running up his leg. Aurelia called a doctor, who found the leg gangrenous and diagnosed Otto as having an advanced case of diabetes, a disease that would have been treatable had he sought assistance in time. For the next few weeks his colleagues covered his classes. A nurse was hired to help, and Sylvia wore a miniature nurse's uniform. On the nurse's first day off, while Aurelia and the children were out, Otto collapsed going down a stairway. A specialist was consulted, and he decided the leg would have to be amputated. The operation crushed Otto Plath's will, and he never rose from his hospital bed, dying a month later of an embolism in his lung.

On the following morning, when Aurelia informed Sylvia that her father had died, she woodenly remarked that she would "never speak to God again." In her introduction to *Letters Home*, Aurelia reported that her eight-year-old daughter insisted on attending school that day, returning with a piece of paper on which she had written "I PROMISE NEVER TO MARRY AGAIN," with a space below for Aurelia's signature. Mrs. Plath signed the promise immediately, noticing that Sylvia sighed as if greatly relieved and pushed her chair against her mother's. Leaning against her arm, she ate the cookies and milk that her mother provided. The little vignette is tender and revealing. Although Sylvia would later berate her mother for her insufficient display of grief on the occasion of her father's death, she intuitively understood from the start that now her mother would become her exclusive source for approval, encouragement and support.

"Psychic Osmosis"

Otto Plath was not entitled to a pension, and the little insurance money was quickly dissipated for medical and funeral expenses. His premature death, however, was only the start of a chain of calamity. To save money, Aurelia's parents moved into her house so that Mrs. Schober would be able to help take care of the children while Aurelia resumed teaching high school. Both children were ill with chronic sinusitis, and Warren had pneumonia. Worried about the future and pressured, Aurelia developed a duodenal ulcer and on two occasions began hemorrhaging so severely she needed to be hospitalized. Then her father lost his job as an accountant because of failing eyesight. Even-tempered, genial, he was able to find work as a steward in a country club, but that meant he had to live on the premises and only return home on weekends. For Sylvia, the strong paternal center represented by Otto Plath was suddenly gone, with no one to replace it. The household was run by women—her mother earning the means and her grandmother in charge of all the domestic details, even the family car, since at that point she was the only one with a license.

In 1942, two years after Otto's death, Aurelia Plath was asked to start a program for medical secretaries at Boston University, a job she would retain for twenty-nine years. In order to be closer to Boston, and because of several faculty wives she knew who lived there, Aurelia moved her family to Wellesley, which was inland and likely to be good for her children's sinus conditions and Warren's asthma. There was enough money for necessities, but matters needed to be managed with a view to economy. Meanwhile, America's participation in World War II had begun.

For Aurelia war tensions were compounded to a certain extent by the predicament of being German while her adopted country was at war with Germany. As compensation, she advocated community principles, partly to assure her own credentials as an American and partly to see to it that her children were accepted without the blemish of Germanic associations. She taught Sunday school at the Unitarian Church. She thought the right books were as important for her children as the right friends, who were mostly the children of other faculty at Boston University. She brought them to concerts and the theater—Sylvia's first play was *The Tempest*. Sylvia studied piano and viola and continued to read poetry with her mother. She was beginning to write her own poems, and after Otto's death

Aurelia heard her daughter recite a spontaneous couplet comparing the moon to a witch. In *Letters Home*, Aurelia noted that the same sort of "psychic osmosis" that had occurred between her mother and herself was now present between Sylvia and herself. The closeness, she knew, could develop into claustrophobia. Such a condition was all the more possible because they had to share a bedroom, a situation that persisted until Sylvia was a junior in high school and Warren was accepted on a full scholarship to Phillips Exeter, a fine prep school in New Hampshire.

Actually, the term "psychic osmosis" is a euphemism for control and maternal dominance, another pattern prevalent in the lives of the writers discussed here. The fathers of Lawrence, Fitzgerald, Miller and Thomas were absent or ineffectual, forfeiting domestic command to mothers who represented authority and convention. The rebellion against the mother is subversive in the case of Lawrence, who never severed the tie or totally repudiated her, and more ambivalent in the case of Miller, whose dual regard of women was always poised between the unobtainable object and her opposite. It is more intangible in the case of Fitzgerald, who struggled unsuccessfully with his matricidal novel without ever finding a way of expressing or integrating his negative feelings, except in his total rebellion against his mother's middle-class morality. Thomas, who refused to relinquish the role of the child, always seemed to search out someone who could offer some kind of temporary nurturing or consolation. Thomas gives the impression of summoning up the entire ambience of his childhood, which he wrote about with stunning effect, rather than a particular parental figure, though all of his life he was in flight from the values of his mother's fundamentalist Welsh faith. Plath seems to have been the most confused by her mother's expectations and her rebellion may have been more inward.

Aurelia Plath's anxiety about being accepted certainly left its stamp on Sylvia. But Aurelia was also a remarkable mother in many ways, who saw what was extraordinary in her daughter and fostered the development of Sylvia's gifts, without ever calculating that those gifts might lead Sylvia along an independent path that was as frightening as it was vital to her identity. Of all the writers here, Plath may have been the most restrained as well as the most nurtured by her mother's influence—a difficult situation in which to maneuver.

Called "Siv" or "Sivvy," Sylvia was an awkward five feet eight when she entered high school, only an inch under her eventual height. She would always be conscious of her height, worried that she was too tall to suit most men. Talkative and capable of a forced cheer, she wanted to be popular and devised strategies toward that end in her diaries, but there were obstacles. As she had once noted herself in a scrapbook she kept, she felt "doomed" always to be on the periphery, an outsider. What she wanted most was acceptance and a feeling of belonging, which was her response to a tremendous pressure to conform, adjust and cooperate that dominated the mood of the postwar era, and which the media did its best to advertise. One of her favorite magazines, the *Ladies' Home Journal* exemplified and preached the joys of family and domesticity, emphasizing the importance of selecting the man whose career would determine his wife's social status and consequent happiness.

Wellesley was an affluent suburb where Sylvia's prospective value as a future wife was compromised by her relative lack of means. There was no money for travel or for fancy summer camps or vacations. For six summers, she spent two weeks roughing it in an inexpensive Girl Scout camp with simple food and facilities. With an insufficient clothing allowance, she babysat to earn extra money. She wanted to go out with boys, and she did date, but the most eligible boys found her either too smart, too competitive or too poor. The mating game of "testing, trying," she noted in the journals, was also frustrating because of the sexual boundaries young women of that era felt obligated to respect. While she felt frustrated by such sexual boundaries, she could "hate, hate, hate boys who display sexual hunger freely." The comment, again from the journals, gets its intensity from the triple repetition that she would later use so passionately in her last poems; in general, the sharp perceptions of her journals, with their devastating honesty and directness, would not be expressed with the same power in her poetry until just before her death.

In *Letters Home*, Mrs. Plath included a segment of her daughter's diary, written when Sylvia was seventeen. In it she stressed her desire for artistic and personal perfection, at one point calling herself the "girl who wanted to be God." At the same time she remonstrates with herself for her egotism, which is contradicted by what she sees when she is transfixed by her image in her mirror. She knows that she is too tall, that her nose is too fleshy, yet she preens before her own reflection. She is left with the polarities of the divine omniscience to which she aspires (realizing that it is foolishness, but also that it is connected to wanting to write) and the blemished beauty in the mirror. In a sense she is mesmerized by the image of her evolving womanhood—staring into the mirror at seventeen must be some avatar of initiation, the cracking voice of a woman still emerging from adolescence, still inhibited by a virginity required by her historical moment and her place in the scheme of things. She is both happy to be in the final stages of her youth and unhappy to be leaving it.

In high school she consistently received the highest grades, driven by a need to excel, to reach for perfection and through such effort to achieve some recognition and control in any situation in which she found herself. To a large extent, she had been conditioned in her obsessive quest to be the best student by parents whose approval was always based on her accomplishment. While she succeeded as a student, that success required hours of effort in study and preparation on top of a full schedule that included basketball and orchestra practice and work on the school newspaper. If all this activity helped develop her organizational capacities and her discipline, the fear of not consistently fulfilling her own high expectations caused a persistent anxiety reflected in insomnia which she tried to alleviate with sleeping pills.

Pills would become the sort of fuel for Plath that alcohol had been for Fitzgerald and Thomas, a way to relieve unbearable tensions of the spirit and mind and jar the space, to rearrange the intolerable humdrum of repetitive events with some ingested agent that, taken frequently and to excess, would galvanize them. Her creative expression is, of course, the consequence of great force, and some artists seem to need a kick-start catalyst.

The only real outlet she had for her anxiety was her writing: diaries, letters, poems and stories, articles for the school paper. In her first year of high school, she gave a few poems to her English teacher, Wilbury Crockett. He had taught a few college classes, he had unusually high standards, and he was impressed by the sensitivity and awareness that he felt in the poems. One that Crockett liked particularly, "I Thought That I Could Not Be Hurt," had been written when Sylvia was fourteen. It projected a dark, otherwise silenced part of herself, an invulnerability to suffering or mental agony that is later amended in the poem by a consciousness of human frailty. The poem indicates that Plath was reading Emily Dickinson without having yet developed a capacity for her concise, surprising images or wry understatement, but, as Crockett recognized, it showed a powerful lyric gift. Crockett was the rare kind of teacher who tries to give his students a lot of individual attention. Occasionally, Sylvia would bicycle over to his house with some special question. He was her English teacher for three years and he saw the enthusiastic, outgoing side that she could present to the world. It was a convincing presentation and Crockett, like most people who knew her, thought she was especially well-adjusted.

Sylvia needed little encouragement to write, and Crockett's support was confirming, but she also felt the need to justify her fledgling literary efforts with the expectation of publication and payment. In another poem, written when she was fifteen, she admitted that she had to write because of an inner voice that would not be stilled, but only the mask she was then still learning to assume of perfect American femininity would explain why she tried so hard to win acceptance in glossy magazines like *Seventeen* or the *Ladies' Home Journal*. In the summer of 1950, after graduating from high school, and after having collected forty-five rejections from *Seventeen* and scouring it to decipher its style, she finally received notice that her sentimental story about a girl falling in love with her tennis teacher, and then a poem, had been accepted for publication.

One result of the *Seventeen* story was the beginning of a long correspondence and friendship with Ed Cohen, a young man four years older than Sylvia, who liked the story and wrote to her because of it. Cohen had dropped out of the University of Chicago and had lived with a girlfriend and in Mexico for a while. He seemed more mature than many of the boys Sylvia had dated. A political radical who attacked the anti-Communist McCarthyism of the period and the American involvement in Korea, he spoke a language that the pacifist Sylvia could appreciate and share. In one of her letters to Cohen she described spending the summer working on a vegetable farm, soiling her hands in the dirt as a means of repudiating her own middle-class upbringing. Recognizing a kindred spirit, she told Cohen that she felt alienated and was capable of a skeptical sarcasm that could be interpreted as callousness, but that really was a way of protecting herself. That sarcasm would become an eminent feature of her last poems, an indelible element in the angry voice she devised for them.

The Scrubbed, Shining, Expectant

Sylvia Plath had been offered a scholarship to Wellesley, but that meant living at home with her mother and a subsequent sacrifice of independence at a time when she felt she needed it most. As it was, she confessed in her journals, she had already been too influenced. The echo of Aurelia's voice in her own frightened her; she could imagine her mother's facial expression emanating from her own face. Her alternative to Wellesley was a partial scholarship to Smith, one of the Seven Sister colleges socially affiliated with the Ivy League and located in Northampton, Massachusetts. To Sylvia, receiving the scholarship, which was mostly financed by an endowment established by Olive Higgins Prouty, a successful romantic novelist, meant she would have to work all the more strenuously to justify it.

Sylvia had a tremendous capacity for worry—another quality she shared with Aurelia—about the threat of nuclear annihilation, about her fear that she could not make her life significant enough to describe in her writing, about her future academic performance, even the concern that she would not receive an A in her first English course. In her letters to Aurelia, she asserted that she was happy, but in her journals she questioned the terms of her identity and expressed a "horrible and overpowering" loneliness. The split between her surface equanimity and her private perceptions was growing and hardening.

As usual, she had the problem of fitting in, of somehow accommodating herself to the forty-seven other women who shared her house, even though she knew she felt naturally more comfortable when with men. One of her subsequent roommates, Nancy Hunter Steiner, has observed that the women at Smith were almost without exception "scrubbed, shining, expectant." Though there were no male students to preen in front of, clothing and coiffure were quite important, skirts had to match cashmere sweaters. Bermuda shorts were worn with knee socks and a button-down shirt. The Smith girl was supposed to be a busy participant, she was being educated for social involvement, though at the same time she tacitly understood "that she was interchangeable with dozens of others just like her." Instead of playing bridge, Sylvia would spend evenings and weekends sequestered in her room, and so was dismissed as a grind. The isolation of her room was connected to her desire to write, which in turn was a function of childhood introversion.

More and more, she was concerned with men and her emerging sexuality. While she was glad she had no male classmates, to whom she would have deferred, according to her mother she felt an "intense craving" for male companionship, which in her journals she connected to the early absence of her father. She attended a lecture on "Sex Before Marriage" and she went out on several blind dates. One of them was arranged by a Jewish classmate who was her best friend in her first semester, Ann Davidow, who would transfer out of Smith in January after contemplating suicide with sleeping pills. The young man was a student at Amherst who told her that when she spoke she was either overdramatic or as innocent as a schoolgirl giving her first report. They saw each other again, and he wanted to see more of her, but he had no spark, she told her mother. Dating, she explained in one of her letters to Aurelia, meant going to Yale or Dartmouth for a weekend, where the major activity would be drinking at a fraternity party.

She had another blind date with a former marine. When she tried to get him to confide in her, he bluntly told her that he wanted to make love. The marine, she felt, was not a bad sort—he had been wounded and like Hemingway had had a hospital affair with his English nurse—but he helped her realize that "most American males worship women as a sex machine." As if confirming so cynical a view of American men, she received a spontaneous visit from Ed Cohen. She had written quite freely to him in her letters of her sexual frustrations, but she had hoped in her journals that she would never have to actually meet him. Impulsively, he had borrowed a family car and driven nonstop from Chicago, appearing disheveled and unwashed just as Sylvia was preparing to return to Wellesley for a weekend. Unsettled by his unannounced appearance, she allowed him to drive her in silence to Wellesley, but then coldly dismissed him. Although Aurelia was surprised, Sylvia had understood her suitor's secret purpose. In a subsequent letter, Cohen acknowledged that he continued to New York, where he was able to gratify himself with another woman. Blaming Sylvia for her bad manners, he announced that he was seeking psychiatric help and suggested that she might benefit by a similar course.

In her journals she argued that she had no intention of yielding her body unless her mind was first satisfied, and she wondered whether she would be lucky enough to find a man who was physically magnetic and intelligent enough to share her spirit. She had been dating a Wellesley neighbor, Dick Norton, whose younger brother Perry had been her childhood playmate. Although she had always been more attracted to Perry, it was Dick who invited her to several weekends at Yale.

A tall, good-looking blond man, Norton was a senior who had been accepted to Harvard Medical School. Sylvia could appreciate his scientific interests and was especially intrigued by his account of a visit to a mental institution as part of a sociology course requirement. Sylvia was excited when he invited her to his senior prom, borrowing articles of clothing from some of her housemates, but was devastated a week later when she learned in a letter that he had come to Smith without warning her to escort Jane Anderson, another Wellesley girl, to a dance. She never expressed her anger to him directly and he continued to write to her. Norton spent two more weekends visiting Plath at Smith, and she attended his graduation at Yale in May with his family, who assumed that Dick and Sylvia were practically engaged. On the surface, she was living the perfect collegiate life featured in *Seventeen* and the women's magazines she read so avidly: an Ivy League boyfriend, dates, proms, invitations to Yale, the prospect of marrying well. Yet she was puzzled because he seemed to regard her more as a pal than as a prospective mate and lover; he still referred to her mother as "Aunt Aurelia" and to her as "dear cousin" in his letters. But she wasn't ready to bring her disquiet to the surface. Instead, during the summer she took a job as a mother's helper in Swampscott, on the Massachusetts coast, so that she could be near Norton, who was working as a busboy in a hotel in Brewster, where his parents owned a summer cottage.

Washing, ironing, cooking, making beds and supervising the play of three small children left her drained, feeling worthless because she had no mental strength left to read a book, think or write. The work was so consuming that she did not have the energy to visit Dick in Brewster when he invited her. When she did manage to see him, he admitted to an affair with a Vassar student who was working as a waitress in the same hotel, in part blaming Sylvia for not having visited him when he needed company.

Dick Norton was a fitting projection of Aurelia Plath's idea of the acceptable husband, the clean-cut neighbor boy who was on his way to making good in America, a fifties dream whose appearance radiated confidence. In time, Sylvia Plath would choose her own version of the acceptable husband, the poet whose interests coincided with her own, but she held tight to the fifties dream of marriage as an expression of "togetherness" and fidelity. Dick Norton's confession of an affair with the Vassar student left Plath feeling deprived and jealous of the pleasures of promiscuity available to men. In her journals she expressed "insidious, malignant, latent" envy of men's abilities to divide their careers and families. It is a perspective that Frieda Lawrence, Zelda Fitzgerald and Caitlin Thomas certainly shared, a feeling that it was luckier and easier to have been born male, that the world was organized by men for their comfort and that women could only share in part of it, according to definitions proposed and instituted by men. But writers have an advantage that Plath availed herself of when she took her revenge on Dick Norton a decade later by exposing his weaknesses as Buddy Willard in *The Bell Jar*.

By questioning Dick's appeal, she had begun to shake herself free of her mother's expectations, but couldn't yet articulate an alternative. Confused and ambivalent, she was not ready to sever the threads of her connection to Dick when she returned to Smith.

As a means of economizing, Plath shared a room with Marcia Brown, an outgoing, confident young woman with many established friendships among the other students. She felt at ease with Marcia, who helped her integrate into college life. She also felt less pressure academically, taking special pleasure in a creative writing course. Two of the stories and five of the poems she wrote for that class appeared in *Seventeen*, and a third story would win a fiction contest sponsored by *Mademoiselle*. Plath was elected to the editorial board of the college literary magazine, to the arts honor society, and she was paid to write press releases for the college.

She was still corresponding with Ed Cohen, whose letters were important to her because he was so outside the mainstream, so disaffiliated, such a clear foil to Dick Norton. She met Cohen again with a friend in Boston, but in person, as had been true the time before, he seemed less compelling than on paper. Even as she sympathized with his radical views, she was attracted as a writer to the privileged world of Smith, and the women she encountered there.

One weekend during autumn foliage, she was invited along with fifteen of her classmates to Maureen Buckley's coming-out party in Sharon, Connecticut. The Buckleys were a wealthy family. One of Maureen's brothers, William F. Buckley, had just written *God and Man at Yale*, a book that was widely read and discussed. The limousines, the spreading lawns and great elms, oaks and maples in glorious golden color, the bedrooms with their balconies and French doors, all contributed to an atmosphere of luxury that she had never experienced on such a scale. She found the air of old-time wealth and snobbery intoxicating, at least for a while. She met a number of Yale seniors—several of whom knew Dick Norton—and a Princetonian, the handsome son of a Russian general who made the romantic setting all the more enticing. When a few weeks later, the Russian invited her to Princeton, she had to discourage him with the excuse of her exams.

Instead, she went up to Harvard to visit Dick Norton. Disguising her as a student nurse, he took her into a maternity hospital and showed her fetuses lined in bottles in one room and an actual birth at which he was assisting in another. The tour may have been Norton's subtle signaling of what he really wanted, a wife who would give him children and family. Sylvia felt he had shifted the grounds of their courtship to an arena where she could not compete successfully, where his authority was clear. In her journals she wondered whether Dick's game all along had been simply domination, and his interest in writing simply a manipulative lever. They were doomed, a favorite word in her journals, endlessly to compete without cooperating. While initially she had been attracted to his scientific interests—on some level, perhaps, surrogates for Otto Plath's—she was repelled when he seemed condescending, like the time he said, in a letter, that poems were only "inconsequential dust."

When she saw him in Wellesley over Christmas, he seemed less inhibited, more intimate in his touching. On a later visit to Harvard that spring, they read Hemingway aloud to each other for seven hours, but by then she realized that she was not in love with Dick Norton, no matter how suitable he seemed. He had already intimated the difficulties he imagined for her as a writer living in a small town, burdened with children. Furthermore, as she admitted in her journals, she was bluntly and concisely "in love only with myself." Though the statement seems like sheer postadolescent narcissism, it is balanced in the journals by periodic bouts of self-belittlement and uncertainty. A word she repeats is "ricocheting," at one point from an awareness of the brevity of life to the "dizzy joy" she feels on the weekend at the Buckley estate, at another between her real feelings and the masks one assumes as part of the "monumental grotesque joke" of existence.

Sylvia began the summer of 1952 working as a waitress in a hotel on Cape Cod. Inexperienced, she was assigned to serve the hotel staff. The work made her conscious of her awkwardness. At five feet nine and almost 140 pounds, she felt oafish and clumsy. There were a number of young men who seemed worth meeting, although she predicted in a letter to her mother that she would have little success because she was not a "drinking flirt" like some of the other girls, but conservative, a quiet, gracious type who tended to be too serious and metaphysical in conversation. Of course, this was the side she needed to put forth to her mother, the reassurance that she was a good girl. Actually, she was capable of considerable boldness with men, as she would eventually demonstrate.

She was jubilant when she learned that she had won the *Mademoiselle* fiction contest, and felt her new surroundings would give her rich material for another story. By midsummer, however, she had become ill with a bad sinus infection and decided she could recuperate better at home. Once there she felt little inclination to return to waitressing, especially when she realized that the five-hundred-dollar prize money was more than what she could have earned.

During the days she needed to recuperate, reading and idling—a rare space unavailable to her during her hectic schedule at Smith—she conceived of the bell jar metaphor that she would later use for her novel. She imagined a community regulated in the repetition of its routine like clockwork, its atmosphere controlled by a sealing, protective dome. She may have read Anaïs Nin's surrealistic story "Under a Glass Bell," but the concept was clearly an outgrowth of her view of the grotesqueness she saw in the world.

Aurelia disapproved of her plan to read and write, feeling, perhaps compulsively, that Sylvia needed to earn money during the summer recess, needed to work continuously as she herself had before meeting Otto Plath and since his death. Aurelia not only taught every summer, she also did babysitting. Through an advertisement in the *Christian Science Monitor*, Sylvia found a mother's-helper job on the Cape. Her employers were amiable, and their children were older and less taxing. But her mother had made a serious mistake in not understanding that Plath needed time out, that she had been driving herself without benefit of her mother's strength, determined fortitude or undivided vision of hard work as its own reward and as a necessary step to future rewards. Her mother's example and attitude put pressure on Plath to pursue success doggedly even when she was tired both physically and emotionally. Plath imbued the possibility of failure with fatality.

In her junior year at Smith, she was required to take a course in the physical sciences that she found both boring and incomprehensible. She was filled with panic and dread that she would fail the course and compromise her academic standing. The prospect was so terrifying that in her journals she expressed the thought of killing herself as a way to escape responsibility. It was a clear and terrible warning. She wondered about Virginia Woolf's suicide and whether work and accomplishment were only a sublimation of a deeper desire for a death, which she saw as a return to the womb.

In a letter to her mother, she admitted that her despair over the course had caused suicidal reflections, "annihilating her will and love of life." Aurelia Plath seems unable to have heard such an appeal, or at least to have fully measured its significance. She believed in expressing gratitude for one's gifts and rewards and in a selfless devotion to the task at hand. While her responses to her daughter's depression attempted to restore her morale, she could not imagine the steps Sylvia might take to relieve her pain.

The physics course had turned Plath's mood. She began experiencing menstrual irregularity; she was overheard quarreling with her mother on the telephone. She suffered severe insomnia, which drove her to the college psychiatrist, who prescribed more sleeping pills. Perceptively, Ed Cohen realized from her letters that she was approaching an "ultimate breaking point" and needed more help from a psychiatrist than sleeping pills could provide.

Dick Norton had also affected her mood. He had contracted tuberculosis and was writing letters to her, sometimes several in a day, discussing books they were reading—D. H. Lawrence's *Women in Love* and J. D. Salinger's *The Catcher in the Rye*. In a strange way, Plath was envious of his leisure to read without having to compete for grades, while her own path seemed full of jarring, leering "fiendish obstacles" that only made her wish "to end the pointless round of objects, of things, of actions."

The dark mood lightened after Thanksgiving. In her journals she wrote that she had decided to cultivate her mask of gaiety, partly because the physics course seemed more manageable, and because at the Norton home in Wellesley she had met a man who excited her. Myron Lotz was Perry Norton's roommate, the strapping son of Austrian immigrants who was on a scholarship to Yale, and had already been admitted to medical school. Tall and athletic, Lotz had spent the previous summer pitching for a semiprofessional baseball team. He was full of an ambition and drive that corresponded to Plath's, and he suggested a healthy vitality that roused her. Lotz invited her to the Yale junior prom, and they began to see each other on weekends.

On one occasion, walking to a cocktail party at the home of a Smith professor, they wandered into the Northampton mental hospital, a strange detour on a date. She heard patients howling behind barred windows. Plath reported to her mother that it was the most "terrifying, holy experience." It made her want to learn "*why* and *how* people cross the borderline between sanity and insanity," and the fact that she was so curious about the place that she led her date through it indicates how deeply implanted in her mind was such a question.

To varying degrees, all of the writers in this book were drawn to such testing. The relativity of sanity is a Nietzschean proposition, as Lawrence understood even in the intensity of some of his rages, as Fitzgerald and Thomas must also have understood in the tormented flights of their drinking. In *Tender Is the Night*, Fitzgerald centered his novel on the question of sanity, and for Miller as well it was an essential concern in the *Tropic* novels. The romantic artist tends to some extent to idealize the insane—or should we use the term "outsane"?—whenever it throttles the social order with profoundly disquieting and unanswerable questions. Plath certainly belonged to this tradition.

She would soon test her own hold on reality, though she could not have known that when she traveled to Saranac Lake in the Adirondacks during the Christmas holiday, more out of duty than devotion, to see Dick Norton, who was recuperating in a sanatorium there. He was reading Thomas Mann's *Magic Mountain*, the great novel about tuberculosis and the diseased mind of modern civilization, and seemed obsessed with the particulars of his own recovery. As though she were part of his plans for recovery, he talked to Plath as if they intended to marry. It was no longer what she wanted, but listening to him, she felt guilty—after all, marrying him seemed the best way to repay her mother for her sacrifices.

The next day, perhaps risking the edges of her self-destructive capacities as a way of purging her guilt, she decided to go skiing even though she had never tried it before. With Dick ostensibly guiding her, although he too had never skied, she plunged down a slope meant for advanced skiers. For a few hurtling seconds, flying free of the earth, tilting in air, she felt a soaring sense of elation and liberation. Suddenly a man stepped into her path. She swerved and fell, breaking her leg, her "fabulous fractured fibula," as she telegraphed her mother. But the bravado of her message to her mother could not conceal the awkwardness and pain of her broken leg and the blow that crashing to the ground represented.

When classes resumed at Smith, she was forced to navigate its snowy campus on crutches with her leg in a cast. She increased her reliance on sleeping pills because the leg hurt at night. In letters to her mother, she mustered a grim cheer, but in her journals she lacerated herself, saying she had lost all delight in living, that she was merely stumbling along blind alleys, that she was also incapable of love. Commenting on a snapshot of herself that she pasted into her journals, she stressed her pouting, disconsolate mouth, eyes that seemed numb and expressionless. Finally, she understood that the cast that she had dragged around the campus (no wonder there are so many things being dragged through her poems) was a concrete symbol of her limitations and her separation from others.

She spent a lot of time in her room that spring. Her irritability and the slowness of her recovery affected her relationship with Lotz adversely. She regarded the news that he had dated someone else as a betrayal even though she went to New York on a weekend with a former boyfriend, and was in the process of charming another prospective suitor. Extremely good-looking, Gordon Lameyer was also from Wellesley, and he also wrote. Completing his studies at Amherst and preparing to serve in the Navy, he met her for a sandwich and a Coke while her leg was still in a cast. Too enthusiastic, raving about her love of Dylan Thomas's poems, she puzzled Lameyer, who did not know quite how to interpret her effusiveness, but planned to see more of her that summer.

Plath's spirits continued to improve, helped by the fact that her leg healed. She had been permitted to audit the second-semester science requirement and took a course in Milton for credit instead. She was elected to Phi Beta Kappa as a junior, an unusual honor, and she was chosen to edit the *Smith Review*, the college literary magazine. In a creative writing class she wrote a villanelle entitled "Doomsday" (written for her father, she said later). She submitted it to the *New Yorker*, which represented to her the acme of literary accomplishment. While the poem was not accepted, she received a personal note suggesting revisions, rather than an impersonal, anonymous form rejection. "Doomsday," along with two other poems, was taken by *Harper's Magazine*. Plath regarded that as her first professional acceptance.

She felt, she noted in a letter to her mother, that she was becoming more adept with the "singing, uncrowded lyric," finding with it a way to free her style from a "static adjectival smothered thought," which had been an unnecessary weight. In another creative writing class she met W. H. Auden, interviewed him and asked him to read a sheaf of her poems. Auden was gracious but warned her of glibness and told her to work on her verbs. She also heard Dylan Thomas reading in Amherst on one of his final American tours, an event that enthralled her. Most exciting of all was the news that she had won a guest editorship at *Mademoiselle* for the summer. She had worked diligently to prepare her application for months since it required several stages, and the magazine had accepted one of her poems, ominously entitled "Mad Woman's Love Song." Now she was heading straight for the literary center of America, New York City.

Broken and Mended

Twenty young women from across America had been selected to help prepare the special August college issue of *Mademoiselle*. They were accommodated in small, simply furnished rooms in the Barbizon, a hotel for women on Lexington Avenue and Sixty-third Street, which was conveniently located a few blocks from the magazine's Madison Avenue offices. Some of them would become glorified interns, typing, filing, and answering telephones. Plath was appointed guest managing editor, which meant she had to read, evaluate and improve all the material that was being considered for the issue, and she worked in the actual managing editor's office.

Cyrilly Abels was a seasoned journalist who understood Plath's potential and bore down on her, expecting her to know more than she could have, and succeeded in making her feel inexperienced. Abels found Plath was always on her guard, unable to relax at work, afraid to violate a decorum she thought was expected in a professional world. Her hair was cut in a champagne-colored pageboy suitable for an apprenticeship, and she was afraid to cross the line between intern and professional.

Plath had prepared a feature on new poets while still at Smith, conducting telephone interviews with five male poets. She had arrived in New York early in June with what she regarded as a finished piece, but Abels found it stiff and demanded a rewrite. Plath found that reworking her material to suit the magazine's lighter touch was frustrating, and the process made her lose confidence. Writing home to her mother, she expressed a premonition that she would not be admitted to a creative writing workshop at Harvard that summer begin taught by short story writer Frank O'Connor, which she very much wanted to attend.

Another depressing event was the execution of Julius and Ethel

Rosenberg, who were found guilty of passing crucial atomic secrets to the Russians. The execution was opposed by many who doubted that the Rosenbergs were guilty. Plath was so distressed by it that at the moment she thought they were being electrocuted, she broke out in hives. The image of the Rosenbergs strapped in the electric chair haunted her, and she would begin *The Bell Jar* "wondering what it would be like, being burned alive all along your nerves."

Plath's politics, like Lawrence's, Miller's, and Thomas's, were essentially bohemian, a view that knew that the artist had to be separate from the state and the social realities it superimposed. Never as anarchistic as Miller, Plath was more like Thomas in that she would permit herself almost no political latitude in her poems, perhaps quite aware that such direct expressions would only date and limit them. Yet, like Thomas, she was sympathetic to a left-of-center perspective, though they both came from middle-class backgrounds, the children of teachers. This may have been an attribute of the romantic need to transcend origins and even values that are deeply imbued.

The month Plath spent in New York was frenetic and overwhelming. Near the end of her stay, she wrote her brother that the experience of the city had moved her from ecstasy to horrible depression, but it had enlightened her. The pace had been "hard and fast." *Mademoiselle* had arranged a variety of functions for the group: gallery openings, fashion shows, movie previews, a formal dance. Plath had been asked to interview writers Elizabeth Bowen and Marianne Moore, though she had wanted to speak to J. D. Salinger. One night Plath and a friend loitered in the hallway of a hotel where Dylan Thomas was staying, but he never returned that night, at least while they waited.

Speaking with writers was a part of the excitement offered by the city, but the *Mademoiselle* sojourn had its fraudulent and staged aspects as well. On one of their first days in New York, the girls were assembled in Central Park for a group portrait in the shape of a human star with Sylvia at its pinnacle. When the picture appeared in the glossy spectacle of the magazine, not a hair was out of place, but actually it had been a sweltering day of 94-degree heat and stagnant, humid air, and everyone had been dressed in wool tartan skirts. More debilitating was a luncheon organized by an advertising agency where the entire group was poisoned by some contaminated crab meat—an event Plath retold in *The Bell Jar*—which helped her repudiate the slick artifice of the fashionable world. But that was the world for which Smith had prepared her.

She took the group poisoning as a general symbol of the costs of illusion.

One evening, she went to a party with a blind date, a Peruvian who beat and almost raped her in a garden, making her feel all the more uncertain about who she was and who she was supposed to be. The pressures of city life may have cracked the self-denying, self-controlled image she had manufactured at Smith. "I felt terribly inadequate," Esther Greenwood, her persona in *The Bell Jar*, says, "The trouble was I had been inadequate all along, I simply hadn't thought about it. The one thing I was good at was winning scholarships and prizes and that era was coming to an end."

The identity she had worked so hard to project was in question, and perhaps no longer suitable for an ominous future. At the very end of the month, just as she was preparing to return to Wellesley, she began throwing her clothes out of the hotel window, clothes for which she had carefully saved and about which she felt guilty. It was a dramatic signal of a coming rupture, as terrible in its way as Zelda Fitzgerald's burning of her clothes in a Hollywood hotel, though no one was aware of it at the time.

Wearing a green dirndl skirt and a white peasant blouse that she had borrowed from a friend, Plath took the train to Wellesley, where her mother met her. In the car, Aurelia told her that O'Connor's workshop had been filled and that she would have to reapply next summer. Despite her premonition, she was devastated by this news, which she interpreted as a rejection, a denial of her competency. She felt she needed the workshop to stimulate her to write, and she was unhappy at the prospect of spending the entire summer in Wellesley sharing a bedroom with her mother, and learning short-hand as a practical skill.

For the first two weeks of July, before leaving for officer candidate school, Gordon Lameyer saw her frequently. They listened to his records of Dylan Thomas, Robert Frost and James Joyce reading their work, and read Joyce aloud to each other. Lameyer wanted to write poetry. Being with him made Plath appreciate the dangers of marrying another writer, the possible ego conflict that could ensue, especially if the woman were more successful. While Plath was never really serious about Lameyer, she usually needed a bevy of suitors to make herself feel accepted. During this period Lameyer remained completely unaware that she was becoming more and more depressed, that her insomnia was so protracted it made her suspect she was going mad.

In her journals, she repeated her desire to crawl into a womb. She knew that doubting herself would only incapacitate her creativity, but she had reached a state of numbness by the middle of July when she could no longer even read with comprehension. She was unable to master shorthand, perhaps because her mother was trying to teach her, and she could barely read her own handwriting. For a few days she had tried to work as a nurse's aide in the Newton-Wellesley hospital, feeding patents who were too sick to feed themselves, but she could not even manage that.

She feared she was trapped in a "masochistic mental hell," which was her way of avoiding responsibility. Despite her constructive intentions, to find a subject for her senior honors thesis, to continue with her own writing, she found herself in a state of "utter nihilistic shock," paralyzed by an anticipation of the "huge man-eating world" and suffocating in a nauseating stasis.

Again and again in her journals she congratulates herself on the good fortune of a loving family, a house in Wellesley, a scholarship to Smith. In sharp counterpoint is a recurrent grief which she is not able to exactly pinpoint. The grief is remembered more precisely in *The Bell Jar*, in which, just prior to her suicide attempt, she went for the first time to her father's grave and laid her face "to the smooth face of the marble and howled my loss into the cold salt rain."

In the middle of July, when her mother noticed some purple gashes on her legs, Plath admitted that she had tried to summon the nerve to cut an artery with a razor. In a voice full of anguish, she exclaimed that she had done it because the world was rotten and that she wanted to die. Mrs. Plath took Sylvia to her family physician, who recommended a psychiatrist. The psychiatrist advised electroconvulsive shock on an out-patient basis, possibly because it was a quick and relatively inexpensive treatment. Cavalier and arbitrary, the psychiatrist did not prepare Plath for her treatment; instead of seeing her during the course of it, he left on vacation. The treatment, a surge of electricity through the brain, filled Plath with a tremendous apprehensiveness that would become a permanent feature of her imagination, and is reflected in the air of threatening menace that hovers over so many of her poems:

> By the roots of my hair some god got hold of me.
> I sizzled in his blue volts like a desert prophet.

In a poem called "The Hanging Man" and in *The Bell Jar*, she would describe being so shaken by the great drubbing jolt that she thought "my bones would break and the sap fly out of me like a split plant." It felt, in short, like the end of the world.

Characteristically, Plath did not tell any of her friends about her treatment, even though she saw Lameyer and was corresponding with Norton and Lotz. Similarly, her mother kept the matter secret, ashamed of her daughter's condition and afraid of the possible costs of caring for a mentally disturbed person in the future.

By the middle of August, as she explained in an unsent letter to Ed Cohen, she had decided to commit suicide as the only alternative to an "eternity of hell" in a mental asylum. She had unsuccessfully tried to drown herself, and she wanted a "quick clean ending...at the height of my so-called career." On the afternoon of August 24, 1953, wearing the same green dirndl skirt and white blouse that she had worn on her return to Wellesley from New York, she formulated a plan. Her mother, thinking she looked especially buoyant, left the house to see a film of Queen Elizabeth's coronation. Her brother, Warren, was at work. While her grandparents were relaxing in the garden, she forced open a steel cabinet that contained her sleeping pills. Along with a jar of water, she took them down into the basement, where there was a narrow crawl space blocked with wood. Removing and then carefully replacing the wood, she sequestered herself in the womblike recess and began swallowing the pills, "one by one by one," as she enumerated in *The Bell Jar*.

When Aurelia returned, she found a note propped up against a vase of flowers on the dining room table stating that Sylvia had gone on a long walk and would not come back until the next day. Alarmed, Mrs. Plath informed the police; neighboring woods were searched, and the Boston newspapers ran a report and her photograph. At lunch, two days later, Warren heard a slight groan coming from the basement. Plath had taken too many of the pills and had vomited enough of them to prevent overdosing. When she regained consciousness in the Newton-Wellesley hospital with an ugly bruise under one eye, she faintly, but with a touch of bizarre irony that would become her signature, told her mother that her attempt had been her "last act of love."

After two weeks she was sent to Massachusetts General Hospital, where she received letters of support from friends and from some of her Smith teachers. Olive Higgins Prouty, her Smith benefactor, interceded and offered to pay so that Plath could recover in McLean Hospital, a private psychiatric facility that specialized in care and rehabilitation. From October through January, Plath was at McLean, visited regularly by Mrs. Prouty, by her high school teacher Wilbury Crockett, and by her mother. She was under the care of a skilled and sympathetic psychiatrist, Dr. Ruth Beuscher, who won her confidence and who persuaded her to resume the electroconvulsive and insulin shock treatments, which brought back her will to live, though ultimately they may have made her all the more hypersensitive, unable to tolerate what she considered rejection or betrayal.

Lifting the Millstone

Warren drove his sister to Northampton to resume her classes early in February of 1954. When the car was already on the Smith campus, it skidded on some ice and spun around, out of control. No one was hurt, but Plath, with a talent for making myth out of mishap, immediately interpreted the event as a rebirth.

Installed in her own room at Lawrence House, she brought with her the reputation of a brilliant student who had been overwhelmed by academic pressure. She became friendly with Nancy Hunter, a Midwesterner of Irish extraction who had transferred to Smith and who Plath decided was her alter ego. In a memoir, Hunter remembered her own surprise on their initial meeting. Expecting to meet someone who appeared alienated or tortured, she instead encountered a young woman who seemed to still have the giddy irrepressibilities of a schoolgirl. Hunter found Plath quite beautiful, with dark eyes, high, pronounced cheekbones and hair dipping over one eye and falling to shoulder length. In certain ways, since her stay at McLean, Plath was much less reserved and spoke freely to Nancy Hunter about her suicide and recovery.

Plath was excited by a course in Tolstoy and Dostoyevsky that she was taking with Professor George Gibian, who would direct her honors thesis. Weekly, she met with the Smith psychiatrist. She saw Myron Lotz and continued writing to Gordon Lameyer, who was at sea, and to Ed Cohen, who had married. She confided to Cohen that what she needed most when she woke shuddering in the night, seized with the terror that she was being led through the cement tunnels leading to the electroshock room at McLean, was someone she could love, someone who would sustain her with the sort of assurance and stability no psychiatrist could provide. It was in part an image of love that was in vogue in the fifties, love that retreated to a house past whose white picket fence no danger or conflict could pass. But in Plath's case it was perhaps also a sign of the romantic burden she would put on love and, by extension, marriage: a poignant dependence on idealized love as a shield against her inner demons. Those inner demons and her own heightened expectations and painful disappointments would tear her apart in her marriage and would find their ultimate expression in *Ariel*, her last poems before her agonized suicide. These poems depleted her, left her "exposed as an x-ray," as she admitted in "Medusa."

Robert Lowell and the critic George Steiner saw her death as integrally related to the imaginative risks of her last poems, arguing that the atmosphere of threatening menace, the confessions of estrangement, terror and failure that she set down so spontaneously in some manner filled her with an unmanageable quality of mortal dread.

Certain of her poems were laced with allusions to the Holocaust, sometimes ironically, sometimes identifying with its victims. Some critics saw the Holocaust metaphors, like the poems themselves, as disproportionate and self-aggrandizing, but she may have felt that only a disaster of such magnitude could fill the dimensions of her terror. Full of sardonic, jeering bitterness, Plath proposed the most grotesque possibilities—like the concluding line of "Lady Lazarus," "I eat men like air"—with a calm aplomb that cannot mask the horror in her voice and the pity and awe at her pain, the catharsis associated with tragedy as an art form, that is experienced by readers of those lines.

The episode at McLean Hospital, frightening as it had been, was also for Plath a rite of passage, in a sense. If she had not quite liberated herself from all of her conditioning as a conventional young woman of her time, she had crossed a line toward her own independence. That was reflected in the men she would now choose for herself, more bohemian in their attitudes and behavior than the men she had previously known. In the spring of the school year, she met Richard Sassoon, a rebellious iconoclast who quoted Nietzsche and Rimbaud and posed as a French existentialist. Slender, only Plath's height, he was raised in Paris, his father a cousin of the English poet Siegfried Sassoon. Sassoon had a cultivated old-world air of hauteur and decadence that Plath admired. They spent several weekends in New York, one of "ecstatic rapport," she noted in a scrapbook, culminating with a "nuit d'amour."

There is only circumstantial evidence to suggest that Sassoon and Plath were lovers at this time. In *The Bell Jar* she would remark that her virginity had weighed like a millstone around her neck during her college years. For a year after her psychiatric confinement, there are no journal entries, and the "night of love" phrase could be an exaggeration to describe torrid petting, which was as far as she had gone with a number of men.

Such dalliances, to use Nancy Hunter's term, were to culminate that summer in a rape. To appear daring, Sylvia had bleached blond streaks in her hair. She registered for the Harvard summer session for an intensive German class, but not for the O'Connor short story workshop that had precipitated her depression. For a year, she had not written a story, finishing only one poem that spring, which she took as a confirmation of her recovery. Sharing a small apartment with Nancy Hunter a short walk from Harvard Square, she saw Gordon Lameyer and a succession of other men, mostly dates who could take her to a play or to a restaurant.

One afternoon, on the steps of Widener Library, she and Nancy Hunter met an extremely tall, gangling, balding man with thick eyeglasses and a perplexed, morose expression. This man, called "Irwin" in *The Bell Jar* and in Hunter's memoir, was a sort of Ichabod Crane who taught biology at another university and was doing research at Harvard that summer. He invited Nancy out for dinner, though she learned with some trepidation when already in his car that dinner was to be at his apartment. Reassuring her, he told her that his landlady was next door and he would keep the door open. After dinner and a bottle of wine, the door now conveniently shut, he pursued her around his brown leather couch until she persuaded him to take her home. She felt sure that his awkward seduction was the evidence of a "depraved hobby," a practice to which he had subjected innumerable young women. Undaunted, Irwin called the next day and spoke to Plath. Hunter warned Plath that Irwin was not to be trusted, but soon he was seeing her, driving her to her psychiatrist, even giving her a key to his apartment so that she might have a private spot to study.

One morning Nancy Hunter woke to discover that Plath had not returned from an evening at Irwin's. Moments later, he was on the telephone explaining that Plath was hemorrhaging, but that she was on her way home. Several hours later, in a pool of her own blood, Plath persuaded Nancy Hunter to escort her to a hospital, where a vaginal tear was sutured. Two weeks later, she would tell Gordon Lameyer that Irwin had assaulted her manually, that she had repulsed him but not before he had cut her hymen with his fingers. This version of events is quite different from what she would write in *The Bell Jar*, in which Esther Greenwood wants to relieve herself of her virginity. This incident and another one that occurred just as Hunter was preparing to take a final, when Plath became hysterical after a migraine attack and insisted that Hunter stay with her and abandon her exam, convinced Hunter that Plath had formed a compulsive dependence on her "alter ego." In her memoir, she stated that Plath saw herself as a suffering victim who needed a symbolic salvation "as though only by being snatched from the brink of death" could she confirm her worth.

Hunter's perception is chilling in its insight. If she, Plath, is worth saving, then a force outside herself, a savior, will give the confirmation sign by snatching her "from the brink." Hunter's comment echoes Plath's confession to Ed Cohen that she needed someone to love and sustain her. Yet the men she sought out and saw during this time of her life seem to have less to do with a search for love and assurance than for adventure—as though she were testing her power as a woman to attract a diversity of men and to achieve a degree of experience and sophistication that would make her more desirable to the kind of man she was preparing herself to meet in the future.

Plath and Hunter remained roommates during Plath's senior year, although the two women were never really close again. Hunter withdrew, afraid of what she had seen during the summer, but actually she had little need to worry. At Smith, Plath was always the perfect Smith girl, critical of others who affected a more bohemian posture. She had restored her hair from her "platinum summer" blond back to its natural sandy brown. The look was more "demure and discreet," she told her mother, right for her graduate school and fellowship interviews. These, and the applications to Oxford and Cambridge universities, to Radcliffe and Columbia, and the many letters of recommendation she had to solicit, took up lots of time.

One of the professors whose recommendation she most valued was the critic Alfred Kazin, who was teaching at Smith during Plath's senior year. Initially, he became interested in Plath when he learned that she was a writer and a scholarship student, therefore not nearly as pampered as many of the Smith undergraduates. Kazin invited her to join his small creative writing class. While she felt appalled by what she called the "weak mealy mouthed apathy" of her classmates, she responded to Kazin and his belief that great art resulted from great passion, and she began writing short stories and poems, some of them influenced by Dylan Thomas.

She was also laboring over her honors thesis on the double in Dostoyevsky, reading Poe's "William Wilson," *Dr. Jekyll and Mr. Hyde*, *The Picture of Dorian Gray*, and an essay on the double or split self by Otto Rank. Although she was unaware of it, her thesis related to the doubleness within herself, the artist trapped in her Smith facade.

She had resumed seeing Richard Sassoon, who had spent the summer in Europe. Sassoon was now demonstrating a sadistic side of his personality, harping in his letters to her about the relationship between pleasure and pain. She had already decided that Sassoon was too short for her (she could not wear heels with him), but was still drawn by the marginal element he represented. One weekend, in New York, he took her to the Museum of Modern Art to see a silent French film about Joan of Arc. Plath found the culminating scene, in which Joan is burned at the stake, cathartic, leading to a purging of her own accumulated tensions. She strongly identified with the scene, and it would recur in refracted versions in *Ariel*.

In late spring, she won a poetry contest at Mount Holyoke College and had a poem accepted by the *Atlantic Monthly*, which she considered almost as important as the *New Yorker*. She was graduating *summa cum laude*, near the very top of her class, but most wonderful of all was the news that despite the heavy odds against her she had been awarded a Fulbright fellowship to Cambridge University. Full of excitement, she telephoned to relay the news to her mother, who was in the Newton-Wellesley hospital about to have most of her stomach removed. Aurelia Plath's persistent ulcer problem had abated but then become greatly aggravated at the time of her daughter's suicide attempt and recovery.

Mrs. Plath managed to attend the Smith graduation after her operation, lying on a mattress in the back of a friend's station wagon as she was driven to Northampton. That summer, while her mother was recuperating, Plath returned to Wellesley. At McLean

Hospital, Dr. Beuscher had advised her to stay away from her mother, and during her senior year she had managed to avoid Aurelia to some extent by spending a lot of time with Sassoon. Mrs. Plath was unimpressed with him. She preferred the handsome Lameyer. Both men were still pursuing Plath, who felt pressured by the fact that so many of her Smith classmates and the former *Mademoiselle* girls were getting married. As one of the bridesmaids at a friend's wedding, she had drunk too much champagne and become hysterical, possibly as much from the pressure she felt about marriage as from the champagne.

In the summer of 1955, partly as a way to escape Lameyer and Sassoon, she began an affair with a young editor named Peter Davison, whom she had met in her last months at Smith. Davison had been a Fulbright fellow and his father was an English poet; Plath was drawn to him because she felt he could give her valuable information about the intricacies of publishing and the British poetry scene. In *Half Remembered*, his autobiography, Davison recalled that she had appeared at his apartment near Harvard deeply tanned, her hair streaked from sun, in a strangely elevated mood, hardly waiting "to be asked to slip into my new bed." When her mother returned from a visit to Cape Cod, Plath introduced him to her. She read him her poems and described her attempted suicide and recovery as if it had all happened to another person. All the while she questioned him relentlessly and voraciously: "I felt as though I was being cross-examined, drained, eaten," Davison remembered. Ultimately, he was "baffled" and "fascinated" by her, as was an entire group of other suitors who might have used the same words. At the end of September, she boarded the *Queen Elizabeth* for Europe.

Blazing Love

Plath was charmed by Cambridge. Every alley was crowded with tradition, she informed her mother, rich with antiquity and the sort of ease that took centuries to form. She delighted in the quaintly cobbled, twisting streets, and the open market full of stalls. She could ride her bicycle, wearing the black gown of the Cambridge student like a sacramental robe, or she could stroll by the narrow river Cam, among the willows on its banks, watching the white swans, the canoes and scows.

Her sloped attic room was on the third floor of Whitstead, a rambling old residence on the edge of the college grounds; she looked out on the red-tiled rooftops of the town and the elegant formal gardens of Newnham College. The program of study was less structured than at Smith, though no less demanding. There would be no exams until after two years of reading. Twice weekly, she met with a tutor, who would read and discuss her essays. She attended large lectures in the mornings by the noted critics F. R. Leavis, David Daiches and Basil Willey on tragedy, literary criticism and English moralists through D. H. Lawrence. Such a course of study, she assured her mother, was an attempt to "build bridges over the whistling voids of my ignorance."

She impressed most of those who met her as extremely capable. One friend, Jane Baltzell, who also had a room in Whitstead, remembered a nervousness expressed in body language, hands incessantly locking and unlocking, her right foot crossed over her left and swinging impatiently in the air. The same restless energy was evident in the way she rode her bicycle, head and shoulders straining forward as she pedaled furiously. Baltzell felt the intensity even when they walked back from the dining commons after the evening meal. Plath would draw quite close as they talked, leaning in with a diagonal pressure that threatened to intersect Baltzell's path.

In the social sphere, she was pleased to learn that there were ten men for every woman at Cambridge, but she soon realized that most of the men were younger and not very sure of themselves. She joined an amateur dramatic society as one way to meet people and played a mad poet and a whore in a yellow dress. She met and liked Mallory Wober, a tall, raven-haired Hercules with red cheeks, she wrote to Olive Higgins Prouty. Wober, who had spent nine years in India, and whose earnest integrity reminded her of her brother, was seeing another woman, but he introduced Plath to various of his friends, widening her circle of acquaintances.

She met a few more men at a number of teas. While on the surface most of them were agreeable, they also seemed dull, in part because they were still undergraduates and a few years younger than she was. In contrast, she was receiving intriguing letters from Richard Sassoon, who was studying at the Sorbonne and who visited her in early December. Over Christmas, she joined Sassoon in Paris, where he showed her the city, and then took her to the south of France by train. Plath was enraptured by France, and she believed she had a mystical vision in a chapel in Vence. She felt more drawn to Sassoon than ever before, even though he had told her about other women and seemed uninterested in any permanent attachment. She informed her mother that Sassoon was more brilliant, intuitive and alive than any of the men she had met in England, but she could not admit to herself that their affair was over, that the trip to France was Sassoon's final fling. In fact, when they parted, he asked her to stop writing to him.

Back in Cambridge she was sobered by the cold cutting winds. Mornings, she could see the frosty chill of her breath in her room, and she would have to crouch over her gas heater to dry her hair or to study. By February, her sinuses were inflamed and her mood depressed. Sleep was like the grave, she wrote in her journals, "worm-eaten with dreams." She became more aware of the brown scar under her eye, feeling her "death spot" more consciously than ever. Most of the time, she wore black. Paranoically, she decided her Whitstead housemates saw her as mad and felt the house was bristling with suspicion, frigidity and hostility. She visited the college psychiatrist as a means of confirming that she was not mad, but in her journals compared herself to Lazarus, resurrected from death but still aware of the liberating escape of suicide.

Feeling isolated and lonely, she concentrated on writing poems. Two had appeared in *Chequers*, an undergraduate magazine, but criticized in the same issue by someone named Dan Huws as stilted and affected. She wondered who Huws was, and she felt slighted, hurt. She would only be able to find the right man for herself if her poems were strong, she thought. It was the same kind of totemistic thinking that drove her to want to be the best student at Smith, where the imagination of anything less than a perfect grade left her feeling hopeless and suicidal, as though she would be rewarded and would find a savior only if she were good enough and performed well enough. The "sweet sestinas" and sonnets she had been writing were too "small for a smashing act of love." She sent a group of new poems and a sketch to the *New Yorker*, anticipating their return. In her journals, after quoting Ophelia's last lines before she drowns herself, she warned herself not to panic, advising that she should stoically endure until spring.

By the end of February she had resolved to visit the university psychiatrist again. On the way to see him, she met an American hawking copies of a crimson pamphlet, the first issue of a poetry magazine called *St. Botolph's Review*. She read the magazine while waiting for her appointment, was struck by several of Ted Hughes's poems, and she determined to meet him.

St. Botolph's Review got its name from a former rectory that had been turned into a rooming house and where one of its principal editors lived. Luke Myers was from Tennessee, and he was a cousin of the American poet Allen Tate. He had refurbished an old chicken coop in the garden of the former rectory. Ted Hughes, a recent Cambridge graduate who had studied anthropology, was one of the *St. Botolph* editors. He was working in London as a reader for a film production company, but whenever he returned to visit Cambridge, he would stay in Myers's crowded shack. He was there on the last weekend in February, 1956, because a big party had been planned to celebrate the magazine's premier issue.

In her journals Plath confessed that she had attended the party because she was beginning to feel like a gargoyle stuck in her room listening to the footsteps on the stairs, sounds of her housemates' visitors. The first purple and gold crocuses were beginning to emerge, and she wanted to meet someone who could help her to recover from Sassoon's rejection. Her escort, a man named Hamish, was sweet, but not the "blazing love" she sought, the man through whom she hoped to "surge force."

When they arrived at the party, someone was playing a piano, others were dancing, and the energy seemed at a peak. She met and danced with some young men, among them Dan Huws, one of the *St. Botolph* editors, an extremely pale and freckled young man who seemed nervous about his disparagement of her poems.

In a journal entry written with a bad hangover on the following day, she related what she termed the "worst thing"—meeting Hughes. The moment she had entered the room she noticed him, a "big, dark hunky boy, the only one there big enough for me, who had been hunching around over women." Hughes suddenly appeared before her, staring directly into her eyes. Quite drunk, Plath began quoting lines from one of his poems which she had read in *St. Botolph's*. Both of them had to raise their voices above the general din of the party, but Plath remembered Hughes's as "colossal." "Colossal" is a word that Plath used frequently in her journals; she would use a version of it in a poem describing her father, and it would become the title for her first book. Usually, the word suggested the size and stature of the man she hoped to one day meet, a man big enough not to be jealous of her creativity.

Hughes led her off to a small room where they could drink some brandy. According to Plath's dramatic version of the events (which Hughes has called overblown), after much shouting and stamping about, he kissed her "bang smash" on the mouth. When he tried to kiss her neck, she bit him on his cheek so that when they emerged from the room blood was running down the side of his face.

As Plath described it, the scene had all the sudden encounter and absurd signature of a Kafka story, a poet dreaming a myth that could satisfy her expectations of a romantic crescendo. Intuitively, she realized that Hughes was the very man who could eclipse Sassoon, a man to whom she could give herself "crashing, fighting." In her journals, events were often seen in terms of violation or rape, and this meeting was presented in such terms. The words "crashing" and "fighting" characterize many of the marriages described in this book. They reveal the romantic's true horror of the mundane and a desire to be engulfed and then opened by the intensity of an experience. For Plath, a passionate encounter had to be cataclysmic to validate itself.

However smitten, Plath did not leave the party with Hughes, but with Hamish, who had brought her there. She spent what remained of the night making disoriented love with him in his room.. The sex was only a sordid displacement of what she wanted with Hughes, who returned to London and to his work reading stories for possible film scripts. But his impact on her had been enormous, and she immediately began to trace it in "Pursuit," a poem about lust, passion and destiny, organized around the paradoxical notion that love's intensity was only the other side of a burning consummation that led to death. Emulating the style of Hughes's own poems, with their penetrating, brutal focus on natural process, she imagined him as a stalking panther, a "black marauder, hauled by love" with herself as his final prey. The poem is balanced between the genuinely harrowing and the turgid, and it exists as an early sign of a real change in her own abilities, a turn away from what she regarded as the coy "small preciousness" of what she had done to that point.

Her theme here is extremely personal in its vision but it calls up something large and elemental. Twinning love and death, it is death-haunted in its implications in a way that approaches her best work. Dylan Thomas too felt a harrowing awareness of death but he raged at the transience of life. Plath, on the other hand, seemed always to summon death, to want it close at hand, to call up its presence both when her life was stagnant and when it was brimming with possibilities. Keats, in "Ode to a Nightingale," one of the most admired expressions of lyrical romanticism, evoking the sweet intensity of ecstasy and pain, declared himself to be "half in love with easeful death." In Plath's case, there is nothing easeful in her contemplation of passion and death—as though only the violence and blackness of death could match the searing intensity of her passion. It is the dark, modern side of romanticism. The poet Stephen Spender associated Plath with Robert Lowell, John Berryman, Theodore Roethke and others of the postwar generation, as poets who all cultivated their hysterias in the manner of Rimbaud. All of them cultivated their despair as angry fuel; they felt a direct, unbearable connection between their interior depression (Lowell and Roethke spent time in institutions and Berryman committed suicide) and the world they inhabited.

For the following few weeks Plath continued to displace her feelings about Hughes by yearning for Sassoon, hoping to see him in Paris on her spring break, even though he had warned her he would be traveling and intended to join the American army. At the same time she planned a trip with Gordon Lameyer from Germany to Italy in a car he would rent. She received no word from Hughes, but she learned that ironically, while she was out drinking with Hamish one night, Hughes and another man she knew, Luke Myers, had come to the rear of Whitstead and thrown mud at what they thought was her window. The incident displeased her; she associated it with Hughes's reputation as an unruly drinker who chased women, and she felt that her name had somehow been improperly besmirched by the mud.

All she could do was occupy herself with her studies, especially a philosophical literature class she took with a James scholar, Dorothea Krook. Plath admired Krook, comparing her favorably to some of the other female dons, who seemed desiccated before their time, Dickensian caricatures full of secondary knowledge, whom she would portray in her poem "Spinsters." Krook had noticed the "concentrated intensity" of Plath's look and its desperate defiance before the first class. Plath was intrigued by Krook's lecture on D. H. Lawrence's *The Man Who Died*, feeling chilled when she learned that Lawrence had died in Vence, where she had felt her mysterious chapel epiphany.

She did see Hughes in London and spent a night with him in a borrowed room without water or a toilet. That night only confirmed what she had previously presumed in her journals, that Hughes was destined to become her "big smashing creative burgeoning burdened love."

Early the next morning, she left for Paris. Polished, mannered, Lameyer was one of the "nice" boys her mother had wanted her to marry, who would have been content accepting only a small part of her. The trip began with an argument over the extent of John Malcolm Brinnin's responsibility for the death of Dylan Thomas, and they continued to bicker and disagree until they reached Rome. Plath felt the fighting was due to the hidden rankling caused by her rejection of Lameyer, and she was happy when he put her on a plane for England.

There she would again meet Hughes, who spent most of April and May in Cambridge. He had been raised in a small town in Yorkshire, where his father had a newspaper and tobacco store. Since his childhood, he had loved the outdoors, hiking, hunting and fishing. He had been writing since he was fifteen. "Derrick-striding" Hughes took Plath on fifteen-mile walks and introduced her to a new vocabulary of woods, animals and earth. She read more of his poems, which she found "terrible and lovely" (in Yeats's oxymoronic sense of a "terrible beauty") and her own work began to show the register of his influence. Hughes's appeal was similar to D. H. Lawrence's: both were suspicious of rational approaches to human problems, both suspected technology and the power of the state, both insisted on the miraculous powers of nature, and both believed that men and women could come together only when they sublimated their egos and allowed each other to reconstitute themselves in marriage. Hughes and Plath, in line with Dylan Thomas, were united in the view that nature was the source of the terrible beauty, an overwhelming divine power that humans could only gropingly understand, if at all. The modern originator of this view is Lawrence, who got it from Blake, and it is the pagan heart of Romanticism. Plath, like Thomas, understood that by discerning a mythic dimension in nature she could make her poems more oracular and universal. She sent one of these "oracles," a poem called "Metamorphosis," to her mother, a poem about a night when she accompanied Hughes in the forest looking for owls in the moonlight. The poem was a testament to the change in her aesthetic.

So many Englishmen, she observed in her journals, found ideas and opinions unfeminine, but with Hughes she felt no awkwardness in communication. He was unpretentious and unassuming. After graduating from Cambridge, he had worked as a rose gardener and a night watchman in a steel plant. She was, she wrote her mother, with the "strongest man in the world," though being with this "hulking, healthy Adam" was a "shattering" event that would "only lead to great hurt." Hughes's voice sounded "like the thunder of

God—a singer, story-teller, lion and world-wanderer, a vagabond who will never stop."

Plath's letters to her mother during the spring of 1956 are full of the "huge humor" she shared with Hughes, whom she characterized as an overgrown Huckleberry Finn. He related his dreams; he told her fairy stories and fables and read horoscopes. Plath typed his poems for him, sending them out to American magazines. He would help make her, she wrote her mother, a poet that "the world would gape at." She felt invigorated by his presence, joyous, infused with a power that spilled over into a flow of new poems. Her own voice was growing, not whining or quailing, she told her mother, but "sweating, heaving." The only shadow that fell on her ecstasy was the news that her grandmother was dying of cancer.

After her mother's death, Aurelia Plath traveled to England in June for a long-contemplated European trip that she was supposed to take with Sylvia. But plans had changed, and in London Aurelia was surprised to learn that Sylvia and Ted were getting married, impulsively, on June 16 because it was Bloomsday, the day on which all of the events in Joyce's *Ulysses* occur. With a special license and Aurelia as their only guest, the wedding was performed in secret— Hughes did not even inform his family because Sylvia was afraid of jeopardizing her Fulbright status. While he went to his parents' home to store the contents of his London flat, Sylvia showed her mother Cambridge. Then, the three set off for Paris, where they separated: Aurelia for her month in Europe alone; Ted and Sylvia, with a rucksack and a portable typewriter, for a summer in Spain.

Return to America

The newlyweds took a bus to Benidorm, a small fishing village of immaculate white houses on the curving Mediterranean. For a month, they rented a room and shared a kitchen in a house that proved noisy and too close to the tourist center. Hughes got badly sunburned, and Plath fell ill with dysentery. Matters improved when they found their own house, which cost no more than their rented room. They wrote mornings and afternoons, with a two-hour beach break during siesta when the beach was uncrowded. Hughes was working on poems and a series of animal fables, Plath on poems and stories. In letters to her mother, she was full of praise for Hughes, the "magnificent, handsome, brilliant" man she mentions in her journals, but she also brooded about an unspecified "wrongness" at the time of the full moon near the end of July.

Even though Spain was inexpensive and they had tried to live economically, they were out of money by the end of the summer. Partly because they were broke, and also to compensate for the mistake of not informing Ted's parents that they had married, they decided to spend a few weeks with them in September before Cambridge classes began. Heptonstall was Brontë country, steep green hills and purpling moors, stone houses and innumerable black stone walls. A few miles away was Mytholmroyd, once a Celtic center, where Ted had been born. Plath was drawn to the mystical, occult dimensions of the country, visited a local witch, and with her husband studied astrology and the tarot. She was delighted near the end of the month when she learned that the *Atlantic Monthly* had accepted "Pursuit," the poem she wrote after meeting Hughes, and that *Poetry* in Chicago wanted another six of the poems she had written since meeting him.

She returned to Cambridge alone, still afraid that her marriage would violate the terms of her Fulbright. She became upset and unable to concentrate, suffering a "hectic suffocating wild depression" because of the separation, she told her mother. She also confided in Dorothea Krook, who advised her to tell the authorities that she had been legally married; when she did, she discovered that her marriage would be no obstacle to completing her studies. Plath found a cheap apartment in an old run-down, inadequately heated house with a bathroom that had to be shared and moved into it with Hughes in the middle of November. Krook remembered how Plath complained about the cold, which Plath found humiliating and degrading, and Krook loaned her a paraffin heater, which helped. As her tutor, Krook saw Plath at least once a week and thought that Plath was radiant in marriage. She realized, however, that Plath had immediately made herself emotionally dependent on her husband and on the idea of marriage, and wondered what would happen should the marriage ever go wrong. Not self-conscious, Hughes was free of most bourgeois inhibitions. Wendy Campbell, a friend of Krook's, commented in a memoir about the raw vitality in Hughes, a ruggedness and an independence that could work both as a source of attraction and possible danger to any relationship.

Reclusive, Plath was busy preparing for exams. She was also preoccupied with a novel that used Cambridge as its setting and with organizing a collection of her poems for submission to the Yale Younger Poets series. Tired of dampness, the cold and gloom of the apartment, the cliquish elitism of the British, she wrote to Smith asking for a teaching position. While she dreaded the role of the

female professor as somehow inimical to her own writing, an
academic career, even a brief one, would be a token of the
normality she always needed as reassurance and a temporary way
out of poverty.

Hughes had found some work reading Yeats over the B.B.C., and
then, by winter, more regular employment teaching for a semester
at a boys' school in Cambridge. Together, he and Plath had studied
anthropology and mythology, and Robert Graves's *The White Goddess*. She had typed a manuscript of Hughes's poems, and another
of her own, and sent them to a number of British and American
magazines, which accepted some poems by each of them. But most
encouraging of all was the news that Hughes's collection, *The Hawk
in the Rain*, which Plath had submitted to a contest at the Ninety-
second Street YMHA in new York, had won first prize; that meant
that the collection would be published in book form by Harper.
Plath wrote her mother that Hughes had written the most powerful
poems since Yeats and Dylan Thomas. She was convinced of his
genius, comforted by his kindness, stimulated by his mind. In
some way, she added, he filled the vacancy, the "huge sad hole," left
by her father. In her journals she acknowledged that their lives had
intertwined so completely that she could not imagine continuing
without him—"I would either go mad, or kill myself," she predicted—again raising the specter of death.

In April, she learned that Smith had offered her a position
teaching three sections of freshman English. Worried about the
reputation Smith undergraduates had for becoming sexually involved with their professors, she dismissed the idea of Hughes also
teaching at Smith, but applied for him to several other colleges in
the vicinity. She heard that her poetry collection had been chosen
as a finalist in the Yale competition, but had doubts about winning
because Auden was a judge and he had not formed a good enough
impression of her work when he was at Smith. After the ordeal of
her exams and the disappointment at not performing on them quite
as well as she had hoped, in June of 1957, she and Hughes crated
their belongings and sailed for America.

At customs in New York, they were greeted by an inspector who
admonishingly waved their copy of *Lady Chatterley's Lover* in the
air. A friendlier reception greeted them in Wellesley: Aurelia Plath
had arranged a large garden party to introduce Ted Hughes to
Sylvia's American friends. After the party, Warren Plath drove his
sister and brother-in-law to a cottage on Cape Cod, rented for the
summer by Aurelia as a belated wedding present.

Both Hughes and Plath intended to use the time for their writing, as they had in Spain. Hughes worked on his animal fables and his poems, and received a number of magazine acceptances during the summer. Plath, still recovering from the drain of her Cambridge exams, struggled to resume work on her novel, putting it aside to work on short stories, which she regarded as a sort of warm-up. She wrote three stories in July, the most substantial of them about a meddling, dominating mother. She knew that what she had done was stilted and artificial, out of touch with her own deepest concerns. She had been reading Virginia Woolf, caught in the mannered recesses of Woolf's involved, self-conscious style, surely the most inappropriate model for the *Ladies' Home Journal* and the *Saturday Evening Post*, the magazines to which she submitted her stories. Still, when they were rejected without editorial comments or encouragement, she felt rebuffed. In her journals, she reiterated her need for articulation and publication as a permanent mark in the flux of things which had less significance otherwise. In August, when her poems were returned by the Yale Younger Poets series, her confidence was badly damaged, even though she herself felt that many of the poems were too arch, ladylike and bland.

Unfortunately, her wavering confidence continued when she began teaching at Smith in the fall of 1957. With seventy freshman themes to correct every week, with lectures to prepare, and conferences with students, she soon found herself depleted by twelve-hour days that left no time for her own writing. Teaching was difficult because she felt shy facing a group, and the pressure was much greater than it ever had been for her as a student. She wrote to her brother, away on a Fulbright in Australia, that she disliked the secondary and derivative atmosphere of the academy, that she preferred reading D. H. Lawrence for the sake of his possible influence on her own writing to discussing what the critics thought of him with unsympathetic undergraduates.

Part of her dissatisfaction can be attributed to a temperamental intolerance for dullness. She felt every moment in the classroom had to be scintillating, charged with energy, an impossible standard. In her journals she admitted the torment caused by an inner demand that she be a paragon, a demonically "murderous" voice of negativity, denial—that of the spoiled little girl. She resolved to battle her demonic inner voice and to accept all flaws, her own and her students', as human and universal. But for Plath it was easier to imagine such a course than to follow it.

While she was struggling with her dissatisfaction over the dy-

namics in her classroom, Hughes was at home, writing produc-
tively. He had broken his foot while getting up from a chair, but that
freak inconvenience did not deter him. *The Hawk in the Rain* was
favorably reviewed by W. S. Merwin in the *New York Times Book
Review* and a new poem had been taken by the *New Yorker*, his
third acceptance by the magazine Plath most admired. All of this
contributed to what she called the "black lid" of her depression. His
productivity was in inverse proportion to hers, and that set off an
anxious tension in her, fear as well as a tacit and illicit jealous
resentment that was more embracing than the usual competitiveness between writers.

For her, his success held an implicit threat. Plath the perfection-
ist, who believed she had to write poems that were worthy of
eliciting love, reveals, in her first journal entry while teaching at
Smith, her underlying fear that the more successful Hughes was,
the more he would find her wanting. She projected writing a story
about a poet husband whose literary subject is his passionate love
for another woman who becomes his muse. She never wrote the
story, but her fugitive fantasy is indicative of her state of mind,
displaced onto a fairly ordinary apprehension of marital infidelity.
That underlying fear never left her and it remained a source of
confusion in the raging, unbalancing jealousy she would feel later,
when she suspected him of actual infidelities that were not merely
her projections for the writing of fiction.

The fall semester exhausted Plath and she spent Christmas with
her husband at her mother's house in Wellesley, recuperating from a
case of viral pneumonia. Hughes had obtained a part-time teaching
job at Amherst for the spring term, which meant they would be able
to save money for a projected year in which neither of them would
have to do anything but write. They had met the poet W. S. Merwin
in Boston, who suggested that it was possible for writers to support
themselves without depending on teaching positions. Such a notion
had great appeal to both Plath and Hughes, who felt trapped in
suburban apartments and burdened by teaching that seemed
invariably to reduce literature to some formula or other, sapping
creative juices in the process.

Both of them were ill, Hughes with a stomach disorder and Plath
with insomnia. In her journals, she wrote that she was sick of
America, which seemed like a line of cars moving from gas stations
to diners. When she informed the head of the Smith English
Department that she did not intend to return for a second year, she
was criticized for her rashness by some of her former professors,

making her feel all the more estranged. Most of her colleagues had been quite distant, except for two of the poets in the department, Anthony Hecht and Paul Roche, who could understand her decision and how it might help her regain a sense of what she called in her journals "life-vision," a perception of meaningful continuities that prevented people like her from going mad.

Another preventative was work. She spent the spring writing a romantic *Saturday Evening Post*–type story, "Stone Boy With Dolphin," a version of her meeting with Hughes at the St. Botolph's party, which she hoped could figure in her Cambridge novel. The story would be told by a Cinderella-like heroine protected by an "unassaultable ego" (which was clearly a projection, since Plath's was as fragile as an egg), a woman enlightened by what in the story she would refer to as the spirit of Zelda Fitzgerald "burning behind the bars of her madness." The tone she wanted would merge elements of Woolf's "neurotic luminousness" with Lawrence's passion. She was rereading much of Lawrence for her Smith lectures, "the breath knocked out of me" by *The Rainbow*, she noted in her journals.

Writing the story filled an immediate need for productive work to relieve the pressures of going mad through idleness, but Plath felt her real work was her poetry, which had been blocked until her spring break at the end of March. In eight days she wrote eight poems based on paintings by Rousseau, Klee and De Chirico, poems that she felt helped free her from the "rococo crystal cage" of Smith. Although the poems were still decorous and controlled, they were written in a frenzy of creativity that anticipated the rush of the *Ariel* poems in her final few months of life. Hughes wrote to his sister that Plath had spent her holiday working twelve hours on some days on these poems, and he wondered what she could be capable of when her academic obligations were ended.

The art-inspired poems were added to a new evolving manuscript collection that was still very much a work in progress, rather than a fully realized and published collection like her husband's. Hughes had been invited to read his poems at Harvard. The event, though sparsely attended because of a snowstorm, provided a thrill Plath could share, even if her own recent work had once again been turned down by the *New Yorker*. In her journals, she commented on the closeness she felt to Hughes, on his comforting care for her, on their mutual vocation, need for solitude, and a love "with no holding back for fear of lies, misuse, betrayal."

On the last day of classes, the perfect closeness she projected in her journals was called into question. Hughes had agreed to meet her in the library after her final class, but she did not find him there. As she emerged from the library, she saw him walking up the road from a necking spot the Smith undergraduates called Paradise Pond, escorting a brown-haired girl in bermuda shorts. Plath had been speculating on the infidelities of several of her male colleagues, and the little vignette of her husband and the girl struck her like a blow, particularly because the student seemed to flee in guilt before she could be introduced. Immediately, Plath concluded that Hughes was enjoying a secret admirer, a belief that led to a physical confrontation in which she scratched his face (repeating or parodying the cheek bite of their initial meeting). This time Plath's suspicions were unwarranted. The young woman was only one of Hughes's Amherst students, whom he had run into while walking to the library just moments before Plath saw him.

Plath and Hughes remained in their Northampton apartment during the summer of 1958, both relieved to be free of the obligations of teaching. Aurelia Plath had repeatedly warned them of the unreliability of free-lance writing as a means of support, practical advice that Sylvia resisted even as it contributed to her anxiety about the future and their plan to return to Europe after a year in Boston. With the prospect of a long period in which she would be able to write, Plath was caught in the "strangled noose" of hysteria and paralysis. Her anxiety was "smothering," she declared in her journals, as if a muscular owl were perched on her chest, its talons clenching and constricting her heart. The result was an inability to write that was not alleviated even by acceptances of poems in the *Nation*, the *Sewanee Review*, and the *New Yorker*, which took two poems at the end of June.

There were quarrels over money and where to live. By the end of the summer they found a small apartment in the Beacon Hill section of Boston. Worried about money, but also searching for subject matter, Plath found a secretarial job in the psychiatric wing of the Massachusetts General Hospital transcribing patients' dreams. The experience gave her the idea for "Johnny Panic and the Book of Dreams," a Kafkaesque story about a secretary in a mental hospital who secretly copies dreams for her own use, is discovered and given electroshock. Plath kept the job for only two months. It gave her a certain distance on material she would use in *The Bell Jar* and it helped minimize her dependence on Hughes—a dependence that had the effect of a whirlpool, she noted in her journals.

Married to a man who was didactic and fanatic in pursuing his own concerns, she observed that living with him was like sharing an outer skin. She wondered whether fame might make him insufferable one day, and whether like vampires they might begin to feed on one another. It was certainly a view that Frieda, Zelda and Caitlin would have understood.

Depressed, struggling with her writing, she resumed analysis with Dr. Ruth Beuscher, her former psychiatrist at McLean, to work on what she realized was her suspiciousness of men, the latent fear that her husband might eventually abandon her as her father had. With Dr. Beuscher's help, she saw that much of her own self-loathing was a displaced hatred of her mother, who enraged her because she represented social conformity. Using a Ouija board with Hughes, Plath would receive messages from a figure called Prince Otto, who served a force called the Colossus, and she told Hughes that her suicide attempt in 1953 had been her way of rejoining her father. Hughes was now connected in her mind to her dead father as a sort of surrogate. In the spring of 1959, she visited Otto Plath's grave in Winthrop, Massachusetts, a scene that she would use in *The Bell Jar* to precipitate her breakdown. She also worked on two poems connected to her father, "Electra at Azalea Path" and "The Beekeeper's Daughter."

Plath used her journals as the place where she habitually expressed her darkest thoughts and premonitions, and in them she recorded the considerable awareness that resulted from her sessions with Dr. Beuscher. In the spring of 1959, she was also drawn to the work of Robert Lowell, a poet who had suffered a breakdown and recovered at McLean. Plath had been impressed by the natural ease she heard in his poems, a power she had only felt previously in her husband's work. Boston was crowded with poets and social opportunities. At dinner, she met Lowell and his wife, Elizabeth Hardwick, and decided to audit his poetry workshop at Boston University. Lowell remembered Plath's "air of maddening docility," a brilliant but tense presence "embarrassed by restraint" and showing the "checks and courtesies of laborious shyness." Mild, unassuming, Lowell tried not to monopolize his workshop, encouraging his students to do the work of criticizing one another's poems themselves. In his workshop, Lowell wanted to relax his students' reliance on traditional forms, favoring instead an open poem written in a very natural diction. He also suggested that, to be effective, a poem's subject should grow out of some personal

experience, a quality reflected in a poem Plath was writing while in
the workshop, "Point Shirley," about her grandmother's house on
the Atlantic.

Plath became friendly with one of the students in the class, Anne
Sexton, a married woman who was from Wellesley and had also
attempted suicide. After class, they would meet for drinks and
dinner with Sexton's lover, George Starbuck, an editor at Houghton
Mifflin who was also in the class and would publish Sexton's
collection of poems, *To Bedlam and Part Way Back.* Sexton's
poems, some of them about her own breakdown, were written with
an honesty and ease of phrasing that appealed to Plath. The formal
openness Lowell proposed in his workshop, his emphasis on a
vernacular, anecdotal toughness, left a deep impression on Plath.
She learned as well from Sexton how a woman of similar circumstances could use her experiences of breakdown and attempted
suicide effectively in poems. She was not as impressed by Starbuck's own imitative poems, and she was dismayed when they were
chosen over hers as the Yale Younger Poets selection.

Plath and Hughes spent the summer on a cross-country trip. He
had been awarded a Guggenheim fellowship and a residency at
Yaddo, a private retreat for artists at Saratoga Springs, New York;
here Plath, pregnant now, had a studio of her own in which to work
and was free for the eleven weeks from most domestic obligations.
But the work did not come easily. She commented in her journals
on the danger of being so close to her husband, with no life separate
from his. The closeness she had sought so desperately she also
found oppressive and threatening—a pendulum swing of moods
that lacerated her. She had difficulty falling asleep, and Hughes
began hypnotizing her at night. He also gave her lists of subjects for
poems, but she struggled with her writing. She intended to work on
stories and a novel, but felt she was handicapped by a lack of real
interest in other people, standing apart from them "enclosed in a
wall of glass."

In her journals, she predicted she would never succeed as a
writer until she opened herself "like an old wound" to her own
experience. Too many of the poems she had written were about
"ghosts and otherworldly miasmas." As a result of the Lowell
workshop, she had discovered a more colloquial voice that had less
of an air of relying on the thesaurus. At Yaddo she wrote the "The
Colossus," which would become the title poem of her first book, a
poem about Otto Plath pictured as an oracular statue, a vast totem

shattered by time, over which she crawls, trying to restore it. In late October, approaching her own twenty-seventh birthday, she began a sequence of seven poems, "Poem for a Birthday," which was more autobiographical than anything she had attempted previously, a poem that reflected on her parents and on aspects of her break-down and recovery. Though "Poem for a Birthday" was clear evidence of a new confessional turn for Plath's work, it still had its elliptical and obscure elements. Her poetry collection had been rejected by six publishers, but she had received a letter from an editor at Heinemann's in England, praising a group of her poems that had appeared in *London Magazine* and asking to see more of her work.

Dragging the Shadow

Plath and Hughes sailed back to England and spent December in Heptonstall. In London in January, already seven months pregnant, she searched for an affordable apartment and found a small, three-room flat in Primrose Square near W. S. Merwin and his wife, Dido. Plath had submitted her poetry manuscript to Heinemann's, which quickly accepted it, an event Hughes celebrated by buying his wife the three-volume edition of D. H. Lawrence's *Collected Poems*.

His own second book of poems, *Lupercal*, was published early in the spring and was very favorably reviewed by A. Alvarez, an influential critic who wrote for the *Observer*. Hughes received the Somerset Maugham award, to be used for travel, for *The Hawk in the Rain*. Almost daily there were invitations to read his poems at schools and universities. He worked on plays and for the B.B.C. The recognition surrounding him as one of the bright lights of British poetry meant an increase in social activities. While Plath liked the opportunity of meeting T. S. Eliot and Stephen Spender, she could often be irritable, rude, aggressive and even antagonistic with certain of Hughes's English friends. Dido Merwin felt that Plath was extremely overprotective of Hughes and particularly jealous of any other woman.

Dido Merwin's observation did not go far enough. Frieda Law-rence and Zelda Fitzgerald had also inserted a discordant note into their husbands' friendships. But Plath must have felt that she too had a right to acknowledgment on her own, acknowledgment she wasn't receiving, as Hughes's fame increased. When A. Alvarez came to interview Hughes for the *Observer*, he thought Plath looked more like a woman in a food advertisement than a poet. In fact, he failed to realize that he had indeed published one of her poems in the *Observer*. Like a number of other people, he saw her as Mrs. Ted Hughes, rather than as Sylvia Plath. For a woman who had tried all her life to excel, whose work staked her claim for recognition, the dismissal by others to the periphery of her husband's life had to be galling.

Perhaps it was in that spirit that she insisted on using the small living room at the Primrose Square flat as her work area. The space in the flat was minimal, even more so when their daughter, Frieda, was born on April 1. That left no room for Hughes to work in, and he set up a borrowed bridge table in a tiny area used for coats in the hall entry until the Merwins, who were spending a summer in France, offered him their study. That eased the problem temporarily, but it was not a permanent solution, and Plath would not find life easier.

The Colossus was published in England in the fall of 1960. It would win no prizes, would receive very little attention, and had no American publisher. Alvarez reviewed it in the *Observer*, cogently perceiving that Plath had not yet formed a consistent voice. Many of the poems were ornate, baroque and rhetorical, as if language and form were a means to keep her inner torment out of the poems. Anne Sexton had observed that Plath's early work seemed confined in a borrowed cage, and many of the poems in *The Colossus* were constricted, cautiously and self-consciously contrived, her diction stilted. The poems, Alvarez noted, were often more imposed on an audience than the process of a discovery. In her journals, Plath had recognized that they were sometimes more brittle and clever than inspired, their themes more scavenged than compelled from some personal need.

Extremely competitive, even with her husband, and as eager as any other writer to have her work acknowledged and admired, Plath was understandably disappointed by the reception of *The Colossus*. For two writers, sharing a small apartment with a newborn child had to create additional strain. Once again, she was finding it hard to write, and the care of an infant compounded the difficulty. In one of the few successful poems she wrote in the spring of 1960, "A Life," she imagined a woman "dragging her shadow in a circle," a relentless image that anticipated the feverish, totemistic fatalism of her final poems.

In January, 1961, pregnant again, Plath suddenly experienced another of her violent outbursts of jealousy. Hughes had been working on a play, meeting theater people, and he had an appointment with Moira Doolan, a B.B.C. producer, in connection with a children's series he had proposed. Doolan called to confirm their appointment. Plath, who happened to answer the phone, irrationally determined from Doolan's voice that she was a younger woman with designs. When Hughes failed to return for lunch as expected, Plath ransacked his papers, the notes for his play and drafts of poems, and burned them. The extremity of her action and use of fire, as it had been when Zelda Fitzgerald burned her clothes, was a significant sign, a warning that some demarcation in the nether-world geography between sanity and insanity was being traversed.

Hughes appeared an hour later to find the apartment in shambles. He confided the details of the incident to Dido Merwin. It must have contributed to the undermining of his confidence in Plath. He had accepted her unpredictable hostilities when they concerned friends, but this attack had been directed at him.

A few days later, Plath suffered a miscarriage, which suggests the extent to which she had provoked herself. Two weeks later, she entered a hospital for a scheduled appendectomy. Since her confinement at McLean, she had dreaded hospitals. She began writing a new series of poems, inspired to some extent by the operation and her recovery. These poems, particularly "Tulips" and "In Plaster," were written quite spontaneously in a voice she characterized as one of "tough prosiness," with an ironic, wry way of detaching herself from her own experience. While she was recuperating, she learned that the New Yorker wanted a first-reading option on her poems, and that Alfred A. Knopf had decided to publish an American edition of The Colossus. Hughes, caring for Frieda and still quite solicitous about Plath, had also received good news: Lupercal had won a prize, and he had been commissioned to write a play for the Royal Shakespeare Theatre.

Late in the spring of 1961, the Hugheses bought a small Morris station wagon to help them find a country house. Plath was pregnant once again and the probability of another child aggravated their concern about space. She had begun The Bell Jar, her novel about her month at Mademoiselle and her subsequent suicide attempt and recovery at McLean, using Merwin's study to write every morning for two months while Hughes took care of Frieda. Plath was at the point in the novel of describing her mother in an astringent, almost caustic tone when Aurelia Plath came to visit in June. While Aurelia saw to Frieda, Plath and Hughes were free to spend a week visiting the Merwins in the south of France. According to Dido Merwin, the visit was a "macabre marathon." Plath fell into one of her inexplicably tormented moods, a strange pouting animosity, over the presence of a woman who was also a guest at the Merwins' cottage, and she became extremely possessive of Hughes.

During the rest of the summer, the Hugheses searched for a house they could afford. In Devon, where real estate was inexpensive and which could be reached by train from London in three or four hours, they found a large old house. Court Green was a dilapidated, thatch-roofed former rectory on several acres dotted by numerous apple and cherry trees. The property had an open, country feeling. With all their savings and with help from their parents, they were able to finance a mortgage. They also met David and Assia Weevil, a young couple who wanted to take over their London apartment.

At the beginning of September, the Hugheses moved into their Devon house. Plath cared for her daughter and organized her house and her garden. She had completed a first draft of her novel, which she wanted published under a pseudonym so as not to give pain to her mother or her American friends. She also received a grant to rework *The Bell Jar* and was happy in her country surroundings. Hughes was doing carpentry for the house, writing a radio play and broadcasting his children's program for the B.B.C. On the surface, things seemed to be going smoothly, but by December, when the weather got cold, the house never seemed warm enough for Plath, who was used to American conveniences like central heating. She was usually depressed by winter, but now she blamed the depression on the menaces of the cold war as well as the cold weather.

On January 17, 1962, she gave birth to her son, Nicholas. The birth was arduous, and caring for two small children and her house never seemed to leave enough time for her writing. She did work on a radio play about childbirth, "Three Women." The play was influenced by Dylan Thomas's *Under Milk Wood*, but lacked its narrative interest and humor and was more of a reflection of Plath's own grim mood.

Instead of improving at the end of winter, Plath's mood darkened. By March she was afflicted with the stinging, itchy sores of chilblains, a reaction to the unprecedented cold of that month.

Another cause of depression was the gradual decline of a neighbor who was dying of lung cancer, an event that reminded her of her father's death. She also began to resent Hughes's London trips for his work with the B.B.C. and that she was still typing his manuscripts and submitting his poems to publications for him. To add to her dark mood, Hughes was tutoring a sixteen-year-old, a girl Plath found dangerously flirtatious.

Plath kept detailed notes on some of the people she met in Devon, material she hoped to integrate someday into her novel about her marriage. At the same time she was writing poems about troubled relationships whose conflicts seemed clearer in her drafts than in the final, obscure versions, almost as if she needed to hide her premonitions from her husband.

In May, she was visited by a new friend, Elizabeth Compton, who lived twenty-five miles to the north and was also married to a writer. There was also a disturbing visit from David and Assia Weevil, the couple who were living in their former London apartment. David Weevil was Assia's third husband, and Plath convinced herself that Assia was no longer passionately attracted to him and that she now had designs on Ted Hughes.

In "Quarrel," a poem written after the departure of the Weevils and the first poem in which Plath used autobiographical material so directly, she alluded to a "groove of old faults, deep and bitter," in which she walked as if trapped in a ring. The poem is an early sign of the haunted, possessed mood of her last poems, an almost alchemical transformation of her paranoia and anger. Reworked into a poem called "Event," it showed Plath examining her marriage with a new, disillusioned perspective. In "The Rabbit Catcher," the next poem she wrote, she compared herself in marriage to the unsuspecting rabbit caught in the constricting noose of the hunter's snare. It was a melodramatic image, reminiscent of her early image of herself as Hughes's prey, but a prospect that had loomed as both exciting and frightening when they had first met was now darkened by an intensity of apprehensiveness and a feeling that the threat to her was real, immediate and inescapable.

When A. Alvarez visited the Hugheses in early June, he remarked on a change in their relationship. Sylvia no longer seemed like a "housewifely appendage to her husband," but assertive and secure in her own home. She was again wearing the mask of the young woman in control of her life. Aurelia Plath visited later that month and failed to notice her daughter's underlying anguish. As *Letters*

Home makes clear, Plath consistently presented her domestic situation in the best of all possible lights to her mother, and was particularly deceptive on the subject of her marriage, as if she constantly felt a need to justify her choices before her mother. Aurelia did not know that her daughter believed that Hughes was having an affair with Assia Weevil. Plath's suspicion was caused by a number of mysterious telephone calls, provoking her poem "The Other," in which she projects Assia as her husband's mistress.

One day in July, as her mother watched, she entered Hughes's attic study and collected some letters and possibly some of the notes for her novel on their marriage. These she burned in a bonfire, after reciting a series of incantations and spells, which mystified Aurelia. Several days later, she accepted a disguised call for her husband that she was convinced was from Assia. Enraged, she tore the telephone wires from the wall.

After this outburst, Hughes escaped to London and Aurelia Plath moved into a room in a nearby cottage, where she remained until her return to America at the beginning of August. By that time Hughes was back at Court Green. Together, they took a trip to Wales and another to London to visit Mrs. Prouty, Plath's former benefactor. On both trips Plath was still pretending that she was happily married, though several weeks later she ran her car off the road in a harmless accident that she later claimed was a suicide attempt. On another trip, this time to Ireland, where Plath intended to spend the winter to escape the Devon cold, Hughes at one point went off on his own, and Plath returned to England alone.

Back at Court Green, she ripped off the mask of domestic tranquility, denouncing Hughes and identifying herself as the innocent victim of his treachery in a series of letters to family and friends. She resolved to break off with her husband, abetted in this decision by her former psychiatrist, Dr. Ruth Beuscher, and supported as well by letters from her mother and Mrs. Prouty. Hughes left Court Green early in September.

During the fall months, Plath began writing the poems of extreme hatred and rage that helped her to exorcise him and the image of her as the perfect housewife. She knew she was writing the best poems she had yet written, caught in a frenzy of creativity that was fueled by her anger. Later, in an introduction to a collection of her short stories, Hughes would observe that she had found her true voice only after accepting her own painful subjectivity as her theme: "the plunge into herself was her only real direction."

But "the plunge" still left her distraught. Unable to sleep, she used sleeping pills. Groggy one morning, she accidently sliced off the tip of one of her fingers with a carving knife. She would use the experience in a poem, and the accident seems like another warning of an irresistible urge to damage herself. She suffered from a recurrent flu and fluctuating fevers, and she lost twenty pounds during the fall months. By October, she had decided on a divorce, and Hughes had agreed to a thousand pounds annually for child support. Plath began riding an old horse named Ariel, and assembling the poems she was writing into a new manuscript to be called *Ariel*. As her father had once done, she was also keeping bees and she wrote seven beekeeping poems. While she remained confident about what she was writing, she was experiencing sharp changes of mood, blaming Hughes for ruining their marriage, and then feeling liberated from it.

In her letters, she condemned Hughes for isolating her in the country, and she decided to spend the winter in London in the hope of finding warmer accommodations than Court Green could provide, and more social contact. When she found an apartment in a Primrose Hill house that Yeats had once inhabited, she was delighted, and she moved into it with her children in early December. With money from Hughes, who regularly visited the children, and money from her mother and Mrs. Prouty, she soon had the place painted white, and she bought herself some new clothes. *The Bell Jar* was being published in England in January, and Plath was hoping to support herself with short prose pieces, and was planning another novel on the dissolution of her marriage.

When Alvarez visited her just before Christmas, she wore her hair loose; it was so long it almost reached her waist. He thought she looked gaunt, her face rapt "like a priestess emptied out by the rites of her cult." Christmas itself was lonely and depressing. January brought with it snow and ice and the coldest weather in fifty years, and Plath had always detested the cold. Again, she and the children succumbed to fevers and the flu. To make matters worse, Howard Moss, the poetry editor of the *New Yorker*, seemed uninterested in the poems she was sending him. *The Bell Jar* was turned down by two American publishers on the grounds that it seemed insufficiently universal, too close to a personal case history. The English reviews, while favorable, were also not glowing.

Early in February, Plath visited Dr. John Horder, a local physician she knew. She complained of depression and of her fears of imminent breakdown. Horder prescribed antidepressants and said he would try to find a hospital facility where she could be helped. Debilitated by the flu, by the fear of resuming electroshock treatments, by sleeping pills and the antidepressants that had not yet changed her mood, she spent a few days with friends until she felt strong enough to return to her apartment.

Around midnight of February 10, she asked her downstairs neighbor for some stamps. Ten minutes later, he opened his door again to find her staring into space in the freezing hallway. All that night, he was disturbed by the sounds of Plath walking above his bedroom. On the next morning, a nurse sent by Dr. Horder was unable to gain entry when she rang Plath's bell. When she smelled gas seeping under the door, she found someone to force it open. Plath was lying on her kitchen floor, her head on a piece of folded cloth in the oven. The door and window cracks had been taped and stuffed with towels. The children, provided with bread and milk, were in their room with its window wide open.

Suicide, Joseph Conrad once wrote, is very often the outcome of mental exhaustion, "not an act of savage energy but the final symptom of complete collapse." We can never know with any certainty whether Plath took her life because she saw herself as betrayed and abandoned by her husband, the perfect marriage of her fantasy ruined by the proverbial other woman, or whether she was terrified by a return of the process of breakdown, electroshock and psychotherapy that she had already experienced. Concentrated in his intensity, Hughes had been a difficult mate, but everyone who knew Sylvia Plath affirms that she was equally difficult.

The rest is the story of posthumous fame, of attention to Plath's life and acclaim for the power of her last poems. For Aurelia Plath, for Hughes and the children, there could be no immediate escape from the repercussions of her death. They would all, as Aurelia Plath observed, be forever "trapped in her past."

A Poisoned Romantic

Illness was a familiar feature of Plath's childhood. The death of her autocratic, seemingly invincible father when she was so young had a terrifying impact that would remain with her always. Her mother suffered from ulcers and her brother from asthma and sinusitis.

But for Plath, in its most benevolent guise, illness was a peculiar route to a kind of leisure that allowed her to idle or read without the purpose of self-improvement, a luxury of sorts in a household that emphasized industry and achievement for its own sake. She would take illness underground, and it would define her life.

Coming of age in the 1950s, she had been in part conditioned by her mother's gnawing anxieties and by the rigid proprieties of that era: the values of adjustment and conformity, of respectability and seemliness. Yet aspects of her upbringing put her in conflict with the value of "fitting in." As a child, her parents had encouraged her to be competitive. At Cambridge, she yearned for a "smashing" love as a way to motivate or energize her artistic self. When she taught at Smith, she wanted to be the most scintillating, brilliant of teachers. As a poet, she longed most of all to appear in the *New Yorker*. As a wife, she wanted her marriage to reach an apogee of perfection and indomitable monogamy. She needed to stand out, to excel, to be noticed and admired. The tension of the conflict between fitting in and being outstanding would resonate throughout her life.

In the fifties, a woman's path was demarcated by husband, children, family ties, owning a house. Plath's favorite magazine was *Good Housekeeping*. Like F. Scott Fitzgerald, she gleaned some of her aspirations from popular magazines, and like both Scott and Zelda she was confused by a period of rapidly evolving sexual definition and expectation. As a young woman, ungainly and a bit awkward, she had been groomed by her mother to wait for the right man, even at the risk of boredom—the future doctor next door whom she was expected to marry as a virgin. At Smith, she was taught that even though she had a mind she could use, the world required her future maternal and domestic competence. Self-denying, self-controlled, she envied the freedom of men to separate career and family, or to advertise their lust and gratify it. Nice girls, she was made to understand, repressed sexual desire till marriage and always kept their worldly ambitions in perspective. Whatever the particular damages imposed on women in that decade, Plath was not alone among her generation of poets in finding the atmosphere of the fifties stifling and disorienting.

Robert Lowell, who is perceived to have dominated the postwar era in American poetry, confided to his friend John Berryman that there was something peculiarly "twisted and against the grain" about the world his generation had lived in, and he summarized their fate when he discerned that they wrote with such single-mindedness intensity that they "almost seemed on the point of drowning." Lowell suffered a series of breakdowns and received shock treatment at McLean, just as Sylvia Plath and Anne Sexton did. Like Plath, several of the poets of her generation took the drastic step of killing themselves—Berryman leaping from a bridge and Randall Jarrell walking in front of a passing car.

Plath, essentially an outsider who needed to be accepted, had the thespian ability of manipulating herself to find the appropriate mask for the moment. Such a talent was perfectly in accord with the subtle demands of the fifties, a code of deceptive shifting to find a face to fit the expectations of any role. No wonder her high school English teacher believed she was so well adjusted. One of her boyfriends, Gordon Lameyer, thought she was enthusiastic when she was deeply depressed, but in the fifties mental problems of any kind were regarded as a kind of deviance and source of shame. On the morning she tried to kill herself by swallowing sleeping pills, her mother thought she looked especially buoyant.

Such are the vagaries of appearances. Plath's masks were an opportunity for a poet who could learn to dramatize realities through them. Her true power, and the ultimate source of her romanticism, would occur only when she was able in her final poems to crash through the masks and use the consequent subjectivity as her subject. The doubleness that was the theme of her Smith honors thesis was paradigmatic, suggestive of the social code of duplicity that dominated the fifties, a code that insinuated the protective value of hiding genuine feeling. Plath had been able to release hers at great personal risk: first the breakdown and electroshock treatments she recorded in *The Bell Jar*, and then the collapse of her marriage.

There is something both wretched and fascinating about the later stages of Plath's marriage that illustrates the impossible demands made by romantics in any time. For Plath, the price of her life had been measured out in the final months of ecstatic creativity and an anguish she could not tolerate. To an extent, like other poets of her generation who felt "twisted and against the grain," she illuminated both the terrible cost and the romantic premium of her mental torment. If Plath was the victim of the extremity of emotional turmoil, her art was its crystalline distillation.

Epilogue

L IVES THAT ARE CLAMOROUS in their contradictions and that
reveal their incongruities and shortcomings can obscure the
qualities that attract us to them and to their larger role in the
history of human thought and attitudes. Each of the writers
discussed in *Passionate Lives* was guilty of follies and absurdities
that exposed the discrepancies between their professed perspec-
tives and their faltering humanity. Their works record how they
reconciled their ideals to their understanding of experience, and it
is to those works that we turn to chart the imaginative expression
of their vision and to measure their artistic mastery. Nevertheless,
beyond functioning as sources of illumination of their work, their
lives are compelling registers of the raw and unreconciled conflicts
that are part of the truth of human experience.

Each of these writers fell in love instantly and obsessively, but
could not sustain the promise of their own intensity. The marriages
that began with passionate impulses and sweeping expectations of
the transforming power of love chafed under the inevitable frictions
of domestic life. Stormy, competitive, full of conflict and at times
violence, the marriages that formed the emotional center of the
lives and works of these writers are not advertisements for domestic harmony.

These marriages expose many of the issues that have separated
the sexes in the twentieth century. Romantically pursuing their
own inclinations rather than perceived notions of marital order,
perhaps echoing Shelley's "universal thirst for a communion not
merely of our senses, but of our whole nature," these writers chose
powerful mates whose spirit seemed commensurate with their own.
Yet, as participants in marriage, they created conditions of perpetual failure. Lawrence, Fitzgerald and Miller made the belligeren-
cies and appeasements of marriage crucial levers for their

311

imaginations, sources of inspiration for their work. Thomas and Plath, who matured in a historical moment when the romantic agony was compounded by despair, integrated that despair into the mosaic of their lives and work.

Despite finding their path to independence blocked by the expectations of their times, neither Frieda Lawrence, Zelda Fitzgerald, June Miller nor Caitlin Thomas easily played the part convention assigned to them. Plath, who stands alone among the women in this volume as a fully realized artist in her own right, was as confounded as the other wives by the lesser role assigned to women in marriage. The others may not have accomplished as much as their husbands, but they were strenuously active in the struggle to identify themselves. Although their expression of identity was confined within the geographical dominion of their husbands' achievements, to varying degrees they contributed to the artistic visions of their mates. In their self-assertiveness, they stubbornly stamp themselves as individuals on our consciousness and they claim our attention.

It may not be totally surprising that the wives presented here are more overtly violent than their husbands, frustrated perhaps by borders that were opened but that could not be crossed. The result for their marriages, as Plath might have put it, was an evolutionary breaking and mending. But, except for Miller's, these marriages endured—testimony that we cannot judge these lives only by their most hysterical moments.

One advantage of even the most bitter rage is that it may give us a glimpse of the other side—an intense demand for new ways of imagining relations between men and women. These writers have given us tests for marital situations that seem representative, and they enable us to see the unfolding opportunities and hazards for women in the twentieth century. These men and women, to borrow Miller's phrase, are all plenipotentiaries "from the realm of free spirits," even if they are failed plenipotentiaries, mired in their own natures and confounded by their own limitations and the limitations of their moment in social history.

They represent lives in transition, and it is perhaps here, in the seam between the confused idealism of these romantic writers and the unfinished expectations they set in motion, that we can trace the course of our still-evolving vision of emotional parity between men and women.

Notes

2. D. H. Lawrence and Frieda

The basic source for all D. H. Lawrence studies is the massive, three-volume *Composite Biography* edited by Edward Nehls (Madison, Wisc.: University of Wisconsin Press, 1957). Nehls gathers many of Lawrence's letters and recollections and some of the reminiscences of his friends. Lawrence's *Collected Letters* were edited by Harry T. Moore (New York: Viking, 1962), who also wrote the standard biography, *The Intelligent Heart* (New York: Farrar Straus & Young, 1954), which was redone and expanded twenty years later as *Priest of Love* (New York: Farrar, Straus and Giroux, 1974). A very good account of Lawrence's peregrinations in England during the war years is *D. H. Lawrence's Nightmare*, by Paul Delany (New York: Basic Books, 1978). An excellent study of the von Richthofens and Frieda's early years, as well as her affair with Otto Gross, is Martin Green's *The Von Richthofen Sisters* (New York: Basic Books, 1974). Green believes that Lawrence was so fascinated by the Germanic elements in Frieda's life that he transposed them into his fiction. He may exaggerate the role Frieda played, claiming that Frieda "guided as well as inspired" Lawrence's writing (p. 362), the living demonstration of what Lawrence could only imagine. A much less accurate account of Frieda is Robert Lucas's biography (New York: Viking, 1972). Otto Gross's letters are at the Humanities Research Center in Austin, Texas. Frieda's account of her life with Lawrence is *Not I, but the Wind* (New York: Viking, 1934), and her *Memoirs and Correspondence* were edited by E. W. Tedlock, Jr. (New York: Knopf, 1964). A group of later letters are found in *Frieda Lawrence and Her Circle*, edited by Harry T. Moore and Dale B. Montague (Hamden, Conn.: Archon Books, 1981). The most important volumes of reminiscences are: Richard Aldington's *Portrait of a Genius But* (New York: Duell, Sloan and Pearce, 1950); John Middleton Murry's *Reminiscences of D. H. Lawrence* (London: Jonathan Cape, 1933) and *Between Two Worlds* (New York: Julian Messner, 1936); Bertrand Russell's bitter recollections in *Harper's* Magazine in February 1953 and in his *Autobiography* (New York: Bantam, 1969); Ottoline Morrell's memoir, *Ottoline at Garsington*, edited by R. Gathorne-Hardy (London: Faber and Faber, 1974); and Cecil Gray's *Musical Chairs* (London: Home and Van Thal, 1948). Katherine Mansfield's *Journal: 1904–22* (London:

Constable, 1962) is a good source, as is her *Letters to John Middleton Murry* (London: Constable, 1951). The best account of Mansfield's marriage to Murry is in Anthony Alper's biography *Katherine Mansfield* (New York: Knopf, 1953, revised in 1972). A useful little critical book is Daniel A. Weiss's *Oedipus in Nottingham* (Seattle: University of Washington Press, 1962). Also helpful is Kingsley Widmer's essay, "Lawrence and the Nietzschean Matrix," in *D. H. Lawrence and Tradition*, edited by Jeffrey Meyers (Amherst, Mass.: University of Massachusetts Press, 1985).

3.   Scott and Zelda

There are more than a dozen biographies of Fitzgerald, and most of them are inferior. "There never was a good biography of a good novelist," Fitzgerald maintained in his *Notebooks*. "There couldn't be. He's too many people if he's any good." The best of the biographies is Arthur Mizener's *The Far Side of Paradise,* originally published in 1949 and then extensively revised in 1965 (Boston: Houghton Mifflin). Mizener is the most scholarly of the biographers, but his interest in theory sometimes is at the expense of the narrative sense that sustains biography. He is best with the early years. Andrew Turnbull's *Scott Fitzgerald* (New York: Macmillan, 1962) does not tell us much that is different from Mizener, except for the period at La Paix where Fitzgerald lived on Turnbull's parents' estate. The book has the zeal and the flaws of an obviously star-struck admirer. Nancy Milford's *Zelda* is one of the first examples of a genre that approaches the artist through his wife (the latest example is Brenda Nora Maddox's retelling of Richard Ellman's biography of Joyce). Milford is not a party-line feminist and, although she favors Zelda's point of view, she doesn't lose her sympathy for Fitzgerald. She quotes more liberally than anyone from Zelda's letters and psychiatric reports, and tells the harrowing story of Zelda's breakdowns and consequent suffering with considerable authority. Many of the other biographies are like James R. Mellow's *Invented Lives* (Boston: Houghton Mifflin, 1984), which tries to justify itself by accumulating detail and establishing atmosphere but has little new insight to offer. Mellow's book seems hurriedly written and is full of errors, even getting the year of Zelda's death wrong on its last page. A more accurate book is an earlier one, *A Critical Portrait*, written by Henry Dan Piper (New York: Holt Rinehart & Winston, 1965), who was able to visit Zelda in her declining years.

Fitzgerald's own reminiscences are collected by Edmund Wilson in *The Crack-Up* (New York: New Directions, 1945), which includes the *Notebooks*, various letters, and essays about Fitzgerald by John Dos Passos, Glenway Wescott and Paul Rosenfeld. Fitzgerald's "How to Live on Practically Nothing a Year" appeared in the *Saturday Evening Post* on September 20, 1924. Fitzgerald's *Letters* are edited by Andrew Turnbull (New York: Scribner's, 1963). Another volume of letters is *The Correspondence of F. Scott Fitzgerald*, edited by Matthew J. Bruccoli and Margaret M. Duggan (New York: Random

House, 1980). Two other volumes of letters are *Dear Scott/Dear Max: The Fitzgerald-Perkins Correspondence,* edited by John Kuehl and Jackson R. Bryer (New York: Scribner's, 1971) and Hemingway's *Selected Letters,* edited by Carlos Baker (New York: Scribner's, 1981). Two useful primary sources are *F. Scott Fitzgerald's Ledger,* edited by Frances Scott Fitzgerald Smith (1972) and *F. Scott Fitzgerald in His Own Time,* edited by Matthew J. Bruccoli and Jackson R. Bryer (Kent, Ohio: Kent State University Press, 1971), a miscellany that includes many of the interviews, the early college writing and several brief autobiographical statements.

There are a number of important recollections, most significant of which is Hemingway's in *A Moveable Feast* (New York: Scribner's, 1964). Two others that were helpful are Morley Callaghan's *That Summer in Paris* (New York: Coward McCann, 1963) and Sheilah Graham's *Beloved Infidel* (New York: Bantam, 1958). A very lively account of the Murphys is Calvin Tomkins's *Living Well Is the Best Revenge* (New York: Viking, 1971). Some of the more illuminating individual essays for me were Edmund Wilson's *Bookman* piece, March 1922, and the essay he collects in his *The Bit Between My Teeth* (New York: Farrar, Straus and Giroux, 1966). I was already well under way with this book when I read his linking of Lawrence, Fitzgerald and Dylan Thomas as versions of the dying god Adonis, but that perception gave me extra impetus. John Mosher's *New Yorker* profile, "All the Sad Young Men," April 17, 1926, was insightful, as were James Thurber's *Reporter* piece, April 15, 1951, and William Troy's essay in *Accent,* which appeared in the fall of 1945. James Dickey's introduction to Fitzgerald's *Poems* (Columbia, S.C.: Bruccoli Clark, 1981) was full of sweetness and soul, and Gore Vidal's intelligent but characteristically acerbic essay, "Scott's Case," was in the *New York Review of Books,* May 1, 1980.

4.   Henry and June and Anaïs

As Norman Mailer has pointed out, literary criticism has made a giant detour around Henry Miller as if his reputation existed in a void. Most of Miller's letters and manuscripts are housed in the Miller collection at U.C.L.A. at Westwood. Several individual volumes of his letters have appeared, the correspondence with Alfred Perlès as *Art and Outrage* (New York: E. P. Dutton, 1961), the letters to Durrell as *A Private Correspondence* (New York: E. P. Dutton, 1963), and the letters to Wallace Fowlie (New York: Grove, 1975). Crucial for the development of this chapter were Miller's letters to his friend Emil Schnellock, which were published as *Letters to Emil* (New York: New Directions, 1989). Another useful collection was *Collector's Quest: The Correspondence of Henry Miller and J. Rives Childs,* edited by Richard Clement Wood (Charlottesville, Va.: University of Virginia Press, 1968), and *Hamlet,* the letters between Michael Fraenkel and Miller (London: Carrefour, 1939). The letters to Anaïs Nin are collected as *A Literate Passion,* edited by Gunther Stuhlman (New York: Harcourt Brace Jovanovich, 1987). Nin's

Diaries are an especially useful source for this chapter, and the most important was the unexpurgated final volume, *Henry & June* (New York: Harcourt Brace Jovanovich, 1986).

For a man with as many friends as Miller seems to have enjoyed, there is very little published reminiscence. The most useful source is Alfred Perlès's *My Friend, Henry Miller* (New York: John Day, 1956). Much less trustworthy is Kathryn Winslow's *Henry Miller: Full of Life* (Los Angeles: Tarcher, 1986). Miller himself was capable of a certain amount of garrulous reminiscence, some of which was collected in interviews. The best of these is "Reflections of a Cosmic Tourist," in *Rolling Stone*, February 27, 1975. The standard interview is the one collected in the *Paris Review Writers at Work* series, edited by George Plimpton (New York: Viking, 1963). The first biography is Jay Martin's *Always Merry and Bright* (Santa Barbara, Calif.: Capra Press, 1978). Martin's book is often impressionistic: he invents conversations and sometimes uses material from the novels as factual occurrence. He also has the annoying habit of quoting practically verbatim from Miller's letters and passing the quotation off as his own. I reviewed Mary Dearborn's *The Happiest Man Alive* (New York: Simon and Schuster, 1991) and Robert Ferguson's *Henry Miller: A Life* (New York: Norton, 1991) in the *Washington Post Book World* on Sunday, May 5, 1991. Dearborn is psychoanalytical where Ferguson is sober and circumspect, more aware of the implicit exaggeration in everything Miller wrote.

Miller criticism, as Mailer suggests, is insubstantial. Mailer's own anthology of Miller's writing, *Genius and Lust* (New York: Bantam, 1977), provides the most intuitive and illuminating critical insights, though they are clearly partisan and in some part intended as a rebuttal to Kate Millet's attack in *Sexual Politics*. Two very sober and intelligent critical studies are William Gordon's *The Mind and Art of Henry Miller* (Baton Rouge: Louisiana State University Press, 1967) and Leon Lewis's *Henry Miller: The Major Writings* (New York: Schocken, 1986). Lewis's introductory chapter exists as the best single review of Miller criticism. An important critical essay is Ihab Hassan's *The Literature of Silence* (New York: Knopf, 1967), and another one is Frederick Crews's "Kinetic Art," which originally appeared as a *New York Review of Books* piece and has been reprinted in his *Skeptical Engagements* (London: Oxford University Press, 1986).

5. Dylan and Caitlin

Thomas was a phenomenon who provoked lots of commentary and reminiscence. Daniel Jones, his best friend in childhood, offers his version of the Swansea days in *My Friend, Dylan Thomas* (New York: Scribner's, 1977), an account which is sometimes unconvincing, as when he argues that Dylan was never frail or sickly as a youth. Jones does not even mention Caitlin, who, of course, wrote three separate accounts of her life with Dylan. The first of these, *Leftover Life to Kill* (Boston: Little Brown, 1957) is the most anguished, an overwrought attempt to assuage her depletion after his death. This was followed by *Not Quite Posthumous Letter to My Daughter* (Boston: Little Brown, 1963) which is less informative, and *Caitlin* (New York: Henry Holt, 1986), which is a sort of oral biography of tape-recorded recollections, edited by George Tremlett. The standard source for the American tours is John Malcolm Brinnin's *Dylan Thomas in America* (Boston: Little Brown, 1955). Pamela Hansford Johnson's recollections are found in *Important to Me* (New York: Scribner's, 1974). Thomas's refreshing own radio talks on his Welsh childhood are collected as *Quite Early One Morning* (New York: New Directions, 1954). A useful volume of letters is the *Letters to Vernon Watkins* (New York: New Directions, 1957). The *Selected Letters* are edited by Constantine Fitzgibbon (New York: New Directions, 1965) but Thomas's beautifully composed letters are tricky material for the biographer because he was so capable of embellishment and exaggeration.

The best biography, though it is quirky, is probably the official one by Constantine Fitzgibbon (Boston: Little Brown, 1965) because it includes a number of crucial letters and documents which are left to speak for themselves. Paul Ferris's biography (New York: Dial Press, 1977) is better on the last years. A useful book of photographs is Rollie McKenna's *Portrait of Dylan* (Owings Mills, Md.: Stemmer House, 1982). Among the most cogent critical essays are William Empson's review of the *Collected Poems* in the *Nation* (May 15, 1954), David Daiches's piece in his book *Literary Essays* (London: Oliver and Boyd, 1956), and Elizabeth Hardwick's essay in *Partisan Review* (Spring 1956). The account of Thomas's thespian qualities by Richard Burton is from *Book Week* (October 24, 1965). I was also helped by Jan Morris's *The Matter of Wales* (London: Oxford, 1984).

6. Sylvia and Ted

The best source for Plath's childhood is *Letters Home by Sylvia Plath: Correspondence, 1950–63*, edited by Aurelia Schober Plath (New York: Harper & Row, 1975). This book has been criticized as presenting a false image of Plath, a version of the dutiful and adjusted daughter. A gloomier corrective is *The Journals of Sylvia Plath, 1950–62*, edited by Frances McCullough and Ted Hughes (New York: Dial Press, 1982).

There has been considerable biographical speculation about Plath, though not all of it facilitated by Ted Hughes, who controls Plath's estate since there never was an actual divorce. Linda Wagner-Martin's *Sylvia Plath* (New York: Simon and Schuster, 1987) is very detailed on the American years through Smith College, and she follows the argument that Hughes bears considerable responsibility for the breakdown of the marriage. Anne Stevenson's *Bitter Fame: A Life of Sylvia Plath* (Boston: Houghton Mifflin, 1989) is skimpy on the early years and quite detailed on the last years in England. Reviewers have attacked her as an apologist for Hughes and his sister Olwyn, who according to Plath's friend Elizabeth Compton, was jealous of her talent and beauty. A number of Hughes's friends, like Dido Merwin, published accounts explaining how difficult it must have been to live with Plath.

Two useful reminiscences of Plath at Smith are by Nancy Hunter Steiner, *A Closer Look at Ariel* (New York: Harper's Magazine Press, 1973) and Gordon Lameyer's "Sylvia at Smith," which is collected in Edward Butscher's *Sylvia Plath: The Woman and Her Work* (New York: Dodd Mead and Company, 1977). Another account of Plath at Smith is in Alfred Kazin's *New York Jew* (New York: Knopf, 1978). Butscher's anthology includes two other remembrances of Plath at Cambridge by Dorothea Krook and Jane Baltzell Koop, and two more on the Devon period by Clarissa Roche and Elizabeth Compton. Another essay on Plath at Cambridge is by Wendy Campbell, in Charles Newman's *The Art of Sylvia Plath* (Bloomington, Ind.: Indiana University Press, 1971). The Newman collection also includes Lois Ames's "Notes Toward a Biography," Anne Sexton's "The Barfly Ought to Sing," on the period when Plath was auditing Robert Lowell's class, and Ted Hughes's "The Chronological Order of Sylvia Plath's Poems." A. Alvarez's account of Plath is in his study of suicide, *The Savage God* (New York: Random House, 1972).

PERMISSIONS

319

Index